Communications
in Computer and Information Science 1416

More information about this series at http://www.springer.com/series/7899

Nirbhay Chaubey · Satyen Parikh ·
Kiran Amin (Eds.)

Computing Science, Communication and Security

Second International Conference, COMS2 2021
Gujarat, India, February 6–7, 2021
Revised Selected Papers

 Springer

Editors
Nirbhay Chaubey ⓘD
Ganpat University
Gujarat, India

Satyen Parikh ⓘD
Ganpat University
Gujarat, India

Kiran Amin ⓘD
Ganpat University
Gujarat, India

ISSN 1865-0929 ISSN 1865-0937 (electronic)
Communications in Computer and Information Science
ISBN 978-3-030-76775-4 ISBN 978-3-030-76776-1 (eBook)
https://doi.org/10.1007/978-3-030-76776-1

This Springer imprint is published by the registered company Springer Nature Switzerland AG
The registered company address is: Gewerbestrasse 11, 6330 Cham, Switzerland

Preface

This volume contains the papers presented at the Second International Conference on Computing Science, Communication and Security (COMS2 2021), held at the beautiful campus of Ganpat University, India, during February 6–7, 2021. COMS2 2021 was held online, wherein the invited guests, keynote speakers, dignitaries, session chairs, paper presenters, and attendees joined a two-day international conference online from their homes through Zoom. The online conference forum brought together more than 155 delegates including leading academics, scientists, researchers, and research scholars from all over the world to exchange and share their experiences, ideas, and research results on aspects of Computing Science, Network Communication, and Security.

The conference was virtually inaugurated by the Indian National Anthem "Jana Gana Mana .." with the online presence of academic leaders and luminaries: Shri Ganpatbhai I. Patel (Padma Shri), President and Patron-in-Chief of Ganpat University, India; the Invited Guest of the program Professor (Dr.) Ian T. Foster, father of Grid Computing and Professor of Computer Science at the University of Chicago, USA; Professor (Dr.) Akshai Aggarwal, Professor Emeritus at the University of Windsor, Canada, and Former Vice Chancellor of Gujarat Technological University, India; Professor (Dr.) Rajkumar Buyya, Director of the Cloud Computing and Distributed Systems (CLOUDS) Lab at The University of Melbourne, Australia; Shri Rasesh Patel, Executive Vice President of AT&T, USA and BOG member of Ganpat University, India; Shri Arup R. Dasgupta, an Eminent Scientist and Former Deputy Director of the Space Application Centre at the Indian Space Research Organisation (ISRO), India; Dr. Mahendra Sharma, Pro-Chancellor and Director General of Ganpat University, India; and Dr. Amit Patel, Pro-Vice Chancellor and Executive Registrar of Ganpat University, India, which declared the conference open for further proceedings.

There were five plenary lectures covering the different areas of the conference: Dr. Ian T. Foster graced the conference with a talk giving insights on "Artificial Intelligence for Science", which discussed the opportunities for AI in science and also highlighted that progress requires much work in applications, learning systems, foundations, and hardware; Dr. Akashi Aggrawal delivered a talk on "Resetting the Universities after COVID-19"; Dr. Rajkumar Buyya addressed "Neoteric Frontiers in Cloud and Edge Computing"; Dr. K. K. Soundra Pandian from the Ministry of Electronics and Information Technology, India, delivered a talk on the "Impact of Emerging Technologies and Challenges in Cyber Physical Systems and Embedded IoT for Industrial Revolution"; and Prof. Arup R. Dasgupta gave a valedictory session talk on "Security and AI – Social Dimensions".

The conference accepted 19 papers as oral presentations (out of the 105 full papers received and critically peer reviewed using the Springer OCS System), which were presented online over the two days. The conference committee formed two session tracks: (i) Artificial Intelligence and Machine Learning and (ii) Networking and

Communication. Each track had five session chairs, all expert professors in their fields and from reputed universities in India and abroad. The first track was led by the following panel members and session chairs: Dr. Savita R. Gandhi, Gujarat University, India; Dr. Maulika Patel, CVM University, India; Dr. Snehal Joshi, Veer Narmad South Gujarat University, India; Dr. Nilesh Modi, Dr. Babasaheb Ambedkar Open University, India; and Dr. Priyanka Sharma, Raksha Shakti University, India. The panel members and session chairs leading the second track were as follows: Dr. Rakhee, University of West Indies, West Indies; Dr. Nikhil J. Kothari, Dharmsinh Desai University, India; Dr. Vishvjit Thakkar, Gujarat Technological University, India; Dr. J.M.Rathod, BVM Engineering College, India; and Dr. Vrushank Shah, Indus University, India.

The selected papers came from researchers based in various countries including Australia, Canada, Japan, Sri Lanka, Malaysia, Bangladesh, and India. All the accepted papers were peer reviewed by three qualified reviewers chosen from our conference Scientific Committee based on their qualifications and experience. The proceedings editors wish to thank the dedicated Scientific Committee members and all the other reviewers for their contributions. We also thank Springer for their trust and for publishing the proceedings of COMS2 2021.

The conference was organized by Ganpat University as a well reputed State Private University established through the Government of Gujarat State Legislative Act No.19/ 2005 on April 12, 2005, and recognized by the UGC under section 2(f) of the UGC Act, 1956, which has a campus spread over more than 300 acres of land with world-class infrastructure and more than 10,000 students on campus. In consideration of its contribution to education in a short period of time, the university has been given Permanent Membership of the Association of Indian Universities (AIU), India, besides having membership of the Association of Commonwealth Universities (ACU), UK, and the International Association of Universities (IAU), France. Ganpat University offers various unique, quality, industry-linked, and sector-focused Diploma, Under-graduate, Postgraduate, and Research level programs (professional and non-professional) in the field of Engineering, Computer Science, Management, Pharmacy, Sciences, Commerce and Social Science, Architecture, Design and Planning, Maritime Studies, Law, etc.

In a nutshell, the conference was full of fruitful discussions, igniting the spirit of research. It was indeed a remarkable, memorable, and knowledgeable virtual conference. The success of COMS2 2021 conference means that planning can now proceed with confidence for the Third International Conference on Computing Science, Communication and Security (COMS2 2022) scheduled for February 2022 at Ganpat University, India.

February 2021

Nirbhay Chaubey
Satyen Parikh
Kiran Amin

Organization

Scientific Committee

Ganpatbhai Patel (Patron-in-Chief and President)	Ganpat University, India
Mahendra Sharma (Pro-Chancellor)	Ganpat University, India
Amit Patel (Pro-Vice Chancellor)	Ganpat University, India
Rajkumar Buyya	The University of Melbourne, Australia
K. S. Dasgupta	DAIICT, India
Mohammed Atiquzzaman	University of Oklahoma, USA
Shri. A. R. Dasgupta	ISRO, India
Akshai Aggarwal	University of Windsor, Canada
Om Prakash Vyas	IIIT, Allahabad, India
Savita R. Gandhi	Gujarat University, India
Sabu M. Thampi	IIITM-K, India
Dipak Mathur	IEEE, India
Sartaj Sahni	University of Florida, USA
Maniklal Das	DA-IICT, India
S. Venkatesan	IIIT, Allahabad, India
Deepak Garg	Bennett University, India
Mohit Tahiliani	NIT, Karnatka, India
Nilesh Modi	Dr. Babasaheb Ambedkar Open University, India
Kevin Dami	University of Detroit, USA
Bala Natarajan	Kansas State University, USA
Virendra C. Bhavsar	University of New Brunswick, Canada
G. Sahoo	Birla Institute of Technology, India
Rajen Purohit	Ganpat University, India
Kiran Amin	Ganpat University, India
Satyen Parikh	Ganpat University, India
Hemal Shah	Ganpat University, India
Nirbhay Chaubey	Ganpat University, India
Rakesh D. Vanzara	Ganpat University, India
Girish Patel	Ganpat University, India
Hamid R. Arabnia	University of Georgia, USA
Sanjay Madria	Missouri University of Science and Technology, USA
Arvind Shah	Georgia Southwestern State University, USA
P. Balasubramanian	Nanyang Technological University, Singapore
Xing Liu	Kwantlen Polytechnic University, Canada

Kalpdrum Passi	Laurentian University, Canada
Ratvinder Grewal	Laurentian University, Canada
Ali Mostafaeipour	Yazd University, Iran
Ramesh Bansal	University of Sharjah, UAE
Neville Watson	University of Canterbury, New Zealand
Yuan Miao	Victoria University, Australia
Shah Miah	Victoria University, Australia
Mohan Kolhe	University of Agder, Norway
Akhtar Kalam	Victoria University, Australia
Pao-Ann Hsiung	National Chung Cheng University, Taiwan
Prateek Agrawal	University of Klagenfurt, Austria
Anatoliy Zabrovskiy	University of Klagenfurt, Austria
Valentina Emilia Balas	University of Arad, Romania
Ashok Karania	EMEA, UK
D. P. Kothari	VIT University, India
H. S. Mazumdar	Dharmsinh Desai University, India
Debajyoti Mukhopadhyay	Bennett University, India
Hiral Patel	Ganpat University, India
Ashok R. Patel	Florida Polytechnic University, USA
Ruoyu Wang	Arizona State University, USA
Kevin Gary	Arizona State University, USA
Tatyana Ryutov	University of Southern California, USA
George Sklivanitis	Florida Atlantic University, USA
Koushik A. Manjunatha	Idaho National Laboratory, USA
Sathyan Munirathinam	ASML Corporation, USA
Yogesh Patel	SalesForce, USA
Priyanshukumar Jha	Amazon, USA
El Sayed Mahmoud	Sheridan College, Canada
Jigisha Patel	Sheridan College, Canada
Pawan Lingra	Saint Mary's University, Canada
Xing Liu	Kwantlen Polytechnic University, Canada
Muhammad Dangana	University of Glasgow, UK
Gisa Fuatai Purcel	Victoria University of Wellington, New Zealand
Gyu Myoung Lee	Liverpool John Moores University, UK
Stefano Cirillo	University of Salerno, Italy
Flavio Vella	Free University of Bozen-Bolzano, Italy
Alessandro Barbiero	Università degli Studi di Milano, Italy
Lelio Campanile	Università degli Studi della Campania LuigiVanvitelli, Italy
Asmerilda Hitaj	University of Milano-Bicocca, Italy
Abdallah Handoura	Ecole Nationale Supérieure des Télécommunications de, France
Gua Xiangfa	National University of Singapore, Singapore
Raman Singh	Trinity College Dublin, Ireland
Ahmed M. Elmisery	Waterford Institute of Technology, Ireland
Shahzad Ashraf	Hohai University, China

Tran Cong Hung	Posts and Telecomunication Institute of Technology, Vietnam
Anand Nayyar	Duy Tan University, Vietnam
Pao-Ann Hsiung	National Chung Cheng University, Taiwan
Seyyed Ahmad Edalatpanah	Ayandegan Institute of Higher Education, Iran
Aws Zuheer Yonis	Ninevah University, Iraq
Razan Abdulhammed	Northern Technical University, Iraq
Moharram Challenger	Ege University, Turkey
Sandeep Kautish	LBEF Campus, Nepal
A. A. Gde Satia Utama	Universitas Airlangga, Indonesia
Eva Shayo	University of Dar es Salaam, Tanzania
Anil Audumbar Pise	University of the Witwatersrand, Johannesburg, South Africa
Sarang C. Dhongdi	BITS Pilani, India
Satyabrata Jit	IIT(BHU), India
Pratik Chattopadhyay	IIT(BHU), India
Amrita Chaturvedi	IIT(BHU), India
Amit Kumar Singh	IIT(BHU), India
Amrita Mishra	IIIT, Naya Raipur, India
Panchami V.	IIIT, Kottayam, India
Bhuvaneswari Amma N. G.	IIIT, Una, India
Jitendra Tembhurne	IIIT, Nagpur, India
Renjith P.	IIIT, Kurnool, India
Sachin Jain	IIIT, Jabalpur, India
Priyanka Mishra	IIIT, Kota, India
Chetna Sharma	IIIT, Kota, India
Eswaramoorthy K.	IIIT, Kurnool, India
Pandiyarasan Veluswamy	IIITDM Kancheepuram, India
Sahil	IIIT, Una, India
Sanya Anees	IIIT, Guwahati, India
Suvrojit Das	NIT, Durgapur, India
Aruna Jain	Birla Institute of Technology, India
Amit Kumar Gupta	DRDO, India
R. Kumar	SRM University, India
B. Ramachandran	SRM University, India
Iyyanki V. Muralikrishna	J.N.Technological University, India
Apurv Shah	M.S. University, India
Bhushan Trivedi	GLS University, India
Manoj Kumar	Infliblnet University Grants Commission, India
U. Dinesh Kumar	IIM, Bangalore, India
Saurabh Bilgaiyan	KIIT Deemed to be University, India
Raja Sarath Kumar Boddu	Jawaharlal Nehru Technological University, India
Kiran Sree Pokkuluri	SVECM, India
Devesh Kumar Srivastava	Manipal University, India
P. Muthulakshmi	SRM University, India
R. Anandan	VELS University, India

Amol Dhondse	IBM India Software Labs, India
R. Amirtharajan	SASTRA Deemed University, India
Padma Priya V.	SASTRA Deemed University, India
Deepak H. Sharma	K. J. Somaiya College of Engineering, India
Ravi Subban	Pondicherry University, India
Parameshachari B. D.	Visvesvaraya Technological University, India
Nilakshi Jain	University of Mumbai, India
Archana Mire	University of Mumbai, India
Sonali Bhutad	University of Mumbai, India
Anand Kumar	Visvesvaraya Technological University, India
Jyoti Pareek	Gujarat University, India
Sanjay Garg	Nirma University, India
Madhuri Bhavsar	Nirma University, India
Vijay Ukani	Nirma University, India
Mayur Vegad	BVM Engineering College, India
N. M. Patel	BVM Engineering College, India
J. M. Rathod	BVM Engineering College, India
Maulika Patel	CVM University, India
Nikhil Gondalia	CVM University, India
Priyanka Sharma	Raksha Shakti University, India
Digvijaysinh Rathod	Gujarat Forensic Science University, India
Kalpesh Parikh	Intellisense IT, India
Balaji Rajendran	CDAC, India
Mehul C. Parikh	Gujarat Technological University, India
G. R. Kulkarni	Shivaji University, India
Amol C. Adamuthe	Shivaji University, India
Shrihari Khatawkar	Shivaji University, India
Snehal Joshi	Veer Narmad South Gujarat University, India
Ambika Nagaraj	Bengaluru Central University, India
Ashok Solanki	Veer Narmad South Gujarat University, India
Aditya Sinha	CDAC, India
Harshal Arolkar	GLS University, India
Binod Kumar	University of Pune, India
Maulin Joshi	Gujarat Technological University, India
Vrushank Shah	Indus University, India
Manish Patel	Gujarat Technological University, India
Ankit Bhavsar	GLS University, India
Seema Mahajan	Indus University, India
S. K. Vij	ITM University, India
Vishal Jain	Sharda University, India
D. B. Choksi	Sardar Patel University, India
Paresh Virpariya	Sardar Patel University, India
Priti Srinivas Sajja	Sardar Patel University, India
C. K. Bhensdadia	Dharmsinh Desai University, India
Vipul K. Dabhi	Dharmsinh Desai University, India
N. J. Kothari	Dharmsinh Desai University, India

Narayan Joshi	Dharmsinh Desai University, India
S. D. Panchal	Gujarat Technological University, India
M. T. Savaliya	Gujarat Technological University, India
Vinod Desai	Gujarat Vidyapith, India
Himanshu Patel	Dr. Babasaheb Ambedkar Open University, India
Chhaya Patel	Gujarat Technological University, India
Jignesh Doshi	Gujarat Technological University, India
Bhaveshkumar Prajapati	Gujarat Technological University, India
Nisha Somani	Gujarat Technological University, India
Desai Archana Natvarbhai	Gujarat Technological University, India
Akhilesh Ladha	Gujarat Technological University, India
Jaymin Bhalani	Gujarat Technological University, India
Dhananjay Yadav	Gujarat Technological University, India
Keyur Jani	Gujarat Technological University, India
Jeegar Trivedi	Sardar Patel University, India

Organizing Committee

Ajay Patel	Ganpat University, India
Ketan Patel	Ganpat University, India
Anand Mankodia	Ganpat University, India
Paresh M. Solanki	Ganpat University, India
Savan Patel	Ganpat University, India
Jigna Prajapati	Ganpat University, India
Pravesh Patel	Ganpat University, India
Ketan Sarvakar	Ganpat University, India
Chirag Gami	Ganpat University, India
Sweta A. Dargad	Ganpat University, India

Contents

Networking and Communications

Artificial Intelligence and Machine Learning

Data Balancing for Credit Card Fraud Detection Using Complementary Neural Networks and SMOTE Algorithm

Vrushal Shah and Kalpdrum Passi(✉)

Laurentian University, Sudbury, ON P3E 2C6, Canada
{vshah1,kpassi}@laurentian.ca

Abstract. This Research presents an innovative approach towards detecting fraudulent credit card transactions. A commonly prevailing yet dominant problem faced in detection of fraudulent credit card transactions is the scarce occurrence of such fraudulent transactions with respect to legitimate (authorized) transactions. Therefore, any data that is recorded will always have a stark imbalance in the variety of minority (fraudulent) and majority (legitimate) class samples. This imbalanced distribution of the training data among classes makes it hard for any learning algorithm to learn the features of the minority class. In this thesis, we analyze the impact of applying class-balancing techniques on the training data namely oversampling (using SMOTE algorithm) for minority class and under sampling (using CMTNN) for majority class. The usage of most popular classification algorithms such as Artificial Neural Network (ANN), Support Vector Machine (SVM), Extreme Gradient Boosting (XGB), Logistic Regression (LR), Random Forest (RF) are processed on balanced data and which results to quantify the performance improvement provided by our approach.

Keywords: Complementary Neural Network · SMOTE · Oversampling · Under-sampling · Class imbalance

1 Introduction

A credit card is an installment card given to clients to empower the cardholder to pay a merchant for products and ventures dependent on the cardholder's guarantee to the card issuer to pay them for the sums in addition to the next concurred charges. The card guarantor gives time to their clients to reimburse later in an endorsed time and charges a specific expense for its services. A fraudulent credit card transaction is an unauthorized withdrawal/expenditure by a person for whom the account was not intended. In simple terms, credit card fraud is defined as when an individual uses another individual's credit card for personal transactions without the knowledge of the actual card holder. Credit Card frauds are among the easiest and most rapidly rising frauds in the modern world. While they provide a seamless service of executing monetary transactions, it also makes the task of detecting a fraudulent transaction equally harder. E-commerce and other

© Springer Nature Switzerland AG 2021
N. Chaubey et al. (Eds.): COMS2 2021, CCIS 1416, pp. 3–16, 2021.
https://doi.org/10.1007/978-3-030-76776-1_1

similar online transactions account for a huge portion (roughly 80%) of such fraudulent transactions.

With the growing number of credit card frauds (Fig. 1), researchers too have shown increasing interest related to fraud detection using classical Machine Learning approaches [1, 5, 7] as well as newer AI based algorithms [6]. But one of the biggest bottlenecks in solving the classification problem (fraudulent transaction vs legitimate transaction) is the imbalance in the transaction data. Since it is obvious that the number of legitimate transactions is far more than the number of fraudulent transactions, it becomes extremely hard for any learning algorithm to be trained on the features of the minority class samples (fraudulent credit card transactions). Various difficulties related with credit card identification include dynamic fraudulent profiles with such transactions looking legitimate; very few datasets available related to credit card transaction with fraudulent exchanges and the ones available being highly imbalanced (or skewed); optimal feature (variables) selection for the models; suitable metrics to evaluate the performance of techniques on skewed credit card fraud data.

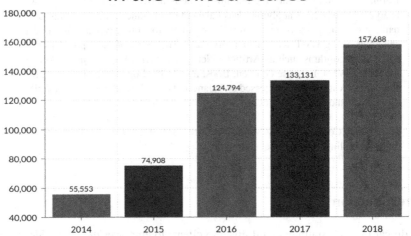

Fig. 1. Credit card fraud reports in the United States

2 Literature Review

Over the past couple of years, different machine learning techniques (supervised and semi-supervised) have gained traction [2, 14]. John O. Awoyemi [1] in 2017 had presented a comparative analysis of existing machine learning algorithms for credit card fraud detection. Among un-supervised approaches, clustering [8] by Vaishali et al. was one of the earliest to have gained popularity but failed to keep up with the growing amount of transaction data as it became computation heavy and results deteriorated significantly with growing number of transactions. The earliest supervised approaches as shown by Dhankhad in [5] include SVM, Random Forest, XGB, etc. have almost all shown considerable improvement over the pre-existing clustering approaches. Dhankhad [5] also experimented with under sampling the majority class to show improvement in performance. It is from this reference that we garner our motivation to first attack the class imbalance itself and analyze the extent of performance improvement.

A few more fundamental challenges in detecting fraudulent transactions have been very well-drafted in [16] and [17]. Any authentic, real-world data will always have an extremely large number of genuine transaction samples while containing only a handful of fraudulent cases. This is probably because fraudulent transactions, although they have increased rapidly over time but are a case of an anomaly in the regular genuine transactions. To make it worse, not all of the transactional data can be made available publicly due to the user-sensitive nature of such data. This makes it extremely difficult to create and validate any kind of detection system. Another important issue to highlight is the practical implementation side. In the domain of banking, fraudulent transactions must be detected in real-time such that it can be blocked before it has been executed. Thus, implying the need for a robust and accurate FDS (Fraudulent Detection systems) which is also capable of providing real-time classification results (classifying between genuine and fraud). It also needs to be easily scalable in order for it to not become obsolete sooner than later.

A random sampling approach is utilized in [9, 10] that reports experimental results describing 50:50 artificial distribution of legitimate/non-legitimate training data. The classifiers achieve the highest true positive rate and low false positive rate, hinting that reducing the class imbalance can result in much better performance. Duman et al. [11] use stratified sampling for under-sampling the legitimate records to a meaningful number. They experiment on 50:50, 10:90 and 1:99 distributions of fraud-to-legitimate cases and report that the 10:90 distribution has the best performance, perhaps owing to its similarity to the real world. Thus, we acknowledge two challenges in an under-sampling approach. First, simply applying a random sampling approach does not solve the problem and second, the resulting balance among the majority and the minority class will also impact the resultant performance of the classifier. To solve these challenges, we apply a comprehensive solution. We choose CMTNN for under sampling because it is a learning-based approach i.e. it learns the features of the majority class (legitimate transactions) and then removes only those samples from the training data that have relatively low information content and would essentially be redundant in training the classifier. This automatically takes care of the second challenge as the resulting balance among the classes would be an optimum balance i.e. one containing maximum information.

3 Dataset Description

The dataset used in this study is taken from ULB Machine Learning Group and description is found on Kaggle [15]. The dataset holds credit card transactions made by European cardholders in September 2013. This dataset describes the transactions that occurred in two days, consisting of 284,807 transactions. The minority class (fraud cases) contains

0.172% of the transactions data. The dataset is highly unbalanced and skewed towards the positive class (as shown in Fig. 2). It holds only numerical (continuous) input variables which are as a result of a Principal Component Analysis (PCA) feature selection transformation resulting in 28 principal components. Thus, a sum of 30 input features (characteristics) are utilized in this study. The details and background information of the features could not be presented due to confidentiality issues. The time column in the data set contains the seconds elapsed between each transaction and the first transaction in the dataset. The 'amount' column is the transaction amount. Feature 'class' is the target column for the binary classification and it takes value 1 for fraud case and 0 for non-fraud case.

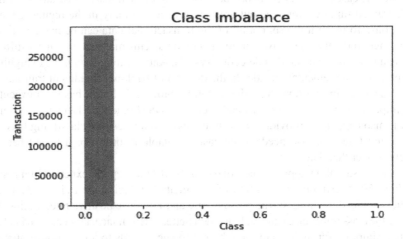

Fig. 2. Class imbalance (Showing Skewness)

It is important to understand that since over 99% of the transactions are non-fraudulent, a prediction accuracy of 99% or more can be achieved by a classifier that always predicts that the transaction is non-fraudulent. Thus, the accuracy metric in itself can be highly misleading in such cases of extremely skewed dataset. Thus, our focus throughout this study has been on improving higher order metrics like AUC (area under the receiver operating characteristics (ROC) curve), accuracy, precision, recall and F-score. While all of these metrics were employed during analysis of CMTNN and SMOTE performance, for visualization purpose and for a clarity in presentation of results, we will be considering only AUC and accuracy metrics.

4   Proposed Method

While we do not propose a novelty in the classification algorithm itself, we bring together different techniques of data analytics (CMTNN and SMOTE) and Machine Learning (SVM, RF, XGB, LR and ANN) in a systematic manner to tackle both data level challenges and learning level challenges. As discussed in the "Dataset" section above, the credit card transaction data used for our experiments is highly skewed towards legitimate transactions as compared to fraudulent transactions.

In our proposed method, we have designed a two-block pipeline (Fig. 3), wherein the first stage deals with Data Balancing Network (balancing the skewness using under sampling and oversampling techniques) and the second stage deals with Classification Algorithms. The second stage is further divided into two sub stages. First substrate deals with algorithms of Classical Machine Learning and the second sub stage deals with algorithms of Advanced Deep Learning.

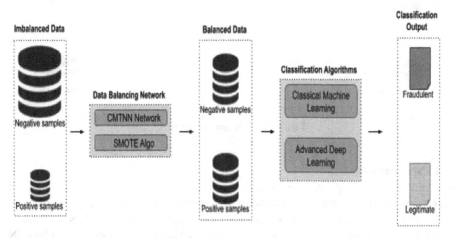

Fig. 3. Proposed pipeline

As shown in Fig. 3, our major focus has been on the first block of our pipeline "Data Balancing Network". It is in this section that we perform the majority of the computation. The beauty of this section lies in the fact that although computationally intensive, the two processes i.e. under sampling (CMTNN Network) and oversampling (SMOTE Algorithm) are actually independent of each other in the sequential sense and therefore can be parallelized (this will be part of our future work).

4.1 Data Balancing Network

Standard data processing techniques like random under sampling and replicative over-sampling have existed among the research community for a long time and have also been successful in several instances. But in our particular case of fraud detection, the aim is not primarily to ease computation (this is usually where normally random sampling proves effective) and replicative oversampling can easily result in overfitting of our classifier. Therefore, in our case we need a data centric or information-theory centric approach to under sampling and oversampling.

Thus, we have used CMTNN Network for under sampling while preserving training samples that provide crucial information for feature learning. For the oversampling part we have used the Synthetic Minority Over-sampling Technique to generate relevant samples for the minority class. Figure 4 Shows the representation of Data Balancing Network

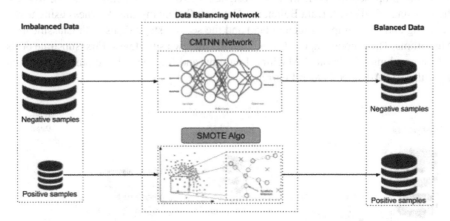

Fig. 4. Data balancing network

CMTNN Network

In recent years, Complementary Neural Networks (CMTNN) based on feedforward neural networks have been proposed to deal with both binary and multiclass classification problems [12, 13]. Instead of considering only the truth information, CMTNN considers both truth and falsity information in order to enhance the classification results. CMTNN consists of both, truth neural network and falsity neural network, based on truth and falsity information. CMTNN with such a structure provides better performance when compared to the traditional feed-forward neural networks [12, 13].

In our design of the CMTNN (Fig. 5), we train two Artificial Neural Networks "Truth NN" and "Falsity NN". Both networks are structurally identical in design (Fig. 5) and follow the same ANN Architecture inherently (Fig. 6). The only difference is that Truth NN uses the original targets/labels while training whereas the Falsity NN uses complementary targets while training.

CMTNN Implementation

CMTNN is applied for the under-sampling problem by employing "Truth NN" and "Falsity NN" to detect misclassification patterns i.e. all the patterns that were classified incorrectly. The intersection of these incorrectly classified samples is then removed from our training data.

- "Truth NN" is trained on the training data keeping the target values as it is to learn a classification function (T).
- "Falsity NN" is trained on the training data with target values complementary to that provided for Truth NN to learn a classification function (F). Both the networks after reaching convergence are used to classify the majority class of the training data individually.

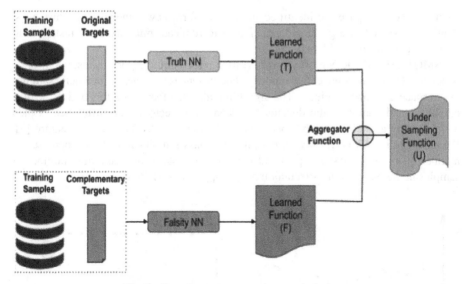

Fig. 5. Complementary neural network design

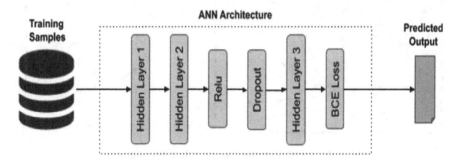

Fig. 6. ANN architecture

- The misclassification patterns i.e. pattern for which the network output is different from the actual output (for Falsity NN actual output is complementary to the actual output of the Truth NN) are stored in Mtruth and Mfalse.
- Then we find the intersection of Mtruth and Mfalse. These intersection samples are stored in Mfinal. The patterns in Mfinal in a sense are output of the aggregated function (U). This aggregated function is just a combination of intersection over the classification functions (T) and (F).
- In the final step, we remove the patterns of Mfinal from our training dataset, thus effectively under-sampling our majority class.

SMOTE Algorithm

SMOTE is an over-sampling technique where it boosts the number of minority class samples by interpolation method. The minority class samples that are close to each other in a search space are identified in order to form new minority class instances. Synthetic instances are generated rather than to replicate minority class instances to avoid the over-fitting problem.

SMOTE (Synthetic Minority Over-sampling Technique) algorithm uses K-nearest Neighbors (KNN) to connect the minority class instances to create the synthetic samples in the space as shown in Fig. 7. The algorithm takes the feature vectors and its nearest neighbors and computes the distance between these vectors. The difference is then multiplied by a random number between (0, 1) and is added back to the feature [4]. We have applied SMOTE only on the minority class samples in order to increase the number of minority class samples and make them equal to the remaining number of samples in the majority class (remaining after applying CMTNN).

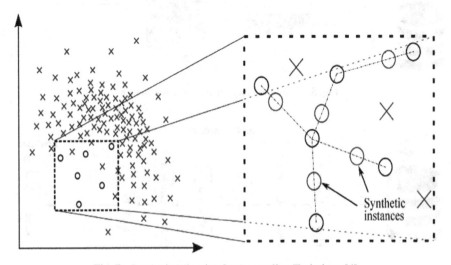

Fig. 7. Synthetic Minority Over-sampling Technique [4]

It is important to note that in our workflow, we start with a huge bias in the number of samples where the minority class constitutes only 0.17% of the total transaction samples. We then under sample the majority class by applying CMTNN and then oversample the minority class to match the number of samples in the reduced majority class.

4.2 Classification Algorithms

After the *Data Balancing Network*, the next block in the pipeline is the *Classification Algorithms* block as shown in Fig. 8. Five classifiers were used to test the model, namely SVM, Random Forest [7], XGBoost [10], Logistic Regression, and ANN [6]. The data after processing from the *Data Balancing Network* is then passed to the *Classification Algorithms* block.

The choice of Classifiers was made based on existing papers that have employed these classifiers for credit card fraud detection or similar tasks, and also on their frequent use in the research community. The ANN classifier follows a simple network architecture of

Classification Algorithms

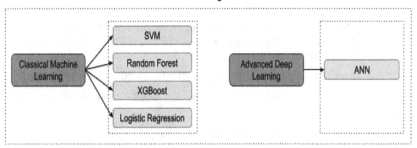

Fig. 8. Classification algorithms

3 Hidden Layers, 1 ReLU block, and *1 Dropout Layer*. The final output of the *Dropout Layer* was passed through a *Sigmoid Layer'* and then fed to *Binary Cross-Entropy Loss Layer*. Structurally, the architecture is identical to that of *CMTNN Network*.

5 Results

5.1 Performance of CMTNN

To solve the class imbalance problem described above, we present our innovative app-roach of utilizing CMTNN [3] and SMOTE [4] in a synergic manner to implement under sampling on majority class and oversampling on the minority class.

Since the CMTNN network has an underlying neural network architecture it is impor-tant to note that differently trained CMTNNs might result in varied extent of under sam-pling (i.e., the final compression achieved over the majority class data). Therefore, we perform an incremental analysis over the training epochs to decide how much (to how many epochs) training would provide optimum results. This analytical exploration is aimed at only finding the optimum extent of training of the CMTNN Network and thus we have used only one classifier at this stage i.e., ANN. We compare the performance of CMTNN+ANN architecture with only ANN in Table 1. A baseline of vanilla ANN at six different levels of training of CMTNN Network for epoch 10, epoch 20, epoch 50, epoch 100, epoch 150 was used.

The detailed results of this analysis are present in Table 1 and Fig. 9 above. Different extent of training the CMTNN network also resulted in different levels of reduction (*due to under-sampling*) achieved in the number of samples of majority class. The amount of reduction (mentioned as *Compression*) in percentage form achieved by varying the number of epochs of training the *CMTNN Network* is presented in Table 1 and also represented in Fig. 10. The compression in the number of samples of the majority class is calculated as percentage of the number of total samples of the majority class before any under-sampling. Figure 10 shows that the level of compression increases with the increase in the number of epochs.

From the results obtained in our exploratory analysis we have observed that any significant compression only starts after the CMTNN Network has been trained for at least 20 epochs. One can also notice that the accuracy and AUC' (area under the ROC

Table 1. Incremental training of CMTNN

Metrics	ANN (Classifier) (No CMTNN)	CMTNN (Balancing Network) + ANN (Classifier) (by varying extent of Training of CMMTNN Network)				
	(No CMTNN)	Epoch 10	Epoch 20	Epoch 50	Epoch 100	Epoch 150
AUC	0.898	0.854	0.659	0.688	0.741	0.670
Accuracy	0.837	0.739	0.340	0.397	0.522	0.371
Compression (%)	0.0	0.02	44.78	49.72	69.83	88.24

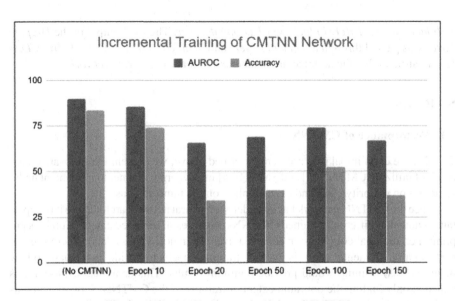

Fig. 9. Analysis of incremental training of CMTNN

curve) metrics are on a rising curve from epoch 20 to epoch 100 but then there is a noticeable dip from epoch 100 to epoch 150 which clearly shows that the number of samples reduced in terms of compression. We achieve optimum performance (in terms of accuracy and AUC) of CMTNN when it is trained for 100 epochs. A compression of 70% in total number of samples of majority class is achieved when the CMTNN Network is trained at its optimum level of performance (epoch 100). Thus, we can conclude that based on our dataset and the underlying neural network architecture of our CMTNN network, we achieve optimum performance (in terms of *Accuracy* and *AUC*) of CMTNN when it is trained for 100 epochs. A compression of 70% in total number of samples of majority class is achieved when the CMTNN Network is trained at its optimum level of performance (*epoch 100*).

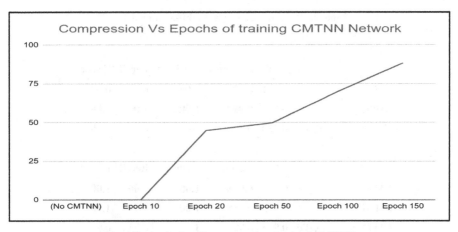

Fig. 10. Analysis of incremental training of CMTNN

5.2 Classification Results

For the larger part of our experimental analysis, we have employed five classifiers, namely *SVM, Random Forest, XGBoost, Logistic Regression and ANN*, one based on advanced deep learning architecture and the remaining four based on traditional machine learning methodologies. Our choice of classifiers for this part of experiment was based on our literature review of existing works on credit card fraud detection in the research community. It is important for the reader to note that the focus of our study is not to explore the best classifier but to explore the effect of the *"Data Balancing Network"* on the performance of the classifiers. Thus, for each of the classifiers we have analyzed them in three different forms i.e., *CMTNN, SMOTE, CMTNN + SMOTE*.

In the CMTNN form, we have applied under-sampling on the majority class and left the minority class as-it-is. In the SMOTE form, we have applied SMOTE based oversampling on the minority class to increase the number of samples to match that of the majority class. In the "CMTNN + SMOTE" form, we have first applied CMTNN based under-sampling on the majority class and then used SMOTE based oversampling on the minority class to increase the number of samples to match that of the modified majority class. Thus, we have created two baselines to compare the performance of our proposed network and all of the classifiers in all of the forms were trained till convergence. The results of this study are presented in Table 2 for each classifier. The performance metrics include AUC, accuracy, precision, recall and F-score.

As evident from the results in Table 2, our proposed approach *"CMTNN + SMOTE"* provides greater AUC than the other two baselines for every classifier while compromising for a small dip in accuracy. To understand the significance of the results obtained in this study, one must also understand why AUC score is more reflective of the classifier's ability to detect fraudulent transactions for our case of highly skewed dataset. Accuracy measures the average of points correctly classified, regardless of which class they belong to. Whereas AUC is a performance metric of the likelihood that given two random points—one from the positive and one from the negative class—the classifier will rank the point from the positive class higher than the one from the negative class. Thus, in a

Table 2. Performance results of different models

ANN

	AUC	Accuracy	Precision	Recall	F-score
CMTNN	0.741	0.522	**1.00**	0.93	0.97
SMOTE	0.796	**0.999**	**1.00**	**1.00**	**1.00**
CMTNN + SMOTE	**0.950**	0.880	**1.00**	0.97	0.98

SVM

	AUC	Accuracy	Precision	Recall	F-score
CMTNN	0.924	**0.998**	**1.00**	**1.00**	**1.00**
SMOTE	0.899	0.988	**1.00**	0.99	**1.00**
CMTNN + SMOTE	**0.953**	0.926	**1.00**	0.93	0.97

Random Forest

	AUC	Accuracy	Precision	Recall	F-score
CMTNN	0.956	0.998	**1.00**	**1.00**	**1.00**
SMOTE	0.880	**0.999**	**1.00**	**1.00**	**1.00**
CMTNN + SMOTE	**0.997**	0.993	**1.00**	0.99	**1.00**

XGBoost

	AUC	Accuracy	Precision	Recall	F-score
CMTNN	0.925	**0.993**	**1.00**	**0.99**	**1.00**
SMOTE	0.937	0.993	**1.00**	0.99	**1.00**
CMTNN + SMOTE	**0.967**	0.965	**1.00**	0.96	0.98

Logistic Regression

	AUC	Accuracy	Precision	Recall	F-score
CMTNN	0.973	**0.999**	**0.99**	**0.93**	**0.97**
SMOTE	0.914	0.972	**1.00**	0.99	**1.00**
CMTNN + SMOTE	**0.932**	0.912	**1.00**	0.99	**1.00**

sense AUC gives a measure of how clearly (*with greater likelihood*) the classifier can differentiate a sample of the positive class from a sample of the negative class, which is undoubtedly the most important part in detection of fraudulent credit card transactions. High scores of precisions, recall and F-score indicates that very small error rate in terms of the false positives is achieved.

6 Conclusions and Future Work

In this paper, we have applied a *Data Balancing Network'* (based on CMTNN and SMOTE) that reduces class imbalance in a skewed dataset. The architecture of the "Data Balancing Network" is independent of the dataset size or type and thus this technique can be extended to any classification task where the dataset suffers from class imbalance problem. It is also important to note that a lot of credit cards fraudulent transactions go unreported, and thus, it results in minority class samples being incorrectly labeled as majority class samples, which further increases the problem in classification. Using 5 different classification algorithms, we have shown that our proposed "Data Balancing Network" boosts the AUC score for all of the five algorithms. Since AUC score tends to be a better reflection of the classification performance for tasks like fraudulent transaction detection, we have established the performance enhancement provided by our proposed network for such tasks irrespective of the classification algorithm employed.

In future, we would implement and analyze the impact of our network on datasets with lower skewness and for a greater variety of classification algorithms to include higher order Deep Learning algorithms as well. CMTNN being a deep learning approach it can be utilized in large data sets (Real time Data Sets such as fraud detection and Loan Approval Datasets) where there is an imbalance problem Another possible scope for future development lies in experimenting with the underlying architecture of the CMTNN network, since the CMTNN network follows a deep learning architecture. This opens up new possibilities of improvement that might be possible by further optimizing the architecture and hyper-parameters of the CMTNN network. The open issues in credit card fraud detection include determining the imbalance in the dataset and to what extend the dataset needs to be balanced to give the best detection accuracy and precision.

References

1. John, O.A., et al.: Credit card fraud detection using machine learning techniques: a comparative analysis. In: 2017 International Conference on Computing Networking and Informatics (ICCNI) (2017). https://doi.org/10.1109/iccni.2017.8123782
2. Kuldeep, R, et al.: Credit card fraud detection using adaboost and majority voting. IEEE Access 6, 14277–14284 (2018). https://doi.org/10.1109/access.2018.2806420
3. Jeatrakul, P., Wong, K.W., Fung, C.C.: Classification of imbalanced data by combining the complementary neural network and SMOTE algorithm. In: 17th International Conference on Neural Information Processing, ICONIP 2010, 22–25 November, Sydney (2010)
4. Promrak, J., Kraipeerapun, P., Amornsamankul, S.: combining complementary neural network and error-correcting output codes for multiclass classification problems. In Proceedings of the 10th WSEAS International Conference on Applied Computer and Applied Computational Science (2011)
5. Emad, M., Far, B.: Supervised machine learning algorithms for credit card fraudulent transaction detection: a comparative study. IEEE Annals of the History of Computing, IEEE, 1 July 2018. doi.ieeecomputersociety.org/https://doi.org/10.1109/iri.2018.00025
6. Abhimanyu, R., et al.: "Deep learning detecting fraud in credit card transactions. In: 2018 Systems and Information Engineering Design Symposium (SIEDS) (2018). https://doi.org/10.1109/sieds.2018.8374722
7. Shiyang, X., et al.: Random forest for credit card fraud detection. In: 2018 IEEE 15th International Conference on Networking, Sensing and Control (ICNSC) (2018). https://doi.org/10.1109/icnsc.2018.8361343
8. Vaishali, et al.: Fraud detection in credit card by clustering approach. Int. J. Comput. Appl. 98(3), 29–32 (2014)

9. Stolfo, S., Fan, D.W., Lee, W., Prodromidis, A., Chan, P.: Credit card fraud detection using meta-learning: Issues and initial results. In: AAAI-97 Workshop on Fraud Detection and Risk Management (1997)
10. Pun, J.K.F.: Improving Credit Card Fraud Detection using a Meta-Learning Strategy. Doctoral dissertation, University of Toronto (2011)
11. Duman, E., Buyukkaya, A., Elikucuk, I.: A novel and successful credit card fraud detection system implemented in a turkish bank. In: 2013 IEEE 13th International Conference on Data Mining Workshops (ICDMW), pp. 162–171. IEEE (2013)
12. Kraipeerapun, P., Fung, C.C.: Binary classification using ensemble neural networks and interval neutrosophic sets. Neurocomputing **72**, 2845–2856 (2009)
13. Kraipeerapun, P., Fung, C.C., Wong, K.W.: Uncertainty assessment using neural networks and interval neutrosophic sets for multiclass classification problems. WSEAS Trans. Comput. **6**, 463–470 (2007)
14. Pozzolo, A.D., Caelen, O., Johnson, R.A., Bontempi, G.: Calibrating probability with under-sampling for unbalanced classification. In: Symposium on Computational Intelligence and Data Mining (CIDM), IEEE (2015)
15. https://www.kaggle.com/mlg-ulb/creditcardfraud
16. Wei, W., Li, J., Cao, L., et al.: Effective detection of sophisticated online banking fraud on extremely imbalanced data. World Wide Web **16**, 449–475 (2013). https://doi.org/10.1007/s11280-012-0178-0
17. Bolton, R.J., Hand, D.J.: Unsupervised profiling methods for fraud detection. Credit Scoring and Credit Control VII", pp. 235–255 (2001)

A Multi Class Classification for Detection of IoT Botnet Malware

Hrushikesh Chunduri[1]([✉]) [iD], T. Gireesh Kumar[2][iD], and P. V Sai Charan[3][iD]

[1] TIFAC-CORE in Cyber Security, Amrita School of Engineering,
Amrita Vishwa Vidyapeetham, Coimbatore, India
`cb.en.p2cys19004@cb.students.amrita.edu`
[2] Department of Computer Science and Engineering, Amrita School of Engineering,
Amrita Vishwa Vidyapeetham, Coimbatore, India
`t_gireeshkumar@cb.amrita.edu`
[3] Department of Computer Science and Engineering, Indian Institute of Technology,
Kanpur, India
`pvcharan@cse.iitk.ac.in`

Abstract. Botnets are one of the most prevailing threats for cyber-physical devices around the world. The evolution of botnet attacks has been rampant and diverse with vast scalability. One of the variants is targeting the IoT ecosystem involving devices not limiting to sensors, actuators, and all kinds of smart devices. Modern-day botnet threats have multiple functionalities rather than targeting devices for DDoS. In this paper, we used the two latest IoT Botnet data sets: IoT-23 and MedBIoT, which consists of modern-day attacks that helped us classify them for more than two classes. We have considered 6 variants of IoT botnet attacks from both the data sets and categorise them into 3 classes. We have used ensemble approaches for multi-class classification where random forest outperformed with an accuracy of 99.88. We have also generated new samples using conditional generative adversarial networks (CTGAN) for testing the efficacy and robustness of our models built.

Keywords: IoT botnet · KNN imputation · Conditional Generative Adversarial Networks (CTGAN)

1 Introduction

1.1 IoT Botnet

An IoT bot is a variant of a traditional botnet with a group of compromised computers, sensors, and smart devices connected over the internet selected for causing damage financially and for illegitimate purposes. According to the recent statistics [14], it is estimated that there might be 75 billion IoT devices connected by 2025, and the economy generated by this could be several trillion by 2030. Contrasting to these numbers [20], researchers at Palo Alto Networks states that 98% of total IoT ecosystem traffic is unencrypted. Over 41% of total attacks are

© Springer Nature Switzerland AG 2021
N. Chaubey et al. (Eds.): COMS2 2021, CCIS 1416, pp. 17–29, 2021.
https://doi.org/10.1007/978-3-030-76776-1_2

due to the vulnerabilities that the devices hold in them, and botnets contribute around 13% of all attacks [20, 21]. An average of five minutes is required to get hold of any IoT device and subjecting towards botnets, these are comparatively easy to advance once the attacker got hold of the device. These statistics pave an imperative role for cybersecurity implementations in every which way possible to curb these at different levels. Basic implementation overview will be a phase wise approach as depicted in Fig. 1 and briefed as follows [1].

Phase 1: Rigorous Scanning and Report Server: The Attacker/Infected bot will continuously scan for open ports, services, and back door vulnerabilities. After a potential victim is found, it is exploited by brute-forcing the login credentials or depending on the attack's functionality, any other attacking strategy can be used. After gaining access to the device, its information [IP address and login credentials] is sent to the report server.

Phase 2: Deploying Payload and Execution: Depending on the vulnerability exploited and device architecture, the corresponding payload is selected and sent to the victim through the report server. After execution is completed, many botnets delete themselves to hide their functionality and kill other critical processes.

Phase 3: C&C Commands and Self Propagation: The above two phases can be considered the first stage of the attack, and many botnets have the ability to propagate through the infected devices for DDoS attacks. Now, the infected devices act according to the Command and Control server's instructions managed by the attacker. While accepting the commands from C&C, infected bots will also have the capability to scan for other devices and propagate the attack simultaneously. This process runs in a loop, causing reflection and amplification of a DDoS attack.

Sophisticated APT malware and botnets have the potential to ex-filtrate data and download malicious files rather than limiting them to Denial of Service [23]. It is essential to restrain the attack in the second phase, and the above mentioned phases are generalized that might not be the same for every variant of attack.

1.2   Briefing on IoT Botnet Attacks

(a) Bashlite: Bashlite [1] is considered the first botnet targeting the IoT devices in 2015 for DDoS attack. This botnet's execution will be in 2 stages where it scans for the devices and then launches the attack. It is not a self-propagated bot, while the other new variants of it are capable. This Botnet mainly targets the devices running SSH/Telnet services and tries to brute force with 6 pre-configured usernames and 14 password combinations. All the commands are in plain text format, and the communication is unencrypted. Also, C&C and IP addresses are hardcoded, which makes the execution obvious and simple.

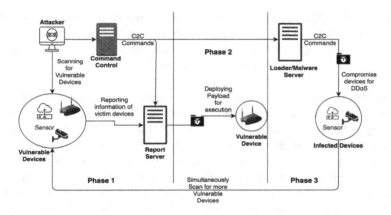

Fig. 1. Basic IoT Botnet execution

(b) Mirai: In 2016, Mirai [1,18] became a predominant and widespread attack in terms of the scalability of damage it has done and challenging the entire security research community. Selecting the victim devices for attack and all the execution strategy to attack are similar for Bashlite and Mirai. So, this can be regarded as the upgraded version of Bashlite with 62 pre-configured login credentials and a self-propagating feature inbuilt. Mirai uses a compact binary protocol to communicate and resolves IP addresses by DNS rather than hard coding them.

(c) Torii: Torii [22] is a more sophisticated, stealthy, and persistent IoT botnet with multiple features causing indefinite damage. This botnet was first noticed in late 2018 and can ex-filtrate sensitive information from the victim devices. Most importantly, this botnet is compatible with most architectures like MIPS, ARM, x86, x64, PowerPC, SuperH, etc., where earlier variants are not capable enough. Unlike traditional botnets, Torii runs a shell script for weak telnet credentials, and depending on the architecture of the device, appropriate payload is downloaded via encrypted traffic. All the exploit codes and commands are encrypted in multiple layers with Advanced Encryption Standard (AES-128) in addition to MD5 hash for checksum. Torii uses 6 different methods to maintain a persistent connection with the infected device and uses TCP port 443 (https) for communicating with command and control. With the anti-debugging feature, the payload hides its identity, which makes it stealthier.

(d) Okiru: Okiru [8] is a Mirai variant spotted in 2018 that specifically targets ARC processors in linux machines and can be considered a target-specific botnet. There are 4 types of pre-configured router exploit codes and 114 hard-coded username/password details for telnet/SSH exploitation. The configuration is encrypted in many stages similar to that of Torii, and there is a high risk probability if the source code is known.

(e) Hakai: Hakai [8] is a variant of Qbot mainly targeting the routers and their vulnerabilities. Rather than telnet/SSH brute-forcing, it only exploits the back-door vulnerabilities and CVE's present in D-link, Huawei, and Realtek routers, which are leading hardware equipment manufacturers.

(f) Muhstik: Muhstik [24] is a new linux variant botnet seen in 2018 mainly targeting GPON routers. The main intention of this variant is Crypto min-ing/jacking attacks for making money. This attack makes use of the remote code execution vulnerability in oracle and php webservers (CVSS-9.8).

The organisation of the paper is as follows: Sect. 1 detailed about the alarm-ing statistics, Phases in executing IoT botnet and briefing on different botnet attacks that are addressed in this paper. Section 2 deals with Related works and the research gap in addressing new IoT botnets. Information regarding the chosen data sets, features considered, extracting the features using network sim-ulator and pre-processing the data are detailed in Sect. 3. Section 4 explains the architectural overview in building the classifier and implementation of CTGAN. Section 5 talks about the obtained results from the list of classifiers used. Finally, in Sect. 6 we conclude our entire work done and give possible insights into future works in this research domain.

2   Related Works

Many works have contributed to address the classification of the attacks in IoT devices [19]. Most of the works have used network simulators for feature extrac-tion, and others have used IDS [16,21] to categorize anomaly detection. In 2018, Mirsky et al. [2] have developed an IDS built on autoencoders for online anomaly detection called "Kitsune". They [2] have developed a feature extractor that consists of the following feature categories (i) Host-MAC&IP (ii) Channel (iii) Network Jitter, and (iv) Socket. They demonstrated their results with anomaly detection of Mirai botnet. In 2018, Meidan et al. [3] introduced a data set called "N-BaIoT" for Mirai and Bashlite attacks considering "Kitsune" [2] features, which have been performed on 9 different IoT devices.

In 2015, Moustafa [4] had created a dataset called "UNSW-NB15" comprising simulated attacks using kali linux and real benign traffic using "IXIA tool". They [4] have used Bro and Argus network simulators to capture the network traffic and overall a 48 feature dataset with 9 different types of attacks. In 2018, Koroniotis et al., [5] came up with a dataset named "Bot-iot" consisting of a realistic testbed to simulate both benign and different types of attack traffic. They [5] have used Argus network simulator for extracting over 30 features and added to it they have simulated 14 flow-based network features. They have also performed machine learning analysis for the obtained dataset and concluded SVM stood out the best.

In 2019, Kang et al., [6] had created an IoT network intrusion data set built on 2 IoT devices. They have simulated attacks using aircrack-ng(kali linux tool). Adding to this, they [6] have used Mirai sample for performing attacks like

UDP flooding and telnet brute-forcing. Recently in 2020, Imtiaz [7] proposed a two-stage flow-based anomaly detection in IoT networks. If the first stage IDS identifies the packet as an anomaly, it will be forwarded to the second stage for further categorization. Their [7] proposed approach stood out best from every classifier with 99.9 accuracy considering flow-based features.

All the above mentioned data sets have limited their works for 2–3 attack samples, and there has been no substantial work and data available for the attacks on IoT devices after 2016. So, to address this, we have considered about 6 variants of botnets, including Mirai and Bashlite. We have preprocessed and classified the data into 3 classes.

The overall aim of this paper is to build a classifier that effectively detects an IoT botnet attack with the best accuracy possible and to have the features and data that have large scalability to fit into multiple families of IoT botnet variants. In detail, our contribution have three objectives mentioned below.

1. As IoT devices are in billions, using generalized Zeek network features and data to solve the problem: early detection of attack by classifying malicious C&C communication
2. Use CTGAN to generate more dynamic data for testing the efficiency of the classifiers built and solve the problem of data insufficiency for torii botnet.
3. Comparisons of different models built on the above mentioned data and choose the best fit classifier.

3   Data Collection and Preprocessing

3.1   Details About IoT-23 and MedBIoT DataSet

IoT-23 DataSet [8]: a labeled data set captured in the Stratosphere laboratory funded by avast software published in January 2020. It has 12 different types of attacks captured on a RaspberryPi with 20 different scenarios [8]. Benign captures are captured over 3 other real IoT smart devices. For all the captures, they have used Zeek Network Simulator [9], having around 18 features and two labels. From all the scenarios given, we have considered only Muhstik, Okiru, and Hakai attacks. MedBIoT DataSet [10]: dataset was created by a researcher Alberto from Estonia, comprising 83 devices, making it a medium-sized network. They [10] have used 3 types of attacks, Mirai, Bashlite, and Torii, as a new variant published in February 2020. They have used "Kitsune" [2] as their entire feature set. To build a classifier, we must have the same attributes so, we made use of fine-grained pcap network captures provided by them to convert all the captures using Zeek Simulator [9]. The reason to choose two data sets is to address more attack scenarios, and the classifier is built on diversified data.

3.2   Log Extraction Using Zeek

Zeek is a network traffic analysis tool [9] that investigates all the traffic for malicious activity. It offers an extensive set of log files separately as output like conn, dns, ftp, files, http, known_certs, smtp, ssl, etc., for both real time traffic and integrated custom inputs. MedBIoT dataset [10] offers separate pcap files for both attack and benign samples. So, we have installed a Zeek simulator on a Ubuntu Virtual Machine for extracting the log files from them. We have given the pcap file as input to the simulator and use Zeek commands to parse the input file to analyze the possible log files it holds and give output in the form of structured ASCII logs as shown in Fig. 2.

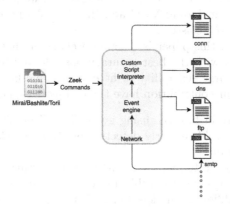

Fig. 2. Log extraction using Zeek

3.3   Samples and Features Considered

Details of the samples considered for building a classifier are mentioned in Table 1. For hakai botnet, only C&C samples are captured, and for Muhstik, we have not considered captured C&C samples as there are in single digits in the dataset. Although substantial work was done concerning Mirai and Bashlite botnet attacks, they are still emerging, and MedBIoT [10] holds new versions of both the botnets. So, to extend the scalability of our work, we have added a good number of samples.

Out of all the 18 features obtained from Zeek, we have selected the below 12 best features for two reasons, one being relevant packet data features (bytes and packets) and data insufficiency is more for other attributes. We have tabulated all the features considered to build the classifiers in Table 2. Apart from benign samples, we have almost considered every sample of C&C and Malicious[1] from the datasets which turns out to be a multi-class classification.

3.4   KNN Imputation

The most important aspect while building a classifier is to train it with appropriate data. We have encountered a few missing values from the features "duration",

---

[1] Malicious includes: Bruteforcing, command injection, and Spreading for DDoS.

Table 1. Statistics of data

Botnet	Benign	C&C	Malicious	Total
Mirai	25000	1700	13000	39700
Bashlite	23000	4450	5000	32450
Torii	500	30	100	630
Hakai	2181	8219	–	10400
Okiru	2663	15687	5000	23350
Muhstik	4536	–	5954	10490
Total	**57880**	**30086**	**29054**	**117020**

Table 2. Generalised 12 features for building classifier

S. No	Feature	Description
1	id.orig_p	Originated port
2	id.resp_p	Received port
3	proto	Protocol name
4	service	Service used for communication (dns, ssl, http etc.,)
5	duration	Total connection period
6	orig_bytes	Total count of payload bytes sender sent
7	resp_bytes	Total count of payload bytes receiver sent
8	conn_state	Connection state
9	orig_pkts	Number of packets that the originator sent
10	orig_ip_bytes	Count of IP level bytes that Sender sent
11	resp_pkts	Count of that the receiver sent
12	resp_ip_bytes	Count of IP level bytes that the receiver sent
13	detailed-label	Benign(B)/c2c(C)/malicious(M)

"orig_bytes", and "resp_bytes". By numerous trial and error attempts with few algorithms, we concluded that missing values fits best with imputing the values through KNN [12]. This algorithm works by considering the weighted euclidean distance of present values, which is calculated from Eqs. (1) and (2). For filling missing data in "duration" attribute, 9, 10, 11, 12 features and for "orig_bytes", "resp_bytes" features 9, 10 and 11, 12 from Table 2 are considered respectively.

$$Distance_{ab} = \sqrt{weightage * square\ of\ present\ values\ distance} \qquad (1)$$

where

$$Weightage = \frac{Total\ Co-ordinates}{Present\ Co-ordinates} \qquad (2)$$

4   Building a Classifier and Implementing GAN

4.1   Ensemble Approach

After preprocessing the data and considering the 12 Zeek Network Simulator [9] features, we need to classify IoT botnet attack samples as benign, C&C, and Malicious which is a multi-class classification. To build a classifier, we have used ensemble models [15,17] which are trained by various weak learners to construct a well-built model. The whole ensemble learning can be mainly categorized into Boosting, Bagging and stacking where we concentrate more on first two categories. The conception for boosting is, wrong learners are given more importance and iterated for becoming efficient. For Boosting, Stochastic Gradient Boosting(GBM) is used to build new base learners by correlating the gradients in the loss function. Loss function can be interpreted as the error between true and predicted values. Next is Bagging, for this, we have RandomForest that works with a culmination of numerous decisions trees. Each decision tree outputs its predictions, and the class with the highest votes is considered the overall prediction. Adding to these classifiers, we have implemented KNN and RadialSVM for a comparative perspective to reveal the ensemble model's effectiveness. As we have considered two different data sets, Fig. 3 mentions the overall implementation steps from extracting raw logs through Zeek simulator and parsing both datasets to form a structured dataset which is directed for classification.

4.2   Applying Conditional Generative Adversarial Networks (CTGAN)

The synopsis for any Generative Adversarial Networks can be termed a two stage process of constructing new samples from the existing data with the generator

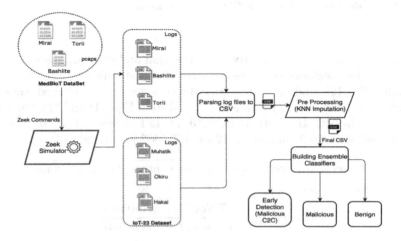

Fig. 3. Implementation architecture

model able to generate new samples, and the discriminator model predicts it's class as real/fake. The usage for GAN's are rampant in image processing which are capable enough to mimic a human faces that haven't been existed. CTGAN, [11] is a variant of GAN to generate synthetic tabular data from numeric and category inputs. It is an advanced version of TGAN [13] mainly in terms of network structure using fully connected networks rather than LSTM for generating column-wise synthetic data. Also, to avoid the model break down for categorical columns, they [11] have designed conditional generator and resample training data. From Fig. 4, we can say CTGAN is used for two purposes, one being to generate data for insufficient Torii samples, which are color coded in blue and are not included in test data. The other reason is to test the effectiveness of our trained model over new data generated. Table 3 will give the statistics of data that is considered to generate the samples and the data generated from them for the respective variant of attack.

Table 3. Statistics of GAN data

Variant	Samples considered	Samples generated
Torii C& C	30	500
Torii Malicious	100	1000
Hakai C& C	5000	10000
Okiru C& C	5000	10000
Okiru Malicious	1000	5000
Muhstik Malicious	5000	10000

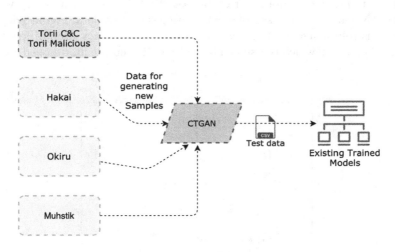

Fig. 4. CTGAN implementation overview

5   Results and Discussion

The whole implementation of the following models is done in R programming language using "caret" package. Initially, we have considered 1,17,020 samples mentioned in Table 1 with repeated cross-validation re-sampling 10 times and 2 repeats for each model. All the results are tabulated in Table 4 with accuracy and kappa values. We have also tabulated Sensitivity which is true positive rate for each class i.e., B:benign, C:C2C and M:malicious in Table 4. Although we have obtained the best accuracy for RandomForest with 99.88, it has a very high time complexity consuming almost 60 min. We achieved slightly less accuracy for gbm with 99.36, but it took 30 min to arrive at that accuracy. On the other hand, SVM and KNN performed well with decent accuracy. Also, from Fig. 5, we can correlate that ensemble approaches are better suited in our case.

Table 4. Results for different classifiers

Classifier	Accuracy	Kappa	Sensitivity
RandomForest	99.88	99.71	99.7 (B), 99.6 (C), 99.6 (M)
gbm	99.36	98.89	99.74 (B), 99.03 (C), 98.67 (M)
SVM	94.72	90.96	94.05 (B), 97.2 (C), 94.00 (M)
KNN	96.14	93.37	95.85 (B), 97.45 (C), 95.68 (M)

For testing dynamic data on our trained models, from Table 3 we have 35,000 new samples of hakai, okiru, and muhstik, excluding Torii samples that are to be added in training data. Also, we have added 5,000 benign samples from the IoT-23 dataset to provide an optimal test dataset. Table 5 gives the accuracy values for CTGAN generated new samples which are passed test data. Figure 6 depicts that gbm is robust against the new data having an accuracy drop of less than 1%. RandomForest, which is assumed to be the best accurate fit, dropped around

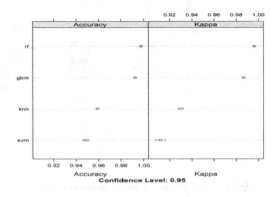

Fig. 5. Accuracy and Kappa statistics for classifiers

8.7%. KNN with a 7.2% drop, SVM can be considered the least fit model with a drastic drop of 27.41%. The overall time complexities from high to low can be interpreted as follows: *RandomForest>Svm>KNN>Gbm*. Though Randomforest performed well, gbm with nearly half time complexity can be considered the best fit model of our implementation.

Table 5. Results of different classifiers for GAN data

Classifier	Accuracy	Kappa
RandomForest	91.18	84.78
gbm	98.75	97.76
SVM	67.31	52.60
KNN	89.21	80.95

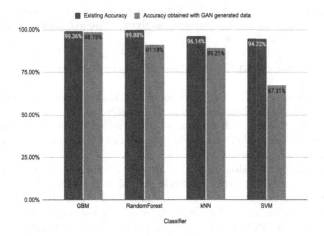

Fig. 6. Variations in accuracy drop for different classifiers

6 Conclusion and Future Work

On a concluding note, our model is effective in classifying the new age IoT Botnets with the best accurate, efficient in time complexity, and optimal feature count. It can efficiently detect malicious C&C traffic, which is crucial for any IoT botnets to advance. To summarize our process and work done, we have addressed the problem of classifying new IoT botnets with two datasets [8,10], and we have efficiently preprocessed the data by imputing missing values with KNN [12] algorithm. We have also tested our model's robustness by generating new samples using CTGAN [11]. We have limited our work to 4 new IoT botnet variants and considered 12 features. In future, we focus to automate the process from feature extraction to prediction stage without any predefined tools which can be used as a plug-and-play method. Also we aim to model an IDS built over our robust models considering more statistical features and also include more variants of attacks.

References

1. Marzano, A., et al.: The evolution of Bashlite and Mirai IoT botnets. In: 2018 IEEE Symposium on Computers and Communications (ISCC). IEEE (2018)
2. Mirsky, Y., et al.: Kitsune: an ensemble of autoencoders for online network intrusion detection. arXiv preprint arXiv:1802.09089 (2018)
3. Meidan, Y., et al.: N-BaIoT-network-based detection of IoT botnet attacks using deep autoencoders. IEEE Pervasive Comput. **17**(3), 12–22 (2018)
4. Moustafa, N., Slay, J.: UNSW-NB15: a comprehensive data set for network intrusion detection systems (UNSW-NB15 network data set). In: 2015 Military Communications and Information Systems Conference (MilCIS). IEEE (2015)
5. Koroniotis, N., et al.: Towards the development of realistic botnet dataset in the Internet of Things for network forensic analytics: Bot-IoT dataset. Future Gener. Comput. Syst. **100**, 779–796 (2019)
6. Hyunjae K., Dong H.A., Gyung M.L., Jeong D.Y., Kyung H.P., Huy K.K.: IoT network intrusion dataset (2019). http://ocslab.hksecurity.net/Datasets/iot-network-intrusion-dataset
7. Ullah, I., Mahmoud, Q.H.: Two-level flow-based anomalous activity detection system for IoT networks. Electronics **9**(3), 530 (2020)
8. Parmisano, A., Garcia, S., Erquiaga, M.J.: A labeled dataset with malicious and benign IoT network traffic. Stratosphere Laboratory, January 2020. https://www.stratosphereips.org/datasets-iot23
9. Zeek Network Security Monitor (2019). https://docs.zeek.org/en/current/intro/
10. Guerra-Manzanares, A., Medina-Galindo, J., Bahsi, H., Nõmm, S.: MedBIoT: generation of an IoT botnet dataset in a medium-sized IoT network. In: Proceedings of the 6th International Conference on Information Systems Security and Privacy (ICISSP), vol. 1, ISBN 978-989-758-399-5, pp. 207–218 (2020). https://doi.org/10.5220/0009187802070218
11. Xu, L., et al.: Modeling tabular data using conditional GAN. In: Advances in Neural Information Processing Systems (2019)
12. Crookston, N.L., Finley, A.O.: yaImpute: an R package for kNN imputation. J. Stat. Softw. **23**(10), 16 p. (2008)
13. Xu, L., Veeramachaneni, K.: Synthesizing tabular data using generative adversarial networks. arXiv preprint arXiv:1811.11264 (2018)
14. Estimation statistics relating IoT. https://www.statista.com/statistics/471264/iot-number-of-connected-devices-worldwide/
15. Anand, P.M., Gireesh Kumar, T., Sai Charan, P.V.: An ensemble approach for algorithmically generated domain name detection using statistical and lexical analysis. Procedia Comput. Sci. **171**, 1129–1136 (2020)
16. Meidan, Y., et al.: ProfilIoT: a machine learning approach for IoT device identification based on network traffic analysis. In: Proceedings of the Symposium on Applied Computing (2017)

17. Ani, R., et al.: IoT based patient monitoring and diagnostic prediction tool using ensemble classifier. In: 2017 International Conference on Advances in Computing, Communications and Informatics (ICACCI). IEEE (2017)
18. Perrone, G., et al.: The day after Mirai: a survey on MQTT security solutions after the largest cyber-attack carried out through an army of IoT devices. In: IoTBDS (2017)
19. Kumar, A., Lim, T.J.: EDIMA: early detection of IoT malware network activity using machine learning techniques. In: 2019 IEEE 5th World Forum on Internet of Things (WF-IoT). IEEE (2019)
20. Statistics relating to attacks on IoT ecosystem (2021). https://threatpost.com/half-iot-devices-vulnerable-severe-attacks/153609/
21. Thomas, A., Gireesh Kumar, T., Mohan, A.K.: Neighbor attack detection in Internet of Things. In: Bhattacharyya, S., Chaki, N., Konar, D., Chakraborty, U.K., Singh, C.T. (eds.) Advanced Computational and Communication Paradigms. AISC, vol. 706, pp. 187–196. Springer, Singapore (2018). https://doi.org/10.1007/978-981-10-8237-5_18
22. Torii IoT Botnet (2018). https://blog.avast.com/new-torii-botnet-threat-research
23. Sai Charan, P.V., Gireesh Kumar, T., Mohan Anand, P.: Advance persistent threat detection using Long Short Term Memory (LSTM) neural networks. In: Somani, A.K., Ramakrishna, S., Chaudhary, A., Choudhary, C., Agarwal, B. (eds.) ICETCE 2019. CCIS, vol. 985, pp. 45–54. Springer, Singapore (2019). https://doi.org/10.1007/978-981-13-8300-7_5
24. Information about Muhstik IoT Botnet (2020). https://unit42.paloaltonetworks.com/muhstik-botnet-attacks-tomato-routers-to-harvest-new-iot-devices/

An AI-Based Solution to Reduce Undesired Face-Touching as a Precautionary Measure for COVID-19

Samir Patel[1] , Hiral Madhani[2] , Samyak Garg[2](✉) , and Madhvik Chauhan[2]

[1] Department of Computer Science and Engineering, Pandit Deendayal Petroleum University, Raisan, Gandhinagar 382007, Gujarat, India
samir.patel@sot.pdpu.ac.in

[2] Department of Information and Communication Technology, Pandit Deendayal Petroleum University, Raisan, Gandhinagar 382007, Gujarat, India
{hiral.mict18,samyak.gict18,madhvik.cict18}@sot.pdpu.ac.in

Abstract. The ongoing health crisis continues to impact all walks of life, demanding radical lifestyle changes, and forcing us to comply with a whole new host of precautionary regulations. Poor hygiene practices are in part responsible for the soaring COVID-19 cases, self-inoculation being one of them. Recent studies in this area have highlighted how face-touching provides us with immediate relief from temporary discomforts such as muscle tension, and is a way of regulating emotions and stimulating memory. This paper is aimed at exhibiting the role of Artificial Intelligence and Machine Learning in developing a fully software-based system to help restrict this instinct. A web application has been designed, which takes in real-time input of a person through a built-in PC webcam, and detects the intersection between the hands and facial regions, resulting in a warning alert as an output to the user. Making use of BodyPix 2.0 in TensorFlow, this novel method has been found to have an accuracy of 91.3%, with proper synchronization and minimum delay in detection. The feasibility of such an approach has thus been discussed herein, giving an insight into how smart hygiene control techniques could help in the management of any such future catastrophes stemming from similar deadly biological agents, lest history repeats itself.

Keywords: Self-inoculation · Artificial intelligence · Machine learning · BodyPix 2.0 · TensorFlow

1 Introduction

Originating in December 2019 as a series of acute respiratory illnesses local to Wuhan, the capital of the Hubei province in central China, COVID-19 caused by the SARS-CoV-2 virus (Severe Acute Respiratory Syndrome Coronavirus-2), has now resulted in a worldwide pandemic affecting about 213 countries and territories of the world. As of 6th September, 2020, nearly 27 million confirmed cases have been reported worldwide, including more than 900,000 deaths (World Health Organization 2020). Despite a history

© Springer Nature Switzerland AG 2021
N. Chaubey et al. (Eds.): COMS2 2021, CCIS 1416, pp. 30–45, 2021.
https://doi.org/10.1007/978-3-030-76776-1_3

of diseases caused by the CoVs (MERS-CoV and SARS-CoV), a new strain of the virus, SARS-CoV-2, has left us totally clueless. Much deadlier than its predecessor varieties, the SARS-CoV-2 is far more contagious, and can be easily transmitted through direct contact with contaminated people or surfaces, as well as via oral-respiratory droplets [1].

Studies have shown that while the SARS-CoV-2 may successfully thrive in aerosols for about 3 h, it can sustain on inanimate surfaces in the form of droplets for a much longer duration (Cardboard: 24 h, Stainless steel: 72 h, Copper: 4 h, Plastic: 72 h) [2]. Through self-inoculation, these contaminated fomites transfer the virus from our hands into our bodies through the facial mucous membranes such as the mouth, eyes and nose [3]. A behavioral study conducted at the University of New South Wales, wherein medical students were kept under observation, has found that people touch their faces about 23 times/h on an average [4]. The alarming statistics regarding self-touch have been explained by scientists, who define the involuntary and spontaneous habit as being intertwined with deeper emotional and cognitive processes [5].

An attempt has been made through this research to explore the possibility of dealing with this instinct by making use of Artificial Intelligence. It has been decades since humans have been training machines to mimic human- like tasks in order to give rise to intelligent systems with the desired potential to augment human capabilities. A subset of AI, Machine Learning (ML), finds extensive use in various fields, computer vision being one of them [6]. It primarily refers to the science that deals with building algorithms that can be trained through data sets to make smart guesses on the basis of pattern recognition. Instead of predefined rigid instructions, machine learning models are fed with sample inputs that enable data-driven predictions as per the actual requirement [7].

A number of innovations have come to the forefront to address the recent happenings. AI-based wearables in particular, are an interesting step towards developing an awareness regarding face-touching by making the user conscious of the exact instance when it happens. These devices give off an alert in the form of a buzzing sensation as soon as the hands enter a pre-calibrated zone near the face. However, it is the forgetfulness associated with the wearing of these smart wristbands, and the complex architecture involved, that demands for the development of a simpler web-based solution. While it may be inconvenient to wear these devices for prolonged periods of time, a detector in the form of an application that runs on a PC could be quite an effective method, considering the rapid digitalization of the modern world.

Founded on the concepts of Neural Networking and Machine Learning, the designed application uses the BodyPix 2.0 model available in TensorFlow for hand and face detection, with any contact resulting in a warning notification to the user. While a number of other object detectors such as R-CNN, MTCNN, YoloFace, DeepFace, SSD, BlazePalm etc. exist, BodyPix is preferred for its enhanced accuracy [8].

Even with more people working from home during the pandemic, people who are still required to show up at work, are forced to prioritize their jobs over their health. Implementing such digital solutions at workplaces could ensure employee safety and well-being to a great extent. This project-based research hence strives to bring to light a digital approach to curb the menace of COVID-19. In this backdrop, a detailed description and analysis regarding the technique and implementation of this model has been presented here, highlighting how this software based outlook with its unique features could indeed make a difference in the current scenario, besides helping the masses get rid of this psychological tendency as a precautionary measure for similar unforeseen future hazards.

2 Proposed System

To achieve the aforementioned objective, an AI-based model has been presented herein, which is capable of dynamically tracking a person's hands and face movements, in an attempt to limit the spread of illnesses exaggerated by self-inoculation. A notable feature of this proposed technique is the choice of BodyPix 2.0 available in TensorFlow for hand and face detection, followed by an accurate warning system in response to intersection between them.

The following steps are involved in the working process:

- The application is opened through any browser.
- Input is fed through an inbuilt PC webcam.
- The presence as well as intersection of hands and face in the real-time image input is detected by the use of BodyPix 2.0.
- A detailed record concerning the number of touches and the time elapsed since the last touch is maintained, and is accessible to the user.
- Each instance of face- touching is brought to notice through an alert notification either in the form of a visual pop-up display on the PC, or through an audible beep sound, or both, as per the user's discretion.

System Implementation

The code has been developed in HTML (Hypertext Markup Language) and JavaScript, offering the exclusive privilege of browser and OS flexibility. The only requirement to run this model is the availability of a PC with a webcam. The system doesn't demand any sophisticated hardware and software, making it increasingly accessible and easy to maintain. Moreover, minimizing the application window anytime doesn't hamper the functioning in any way, allowing the user to carry on any sort of work on the PC. An offline mode of implementation is permissible too, provided the availability of a cache server facility in the browser. Figure 1 summarizes the steps involved.

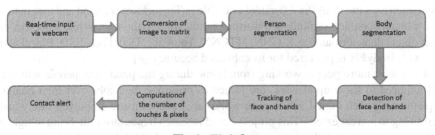

Fig. 1. Work flow

3 Methodology and Algorithmic Explanation

This section is aimed at offering a deep insight into the underlying concepts governing hand and face detection in BodyPix 2.0. The associated technology and techniques adopted at each step of the work flow presented earlier, have also been discussed comprehensively.

3.1 Introduction to BodyPix 2.0

BodyPix 2.0 is an open source machine learning tool introduced by Google, an update to the previous version with enhanced functionalities. It is based on the ResNet50 model, which is a convolutional neural network making use of the ImageNet database [9]. Rooted in the concept of deep learning, the model has been prepared to perform real-time semantic pixel-wise segmentation of an image in accordance with a person as well as the twenty-four body parts, which are treated as classes. It makes use of TensorFlow.js, the JavaScript library to deploy Machine Learning algorithms, and can be run through a browser [10].

The availability in browser is an added advantage that allows it to access to web APIs such as Canvas Compositing due to which it becomes possible to achieve the following effects on the canvas of the web page [10, 11]:

- Foreground and background masks
- Colored masks indicating different parts of the body
- Pixelated masks
- Blurring the bodyparts
- Blurring the background (Bokeh effect)

It is because of these features that BodyPix finds extensive use in video editing and photography.

As compared to the first version, the release of BodyPix 2.0 marks various developments such as multi-person support, a new refined ResNet model, tolerance for different image sizes, weight quantization and an API. Furthermore, improved accuracy is achieved, owing to some technological modifications, such as the up-sampling of the segmentation logits. This ensures that a higher resolution is achieved before the sigmoid function is applied to calculate the probability score of each pixel [12].

A few different versions of BodyPix exist, with fundamental differences concerning inference time and performance time, mainly due to the use of different network architectures, such as ResNet50 and MobileNetV1. While the MobileNet architecture is considered to be smaller and efficient, ResNet is preferred for its higher accuracy, and works well with more powerful GPUs [13].

3.2 Working

The complete algorithm can be divided into 3 main phases:

a) Person Segmentation
b) Body Segmentation
c) Intersection detection

a) Person Segmentation

The most basic step involves distinguishing human figures if any, from the background of an image. The real- time input which is taken in the form of a 2-D matrix, is internally treated as a linear array whose dimensions are determined by the number of pixels. Person segmentation fundamentally deals with segmenting an image into pixels followed by a binary decision for each one of them in order to categorize them into two groups: pixels that contain a person, and those that do not. This is achieved through the sigmoid activation function, which assigns a float value in the range 0–1 to every pixel of the image, indicating the probability of the presence of a person in that particular pixel. Only defined in the range 0–1, the function finds extensive use in models where probability is to be predicted as an output.

A segmentation threshold, decided by the user, then converts these float values into absolute zeros or ones. This threshold refers to the minimum score a pixel must have after sigmoid activation to be considered a part of a person. For instance, setting a threshold of 0.6 would ensure that float values in the range 0 to 0.6 would be converted to zeros making those pixels a part of the background, whereas the remaining values over 0.6 would be turned to ones. A higher value of segmentation threshold results in a tighter crop around a person. However, this may at times cause the obtained segmentation mask to leave out some pixels that are actually a part of the person [14].

Figure 2 provides a holistic view of all the steps involved.

Fig. 2. (From L to R) - Input image, intermediate stage after sigmoid activation, final result after thresholding [10]

The input can be resized before inference by setting the internal resolution to low, medium, high, full, or simply a percentage value between 0 and 1. A larger value implies more accuracy, but slower prediction time. For detecting and segmenting more than one person individually, a variant of the same method is used. This application has however been designed taking into consideration only a single user.

The output thus obtained at the end of this process is essentially a one-dimensional array X [m * n], where m and n are respectively, the length and width of the input image in terms of pixels. Each element of the array is either a 0 or 1, corresponding to the value assigned to each pixel.

b) Body Segmentation

One of the most useful features of BodyPix is its ability to identify various parts of the body. The input image is segmented into pixels, and each is given an integer value in the range of 0 to 23 as illustrated in Table 1, specifying the particular body part that the pixel is associated with. Pixels that do not belong to a human body, are considered to be a part of the background and are assigned a value of −1 [14].

Table 1. Body parts corresponding to their predefined IDs [14]

ID	Part name	ID	Part name
0	Left face	12	Front torso
1	Right face	13	Back torso
2	Upper left arm (front)	14	Upper left leg (front)
3	Upper left arm (back)	15	Upper left leg (back)
4	Upper right arm (front)	16	Upper right leg (front)
5	Upper right arm (back)	17	Upper right leg (back)
6	Lower left arm (front)	18	Lower left leg (front)
7	Lower left arm (back)	19	Lower left leg (back)
8	Lower right arm (front)	20	Lower right leg (front)
9	Lower right arm (back)	21	Lower right leg (back)
10	Left hand	22	Left foot
11	Right hand	23	Right foot

The same process as before is repeated again, but this time with an output tensor P comprising of 24 channels. So for each position in the image, we need to make the best possible prediction among the 24 channels. The optimum body_part_id having the maximum probability is chosen through the formula given below [10, Eq. (1)], where (u,v) indicates the position of each pixel of the tensor P during inference.

$$body\_part\_id = argmax\,(P\,(u,\,v,\,i)),$$
$$i \in I, where\ I = \{0,\,1,\,\ldots,\,23\} \tag{1}$$

The resulting image thus contains pixels having values from 0 to 23, indicating which body part they belong to. The output obtained from person segmentation comes handy here. In body segmentation, all the pixels from the previous stage having float values less than the segmentation threshold are assigned a value of −1. This aids in separating the background from the person, along with an accurate detection of the twenty-four body parts (Figs. 3 and 4).

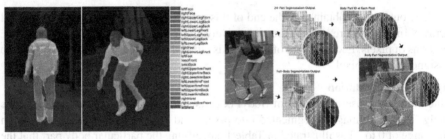

Fig. 3. Body part segmentation [10]

Fig. 4. Combining the output of 24-channel body segmentation and person segmentation [10]

The final image is primarily a matrix constructed from a linear array with appropriate pixel labelling, resulting in the desired mask being applied on all the people in a merged manner. If segmentation needs to be done individually for different people, an alternative API method based on the same concept is employed.

c) Intersection Detection

For detecting the intersection, two separate arrays are required, namely *Hand_array* and *Face_array*. Algorithm 1 describes the main steps involved for obtaining them.

Algorithm 1: Deriving the Hand_array and Face_array

Input: int Array(sourceVideo.width, sourceVideo.height)
Output: Hand_array and Face_array

1. **if** nose=true and left_eye=true OR right_eye= true
2.   Face_array(pixval)
3.   **if** pixval= 0 OR 1
4.   return pixval
5.   **else**
6.   return -1
7. **end if**
8. Hand_array (pixval)
9.   **if** pixval=10 OR pixval=11
10.   return pixval
11. **else**
12.   return -1

The presence of a nose and at least one eye is considered necessary for the identification of a face. The condition for the same is mentioned in Step 1 of Algorithm 1. Step 3 judges the value assigned to each pixel of the incoming video. The pixel value '0' indicates left face, whereas the pixel value '1' indicates right face, according to Table 1. These values are entered into *Face_array*. Any other pixel value emphasizes the absence of a face at that particular pixel. A value of –1 is assigned to the array at all such instances.

Similarly, step 9 checks whether the pixel value corresponds to 10 or 11, which refers to the left hand and right hand respectively. If it does, the value is returned to *Hand_array*. Otherwise, the value –1 is returned.

The linear arrays *Face_array* and *Hand_array* are then converted into matrices, and taken as input by the function *touchingCheck*, as depicted by Algorithm 2.

Algorithm 2: Detecting intersection

Input: matrix1, matrix2, padding
Output: count //Counts the number of intersecting pixels

function touchingCheck(matrix1, matrix2, padding)
1.	Initially, count = 0;	c_1
2.	**for** (let y = padding; y < matrix1.length -padding; y++)	$c_2 n$
3.	**for** (let x = padding; x < matrix1[0].length -padding; x++)	$c_3 n^2$
4.	**if** (matrix1[y][x] > -1) //Checks the presence of face pixels	c_4
5.	**for** (let p = 0; p <padding; p++)	$c_5 n^3$
	// if the hand is left or right, above or below the current face segment	
6.	**if** (matrix2[y][x - p] > -1 OR matrix2[y][x + p] > -1 OR	
	matrix2[y - p][x] > -1 OR matrix2[y + p][x]> -1)	$c_6 n^3$
7.	count **increment**	$c_7 n^3$
8.	**end if**	
9.	**end** for	
10.	**end if**	
11.	**end** for	
12.	**end** for	
13.	**return** count	

C_1, C_2, C_3, C_4, C_5, C_6 and C_7 here, are the costs associated with each statement, while n denotes the number of rows or columns present in the matrices (for complexity analysis, it has been assumed that both the matrices are square matrices of order n).

The variables *matrix1* and *matrix2* represent *Face_array* and *Multihand_array* respectively, whereas the variable *padding* is the space left between the contents and the border of the web page.

The first two *for loops* (steps 2 and 3) are associated with reading the matrices. Step 4 checks for the presence of a face in the frame for detecting intersection. If the face is present, it checks the values of those elements in *matrix2* that are present till the value of *padding*, towards the left, right, upward and downward directions.

In step 5 and 6, it can be seen that if:

- matrix2[y][x − p] > −1, the column number decreases as p increases. Hence, the elements present to the left of the pixel in the same row are read.
- matrix2[y][x + p] > −1, the column number increases as p increases. So, the elements present to the right of the pixel in the same row are read.
- matrix2[y-p][x] > −1, the row number decreases as p increases. Therefore, the elements present above the pixel in the same column are read.
- matrix2[y + p][x] > −1, the row number increases as p increases. Thus, the elements present below the pixel in the same column are read.

Any of these four conditions where the value is greater than −1, indicates the presence of a hand. Since these are nested under the main *for loop* in step 4 which identifies the presence of face pixels, the whole algorithm successfully detects an intersection whenever the conditions stated in step 4 and step 6 are fulfilled. Upon detection, the value of the *count* variable is increased, which keeps a track of the number of intersecting pixels.

This whole process of checking continues for all the values of x and y due to the first two *for loops* (step 2 and step 3).

Complexity of the function is given by Eq. 2 stated below.

$$C(n) = C_1 + C_2 n + C_3 n^2 + C_4 + C_5 n^3 + C_6 n^3 + C_7 n^3$$
$$\therefore C(n) = O(n^3) \tag{2}$$

The function created for intersection detection thus has an algorithmic complexity of $O(n^3)$, where n defines the number of rows or columns in the matrices passed as a parameter to this function.

To sum up, the function *touchingCheck* firstly reads the whole matrix to check whether a face pixel is present nearby. If it finds the face pixel, it then checks the position of hands, considering four possibilities: left, right, above the face segment and below the face segment. If at least one of them is true, the function concludes that an intersection between the face and hands has occurred.

4 Comparative Analysis of Existing Detection Methods

4.1 Available Models

Apart from BodyPix 2.0, a number of other models exist that can be used for detecting hand-face intersection. Listed below are some of the most widely used techniques in this domain [15].

a) OpenCV Haar Cascades Classifier:

One of the most successful feature based detection algorithms was suggested by Paul Viola and Michael Jones [16]. The classifier is based on the concept of machine learning, where it is trained through a large set of negative and positive images, after which it begins extracting Haar features from each image fed to it (Figs. 5 and 6).

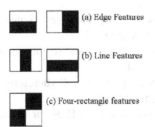
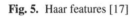

Fig. 5. Haar features [17]   **Fig. 6.** Applying Haar features on training images [16]

The feature chosen here for instance, is based on the general fact that the region surrounding the eye is darker than the adjoining nose and cheek regions. From about $160000+$ features, Adaboost is used to select the best ones [17].

The OpenCV library written in C language makes this detection model extremely fast to implement. However, this comes at the cost of accuracy, as this algorithm is unable to perform well when encountered with side faces, and finds it difficult to handle different poses and illumination changes.

b)   DLib Histogram of Oriented Gradients (HOG):

The fundamental operating principle here is to draw out features into a vector and then feed it into a classification algorithm that would detect an object's presence in a given region. The drawback with this implementation is its inability to detect faces at various angles, and is thus best known as a frontal face detector [18].

c)   DLib Convolutional Neural Network (CNN):

This method deals with the major problem faced by HOG, and is capable of detecting faces at almost all angles. However, being computationally heavy, it isn't suitable for real-time video [19] (Fig. 7).

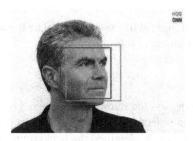

Fig. 7. Comparison between DLib HOG and DLib CNN [19]

d)   Multi-task Cascaded CNN (MTCNN):

Comprising of 3 networks in a cascade, MTCNN is one of the most popularly used models today. It detects the bounding boxes of images, along with the facial landmarks. This method is preferred over OpenCV Haar Cascade for its higher accuracy, although it requires higher run time [20].

e)   YOLOv3:

YOLOv3 which makes use of Darknet-53, is basically a Deep CNN, which implies large architectural complexity. It is capable of detecting objects of various sizes, and is relatively faster than MTCNN. For the detection task, 53 extra layers are added onto it, making YOLOv3 a convolutional neural network comprising of 106 layers in total. This method is very accurate and almost without any error. However, due to its complex nature, more computational resources are required, and the model may function slowly and require a higher run-time on mobile devices [21] (Fig. 8).

f)   MobileNet SSD Face Detector:

Similar to YOLOv3, SSD too is a deep convolutional network. It is quite accurate, and works well in the case of different poses, occlusion and illumination. YOLOv3 however, outperforms this detection tool. Even though the inference speed is reasonably good, it is not enough to function well on low-end GPU or mobile devices [22].

The performance of object detection models is generally measured in terms of the following parameters [23, 24]:

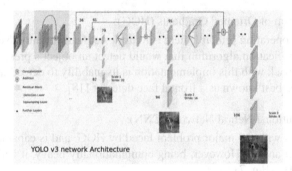

YOLO v3 network Architecture

Fig. 8. YOLOv3 network architecture [21]

a) Mean Average Precision (mAP): It is used to calculate the accuracy, which is found through the following formula [24, Eq. (3)]:

$$precision = \frac{tp}{tp + fp} \tag{3}$$

Here *tp* (true positive) depicts the number of predicted regions which rightly predicted the presence of an object (face/hand) in them. *fp* (false positive) represents the number of areas that falsely identified the background as an object (face/hand) containing region.

b) Inference time: This is used to measure the complexity of performance, and refers to the total time a model needs to perform detection task on a single image. The complexity of a model may also be determined through resource usage (CPU, GPU and RAM).

A graphical conclusion is presented below, which is the result of an experimental study [24], performed using the WIDER Face dataset. The device used was Dell Inspiron 15 7577, with the following hardware specifications:

RAM: 16 GB

GPU: Nvidia GeForce GTX 1060

CPU: Intel Core i7–7700HQ Quad Core Processor (Figs. 9 and 10)

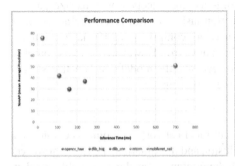
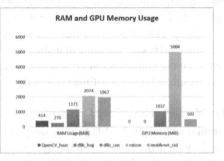

Fig. 9. Accuracy & complexity analysis (CPU used for model no. 1 and 2, GPU used for model no. 3, 4 and 5) [24]

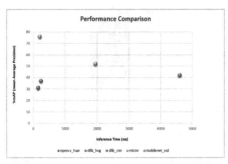
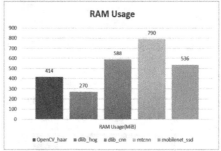

Fig. 10. Accuracy & complexity analysis (CPU implementation for all the models) [24]

4.2   Purpose of Choosing BodyPix 2.0

All the methods discussed above adopt a similar approach, i.e., the desired objects (here, face and hands) once detected, are enclosed by a rectangular bounding box that describes the target location. A major issue that arises in this case, is that often, a large portion of the rectangle may not be even containing the specified object, reducing the actual accuracy of implementation when an intersection between objects is to be detected. Here, in this application, while using other techniques for detection, it may happen that a false intersection may be identified due to the above-mentioned problem, and the person may be notified even though a measurable distance exists between the hands and the face. BodyPix 2.0 overcomes this drawback by providing the shape of the contour much similar to the actual shape of the human body. A tighter crop around the person ensures that the segmentation mask thus obtained is a true outline of the hands and faces, with no extra space from the background enclosed within. The much greater accuracy achieved overweighs the slight delay that may occur due to higher processing time.

Another privilege of using this model is the assurance of minimum clash/conflict. The person segmentation technique employed removes the unnecessary background from the image before any further procedure occurs. The focus here, is hence only on the object of interest. In other algorithms, the background and unnecessary details may add to the confusion, and it might happen that multiple persons may get detected, negatively affecting the correctness of the outcome.

5   Experimental Results

Once the user grants permission, real-time input is constantly taken in through the webcam. The model is loaded when the user permits usage of webcam for the particular file (Fig. 11).

The system is designed to give a notification to the person sitting in front of the PC as soon as the hand touches the face. The user is offered the choice of a visual pop-up display/an audible beep sound or both, as an alert (Figs. 12 and 13).

Fig. 11. Initial display

Fig. 12. Segmentation mask   **Fig. 13.** Notification display on contact detection

Additionally, the tracker on the side provides some useful statistics to the user. Data regarding the number of touches and the time elapsed since the last touch helps the user to take a mental note and become more conscious.

5.1 Accuracy Determination

For finding the accuracy of detection, a screenshot of the application window was taken, wherein the face of the person identified by the model, is shaded in violet. Rectangles of different sizes drawn in the violet portion that extends beyond the face, helps in determining the error in identification. The summation of all the pixels enclosed by each such rectangle, gives the total number of pixels detected incorrectly. Face pixel count is given by the machine learning model and is obtained from the console section of the web page. Table 2 represents the values obtained experimentally, which are used to calculate the Mean Average Precision (mAP) (Fig. 14).

Using Eq. (3), mAP is calculated for each observation. A mean of all these values gives the overall accuracy of the model, which is found to be 91.3%, which means that for every 100 pixels taken from the input, about 91 of them correctly detect the intersection, contributing to an error rate of 8.7%.

The inference of the above experiment is that the accuracy depends on the distance between the person and the webcam, which is the real reason behind the difference in the precision values for each observation. The user's position should neither be too near, nor too far from the webcam.

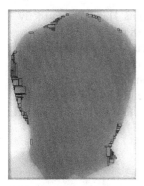

Fig. 14 Pixels falsely
detected as the object

Table 2. Error involved in detection

Sr. no.	Number of face pixels	Number of incorrect pixels	Ratio of incorrect pixels to face pixels	Mean average precision
1.	43672	4075	0.093	0.907
2.	45762	4112	0.089	0.911
3.	31614	2781	0.088	0.912
4.	35146	2959	0.084	0.916
5.	32471	2643	0.081	0.919

5.2 Determining the Response Time

Experimental data obtained through multiple trials as shown in Table 3, gives the response time of the model in accordance with the web browser used. This is the time required by the system to respond to the user through a notification in case of a hand-face intersection.

Table 3. Response time in seconds

Sr. no.	Chrome	Firefox	Internet explorer
1.	0.41	0.46	0.42
2.	0.43	0.43	0.43
3.	0.40	0.45	0.44
4.	0.45	0.45	0.45
5.	0.43	0.41	0.43
6.	0.43	0.46	0.45
7.	0.42	0.42	0.42
8.	0.43	0.44	0.44
9.	0.44	0.40	0.42
10.	0.46	0.45	0.46

CPU configuration: i3-6006U CPU @ 2.00 GHz 2.00 GHz
RAM: 8 GB

It can thus be inferred that the model has nearly the same response time irrespective of the choice of web browser.

General observations:

i) Optimum distance between the object and the device, and appropriate lighting is necessary for accurate results. It has been observed that while the face is rightly identified, hands are not properly detected in case of dim lights. Hands are correctly recognized in the range of 1 foot (0.3 m) to 4.75 feet (1.4478 m).

ii) Inability of BodyPix to deal with 3-D: The image is taken as a two-dimensional input, which at times results in false detections. A hand in front of the face may be identified as an intersection, based on the two-dimensional treatment of objects, even though it may not necessarily be touching the face. Specific hardware or sensors capable of considering distances, would be required along with BodyPix, to address this shortcoming.

6   Conclusion

This research concludes the success of a web-based application to restrict the human tendency of self-inoculation. A user-friendly solution has been introduced that alerts a person at every instance of contact, to keep their hands off their faces with an aim to ward off illnesses. The feature of detection through segmentation mask allows the user to analyze the precise facial regions which are frequently in contact with the hands. A high accuracy of 91.3% achieved through BodyPix 2.0 in TensorFlow as discussed above, makes it a preferred choice over all other object detection methods. With virtually no hardware requirements and a manageable software size, the model is highly compatible, platform independent, and easy to implement. The utility of this solution lies in the fact that it is not just limited to the pandemic times, but could be used as a preventive measure to give up the habit of face-touching altogether.

Conflicts of Interest/Competing Interests.   The authors declare that no conflict of interest exists

References

1. Khasawneh, A.I., et al.: Medical students and COVID- 19: knowledge, attitudes, and precautionary measures. a descriptive study from Jordan. Front. Publ. Health **8**(263), 2 (2020)
2. Jayaweera, M., Perera, H., Gunawardana, B., Manatunge, J.: Transmission of COVID-19 virus by droplets and aerosols: a critical review on the unresolved dichotomy. Environ. Res. **188**, 4–5 (2020)
3. Rahman, J., Mumin, J., Fakhruddin, B.: How frequently do we touch facial T-Zone: a systematic review. Ann. Global Health Art **75**, 1 (2020)
4. Kwok, Y.L.A., Gralton, J., McLaws, M.-L.: Face touching: a frequent habit that has implications for hand hygiene. Am. J. Infect. Control **43** (2015)
5. Mueller, S.M., Martin, S., Grunwald, M.: Self-touch: Contact durations and point of touch of spontaneous facial self-touches differ depending on cognitive and emotional load. PLOS ONE (2019)
6. Esposito, F., Malerba, D.: Editorial: Machine Learning In Computer Vision. Applied Artificial Intelligence. Italian Association for Artificial Intelligence, Bari (2010)
7. Simon, A., Deo, M.S., Venkatesan, S., Babu, D.R.R.: An overview of machine learning and its applications. Int. J. Electric. Sci. Eng. **1**(1), 22 (2016)
8. Visée, R.J., Likitlersuang, J., Zariffa, J: IEEE Transactions on Neural Systems and Rehabilitation Engineering, p. 2 (2020)

9. BodyPix 2.0 – Person Segmentation in the Browser. Adafruit, 20 Nov. 2019. https://blog.ada fruit.com/2019/11/20/bodypix-2-0-person-segmentation-in-the-browser-tensorflow-machin elearning-deeplearning-tylerzhu3-oveddan/. Accessed on 15 Oct 2020
10. [Updated] BodyPix: Real-time Person Segmentation in the Browser with TensorFlow.js. TensorFlow, 18 Nov. 2019. https://blog.tensorflow.org/2019/11/updated-bodypix-2.html. Accessed on 17 Oct 2020
11. Vino, M.: Edit live video background with WebRTC and TensorFlow.js. Francium Tech, 30 April 2020. https://blog.francium.tech/edit-live-video-background-with-webrtc-and-ten sorflow-js-c67f92307ac5. Accessed 15 Oct 2020
12. [BodyPix] single person detection in latest bodypix. GitHub, 17 Dec. 2019. https://github. com/tensorflow/tfjs/issues/2547. Accessed on 15 Oct 2020
13. BodyPix: Person Segmentation in the browser. SymmetricalDataSecurity, 10 Oct. 2019. http://symmetricaldatasecurity.blogspot.com/2019/10/bodypix-person-segmentation-in-browser.html. Accessed 15 Oct 2020
14. BodyPix- Person Segmentation in the Browser. https://github.com/tensorflow/tfjs-models/tree/master/body-pix#person-segmentation. Accessed on 18 Oct 2020
15. Aniket, M.: Facial recognition algorithms. Engati. https://www.engati.com/blog/facial-rec ognition-systems. Accessed 15 Oct 2020
16. Viola, P., Jones, M.J.: Rapid object detection using a boosted cascade of simple features. In: Proceedings of the conference on Computer Vision and Pattern Recognition, vol. 1, p. 3, Feb 2001
17. Face detection using Haar Cascades. OpenCV-Python Tutorials. https://opencv-python-tutroals.readthedocs.io/en/latest/py_tutorials/py_objdetect/py_face_detection/py_face_dete ction.html. Accessed on 16 Oct 2020
18. Johnston, B., de Chazal, P.: A review of image-based automatic facial landmark identification techniques. EURASIP J. Image Video Process. **13**, 7 (2018)
19. Arun, P.: CNN based face detector from dlib. Towards Data Science, 17 April 2018. https:// towardsdatascience.com/cnn-based-face-detector-from-dlib-c3696195e01c. Accessed on 16 Oct 2020
20. Zhang, K., Zhang, Z., Li, Z., Qiao, Y.: Joint face detection and alignment using multi- task cascaded convolutional networks. IEEE Signal Process. Lett. **23**(10), 1–2 (2016)
21. Ayoosh, K.: What's new in YOLO v3? Towards Data Science, 23 April 2018. https://toward sdatascience.com/yolo-v3-object-detection-53fb7d3bfe6b. Accessed 10 Oct 2020
22. Ranjan, R., et al.: A fast and accurate system for face detection, identification, and verification. IEEE Trans. Biometric. Behav. Ident. Sci. **1**(2), 4 (2019)
23. Padilla1, R., Netto, S.L., da Silva, E.A.B.: A survey on performance metrics for object-detection algorithms. In: Proceedings of International Conference on Systems, Signals and Image Processing (IWSSIP) (2020)
24. Dwiyantoro, A.: Performance showdown of publicly available face detection model. Node-flux, 30 April 2018. https://medium.com/nodeflux/performance-showdown-of-publicly-ava ilable-face-detection-model-7c725747094a. Accessed on 10 Oct 2020

DDoS Attack Detection Using Artificial Neural Network

Abhinav Shah$^{(\boxtimes)}$, Digvijaysinh Rathod , and Dharmesh Dave

National Forensic Sciences University, Gandhinagar, India
{digvijay.rathod,dharmesh.dave}@gfsu.edu.in

Abstract. Distributed Denial of Service (DDoS) attacks grow rapidly and cause a serious risk to network security. DDoS attacks intentionally occupy resources such as computing power and bandwidth to deny the services to potential users. So the automatic identification of DDoS attacks is very important. Machine Learning is the proven technology for the identification of such attacks. Over the decade many researchers have taken detection of DDoS attacks as the research objective and succeeded as well. However many more research needs to be explored in the identification of DDoS attacks due to the inefficiency of their techniques in terms of performance, accuracy, identification, and collection of data, normalized data set, feature reduction, and computational cost. We tried Back Propagation Neural Network (BPNN) with supervised machine learning technique to recognize the DDoS attacks at Network/Transport layer. We experimented with a dataset consisting of 4 lakh records of synthetic data, out of which we used 70% of the dataset for training purpose and performance measure on the rest 30% of the dataset. Our experimental results show that 97.7% of DDoS attacks were successfully identified and this technique does not decrease performance and can be easily spread out to broader DDoS attacks.

Keywords: Machine learning · Cyber security · Synthetic dataset · Back propagation Neural Network · Supervised learning · DoS · DDoS

1 Introduction

In the current era of technology, modern human beings rely on technology for their business, education, entertainment, trading and day by day activity because of the huge research and development on the internet, web and mobile technologies. Internet brought biggest revaluation in the computing and communication world by using standard internet protocol, any human being can access their social sites, bank account, trading, money transfer is very easy [1]. Even organization can run their business through mobile application, web application, and data center all around the world. There are people termed as "attacker" in the world whose intension is malicious to gain political gain [33], financial gain [32] and destruction [34] by lunching cyber-attacks including DDOS attack.

Denial of Service (DoS) was formerly introduced by Gligor [35] in the operating system framework [36] but afterward it was used for network context also. Attacker carried out Denial of Service attack (DoS) [38] by pushing huge amount of traffic to the server using a single system. Distributed Denial of Service attack (DDoS) [39] is executed with the same goal of DoS by deploying numerous systems at various geographical location. In 2000, DDoS attacks massively affected the operation of major well known internet corporations such as Amazon, eBay, Yahoo, and CNN. DDoS attacks put down the network (network links, network devices, and server), internet infrastructure, and communication technology with illegitimate traffic. DDoS attacks were always the first choice of the attacker to degradation or complete denial of service [37] of the internet based business of any organization that results in a huge financial or reputation loss.

Attackers can use automated tools like LOIC (Low Orbit ION cannon) – Use TCP, UDP, and HTTP Dos attacks; HOIC (High Orbit ION cannon) – generate an enormous number of HTTP GET and POST request, RIDY – send the HTTP POST request with a lengthy content-length header filed; Slowloris – Slow DoS attack but open multiple threats which send HTTP GET request; HTTP Unbearable Load King (HULK) - uses obfuscation method to create unique flood requests; PyLoris – creates an open full TCP connections and manages to hold them as long as possible and OWASP DoS HTTP POST – generate a huge amount of HTTP GET and POST request [40]. Attackers botnet [44] to carry out DDoS attacks to steal data, send spam or access the devices and their connection. We refer botnet [41] as internet linked devices and each of them is executing one or many bots, bot refers to an automated software application that runs the automated task. Nowadays, attackers also use more sophisticated ways to perform DDoS attacks through system vulnerabilities [42] or the use of bot dropper – a piece of malware [43]. Acharya et al. [46] has discussed about DDoS attacks based on TCP/IP protocol vulnerabilities.

Based on the network protocol layer, DDoS attack is broadly classified into three/four layers – The Network/Transport layer and seven-layer – Application layer [44–46]. Three/Four-layer DDoS attack – This layer DDoS attacks consume more bandwidth of server and is launched at the half-opened connection of TCP, UDP, ICMP, and DNS protocols [3]. Seven-layer DDoS attack – This layer DDoS attack consumes less bandwidth and use layer seven protocol such as HTTP, DNS, VoIP, and SMTP. Layer seven DDoS attacks exhaust the webserver resources by sending a huge number of login requests, search requests, etc., and difficult to detect by the IDS and IPS because the connection is already established and requests could seem to be from legitimate users.

Artificial Neural Network (ANN) [59] is a computing model and component of artificial intelligence which is used to imitate the functioning of a human brain. The neural network model has three processing elements that receive input and deliver outputs based on their predefined activation functions. ANN has three-layer starting with input, output, and hidden layer and each individual layer may have several nodes. There are two categories, one is supervised learning neural networks (SLNNs), and other one being unsupervised learning neural networks (ULNNs). The difference between these two types is that SLNN are labeled and provide deep analysis of the data while the ULNN does not determine under such intelligence [56]. The following main aspect are acknowledged to establish the capability of the network [57]: the design of the ANN model, the training method, and the selection of parameters/attributes used in training.

All of these elements make the composition of optimized ANNs a challenging problem [58]. In this research paper, we used a Back-Propagation Neural Network in the proposed model.

The Experiment is executed on a laptop with i7-4500 CPU @ 1.80 GHz 2.40 Ghz Intel Processor with 12 GB RAM.

In this paper, the author proposed a model with Back Propagation Neural Network (BPNN) algorithm to identify DDoS attacks at Network/Transport layer. As we discussed earlier, attackers use half-open TCP, UDP, ICMP, and DNS protocol to carry-out the DDoS attacks because of ease in implementation, practicality, and online documentation of TCP, UDP, and ICMP protocols [47]. This is the motivation to consider the network/transport layer - TCP, UDP, and ICMP protocol to detect the DDoS attacks. The later part of the paper is formulated as, Sect. 2 briefly discuss the relevant work carried out in the latest research paper in this domain, Sect. 3 describes the data set that was utilized to train our model, Sect. 4 describes the normalization techniques that were used to convert the data into a normalized form. Further on Sect. 5 describes the Back Propagation Neural Network (BPNN) algorithm. This section also describes how the BPNN model was used to train the dataset. Section 6 describes the results that were generated after training the model. Section 7 draws the conclusion and culminates the research paper.

2 Related Work

In this segment, we summarized the survey of the research papers relevant to TCP based DDoS identification and DDoS attack identification using Artificial Neural Network.

Jiao et al. [18] had proposed TCP-based DDoS detection model which focused on to detect fixed source IP attacks as well as random source IP attacks. The Author implemented two decision tree classifiers algorithm, to differentiate malicious traffic from normal traffic. Al-Duwairi et al. [19] recommended a pairing-based filtering (PF) scheme to detect reflector based DDoS attacks which are based on TCP, UDP, ICMP, and DNS protocols. Chen et al. [20] proposed defense scheme against shrew DDoS attacks using TCP flow. Gao et al. [21] used a proactive test methodology to identify malicious TCP flow and also shown simulation results. Jun et al. [22] Used packet sampling-based detection and flow entropy mechanism against DDoS attacks. Gavaskar et al. [4] have shown three counters algorithm to detect TCP SYN flooding. Bedi et al. [17] presented a game-theoretic model to protect against DoS/DDoS attacks on TCP-friendly flows. Noh et al. [31] proposed a methodology that reckons the correlation of number of TCP flags with total number of TCP packets to identify the DDoS attacks. Krishna et al. [45] measured TCP-SYN based DDoS attacks with the protection feature provided by Microsoft. Redhwan et al. [48] proposed a framework for an intelligent ICMPv6 DDoS flooding-attack with a success rate of 98.3%. Khandelwal et al. [49] presented methodology to identify DoS attack by implementing a Back-Propagation Neural Network (BPNN) and authors considered parameters such as frame length, flow rate, and CPU usage. The detection ratio was 96.7%. Ahmad et al. [50] proposed a methodology that uses multiple layered perception architecture and resilient backpropagation. Arun et al. [51] proposed an algorithm by combining the ensemble of Neyman Person cost minimization and Resilient Back Propagation (RPB). The authors tested the proposed algorithm with a publicly available dataset and their own lab datasets also. Li et al. [52] proposed a technique to detect DDoS attack based on neural networks. Ali et al. [53] presented DDoS attack identification using a combination of Back Propagation Artificial Neural Network and Artificial Bee Colony [53]. Shah et al. [54] demonstrated that a reduced dataset do not have any limitation as correlated with full dataset and BPNN can point to a finer model. Amruta et al. [55] proposed methodology for DDoS identification artificial neural network and tested their own lab dataset. Saied et al. [47] applied an Artificial Neural Network (ANN) to identify DDoS attacks and tested with old data set and up to date data set generated in the lab simulation. Andropov [17] proposed methodology for network anomalies using a multilayer perceptron and trained with backpropagation. Proposed methodology tested with data set collected from ISP. Wankhede et al. [28] had used a neural network to detect DoS attack on CIC IDS 2017 dataset. Zekri et al. [29] had designed a DDoS detection system to mitigate the threat and concluded the results of various machine learning techniques. Kumar et al. [30] had used the MeanShift algorithm to detect network attacks and achieved an accuracy of 81.2% and the prediction rate of 79.1%.

Our literature shows that various authors carried out research in the DDoS identification but some of the important points such as inefficiency of their techniques in terms of performance, accuracy, identification, and collection of data, normalized data set, feature reduction, and computational cost. Some of the researches only consider the TCP SYN flag only to identify the DDoS attacks. We proposed Back Propagation Neural Network (BPNN) with supervised machine learning to detect the DDoS attacks at the Network/Transport layer considering all these important factors.

When looking in [5], the author had used the Recurrent Neural Network (RNN) model for predicting intrusion detection and to study binary and multiclass classification. The performance of this model gave an accuracy of around 83%. Figure 1 describes the result of the RNN model.

	KDDTrain⁺	KDDTest⁻	KDDTest²¹	Time
Hidden Nodes = 20, learning rate =0.01	99.40%	79.37%	60.76%	4155
Hidden Nodes = 20, learning rate =0.1	99.79%	83.18%	68.23%	3900
Hidden Nodes = 20, learning rate =0.5	99.81%	83.09%	67.84%	3331
Hidden Nodes = 60, learning rate =0.01	99.39%	78.72%	59.54%	4135
Hidden Nodes = 60, learning rate =0.1	99.79%	81.06%	64.08%	4613
Hidden Nodes = 60, learning rate =0.5	99.87%	83.11%	67.82%	3946
Hidden Nodes = 80, learning rate =0.01	99.29%	79.16%	60.34%	4324
Hidden Nodes = 80, learning rate =0.1	99.81%	83.28%	68.55%	5516
Hidden Nodes = 80, learning rate =0.5	99.85%	82.66%	66.99%	4478
Hidden Nodes = 120, learning rate =0.01	99.28%	78.55%	59.25%	4786

Fig. 1. Result of RNN model

From the above researches, we can conclude that Neural Network has given higher accuracy for deep learning as compared to different existing techniques. So, taking that into count here authors have tried Back Propagation Neural Network (BPNN) algorithm. The purpose of using this algorithm is that, the BPNN model will use a different approach as compared to other algorithms. In the BPNN model [6] it starts with randomly generating the weights and tries to minimize the prediction error after each iteration. The next section covers the dataset.

3 Data Set

Data Set plays the most important roles in machine learning. Data has data type [7] and it is a raw fact that can be in any form either a database dump or an excel sheet consisting of various records. Data can be structured or unstructured. The data type of data can be a number, string, date, decimal, etc. Sometimes dataset might contain categorized data also.

In this paper, we used synthetic dataset [2] that have been used for performing training and testing using machine learning. The reason behind generating a synthetic dataset is to meet exact conditions or requirements which may not be available in the real-time scenario [23]. Many datasets are available to perform machine learning, but in such cases, the authenticity of data is not proved, so in that case a synthetic dataset can be very useful. Another benefit is, it helps to achieve the desired result by applying some modifications in the algorithm [24]. It is very important to understand and validate the data before moving to the training phase. Identifying all the parameters from the dataset is necessary. Once the parameters are identified, prepare it for training. The next section describes generating and preparing the dataset for training.

3.1 Data Preparation

Data preparation is another important part of machine learning. Once the data has been generated, prepare it for machine learning. Sometimes this part needs more attention because when the data is acquired, it doesn't fit exactly into the training model as it is. So, to avoid this kind of problem it is necessary to prepare a complete dataset into a fixed format for processing.

The following Pseudocode has been used to generate the data set and the same data was used in the training model.

```
Define protocol list
Define flag list
Create IP Address function
  Iterate for 4 octets of IP address
    For each octet initialize random values from 1 to 254
  Join all the values of each octet with decimal
Create Protocol function
  Select random protocol from the protocol list
Create Source Port function
  Select random port number between 1 and 65534
Create Destination Port function
  Select random port number between 1 and 65534
Create Syn flag function
  Select random value from the flag list
Create Push flag function
  Select random value from the flag list
Create Ack flag function
  Select random value from the flag list
Create Fin flag function
  Select random value from the flag list
Create generate data function
  Open a csv file in writing mode
  Iterate the loop 4 lakh times
    Write values into the file by calling each function
Call function generate data
```

What we kept in mind while preparing the dataset [8]:

Identifying the Data. It is very important to identify data that will be the part of data set. We will use the dataset to predict attacks. We need to consider the classification, clustering, regression, etc., techniques while identifying the data. In this paper, the author carried out a prediction of DDoS attacks based on TCP flags, so in such case data related to TCP flags must be present in the dataset.

Create Data Collection Technique. It is necessary to have a good data collection strategy/technique. In this paper, the author has generated synthetic data to train the model.

Formatting the Data. Once the data is acquired, it is necessary to convert it into a proper format because it may not be in the proper format. This data can be termed as dirty data. In machine learning, it is important to clean data, to get the desired output [8]. In this paper, the author generated data set manually, so no need to clean the data.

Handling Missing Values. When dealing with the dataset, there might be a case where the data set has missing values. In such case, proper techniques need to be applied to replace missing data with a dummy value (e.g. N/A for categorical data and 0 for integer data), either replace the missing value with the average value or else fill up the missing value with most frequent value occurring in the dataset. This process can be automated by applying various algorithms or scripts that automatically replace the missing values according to the given dataset [8]. In this paper, author didn't get any instance to handle missing values as the data was generated manually.

3.2 Sample Data Set

This section will discuss about the dataset which was generated through a script and was used to train the model. The generated dataset consists of 8 different parameters and their description shown in Table 1. We choose these parameters because combinations of TCP flags can be a surveillance [25] activity made by the attackers to form a large attack. Similarly, in another reference [26], the author has stated that improper combinations of the TCP flag can lead to DDOS attack and can be considered a starting point for a more advanced attack. In another reference [27], the author stated that TCP null attack could be used to perform a large attack. So, considering these references, we have selected the given parameters which will help in detecting a network attack.

Table 1. Data description of dataset

Sr. no.	Parameters	Description	Data type	Sample data
1	Ip address	It describes the source IP address in decimal	Integer	185704401
2	Protocol	It describes the protocol name	String	TCP
3	Source port	It describes the source port	Integer	6152
4	Destination port	It describes the destination port	Integer	5396
5	Syn flag	It describes whether synchronization flag is present or not	String	Yes
6	Push flag	It describes whether push flag is present or not	String	No
7	Ack flag	It describes whether acknowledgment flag is present or not	String	Yes
8	Fin flag	It describes whether finish flag is present or not	String	No

In machine learning the training is done on the historic data, so we executed a script which generated the dataset. Script has generated 2.8 lakh data for training and another 1.2 lakh data for testing. Figure 2 describes the sample data from our dataset.

The dataset consists of 8 different parameters as listed below in Table 1.

Sr No.	Ip_Address	Protocol	Source_Port	Destination_Port	Syn Flag	Push Flag	Ack Flag	Fin Flag
1	3300686739	TCP	8319	36878	No	Yes	No	No
2	2503966511	TCP	38410	32098	No	Yes	No	No
3	4044354010	TCP	57680	41762	No	Yes	Yes	Yes
4	3680851305	TCP	21471	45112	No	Yes	No	No
5	1032064743	TCP	6134	27581	Yes	No	No	No
6	3201104532	TCP	11768	1847	No	Yes	Yes	Yes
7	4110260403	TCP	43782	19022	No	No	No	Yes
8	3016709091	TCP	6963	23785	Yes	Yes	No	Yes
9	3379856516	TCP	29202	32254	Yes	Yes	No	Yes
10	3320918973	TCP	46173	46890	Yes	Yes	No	Yes
11	2227358050	TCP	45461	12902	No	Yes	Yes	Yes
12	2554164731	TCP	61799	36885	Yes	No	Yes	Yes
13	3732327019	TCP	1106	60736	No	No	Yes	Yes
14	4124942521	TCP	42302	44798	Yes	Yes	Yes	No

Fig. 2. Sample data

3.3 Feature Reduction

Data is being generated daily in a huge amount and only some portion is being used for processing. Feature reduction means removing some parameters/attributes/features from the training model [9]. Considering the advantages, it reduces the space required to save data and takes less time to process it. It removes the redundancy hence giving more accuracy to the model. Looking on the other side it may produce some limitations which can lead to data loss and can affect the accuracy of the model [10].

When considering the synthetic dataset [2] it doesn't require feature reduction because the data is already generated with necessary features/parameters. So, in this case, the dataset will remain the same with feature reduction. The next section describes about the normalization.

4 Normalization

Normalization is an important part of dataset preparation. It is necessary to normalize the data before moving for the training part. There is a vast difference when the model is trained with and without normalized data. According to Jaitley et al. [11], we can determine that the efficiency of the model without normalization is 48.80% and the accuracy of the model with normalization is 88.93%. Figure 3 describes the difference between accuracy of model without normalized data and with normalized data.

Moving further in this section, the author now has good clarity about the parameters which would be needed for the training process. Machine only understands numeric data, so here it is required to convert the dataset into normalized form. Normalization is all about converting a given range of values into a specific machine-readable format without changing its original value [11].

Here when the author looks in the dataset, he found that the data type of data in the generated data set is in the string and numeric form, and therefore he has chosen Min-Max algorithm to normalize numeric value and label encoding technique for

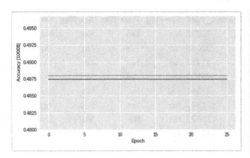 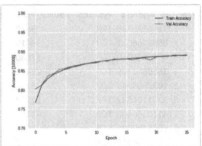

Fig. 3. Accuracy of model without normalized data and with normalized data.

normalizing string data. Yin et al. [5] used the same algorithm to normalize different features/parameters and convert them in the range of 0 and 1. As the author has used synthetic datasets and it does not have any outliers, so in such cases, the Min-Max algorithm is most suitable. It also gives assurance that features will have the exact scale [12]. In the next subsections, the author has described both the technique.

4.1 Min-Max Algorithm

Min-Max algorithm is a technique that is used to normalize numeric data. Here linear conversion is done for the given values of a dataset [13]. In this algorithm, the least and greatest value is fetched from the entire data, and then each value is converted to a new value using the given formula. One advantage of this algorithm is that it will give you the exact value for your given scale. Equation 1 describes the Min-Max Algorithm.

$$v' = \frac{v - \min(A)}{\max(A) - \min(A)} (\text{new\_max}(A) - \text{new\_min}(A)) + new\_\min(A) \qquad (1)$$

Here in the given formula, A is considered as an attribute value in a given dataset, min(A) is the lowest value of an attribute A. max(A) is the highest value of an attribute A. new_min(A) and new_max(A) is the new range of minimum and maximum values. Usually in the Min-Max algorithm new range is considered between 0 and 1. Here v' is the new data for a given value in A.

Considering the dataset in this paper Min-Max algorithm was used for all the numeric values. All the numeric data was converted in the range of 0 and 1. For a given attribute minimum value would be 0 and the maximum value would be 1.

4.2 Label Encoding

As mentioned earlier that machine only understands numeric values [14], but every time it may not be possible to have data in a numeric format for a given dataset. So, in such cases label encoding is done for that data. Label encoding is like assigning a unique id for each different value. Label encoding is generally used for categorical data. So, for example, if we have three different categorical values then we will assign each value with a unique number to represent that data.

Now considering the dataset in this paper, there are various attributes whose values are in string format, so label encoding would be used for such attributes. Table 2 describes the label encoding technique.

Table 2. Label encoding for normalization

Protocol (In Text)	Protocol (In Number)
ICMP	1
TCP	2
UDP	3

From Table 2 it is concluded that for each protocol, a unique number/id is assigned. So now a given protocol will be represented by a number and would be associated with the same after normalization.

4.3 Normalized Data Set

In this section, the author will have a better insight into the data after the process of normalization. As mentioned earlier that dataset consists of 4 lakh record (2.8 lakh for training and 1.2 lakh for testing), so to do normalization for each record would be a very time consuming and tedious task. In order, to avoid that thing a python script was executed by the author that will automatically do the normalization for the dataset. Once the script was executed, an excel sheet was generated containing normalized data.

The following Pseudocode contains the Min-Max algorithm and label encoding method to map it with the dataset.

```
Create function for reading original data
  Open a file in read mode
  Iterate till end of the file
    Append each parameter value in a separate list

Create function for Ip Address, Source Port and Destina-
tion Port separately
  Sort the list and remove duplicates
  Apply min-max algorithm in the IP address, Source port
and destination port list respectively
  Use dictionary to store key and value
  Open file in write mode
    Write the dictionary items in a file

Create function for Protocol, Syn flag, Push flag, Ack
flag and Fin flag respectively
  Sort the list and remove duplicates
  Apply label encoding method
  Open a file in write mode
    Write the values in a file

Call function for reading data
Call different functions individually to do unique map-
ping
```

Now the given Pseudocode is used for mapping normalized value with original value and forming a normalized dataset.

```
Create a function to read data from various files
  Open the files in read mode
  Iterate till the end of files
    Append the data into dictionary

Create a function to define attack
  If all the flags are not present than
    Return 1
  If all the flags are present than
    Return 1
  If syn and fin flag are present
    Return 1
  If only fin flag is present
    Return 1
  Else return 0

Create function to read original data
  Open the file in read mode
  Iterate till end of file
    Append the data in the original data list

Create function to generate normalized file
  Open a file in write mode
  Iterate the original data list
    Use dictionary to retrieve normalized value for each
record
    Write the values in the file

Call function to read data from various files
Call function that reads original file
Call function to generate normalized file
```

From Fig. 4 it has been concluded that data has been normalized. For attributes Source_Port, Destination_Port and Ip_Address the Min-max algorithm was used which scales the value between the range of 0 and 1. For the rest of the attributes label encoding method was used. The last column in the figure is the derived attribute. The given attribute is derived based on the values of Syn, Push, Ack, and Fin flag. The prediction is done based on the flags received during the transmission.

A normalized dataset has been generated and can be used for training the model. In the next section author discuss about the neural networks.

Ip_Address	Protocol	Source_Port	Destination_Port	Syn Flag	Push Flag	Ack Flag	Fin Flag	Attack_Happened
0.770623867	1	0.126928418	0.562724124	0	1	0	0	0
0.583656269	1	0.586101659	0.489783773	0	1	0	0	0
0.945141444	1	0.880151984	0.637251461	0	1	1	1	0
0.859837688	1	0.327621198	0.688370745	0	1	0	0	0
0.23824275	1	0.093586437	0.420856668	1	0	0	0	0
0.747254753	1	0.17955839	0.028169014	0	1	1	1	0
0.960607801	1	0.668075626	0.290250713	0	0	0	1	1
0.703982383	1	0.106236553	0.362931653	1	1	0	1	1
0.789202764	1	0.445592297	0.492164253	1	1	0	1	1
0.775371798	1	0.704561061	0.715502113	1	1	0	1	1
0.518744124	1	0.693696306	0.196862649	0	1	1	1	0
0.595436365	1	0.943005814	0.56283094	1	0	1	1	1
0.871917575	1	0.016861734	0.926784979	0	0	1	1	0
0.964053277	1	0.645491584	0.683579265	1	1	1	0	0

Fig. 4. Normalized data set

5   Back Propagation Neural Network

Back Propagation (BP) [48] is a part of Artificial Neural Network (ANN) [59], that consists of different interlinked nodes and the learning is based on Deepest Descent Technique. Neural network is used widely when you are dealing with a large dataset. Figure 5 describes the Back Propagation Neural Network (BPNN) model.

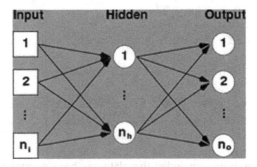

Fig. 5. Back Propagation Neural Network model

Back propagation Neural Network (BPNN) [48] is a commonly used algorithm to predict the outcome of a model. This algorithm gives accurate results for supervised learning as compared to different existing algorithms. The reason for choosing this algorithm is to check the difference between the desired output and the predicted output for a given set of inputs. In this paper, the desired output is already passed during the training and the predicted output is generated by a model based on the training. Here only one output would be generated and that would be whether the attack happened or not. In the neural network, the algorithm is divided into two parts.

First is the learning part in which the entire dataset would be trained, and during the training phase, various patterns would be identified according to the dataset fed into the network. Once the training part has been completed, the testing phase will be initiated. During this phase again some data would be fed into the network which will try to find out the patterns which were formed during the training phase. The goal would be to identify the pattern formed during the training phase.

The output will be produced based on the learning it has made during the training part. The goal of this algorithm is to reduce the error rate of predicted output from the desired output [15]. In the next section, author describes about the algorithm.

5.1 Algorithm

In this section the Pseudocode for the BPNN algorithm is provided. Figure 6 describes the Pseudocode for the Back Propagation Neural Network.

---

1. **Input a set of training examples**

2. **For each training example x:** Set the corresponding input activation $a^{x,1}$, and perform the following steps:

   o **Feedforward:** For each $l = 2, 3, \ldots, L$ compute $z^{x,l} = w^l a^{x,l-1} + b^l$ and $a^{x,l} = \sigma(z^{x,l})$.

   o **Output error $\delta^{x,L}$:** Compute the vector $\delta^{x,L} = \nabla_a C_x \odot \sigma'(z^{x,L})$.

   o **Backpropagate the error:** For each $l = L - 1, L - 2, \ldots, 2$ compute $\delta^{x,l} = ((w^{l+1})^T \delta^{x,l+1}) \odot \sigma'(z^{x,l})$.

3. **Gradient descent:** For each $l = L, L - 1, \ldots, 2$ update the weights according to the rule $w^l \rightarrow w^l - \frac{\eta}{m} \sum_x \delta^{x,l}(a^{x,l-1})^T$, and the biases according to the rule $b^l \rightarrow b^l - \frac{\eta}{m} \sum_x \delta^{x,l}$.

Fig. 6. Back Propagation Neural Network (BPNN) pseudocode

5.2 Back Propagation Neural Network (BPNN) Model

To get better understanding of BPNN Model, it has been divided into different modules.

Back Propagation Preparation. Back Propagation is prepared into three parts: training set, testing set, and learning rate. The training set consists of all the input and output patterns which are passed to train the network. The testing set is the selection of input and output patterns which are used to access the neural network performance.

Calculating Error in Each Output Neuron. Error for each output neuron can be calculated using the given formula.

$$d_{pj} = (T_{pj} - O_{pj})O_{pj}(1 - O_{pj}) \tag{2}$$

Here in the given formula d_{pj} is the output neuron error. O_{pj} is the actual output value for pattern p where output neuron is j and T_{pj} is the target value for pattern p where output neuron is j.

Calculating Error in Each Hidden Neuron. Error for each output neuron can be calculated using the given formula.

$$\delta_{pj} = O_{pj}(1 - O_{pj}) \sum_{k} \delta_{pk} W_{kj} \tag{3}$$

Here in the given formula δ_{pj} is the hidden neuron error. δ_{pk} is the error signal of a post-synaptic neuron k and W_{kj} is the weight of the connection from post-synaptic neuron k to the hidden neuron j.

Calculating and Applying Weight Adjustments. Measure weight adjustments DW_{ji} at time t with the given equation.

$$DW_{ji}(t) = \eta d_{pj} O_{pi} \tag{4}$$

Applying weight adjustments according to the given equation.

$$W_{ji}(t + 1) = W_{ji}(t) + DW_{ji}(t) \tag{5}$$

Adding momentum in the equation.

$$a * DW_{ji}(t - 1) \tag{6}$$

Figure 7 describes the BPNN model formed for detecting network attack.

As shown in Fig. 7, eight input units were used for different parameters which are IP address, protocol, source port, destination port, push flag, syn flag, ack flag, and fin flag. Further moving on eight hidden units are used, and finally, one output unit is there because only one output would be returned either 0 or 1. Random weights would be assigned for each input unit and hence the learning starts. Learning will be done until the predicted output is not nearer to the actual output. In the next section, we will discuss results generated by the BPNN algorithm.

6   Results

We have generated dataset, created unique files for normalizing the data, created manual output files to predict DDoS attack using BPNN modal, and finally we created the confusion matrix. Table 3 shows that 4 lakh records - data set is generated with 8 parameters using the python script wrote by the author within 10.2 s.

Table 4 shows that unique files is generated after applying Min-Max Algorithm and Label Encoding Method within 4.9 s.

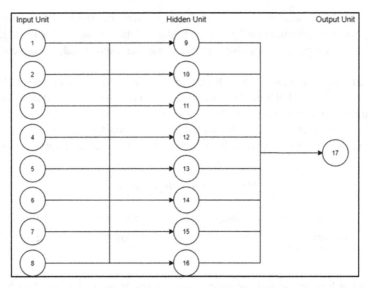

Fig. 7. Back Propagation Neural Network for detecting network attack

Table 3. Output of generated dataset

Sr. No.	No of records	No of parameters	Type	Time
1	4,00,000	8	CSV file	10.2 s

Table 4. Unique files created after applying Min-Max algorithm and label encoding method

Sr. No.	No of records	No of unique file created	Type	Time
1	4,00,000	8	CSV file	4.9 s

Table 5. Output of normalized file

Sr. No.	No of records	No of files created	Type	Time
1	4,00,000	4	CSV file	7.5 s

Table 5 shows normalized file by mapping unique file (Table 4) that was generated earlier with the original dataset. For that author wrote python script and normalized file was generated within 7.5 s to normalize 4 lakh records.

The script also divided the normalized data in the ratio of 70:30. 70% of normalized data was passed for training and 30% of normalized data was passed for testing. Apart from this actual output file was also created which was used in calculating confusion matrix.

We used 70% of data set (2.8 lakh samples) to train and 30% of data set (1.2 lakh sample) for test using BPNN model. The model was processed for 1000 iterations with 4 hidden units and learning rate as 0.5.

Table 6 shows that BPNN model took 4 h and 16 min to generate the output and stored the same result in a separate file, which was used to calculate confusion matrix.

Table 6. Output of BPNN model

Sr. No.	No of records	Training samples	Testing samples	Time
1	4,00,000	2,80,000	1,20,000	4 h 16 min

The author has showcased the output in the form of confusion matrix which will help to get a better understanding of the results. Before moving into it let us define some important terms used in confusion matrix.

Confusion matrix contain two classes one is manual and other one is predicted, and within each class two types of output are present positive and negative [16].

True Positive (TP): The observation was positive, and model predicted as positive.
True Negative (TN): The observation was negative, and model predicted negative.
False Positive (FP): The observation was positive, and model predicted as negative.
False Negative (FN): The observation was negative, and model predicted positive.
Classification Rate/Accuracy: This term defines the overall accuracy of the model in predicting the output. It can be calculated with the given formula.

$$Accuracy = \frac{TP + TN}{TP + TN + FP + FN} \tag{7}$$

Recall: This term describes how often the model predict yes, when the output is already yes. It can be calculated with the given formula.

$$Recall = \frac{TP}{TP + FN} \tag{8}$$

Precision: This term describes how often the result is correct when it predicts yes. It can be calculated with the given formula.

$$Precision = \frac{TP}{TP + FP} \tag{9}$$

F-Measure: This term is defined when we want to compute Recall and Precision at same time. It can be calculated with the given formula.

$$F - Measure = \frac{2 * Recall * Precision}{Recall + Precision} \tag{10}$$

Table 7 shows the confusion matrix that has been generated for the BPNN model. Here four different values are calculated that is True Positive, False Positive, True Negative, and False Negative. True positive is the value, for which output was true and the model identified it as true. False positive is the value, for which output was false and model identified it as true. True negative is the value, for which output was false and model identified it as false, and False negative is the value, for which the output was true and model identified it as false.

Table 7. Confusion matrix

	Class I predicted	Class II predicted
Class I actual	73177 (TP)	1712 (FN)
Class II actual	989 (FP)	44122 (TN)

Table 8 describes the Accuracy, Precision, Recall, F-Measure score. Accuracy means overall accuracy of the BPNN model. It describes how much the BPNN model was able to predict the correctness of the testing samples that is attack happened or not happened. Precision defines the value of how much time the result was true, that is attack happened when model predicted it as true, which include both the cases that is attack actually happened and other one being model mistakenly predicted it as attack happened. Recall defines the value of how much time the model predicted true that is attack happened, when the output was actually true irrespective of what the model predicted. F-Measure is the value when Precision and Recall both are calculated at the same time.

Table 8. Accuracy, Recall, Precision, and F-Measure score

No of records	Accuracy	Recall	Precision	F-Measure
1,20,000	0.977	0.98	0.97	0.98

7   Conclusion

The Back Propagation Neural Network (BPNN) produces great accuracy for predicting the output. From the results section, it was concluded that the BPNN model was able to achieve 97.7% accuracy in detecting DDoS attack and the time taken to generate output was quite less, when compared with the results obtained from different researches, as mentioned in literature review section. This model can still be refined by adding some more parameters in the training. This thing can be considered for the future scope.

References

1. The Internet Revolution is the New Industrial Revolution. https://www.forbes.com/sites/mic hakaufman/2012/10/05/the-internet-revolution-is-the-new-industrial-revolution/?sh=68b 916cf47d5. Accessed on 29 Nov 2020
2. Synthetic Dataset Generation for ML using Scikit Learn and More. https://towardsdatas cience.com/synthetic-dataset-generation-for-ml-using-scikit-learn-and-more-beab8cacc8f8. Accessed on 29 Nov 2020
3. Chang, R.K.C.: Defending against flooding-based distributed denial-of-service attacks: a tutorial. IEEE Commun. Mag. **40**(10), 42–51 (2002)
4. Gavaskar, S., Surendiran, R., Ramaraj, E.: Three counter defense mechanism for SYN flooding attacks. Int. J. Comput. Appl. **6**(6), 12–15 (2010)
5. Yin, C., Zhu, Y., Fei, J., He, X.: A deep learning approach for intrusion detection using recurrent neural networks. IEEE Access **5**, 21954–21961 (2017)
6. Backpropagation Step by Step. https://hmkcode.com/ai/backpropagation-step-by-step/. Accessed on 29 Nov 2020
7. Data, Learning and Modeling. https://machinelearningmastery.com/data-learning-and-mod eling/. Accessed on 29 Nov 2020
8. Preparing Your Dataset for Machine Learning: 8 Basic Techniques That Make Your Data Better. https://www.altexsoft.com/blog/datascience/preparing-your-dataset-for-machine-lea rning-8-basic-techniques-that-make-your-data-better/. Accessed on 29 Nov 2020
9. Bahrololum, M., Salahi, E., Khaleghi, M.: Machine learning techniques for feature reduction in intrusion detection systems: a comparison. In: Fourth International Conference on Computer Sciences and Convergence Information Technology, pp. 1091–1095. Seoul (2009)
10. The Ultimate Guide to 12 Dimensionality Reduction Techniques (with Python codes). https://www.analyticsvidhya.com/blog/2018/08/dimensionality-reduction-techniques-pyt hon/. Accessed on 29 Nov 2020
11. Why Data Normalization is necessary for Machine Learning models. https://medium.com/ @urvashilluniya/why-data-normalization-is-necessary-for-machine-learning-models-681 b65a05029. Accessed on 29 Nov 2020
12. Normalization. https://www.codecademy.com/articles/normalization. Accessed on 29 Nov 2020
13. Data Normalization in Data Mining. https://www.geeksforgeeks.org/data-normalization-in-data-mining/. Accessed on 29 Nov 2020
14. ML|Label Encoding of datasets in Python. https://www.geeksforgeeks.org/ml-label-enc oding-of-datasets-in-python/. Accessed on 29 Nov 2020
15. An introduction to Artificial Neural Networks (with example). https://medium.com/@jam esdacombe/an-introduction-to-artificial-neural-networks-with-example-ad459bb6941b. Accessed on 29 Nov 2020
16. Confusion Matrix in Machine Learning. https://www.geeksforgeeks.org/confusion-matrix-machine-learning/. Accessed on 29 Nov 2020
17. Andropov, S., Guirik, A., Budko, M., Budko, M.: Network anomaly detection using artificial neural networks. In: 20th Conference of Open Innovations Association (FRUCT), pp. 26–31. St. Petersburg, (2017)
18. Jiahui, J., Ye, B., Zhao, Y., Stones, R.J., Wang, G., Liu, X., Wang, S., Xie, G.: Detecting TCP-based DDoS attacks in Baidu cloud computing data centers. In: 2017 IEEE 36th Symposium on Reliable Distributed Systems (SRDS), pp. 256–258. IEEE (2017)
19. AI-Duwairi, B., Manimaran, G.: Distributed packet pairing for reflector based DDoS attack mitigation. Comput. Commun. **29**(12), 2269–2280 (2006)

20. Chen, Y., Hwang, K.: Tcp flow analysis for defense against shrew ddos attacks. In: IEEE International Conference on Communications, pp. 1–8 (2007)
21. Gao, Z., Ansari, N.: Differentiating malicious DDoS attack traffic from normal TCP flows by proactive tests. IEEE Commun. Lett. **10**(11), 793–795 (2006)
22. Jun, J.-H., Lee, D., Ahn, C.-W., Kim,, S.-H.: DDoS attack detection using flow entropy and packet sampling on huge networks. In: 13th International Conference on Networks, Nice (2014)
23. The Ultimate Guide to Synthetic Data in 2020. https://research.aimultiple.com/synthetic-data/. Accessed on 29 Nov 2020
24. Do You Need Synthetic Data For Your AI Project? https://towardsdatascience.com/do-you-need-synthetic-data-for-your-ai-project-e7ecc2072d6b. Accessed on 29 Nov 2020
25. Intrusion Prevention TCP Bad Flags. https://fortiguard.com/encyclopedia/ips/12145/tcp-bad-flags. Accessed on 29 Nov 2020
26. ACK-PSH-SYN-FIN Flood. https://kb.mazebolt.com/knowledgebase/ack-psh-syn-fin-flood/. Accessed on 29 Nov 2020
27. TCP Null Attack. https://ddos-guard.net/en/terminology/attack_type/tcp-null-attack. Accessed on 29 Nov 2020
28. Wankhede, S., Kshirsagar, D.: DoS attack detection using machine learning and neural network. In: 2018 Fourth International Conference on Computing Communication Control and Automation (ICCUBEA), pp. 1–5. IEEE (2018)
29. Zekri, M., El Kafhali, S., Aboutabit, N., Saadi, Y.: DDoS attack detection using machine learning techniques in cloud computing environments. In: 2017 3rd International Conference of Cloud Computing Technologies and Applications (CloudTech), pp. 1–7. IEEE (2017)
30. Kumar, A., Glisson, W., Cho, H.: Network attack detection using an unsupervised machine learning algorithm. In: Proceedings of the 53rd Hawaii International Conference on System Sciences (2020)
31. Noh, S., Lee, C., Choi, K., Jung, G.: Detecting distributed denial of service (DDOS) attacks through inductive learning. In: International Conference on Intelligent Data Engineering and Automated Learning, pp. 286–295. Springer, Berlin (2003)
32. Bangladesh Bank robbery. https://en.wikipedia.org/wiki/2016_Bangladesh_Bank_heist. Accessed on 15 July 2020
33. Ottis, R.: Analysis of the 2007 cyber attacks against estonia from the information warfare perspective. In: Proceedings of the 7th European Conference on Information Warfare, p. 163 (2008)
34. Record-breaking DDoS attack in Europe hits 400 Gbps. CNET (2014). http://www.cnet.com/news/recordbreaking-ddos-attack-in-europe-hits-400gbps/. Accessed on 15 July 2020
35. Lakshminarayanan, K., Adkins, D., Perrig, A., Stoica, I.: Taming ip packet flooding attacks. ACM SIGCOMM Comput. Commun. Rev. **34**(1), 45–50 (2004)
36. Gligor, V.D.: A note on denial-of-service in operating systems. IEEE Trans. Softw. Eng. **3**, 320–324 (1984)
37. Bawany, N.Z., Shamsi, J.A., Salah, K.: DDoS attack detection and mitigation using SDN: methods, practices, and solutions. Arabian J. Sci. Eng. **42**(2), 425–441 (2017)
38. Wang, B., Zheng, Y., Lou, W., Hou, Y.T.: DDoS attack protection in the era of cloud computing and software-defined networking. Comput. Netw. **81**, 308–319 (2015)
39. McGregory, S.: Preparing for the next DDoS attack. Netw. Secur. **5**, 5–6 (2013)
40. DoS attacks: What are the popular DoS attacking tools? (2017). https://www.greycampus.com/blog/information-security/dos-attacks-tools-and-protection. Accessed on 15 July 2020
41. Botnet. https://en.wikipedia.org/wiki/Botnet. Accessed on 15 July 2020
42. Hunter, P.: Distributed Denial of Service (DDOS) mitigation tools. Netw. Secur. **5**, 12–14 (2003)

43. Sood, A.K., Enbody, R.J., Bansal, R.: Dissecting SpyEye–Understanding the design of third generation botnets. Comput. Netw. **57**(2), 436–450 (2013)

44. Hoque, N., Bhattacharyya, D., Kalita, J.: Botnet in DDoS attacks: trends and challenges. IEEE Commun. Surv. Tutor. **99**, 1–1 (2015)

45. Krishna, V.H., Kumar, S.: Effectiveness of built-in security protection of microsoft's windows server 2003 against TCP SYN based DDoS attacks. J. Inform. Secur. **2**(03), 131 (2011)

46. Acharya, S., Tiwari, N.: Survey of DDoS attacks based on TCP/IP protocol vulnerabilities. IOSR J. Comput. Eng. **18**(3), 68–76 (2016)

47. Saied, A., Overill, R.E., Radzik, T.: Detection of known and unknown DDoS attacks using artificial neural networks. Neurocomputing, **172**, 385–393 (2016)

48. Saad, R.M.A., Anbar, M., Manickam, S., Alomari, E.: An intelligent icmpv6 ddos flooding-attack detection framework (v6iids) using back-propagation neural network. IETE Tech. Rev. **33**(3), 244–255 (2016)

49. Khandelwal, M., Gupta, D.K., Bhale, P.: DoS attack detection technique using back propagation neural network. In: 2016 International Conference on Advances in Computing, Communications and Informatics (ICACCI), pp. 1064–1068. IEEE (2016)

50. Ahmad, I., Abdullah, A., Alghamdi, A., Alnfajan, K., Hussain, M.: Intrusion detection using feature subset selection based on MLP. Sci. Res. Essays **6**(34), 6804–6810 (2011)

51. Arun, P.R.K., Selvakumar, S.: Distributed denial of service attack detection using an ensemble of neural classifier. Comput. Commun. **34**(11), 1328–1341 (2011)

52. Li, J., Liu, Y., Gu, L.: DDoS attack detection based on neural network. In: 2010 2nd International Symposium on Aware Computing, pp. 196–199. IEEE (2010)

53. Ali, U., Dewangan, K.K., Dewangan, D.K.: Distributed denial of service attack detection using ant bee colony and artificial neural network in cloud computing. In: Nature Inspired Computing, pp. 165–175. Springer, Singapore (2018)

54. Shah, B., Trivedi, B.H.: Reducing features of KDD CUP 1999 dataset for anomaly detection using back propagation neural network. In: 2015 Fifth International Conference on Advanced Computing and Communication Technologies, pp. 247–251. IEEE (2015)

55. Talhar, N.: Effective denial of service attack detection using artificial neural network for wired lan. In: 2016 International Conference on Signal Processing, Communication, Power and Embedded System (SCOPES), pp. 229–234. IEEE (2016)

56. Anzai, Y.: Pattern Recognition and Machine Learning, pp. 89112. Academic Press, London (2012)

57. Celal, O., Karaboga, D.: Hybrid artificial bee colony algorithm for neural network training. In: 2011 IEEE Congress of Evolutionary Computation (CEC), pp. 84–88. IEEE (2011)

58. Yao, X.: Evolving artificial neural networks. Proc. IEEE **87**(9), (1999)

59. Graupe, D.: Principles of Artificial Neural Network, pp. 5994. World Scientific Publishing Co. Pte. Ltd, Singapore (2007)

Click Ad Fraud Detection Using XGBoost Gradient Boosting Algorithm

Nayanaba Pravinsinh Gohil$^{(\boxtimes)}$ ⓘ and Arvind D. Meniya ⓘ

Department of Information Technology, Shantilal Shah Engineering College, Bhavnagar, Gujarat, India

Abstract. The growth of the online advertising industry has created new business opportunities on the Internet. Companies and advertisers are turning to digital ad platforms like never before to compete for the attention of their audience. In this environment, actions such as clicking an ad result in financial transactions among advertisers, advertising networks and publishers. Since these new opportunities have financial impact, fraudsters have been trying to gain illegal advantages and profit through them. Mitigating the negative effects of illegal traffic is extremely important to the success of any marketing endeavor. Today, false clicks that waste budgets and don't generate any meaningful value or revenue are costing advertisers billions of dollars. These are the biggest challenge PPC (Pay Per Click) marketers face, although there are efforts made by the advertisers to block fake traffic, they still try to find leading security strategy to identify click fraud. This paper analyzes the click fraud mechanism, focusing on its detection and methods of solution used in recent cases, we try and explain various fundamentals related to online advertising. The objective of this research is to propose solution for click ad fraud present in online advertising using the XGBoost Gradient Boosting algorithm and this model provides the accuracy of 96% with a set of hyperparameters along with features that can be implemented on datasets related to click frauds.

Keywords: Online advertising · Click fraud · XGBoost algorithm · Machine learning

1 Introduction

Today the world tends to be online always to keep up with the ever-changing technologies and to be part of this era of digitization. It is estimated that 57% of the world's population now has Internet access. And that number is growing rapidly [1]. Research also shows that people around the world now spend significantly more time on the Internet than they watch TV [2]. This global phenomenon has opened up new opportunities for online marketing. Companies and advertisers are turning to digital ad platforms like never before to compete for the attention of their audience.

With the increased need for an online presence and overall market demand, digital ad spending is projected to be $ 237 billion, or 44% of all global ad spending [3]. It greatly surpasses television as the most popular marketing channel in use today. Despite the fact

© Springer Nature Switzerland AG 2021
N. Chaubey et al. (Eds.): COMS2 2021, CCIS 1416, pp. 67–81, 2021.
https://doi.org/10.1007/978-3-030-76776-1_5

that more and more marketers are starting to use contextual and digital advertising, problems such as clicks (ad click fraud, click fraud, clicks are the same terms) can significantly complicate the creation of successful marketing campaigns. There are different forms of fraud such as botnets, click farms, impression fraud, etc. that occur in online advertising. However, they all have a detrimental effect on the marketing effectiveness of any company. Consequently, marketers need to track and understand sources and explore specific ways to identify each of these different types of wasted clicks, in order to create effective defense mechanisms.

The paper provides the overview of the online advertising network, various advertising models and online advertising frauds. Then click ad fraud and its sources are mentioned along with problems faced in detecting it; later the recent methods used for detection and prevention are discussed. And then proposed XGBoost model is given with details of how it was implemented along with datasets used and we get accuracy of 96%. Lastly in basic research we compare our work with some recent approaches and also other boosting algorithms.

1.1 World of Internet Advertising

Paid online advertising has become the norm for businesses of all sizes. More than half of the world's companies already have a well-established digital marketing strategy. Competition for top positions in PPC (Pay Per Click) placements is very high. Unlike the early days of digital marketing, advertisers today have a wide range of tools to enable them to launch, customize and optimize campaigns. Many companies choose to invest in PPC campaigns because they are easy enough to set up, relatively affordable and provide almost instant feedback [4]. In addition, they level the advertising field to a certain extent and enable new, smaller companies to compete with leading brands for top positions even at the start of market entry. Modern paid Internet advertising is also attractive because it implements [5] as:

Optimal Integration. Companies can implement a range of digital solutions that help track, edit and monetize their PPC campaigns. Modern platforms like Google Ads allow full integration with such tools to help advertisers create safe and profitable campaigns.

Various Formats. Ad networks also offer the ability to serve ads in a variety of formats. These are simple texts, graphic banners, multimedia, native advertising and much more. Each particular type of ad has its own advantages and disadvantages, which is why most companies tend to split their resources to run multiple campaigns in different formats.

Variety of Advertising Models. With the advent of new delivery formats, publishers and ad networks have also developed different bidding models that can be beneficial for marketers. While PPC may be the most well-known model, other popular payment options include but are not limited to:

- CPM - Cost per 1000 impressions
- CPA - Price Per User Acquisition or Sale
- CPL - Price for getting a lead

- CPI - Price per install

Measured Metrics. In the early days of digital advertising, marketers had very few statistics. Advertisers today can dive into a sea of data that is available directly through their marketing and analytic tools. Sellers can now instantly access important statistics like the price of each lead or the number of conversions generated by a specific campaign.

1.2 Online Advertising Fraud

The online advertising model works on very definitive principles, it comprises of various parties like advertisers, publishers and user. There are various models of advertising involved here which depends on the type of business, advertisement and price the advertiser agrees upon. Figure 1 depicts the example of advertising model; it shows the legitimate and illegitimate clicks in the PPC model.

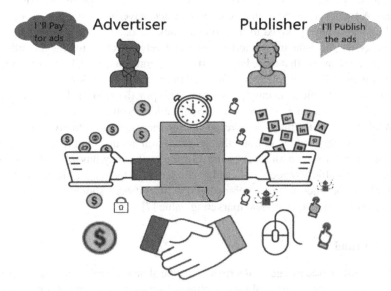

Fig. 1. Online advertising

The publisher and advertiser on bases of the factors involved come up with an agreement they both adhere to along the process of flow in the advertising network. The revenue system in online advertising and loss advertiser faces if click fraud is present in the network. The click in red show the illegitimate clicks while money in red is loss of the advertiser due to fraud click. For example, if 30 clicks in 100 clicks are illegitimate then if the advertiser pays 100 rupees for, they suffer loss of 30 rupees as those clicks were never viewed by legitimate users rather could have been just bots trying to navigate through the network.

The biggest problem with the digital marketing industry is that it operates on the assumption that most, if not all, traffic comes from "legitimate" sources. Marketers by default think that all digital interactions like clicks and views from ad providers like Google and Bing come from people who have some marketing value. However, the fact is that more than half of all Internet traffic is generated by software scripts called robots or bots [6].

Bots visit sites for a variety of reasons. Regardless of their goals, they generate a huge amount of traffic that is reflected in PPC campaigns. This means that even if a large number of visitors come to the site, there is an equally high chance that many of its users have no value at all. Aside from bots, marketers need to understand that there are various sources of illegal ad traffic that can lead to interactions that are useless for them. These non-revenue-generating clicks are of little value to advertisers, but they are still associated with relevant ad traffic and therefore have a huge impact on the effectiveness of digital marketing campaigns [7].

There is no realistic estimate of the percentage of Internet traffic that actually has marketing value, so it is impossible to accurately measure the entire volume of illegal clicks. We know that about a third of ad clicks are fraudulent. But a large number of clicks from real people do not lead to conversions either. It's just a fact of the existence of a business. Ad sellers must commit resources to protect advertisers' budgets. Google and other ad networks have pledged to fight illegal clicks in one way or another. However, in most cases, the mechanisms created do not effectively detect or stop illegal traffic [8].

Moreover, the model that these large platforms operate on is actually encouraging an increase in illegal clicks. While this is frowned upon, almost all businesses fall into the trap of buying web traffic from multiple sources. This practice is to pay for a certain number of unique visitors. They are redirected to the seller's website to achieve the desired goals. While this practice may sound reasonable in theory, it can actually increase your chances of being targeted by ad fraudulent clicks. Even the most influential companies in the world cannot screen all or even most of the traffic they buy from third parties. This means that traffic providers can easily generate huge numbers of bogus visitors in the form of bots or other means, combine them with legitimate sources and charge sites to redirect visitors that have no real marketing value [7].

1.3 Click Fraud

Click fraud is often used as a general term to describe all non-revenue traffic sources such as robots, competitors or criminal organizations. However, in its purest form, ad click fraud can be defined as a fraudulent interaction between a user and a PPC ad that is used to illegally obtain money from marketers. These fraudulent users can be humans, robots, or a combination of both. Unfortunately, illegal clicks can ultimately account for a huge part of a company's PPC spending. In addition, all ad click fraud cases have a culprit, be it a competitor or an organization, that in some way benefits from the depletion of the company's PPC budget, which makes the problem complex and confusing [9]. There are several possible reasons and interests for using Click Frauds such as:

- Own profit, since the publisher site wins by click.
- Financial loss, usually made by competitors of the advertiser who although successful, make him pay for irrelevant clicks

- Self-promotion, a sub-item from the previous case. Whoever commits fraud spends financial resources of competitors with ads in the same research area, therefore can better promote their own ad and acquire human with higher quality than the opposing companies
- Defamation, when fraud is made with the aim of being detected and damaging the reputation of the website that publishes the ad, and may even exclude it from the contract with advertiser or ad network.

1.4 Sources of Click Fraud

Illegal clicks can come from a variety of sources. Many of these clicks are definitely malicious, but the origins of some others may be more obscure. Knowing where to expect click fraud from and knowing what your business is suffering from is the first step to solving this problem. Finding the origin of illegal clicks will help advertisers identify patterns that are inherent in these malicious interactions.

Unethical Competitors. The most obvious suspects in click fraud are competitors. They will always look for a way to gain an edge, especially in highly competitive fields. Worst of all, spending a company's PPC budget to prevent ads from showing to potential customers isn't difficult at all. Competitor click fraud can also manifest itself in the form of repeated clicks on ads from one device or hundreds of clicks from multiple devices, depending on the complexity of the methodologies used. Some less ethical companies may even hire third parties to click on your ads on their behalf [10].

Bots and Cawlers. Bots generate over half of all Internet traffic and are the main source of illegal clicks. While many bots are designed to perform productive tasks, some can still engage in illegal interactions with ads on a regular basis. Today, millions of search robots perform many functions, both good and bad. They check for broken links, collect SEO data, retrieve content and track security vulnerabilities. They make up a significant part of the pay-per-click traffic ecosystem. Sophisticated robots that mimic human behavior can spoof their device type, accept and remember cookies, simulate mouse movement, and even fill out forms to fake conversions [10]. In some cases, even good bots can become scams and click on ads while interacting with websites or search engines. This can easily lead to wasted expenses, even if the bot was not designed to negatively impact marketing campaigns.

Proxy Clicks. The growing demand for privacy and ways to circumvent Internet censorship from certain regions has increased the popularity of proxy servers in recent years. Proxies allow Internet users to hide and spoof their IP address, ISP data, or physical location. Most advertisers use geo targeting in their campaigns. Since proxy servers change the location of users, for ad networks, most of the clicks generated by proxies are illegal. The resulting impression will be based on a false and misleading location and network data provided by the proxy. You will receive incorrect clicks, which will negatively affect your marketing data. Proxy networks are very popular among scammers. They are designed to provide anonymity, hide data, and deceive both humans and detection systems. Marketers facing high recurring clicks through proxies should check their campaigns to minimize the analytics and financial impact of the proxy [11].

Click Farming. Click fraud can also be carried out on offshore click farms. They are specially crafted for fraudulent interactions with websites, social platforms or ad networks. Their sole purpose is to artificially inflate, manipulate, or distort the status of a product or service [10]. Working from remote locations where they are unlikely to have trouble with the authorities, these organizations use hacking tactics to generate fake traffic that can be a combination of human and robot work.

Dissatisfied Customers. Disgruntled consumers can be another source of unnecessary clicks that many marketers fail to identify. All seasoned business owners understand that it is impossible to please all clients. Complaints are a natural part of any business. While consumers most don't understand PPC marketing models, disgruntled sociopaths are known to pose a serious threat to marketers. An angry customer can not only write bad reviews online, but they can repeatedly click on your ads to increase your spending [7].

Shadow Publishers. Websites and mobile apps that publish shady advertisements are known to use illegal methods to improve the performance of their platforms. Many of them rely on bogus traffic that mimics human behavior. These groups are building websites and flooding them with massive amounts of bot-generated traffic. After obtaining the necessary statistics, these websites join ad networks as publishers. Then they start to monetize false clicks at the expense of unsuspecting companies [12].

1.5 Problems of Detecting Click Fraud

There is no doubt that ad click fraud can cause serious harm to advertisers. When executed effectively, it merges dangerously with regular traffic. Some of the most obvious ways to identify fraud are network assessments, behavioral analysis, and device signature tracking. Bots, competitors and other sources of invalid traffic often come from poor quality networks. In addition to the fact that click fraud is difficult to detect, the lack of standardization and overall quality control in the PPC industry also plays an important role in the ubiquity of increasingly expensive but useless traffic. Marketers must take responsibility and continually invest in the security of their campaigns. Despite these challenges, click fraud can be detected and prevented.

2 Related Work

Illegal clicks and ad fraud are a harsh reality that marketers face. Ignoring illegal clicks will only lead to financial problems. Companies need to protect their investments and find ways to change the current situation. Bot owners and the people who hire them have no incentive to change their behavior. Thus, advertisers need to fight fraud themselves. Advertisers can monitor traffic quantity and quality, dictate compensation to large publishers if they doubt traffic authenticity. Because of this, third party clicking manipulation solutions have started to flourish. a lot of the advertisers who have lost confidence in the search engine companies turn to those third-party clients who manage their advertising campaigns by click. Many of these third-party firms have developed and offered on the market click fraud detection services using their own matrix. It reveals the techniques used to detect fraudulent traffic and as trade secrets, they also retain solutions. Research practices can be split into two categories for click fraud detection:

1. A group suggests alternative business models for the Pay-Per-Click system.
2. Other group attempts to find click fraud solutions in the Pay-Per-Click payment model.

In recent studies, following approaches have been considered in terms of evaluating different click fraud. There are various means for detection and prevention of click fraud, here we try to identify and walk through some of widely used recent techniques.

Thejas G.S. et al. provided a deep learning approach as a solution. They used the dataset from TalkingData company and built a multilayered Neural Network with an attached autoencoder. This autoencoder makes it more precise and secure [13]. Nagaraja et al. used timing patterns to classify fraudulent activities by motoring the clicking traffic; they have used dataset formed from a university network [14]. Riwa Mouawi et al. suggests a new crowdsource-based system called Click Fraud Crowdsourcing (CFC), which works with both advertisers and ad networks to protect both parties against potential fraudulent clicking acts. This platform handles ad tracking and ad clicks and tracks redirected user activity on the advertiser's website. It is capable of tracking the length of the client on each advertisement website and at the same time collecting numerous ad query information corresponding to different ad network-publisher-advertiser combinations; they have used their self-made dataset and suggest to add a new component CFC to the ad network [15]. Xin Zhang et al. proposed CS BPNN architecture for click fraud detection and then they use ABC to optimize BPNN connection weights and feature selection synchronously. The dataset used by them was provided by BuzzCity company [16]. Sawsan Almahmoud et al. provide a hybrid approach by combining rule based with Machine learning algorithm that works best with the features selected from the rule-based system and have used dataset from Waseet which is popular company in the Middle East [17]. M. Gabryel introduced an algorithm for fraud detection based on criteria obtained from the advertiser's websites through a special Javascript component; these calculated features attempt to capture end-user interaction with the website, such as the number of pages visited, page scrolling, keystroke data and other client-side information. They used the dataset provided by an online shop operating in Poland and they proposed use of three algorithms as part of solution technique which includes TF-IDF matrix for text mining, Differential Evaluation for evaluation and KNN algorithm for classification [18]. Elena et al. used a public four-day dataset from TalkingData company that manages 200 million clicks. They used the LightGBM algorithm on this large dataset this model compensates categorical values and data unbalance. Engineering features and selection helped them step by step to improve detection performance [19]. Fallah et al. developed a KNN-based click fraud classification technique with a counter field introduction to overcome the high memory consumption associated with this method of classification. They assessed their algorithm's performance on a data set collected from a search engine called parsiijoo and focused on user session information such as search engine user clicks and IP address [20].

3 Proposed Solution

The work aims to identify in a set of clicks which are fraudulent and which are genuine. So, through a database data that contains all the information, with all types of operations, the objective is to build a model that is able to identify which operations have the signs of fraud at the time.

The procedure adopted in this work has some stages as shown in Fig. 2, which are the Exploratory Data Analysis, preprocessing, feature engineering, selection of features, capturing key relations between features and effective application modeling, all steps were performed using the Python programming.

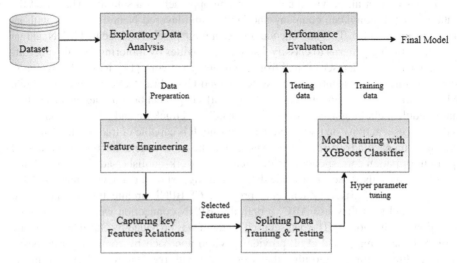

Fig. 2. Proposed methodology

3.1 Dataset

The data used in this work is real time dataset available on Kaggle [21] and was obtained by the company TalkingData. The first stage of the work was to identify the information available to assess which features are more likely to compose the proposed model. The database used in this work contains ad click actions collected from a Chinese mobile platform over a span of four days. It has millions of click data which is distributed over eight attributes. The attributes are shown in the Table 1 with a precise description of each, among this attribute seven features are considered as independent attribute while one feature is dependent attribute. The implementation is in python, where the ratio of train to test data is 3:2 by choosing the rows in the dataset randomly.

There are no missing values in the data set, however the data is unbalanced, the target Class variable has binary values, 0 for normal transactions and 1 for possibly fraudulent, in which the second represents 0.25% of the data. Only about 0.25% of clicks are 'fraudulent', which is expected in a fraud detection problem. Such high-class imbalance is probably going to be the toughest challenge of this problem.

Table 1. TalkingData attributes

Attributes	Description
ip	ip address of click
app	app id for marketing
device	device type id of user mobile phone
os	os version id of user mobile phone
channel	channel id of mobile ad publisher
click_time	ad timestamp of click (UTC)
attributed_time	if user download the app after clicking an ad, this is the time of the app download
is_attributed	the target that is to be predicted, indicating the app was downloaded

3.2 Exploratory Data Analysis

In this stage of the work, detailed evaluations were carried out on the basis of data to ensure the consistency of the data that will be used in the model, thus being able to mitigate problems due to data inconsistency/problems. The goal of search analysis is to "find out" a data set that will do the rest. It smoother the process of modeling in three main ways:

1. We will get valuable data cleaning tips which help in making the model.
2. We will be thinking about ideas for Feature Engineering which can bring your models from good to excellent.
3. We will get a "view" of the data set that will help you communicate the results and increase efficiency.

In EDA, we would start with basic analysis and then explore the data further. Univariate and Bivariate analysis are performed to know the data thoroughly. The Number of unique values in each column of the dataset can be observed in the Fig. 3.

As anticipated ip has the greatest number of unique values and channel being the one with the least number of unique values. All the columns apart from click time are originally integer type though we observe that they are all actually categorical type in general.

3.3 Feature Engineering

In this step, the selection of features that have greater power to explain the response variable present in the database, thus selected for composing the model. Let's now derive some new features from the existing ones. There are a number of features one can extract from click_time itself, and by grouping combinations of IP with other features.

Capturing Key Features. We create datetime variables using a function designed for the purpose. The function takes in a dataframe, adds date/time based columns to it, and

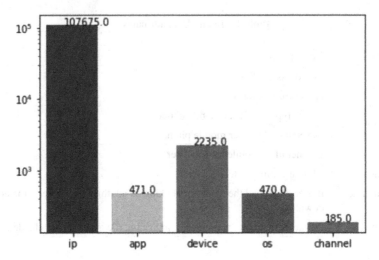

Fig. 3. Unique values per feature

returns the modified dataframe. We use our function that takes in a dataframe and creates these features. The function first of all creates groupings of IP addresses with other features and appends the new features to the df and then merge the new aggregated features with the df. This feature added explicitly would help the model for better prediction.

4 Modelling

The models used in this work are implemented through "software free reps" that do not need a commercial license to be used. So, it was Python programming language was used with the scikit-learn project, developed by Pedregosa et al. (2011), which has the implementation of the main models that use machine learning techniques. Additionally, Python libraries that have functionalities that facilitate the work of implementing models using learning machine code, they being NumPy, SciPy, Matplotlib and Pandas [22].

For our problem click fraud we found XGBoost as an algorithm that gives answers to all the questions like consistency with business objective, scalability, accuracy, speed and other important criterion affecting the choice of algorithm is the complexity of the model. Extreme Gradient Boosting or XGBoost is a gradient boosting algorithm library that is designed to solve modern data science issues and resources. It leverages the bagging boosting and stacking strategies and is bundled in an easy-to-use library [23]. Some of XGBoost's major advantages are that it is highly scalable/parallel, easy to implement, and usually outperforms other algorithms. This machine learning algorithm can be made more complex or ease in depending on the number of parameters or the choice of some hyperparameters. XGBoost's outperforms other algorithms due to its ability to predict fraud click rather than interpretability that is emphasized in the case of click fraud.

We build model to predict the variable is_attributed (downloaded). The first step is to create x and y train that is to split data in train and test/validation sets and to check the average download rates in train and test both as it should be comparable. Secondly, we shall fit model on training data with default hyper-parameters (subsample, learning_rate, max_depth etc.). And then would make predictions and evaluate the same. Finally, we now try changing hyper-parameters using k-fold CV and then use grid search CV to find the optimal values of hyper-parameters. The result shown in Fig. 4 depicts that a subsample of 0.6 and learning rate of about 0.2 seems optimal. Hence, we build final model with the chosen hyper-parameters as 'learning_rate': 0.2, 'max_depth': 2, 'n_estimators': 200, 'objective': 'binary:logistic', 'subsample': 0.6.

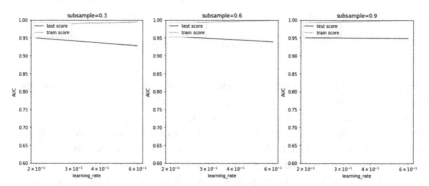

Fig. 4. Sub sample and learning rate of XGBoost

We try other variants of boosting (adaboost, gradient boosting and XGBoost), tune the hyperparameters in each model and compare the performance of each model on 2 different datasets.

5 Results and Analysis

5.1 Model Evaluation

The model evaluation step is carried out to assure the prefect of perfection of the given model; for this sole purpose we use different databases to check the accuracy of the given model. We have implemented the algorithm with specific hyper-parameters on one more database along with the main database TalkingData from Kaggle, sample data is shown in Fig. 5.

	ip	app	device	os	channel	click_time	is_attributed
0	33924	15	1	19	111	2017-11-09 04:03:08	0
1	37383	3	1	13	280	2017-11-09 04:03:08	0
2	56758	15	1	10	245	2017-11-09 04:03:08	0
3	7722	9	1	25	145	2017-11-09 04:03:08	0
4	7811	15	1	13	430	2017-11-09 04:03:08	0

Fig. 5. Sample data from TalkingData dataset

The database is Advertising [24] it is also dataset openly available on Kaggle which has 10 features, sample data is shown in Fig. 6.

	Dailytime	Age	Area	Daily	Ad	City	Country	Timestamp	Clicked on Ad
0	68.95	35	79776	3	1	17	280	3/27/2016 00:53	0
1	80.23	31	114904	3	1	18	402	4/4/2016 01:39	0
2	69.47	26	106136	3	1	19	280	3/13/2016 20:35	0
3	74.15	29	69070	12	1	13	245	1/10/2016 02:31	0
4	68.37	35	10238	18	1	20	121	6/3/2016 03:36	0

Fig. 6. Sample data from advertising dataset

Firstly, we implement our designed model on TalkingData and then on Advertising dataset with the same hyper parameters. The features designed are generalized so any data could fit the model and provide good accuracy.

The model applied on TalkingData gives accuracy of 0.96 and on Advertising it gives accuracy of 0.93 as shown in Table 2, on an average this model provides accuracy on basis of area under ROC curve which is 0.93 to 0.96 for dataset we have applied it to. We also implemented this XGBoost model on this datasets to evaluate its performance.

Table 2. TalkingData attributes

Dataset used	XGBoost
TalkingData	0.96
Advertising	0.93

5.2 Comparing Results

In this step, all the techniques used in this research work will be analyzed jointly, aiming to identify the one that has superior results. When evaluating all the results the answer cannot be direct because there is a "Lose-and-win" when we evaluate all the results together, and each of the methodologies has its advantages and disadvantages. Thus, after the execution of all models we were able to verify that the use of using XGBoost model response variables is completely plausible, thus being a classifier with good ability to identify cases of click fraud, without undermining the accuracy of the model as from Table 3.

We have implemented XGBoost Algorithm on TalkingData and Advertising database and also implemented two other algorithms on the same databases. The other algorithms are AdaBoost and Gradient Boosting and the modeling was carried out the same way as of XGBoost with some changes in hyper parameters for these 2 algorithms. It is important to note that features were kept same for all the algorithms being the grouped features designed during the feature engineering step. This step of implementing different

Table 3. Comparing results of different boosting algorithms

Dataset used	AdaBoost	Gradient boosting	XGBoost
TalkingData	0.94	0.82	0.96
Advertising	0.94	0.91	0.93

algorithm with same features and dataset assures the accuracy and liability of XGBoost when compared with other gradient boosting algorithms.

After implementing our model on 2 datasets and other boosting algorithms we try to compare it with some recent methods using basic research. Table 4 describes various recent approaches used in the field of click fraud detection and the comparison keeping

Table 4. Comparison of recent approaches with proposed model

S/N	Paper title	Database	Method	Findings
1	Deep Learning-based Model to Fight Against Ad Click Fraud - ACM 2019 [13]	TalkingData	Machine learning	They built a layered Neural Network with an attached autoencoder
2	Clicktok: Click Fraud Detection using Traffic Analysis – ACM 2019 [14]	Self-made from a university network	Traffic Analysis	Leveraged timing patterns of click traffic to identify fraudulent acts
3	Crowdsourcing for click fraud detection EURASIP Springer 2019 [15]	Self-made from a university network	Traffic Analysis	They propose an altogether new ad network component CFC
4	Exploring Non-Human Traffic in Online Digital Advertisements: Analysis and Prediction – ICCCI Springer 2019 [17]	Waseet is popular in the Middle East	Machine learning and rule based	They provide a hybrid approach by combining rule based with machine learning algorithm that works best with those features
5	Light GBM Machine learning algorithm to online click fraud detection – IBIMA 2019 [19]	TalkingData	Machine learning	LightGBM is used and categorial values and data unbalance are compensated by the model
6	Click Ad fraud detection Using XGBoost Gradient Boosting Algorithm [Proposed]	TalkingData and Advertising	Machine learning	The method uses XGBoost algorithm to propose model implementation and verify on 2 datasets. Also gives some features that are usually found in most of the click datasets

in consideration the datasets and method followed. We lastly compare our proposed method with those already present approaches using basic research.

5.3 Evaluating the Features Selected for Models

In this stage of the work, the features selected by the method will be evaluated. Sequential selection method, using the XGBoost classifier, for the models that use machine learning along with Data Science techniques.

All the features are important for modeling but ip and date served as most elite features of any click fraud related databases as they help in detecting the fraud when combined with other features of the dataset. The features related to timestamp and click attribute are commonly present in the training of all models, regardless pending the response variable was the one that identifies the number of people responsible for fraud. However, due to the characteristics of the database available all models are directly related to variables related to consultation and inclusion of restrictions.

6 Conclusion and Future Work

We analyze some detection techniques used presently in different solution domains. And propose potential solution for click fraud using XGBoost gradient boosting algorithm and implement the model designed on the TalkingData dataset. We also implement the model tuned with specific hyper parameters on another dataset for evaluation of the prefect of the model given by us and get a generous accuracy also. Then we compare the XGBoost designed model with other gradient boosting techniques on both the dataset for proper validation. This monograph featured that is implemented in the proposed method is capable of reducing Click Fraud giving good accuracy while keeping in mind important parameters of click fraud analysis and detection. Click fraud not only disturbs the budget advertisers but also how bots are used to corrupt your valuable data.

We find that the research in machine learning and deep learning are promising and provide with accurate solution to the problem of click fraud. And there is potential for more solutions in this domain. We need to explore further blockchain as it can be prominent and more accurate solution for click frauds by moving advertising network on a distributed and trusted environment. Hence, it's important to be aware and evolving to come up with solutions to circumvent and prevent them. Defense Strategies must be further and further improved.

References

1. Lin, Y. https://www.oberlo.in/blog/internet-statistics. Accessed 25 Nov 2020
2. Keelery, S. https://www.statista.com/statistics/1040905/india-opinion-timespent-online-than-tv/. Accessed 25 Nov 2020
3. Handley, L. https://www.cnbc.com/2017/12/04/global-advertising-spend-2020-online-and-offline-ad-spend-to-be-equal.html. Accessed 25 Nov 2020
4. Braccialini, C. https://blog.hubspot.com/marketing/online-advertising. Accessed 25 Nov 2020

5. Globsyn Business School Online, Digital Marketing Course (2020)
6. Kshetri, N., Voas, J.: Online advertising fraud. Computer **52**(1), 58–61 (2019). https://doi. org/10.1109/MC.2018.2887322
7. SEJ search engine journal. https://www.searchenginejournal.com/clickcease-howmuchppc-fraud-costing-your-business/357328/. Accessed 25 Nov 2020
8. IPQuality score. https://www.ipqualityscore.com/articles/view/17/what-is-payper-click-ppc-fraud. Accessed 25 Nov 2020
9. Serrano, T. https://thriveagency.com/news/what-is-click-fraud-and-how-do-youprevent-it/. Accessed 25 Nov 2020
10. Lynch, O. https://www.cheq.ai/what-is-click-fraud. Accessed 25 Nov 2020
11. Digital element. https://www.digitalelement.com/identify-proxiesfight-clickfraud-and-was ted-impressions/. Accessed 25 Nov 2020
12. Whats new publishing. https://whatsnewinpublishing.com/publishers-shadowtraffic-pro blem-why-your-traffic-numbers-are-off-by-20/. Accessed 25 Nov 2020
13. Thejas, G.S.: Deep learning-based model to fight against ad click fraud, pp. 176–181 (2019). https://doi.org/10.1145/3299815.3314453
14. Nagaraja, S., Shah, R.: Clicktok: click fraud detection using traffic analysis, pp. 105–116 (2019). https://doi.org/10.1145/3317549.3323407
15. Mouawi, R., Elhajj, I.H., Chehab, A., et al.: Crowdsourcing for click fraud detection. EURASIP J. Info. Secur. **2019**, 11 (2019). https://doi.org/10.1186/s13635-019-0095-1
16. Zhang, X., Liu, X., Guo, H.: A click fraud detection scheme based on cost sensitive BPNN and ABC in mobile advertising, pp. 1360–1365 (2018). https://doi.org/10.1109/CompComm. 2018.8780941
17. Almahmoud, S., Hammo, B., Al-Shboul, B.: Exploring non-human traffic in online digital advertisements: analysis and prediction (2019). https://doi.org/10.1007/978-3-030-283 74-257
18. Gabryel, M.: Data analysis algorithm for click fraud recognition (2018). https://doi.org/10. 1007/978-3-319-99972-236
19. Minastireanu, E., Mesnita, G.: Light GBM machine learning algorithm to online click fraud detection. J. Inf. Assur. Cybersecur. (2019). https://doi.org/10.5171/2019.263928
20. Fallah, I.M., Zarifzadeh, S.: Practical detection of click spams using efficient classification-based algorithms. Int. J. Inf. Commun. Technol. Res. **10**, 63–71 (2018)
21. Kaggle.com, TalkingData AdTracking fraud detection challenge (2018). https://www.kaggle. com/c/talkingdata-adtracking-fraud-detection. Accessed 25 Nov 2020
22. Great learning academy, data visualization in python course (2019)
23. Chen, T., Guestrin, C.: XGBoost: a scalable tree boosting system, CoRR, abs/1603.02754 (2016)
24. Kaggle.com, Jose, Advertising dataset by Jose Portilla and Pierian Data (2018). https://www. kaggle.com/fayomi/advertising. Accessed 25 Nov 2020

A Natural Language Processing Approach to Mine Online Reviews Using Topic Modelling

Usman Ahmad Usmani[✉], Nazleeni Samiha Haron, and Jaafreezal Jaafar

Universiti Teknologi Petronas, UTP, 32610 Seri Iskandar, Perak, Malaysia

Abstract. Artificial Intelligence is about how computers and humans communicate, and how we interact with language abbreviations. The ultimate purpose of the NLP is to connect in a way people can understand and reciprocate. Social networking messages have become a key source of consumer education. Sellers take online feedback to know if a potential buyer is a big part of their market. However, when such online reviews are too broad and/or extremely detailed, both buyers and sellers benefit from a mechanism that quickly extracts key insights from them. In this research paper, we used natural language processing to evaluate feedback from the language-processing community. Other data are included in the assessment of our peers.

1 Introduction

Online product reviews provide marketers with useful information on consumers' reactions, which helps marketers to respond quickly to changing circumstances. Analysis and clinicians have gradually been paying attention to this particular data over the past few years (Laroche et al. 2005; Gopal et al. 2006). Though online voices of the consumer (VOC) are free text, they have proven to reflect the fundamental aggregate characteristics (Campbell et al. 2011; Godes and Mayzlin 2004; Duan et al. 2008; Shao 2012) and provide improvements in traditional marketing operations (Onishi and Manchanda 2012). Given the simple fact that a barrier exists that prohibits all products from offering better service. The amount of knowledge available on the Internet is limitless, incomparable, and without precedent (Godes et al. 2005). Incomplete data collection methods allow businesses not to correctly determine the competitive environment in the industry [1]. However, these points of view and market structure influence how a product is made, advertised, and sold. Through this practise, businesses replace increasing quality scores with product review material. In Chintagunta et al's report. The relationship between movie ratings and movie sales is calculated by how well movies perform online (2006). Book sales are examined by how their scores are calculated. Market structure benefits from developing relationships between rival brands through brand switching data, brand associative data, and set-up (John et al. 2006). Researchers are also able to manage customer knowledge drawn from online product feedback through the efficient use of natural language processes (Feldman et al. 2007). Lee and Bradlow (2011) created an algorithm to leverage input from online product reviews [2] (Fig. 1).

Thousands of various types of content can be found online, which can be used to disseminate messages. People's opinions are a source of information about a given topic.

© Springer Nature Switzerland AG 2021
N. Chaubey et al. (Eds.): COMS2 2021, CCIS 1416, pp. 82–98, 2021.
https://doi.org/10.1007/978-3-030-76776-1_6

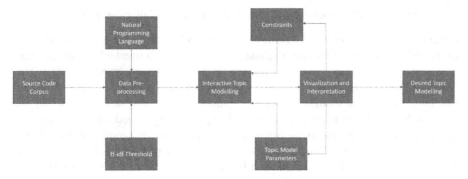

Fig. 1. An architecture overview of interactive topic modelling.

The stability of a company helps it to grow, sell and retain customer relationships [3]. This is why businesses ask customers for input. Although well designed and performed surveys offer the highest quality estimates, they are the most expensive to perform. Affective analysis has been studied as methods for quantifying sentiment, especially in recommendation systems [4]. These strategies seek to restore the sense of positive, negative, and neutral terms and sentences in text. Two essential aspects of sentiment analysis are general feelings and how they play into learning new facts. The content of the document is ambiguous about the emotions involved in the issue. In fact, you can be unhappy with the engine sounding out of tune if you think that the engine is satisfactory. These different customer needs become as important to the manufacturers as their overall satisfaction [5]. A successful e-commerce site must have positive online customer feedback. The individual product reviews will cause travellers to buy a range of products and increase travel volumes. Although product requirements and cost are essential (no buyer would purchase a TV which is too big for his/her living room), it is the influence of others opinions which allowed the purchase decision. Review also takes into account considerations such as accuracy and durability. People all over the world benefit from all of the research we have done about them [6].

1.1 Feedback of Products

Consumer feedback would enable businesses to improve and strengthen the products and services that have already been developed. These two styles of sentiment analysis deal with the issues being studied. The first phase would list the common attributes of objects, and the second phase would include a review of their features. I will present a process model today which focuses on the factors that impact customers' satisfaction. Managed and unattended financial management approaches can be divided into two groups, using both emphasis and delivery. Managed approaches include training on data that has been pre-labeled. Supervised approaches may be effective, but manual work is also required. A model needs to be built to classify unclassifiable data. Topic modelling is a methodology that helps to find particular subjects and the general patterns of topics [7]. The topic models are effective for a variety of applications including organising, cataloguing and communicating large quantities of text data.

1.2 Recovery of Information from Unstructured Text, Collection of Functions

By training a topic model based on bursary text, topics like "bid", "trading," "dividend", "exchange" and so on are created. The image illustrates how a standard model operates, but different types of goods and services on the Web need to be analysed separately. The architecture must be relatively complex and must easily accommodate several programming languages. Topic modelling using techniques such as random forest has become increasingly popular as a method for recognising latent topics and topics in texts [8]. Subject-modeling is based on the premise that documents are sampled from a distribution composed of randomly mixed words. Although topical models benefit from the relationship between words and topics, it is highly inaccurate to disregard word order. Relaxing the presumed notion of BAG OF WORDS should strengthen our models for latent aspects inference, particularly with documents that account for the structure of sentences. This paper explores sentence structure and the forms in which word order, thematic relations and syntactic relations are used [9] (Fig. 2).

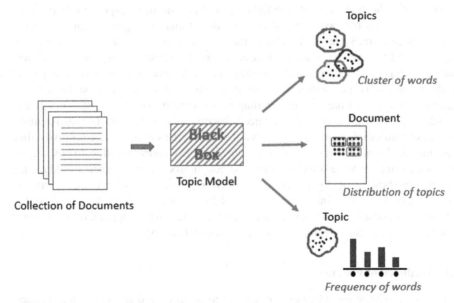

Fig. 2. Flow chart of topic modelling for a collection of documents.

Many studies have shown that customer feedback is essential to both revenue and market growth. Sincerely because what the general public thinks of a product plays a key role in what the public perceives as potential sales success, it is important that the thoughts and feelings expressed in the subsequent reviews be recognised because collectively these reviews represent "the wisdom of the public" and can provide a very reliable indicator of potential sales success [10]. The paper provides the means to make knowledge actionable through the means of designing models and algorithms. Calculations may be made about the future sales of a product using the use of models and algorithms. Previous studies have used review scores or the size of the relation to predict the sales trend without understanding how positive or negative consumers feel about the product. The amount of feedback and sales spikes is strongly correlated, but there are more nuanced explanations behind the relationship. The bulk of how someone is feeling may be better at predicting how they will feel than how much they drink. The previous studies have not properly accounted for the effects of the feedback or the tests' validity. Not all publications are valid. The content of the feedback can vary widely because there is a lack of transparency in the process. Definitions of "poor" reviews include very short, unsubstantial comments like "this book sucks," or lengthy and repetitive reviews that are simply duplicates of the descriptions of the product. Negative reviews, badly written reviews, or even spam reviews can significantly reduce the chances that the review will be useful. Goods delivery is a dynamic domain that needs detailed knowledge on several important factors. This paper focuses on the issues surrounding the predictability, success, and analysis of Hollywood movies. In order to forecast box office figures, three factors need to be measured. Various elements including audience response, previous uses of the word, and an evaluation of content were evaluated. We begin by addressing the manner in which reviews convey feelings, and how this effects various computational text mining applications. Feedback ratings that are positive or negative are often not fully reflective of how the end user really feels In analysing sentiment, we interpret the sentiment in the examination as the product of an input of a number of hidden variables and propose a novel method for sentiment analysis, referred to as Sentiment PLSA. (SSPS) [11, 12]. Unlike traditional academic PLSA, S-PLSAs offer priority to dysfunctional behaviours to feelings, attitudes and emotions. Instead of using vanilla and all the words, we mainly concentrate on the phrases that have to do with feeling, in comparison to the single-word approach. Our research adopts certain terms, taking into account the language advocated by Whitelaw et al. Good progress was achieved by the use of appraisal terms in the comparatively lower number of words used in classifying film reviews. To contribute to the features in the S-PLSA scores, the evaluation words are used [14]. A comparison of the past sales of the product and how other films do. The model used to analyse the data is the Autoregressive (AR) model, which is commonly used for understanding data across time series issues. In order to combine sentiment awareness with word embeddings, we propose a model in which sentiment is modelled [13]. A modern demand forecasting model. Extensive research reveals that the ARSA model is capable of testing both our assumptions and projected revenues [15].

1.3 Semi-supervised Topic Modelling in Tweets Based on Topic Modelling

Information already learned by an algorithm greatly affects the efficacy of that algorithm. "Tweets" are short-length texts which require more sophisticated content for them to be understood. Social media use shifts the association of the word with a topic.

A keyword tag cannot be repaired if it is broken. Through our partnership with external experts, we have devised a system for applying keyword tagging to various goods. Now, keywords will be added depending on the time slice. The evaluation of the language model suggests that it is effective in categorising words.

1.4 Topic Modelling for Social Media in the Restaurant Based Industry

McDonald's Corporation announced a drop in US sales internationally during the second quarter of 2020 due to the COVID-19 pandemic. The COVID-19 epidemic has inundated McDonald's and Burger King, which has made it very difficult for them to keep up. COVID-19 has encouraged customers away from restaurants to eat food, which has changed the food consumption industry. In order to keep their customers satisfied during a COVID-19 outbreak, fast-food restaurants rely on various food services so that customers can return to the restaurant after the outbreak is over due to their previous level of service satisfaction.

Progress occurs when the product or service is happier for consumers than the competition. Even in the fast-food industry, keeping the trust of a customer is one of the key tasks. To ensure that customers remain, loyalty in the fast food industry is important. Customer loyalty is of critical importance to the survival of the fast-food chain, and their orders will inevitably be boosted.

Previous studies have asked clients about factors affecting satisfaction in the catering industry using interviews, surveys, or telephone interviews. In addition, this form of study requires a great deal of labour power and material resources, lacks a large amount of data, has poor data collection timeliness, and is vulnerable to bias. Participant interviews and surveys during COVID-19 will yield a greater amount of information at a faster rate. While EWOM has been gaining popularity in the last decade, there is not enough research on how it is actually thought about by group users. Consumers also share the brand with their personal experiences. Consumer use of social media can show the true emotions of customers and thereby impact product loyalty, all of which is beneficial to advertisers. In purchasing utilities, lodging, and shopping, these online marketing influencers can influence the purchase intentions of other internet users and have become one of the primary sources of customer preference.

Online assessment platforms such as star ratings and reviews provide clients with tools to provide feedback on their purchases. Vásquez discovered the different verbal activities in which clients engage, including (but not limited to) constructive interactions, expectations, suggestions, content adjustments, and alerts. Consumers in the catering industry also read reviews from other clients. Reviews are typically more valued than other sources; they are more likely to impact customers. When good reviews are provided by buyers, they inspire others to purchase the item, which is highly sought after by e-commerce suppliers. The main hypothesis of the paper is that the behaviour of the e-contact WOMs will affect the choices of the rivals, which in turn will contribute to market rivalry.

The remainder of the study paper discusses how and the methodological findings of the online survey were conducted. At the end of this post, the conclusion is further discussed.

2 Related Work

Topic modelling has appeared in various forms in different styles of study [61, 62]. The prepositional phrase has been used infrequently in the context of an exploratory literature review. In addition, LDA, as it is very widely used and is a simple statistical model, is the preferred topic modelling tool [51–55]. Though other research methods may be used, the aim of this paper is to create a scholarly journal [56]. Adaptability and applicability are considered when topic modelling methods are used and LDA is used to define themes [57]. Various other techniques can be used in the context to provide detailed evaluations of the strengths and weaknesses of models. The LDA machine learning system uses a probability-based classification method for topics from a series of documents [58, 60]. A subject is a set selection of words for use in a document or presentation. Various statistical tests are used to analyse words in a language and calculate the likelihood of the distribution of different words (the hidden structure of topics). The technique's approach focuses on how words connect to each other in a sentence rather than word choice. The method is how often a word is used and how often. Presumption is presumed when the most widely used words are used in a topic. If LEAN is a subject of the paper, it is likely that the author is familiar with the JIT and Kanban methodologies. The findings show the most common topics and the highest use of those topics. For each article, the probability of a product is calculated, providing a count of the number of subjects the article discusses. The framework is a step-by-step process in which the use of the framework in the context of a case is defined and the sample code for analysis is shared, enabling others to use the framework for their own literature review. In the book, an adequate introduction to LDA is stated [51]. The code is based on a mathematical language that is open source and can be easily modified for other purposes. To lower the cost of time the reviewer spends, the methodology for exploratory literature reviews can be automated. For automated Business Process Management, the success of a similar online service that was automated was an inspiration for system automation [59]. They find that topic modelling can be automated and say that by using a good tool for topic modelling, it can easily generate good results, but the method relies on the ability of people to find the right data, lead the analytical journey, and interpret the results. Various methods have been suggested to detect the textual data dimension. The theoretical analysis of unaccounted data deals with the previously proposed work [16].

However, both approaches lack a deep study of semantic aspects [17, 19]. They are not feasible because the processing of large volumes of labelled data needs more energy than it is worth. Unsupervised methods have been shown to be useful for describing a number of predefined words. Topics are discovered by uniquely defining the structure within the complex collection of documents [18]. Both papers convey the idea that papers contain a central idea and that the distribution of the central ideas within a paper is defined by the word distributions. Using cooperative semantic representations, we are able to identify aspect words based on aspects of the data they represent. Current topic modelling approaches are very quick, but also require laborious data cleaning. Their comprehension of linguistics is poor since they do not agree that words are formed individually. It is a ranked list of products. A single term is the theme model representing a single theme in a corpus [20]. The second major flaw of current model-based methodologies is failing to treat word order as a significant factor. It is oversimplified. Researchers have been exploring this subject lately, so it is one worth further examination. Dirichlet's hierarchical model was combined with the bigram and thematic models to create a Bayesian model [22]. The Wallach model does not account for word or phrase unigrams, and does not consider series n-grams or phrases. The concept of LDA collocation was not originated by Dr Steyvers and Professor Griffiths. The paper provides a new set of standards on which to determine what word or sentence forms a word or a sentence should have. The proposed model in the paper is advantageous since it uses sentence structure in a text and the co-occurrence statistics between words in LDA [21]. The Collocation Model was improved by Wang et al. by presenting the Topical N-gram Model (TNG) in which the consecutive terms were introduced to the model to determine whether "n-grams" should be generated for the consecutive terms. This model is extended to deal with sentences instead of a single document and also to take into account the multivariate nature of a phrase. With this model, words are created in the correct placement of other words in a text [23–25]. The study approach by Gruber et al. is close to that of Markowich and Wu's method. They claim that all words in the same sentence have the same subject, and the likelihood that two different words would belong to the same sentence is strong. Markov's model successfully extracts the message, but isn't as accurate when it comes to detecting certain patterns such as certain nouns. We want to expand current sentiment analysis subject models to identify multiple emotions. A thematic model is chosen that relies on the use of Unigrams and Phrases. In conventional approaches, these subjects fall short when trying to describe how they are expressed in literature. Our model assumes that a Markov chain is created by the words in a sentence, and the most similar are the words with the most similar sections. We therefore propose a new approach to the automated extraction of sentences that may refer to sentencing [26]. The lexicon is used to cluster multiword descriptors to enhance how a mathematical model is used for text. Our work is transferable between other disciplines allowing transfer learning between various domains. An algorithm that detects hidden patterns in a collection of documents by using a statistic on word frequencies [27–29]. The performance is a complex set of topics that seem to be somehow connected. Documents may have any number of subjects, in any combination. of the subject sometimes occurs in papers and/or their sense is not popular outside. The researcher discusses how the case should be interpreted depending on the continuity of the statement (Chang et al. 2009). The accuracy of the subject models determines its relevance to social scientists. In the case of journalism analysis, the model's collection of topics would preferably include subject categorization or context based on basic theory, such as the list of issues used by the Comparative Agendas Project that uses categories of legislative and journalistic text, such as macroeconomics, international relations and crime (Jones and Baumgartner 2005) [30, 31]. Regardless, the subjects are discussed by analysing patterns of co-occurrence that are not necessarily related to theoretical principles. TIt is plausible to have a general concept or context defined in the abstract sense, but terms may also be written or spoken in different ways. (A natural disaster, for example [33] rs) and frames, that are created, at least potentially, by particular word patterns co-occurring as well [32–35]. After the tragedy at the Chernobyl nuclear power plant, this essay criticises Soviet inaction. The text is underlined with the words taken from the main idea. Subjects were categorised automatically by the model, but the researchers described and specified the topics based on an analysis of variables. This sentence demonstrates many of the usual topics discussed in LDN [36–39]. This paper clearly reflects the context of the article because of the difficulty in selecting a single topic for this paper in a coding scheme obliged to include a single topic per text.

Second, since they are minor words, such as prepositions and determiners, you can see that subjects are not included in the algorithm.

3 Method

For our survey, we surveyed over 5000 Amazon Apparel product reviews. Our goal is to recognise key terms from the customer's feedback. These groups are used to decide whether consumers prefer the given product. There are different ways to get topics out of an email. Some are discussed more frequently than others [40–43]. Techniques of non-negative matrix factorization. The LDA, a commonly used exploratory technique for selecting themes from a selection of documents, will be discussed in this article. LDA claims the papers are composed of many separate sub-topics [44–48]. The phenomena are clarified by the probability of witnessing them. The LDA will recognise the most critical problems that must be resolved in the first place. Now we have a model for extracting online feedback based on a subject approach.

Algorithm for mining online reviews using topic modelling
1)First load all the necessary libraries.
2)Start with the data preprocessing

- def freq_words(x, terms = 30):
- all_words = ' '.join([text for text in x]) all_words = all_words.split() fdist = FreqDist(all_words) words_df =pd.DataFrame({'word':list(fdist.keys()), 'count':list(fdist.values())})
- remove unwanted characters, numbers and symbols df['reviewText']= df['reviewText'].str.replace("[^a-zA-Z#]", " ")
- from nltk.corpus import stopwords stop_words = stopwords.words('english')

3)Removing the Stop Words

- from nltk.corpus import stopwords stop_words = stopwords.words('english')
- tokenized_reviews = pd.Series(reviews).apply(lambda x: x.split()) print(tokenized_reviews[1])

4)Building an LDA model

- dictionary = corpora.Dictionary(reviews_2)
- Creating the object for LDA model using gensim library LDA = gensim.models.ldamodel.LdaModel
- Build LDA model lda_model = LDA(corpus=doc_term_matrix, id2word=dictionary, num_topics=7, random_state=100, chunksize=1000, passes=50)

5)Topics Visualization

- pyLDAvis.enable_notebook()
- vis = pyLDAvis.gensim.prepare(lda_model, doc_term_matrix, dictionary)

LDA is a technique of matrix factorization. Any corpus (document collection) can be interpreted in vector space as a document-term matrix. [49] The matrix below displays a corpus of N documents D1, D2, D3 … Dn and M terms vocabulary size W1, W2 .. Wn. Wn (Fig. 3 and Fig. 4).

Fig. 3. Data preprocessing and cleaning

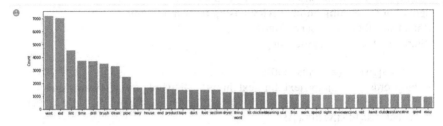

Fig. 4. Most common words in our reviews dataset

In the definition of I J cell, WJ is consolidated. Latent Dirichlet Allocation (LDA) assigns labels that are then converted into lower-dimensional probability matrices M1 and M2 to the words in this article. M1 is the matrix of content-topics and M2 is the set of terms matrix of dimensions (N, K), (K, M), where N is the number of articles, K is the number of subjects, and M is the size of the vocabulary. M2 is the set of terms matrix of dimensions (N, K), where N is the number of articles, K is the number of subjects, and M is the size of the vocabulary. This approach is improved by the use of sampling methods [50]. This includes every vowel in every consonant and moves the subject of the paper to a new one (Fig. 5).

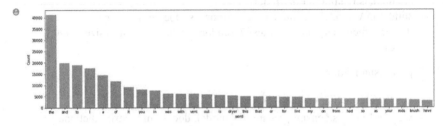

Fig. 5. Plotting the most frequent words and see if the more significant words have come out

The word "w," which has been allocated to a new subject "k.", is described as a combination of two probabilities. P1 – how many of the influential terms are currently described in d. P2 = the proportion of assignments to the topic t that professor w assigns to the topic t in the term. The subject assignment is changed to an entirely new topic relating to the likelihood that each student's product will be better than the other student's product. There is a list of probability tables only if words and topics have been assigned in the correct way. This is the probability that the subject will produce a term, so it makes sense to adjust the probability of what the subject will produce to a new probability . The iterative clustering algorithm reaches a steady state where the document subject and topic term distributions are relatively solid.

To keep your Jupyter Notebooks or your other Python development environment up-todate, please do so by following these instructions. We will use the LDA algorithm to learn a series of topic terms from our online research data set. To import the data for review, first place the data in a folder and then use the pandas read json function to read it. It is an efficient method to search for errors after processing the data. How do we plot a bar chart and what are the most frequently used words on the data? The most frequent grammatical forms are 'the,' 'and,' etc. These terms don't matter and just repeat what we already know. We need to delete these words. We'll begin with the assignment of terms to unique indices in the corpus. Then we will show the Document Term matrix (v2) using the Dictionary (D). Throughout our article, we will use the PyLDAvis library. The visual representation illustrates the subject, the key terms, and various images and diagrams.

Other NLP approaches are used to enhance understanding and learning. Some considerations are discussed below.

Summarize the essense of the essay in a few sentences and a short summary. What organisations are most popular and what are the most famous products?

Using the classification system based on what the analysis shows. This will help us decide how useful the scheme can be, as well as what can be omitted.

Sentiment analysis can be used for improved goods and services, and for improving customer emotions.

Retrieving knowledge saves us from having to think up how to use each object. The article accurately describes the thoughts and viewpoints of other people. However, the results do not provide a hint of the kind of comments they are. This definition expands information retrieval by predicting not only the subject to be discussed, but also the emotions it will evoke (Figs. 6, 7, 8, 9, 10, 11 and 12).

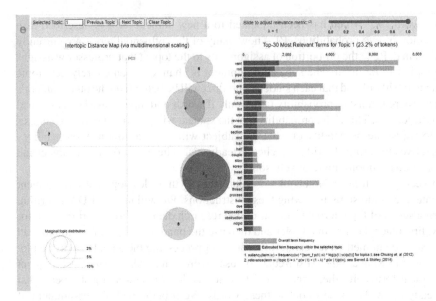

Fig. 6. Interactive visualization of topics

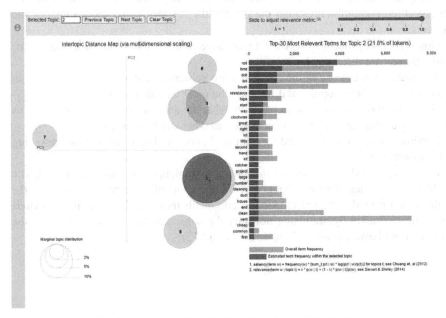

Fig. 7. Interactive visualization of topics at clicked values

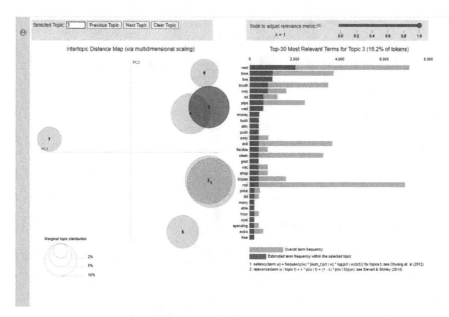

Fig. 8. Interactive visualization of topics at clicked values

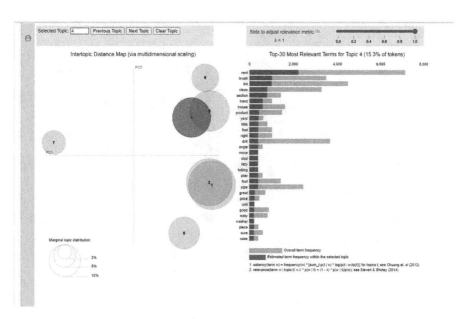

Fig. 9. Interactive visualization of topics at various clicked values.

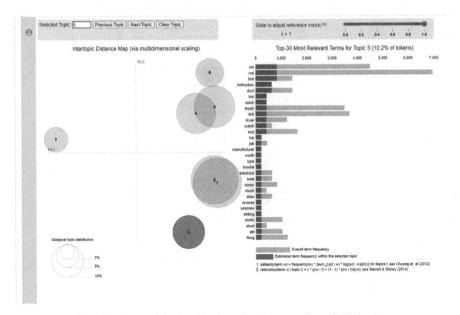

Fig. 10. Interactive visualization of topics at various clicked values

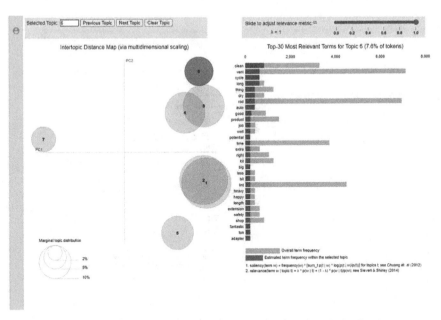

Fig. 11. Interactive visualization of topics at various clicked values

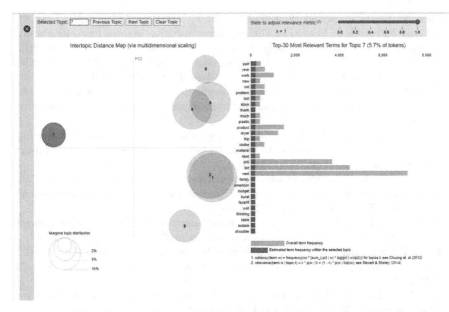

Fig. 12. Interactive visualization of topics at various clicked values

4   Conclusions

Using Natural Language Processing, we look up online feedback, and examine the reviews for correlations across phrases. We offer an algorithm for indexing, mining and extracting online feedback. Text mining applications provide researchers with a number of tools for analysing realistic assumptions, costs and descriptions of vast volumes of different documents, which opens up new data sources that were previously inaccessible. We map the most frequent phrases, disregarding the order of the words, and use rectangles to represent each subject. Topic modelling is not necessarily suitable for all data sets, and when it is used, the performance may be less than optimal. For example, when the text is small (e.g., open-ended questions from a survey), extremely large (e.g., email), noisy (e.g., text from websites) and the individual documents quite short (e.g., Tweets), a subject model will struggle to generate a useful model. One approach to testing our topic models is to validate our models with real data. Text mining is not a replacement for human research, but rather an enhancement to it.

References

1. Ma, B., Zhang, D., Yan, Z., Kim, T.: An LDA and synonym lexicon based approach to product feature extraction from online consumer product reviews. J. Electron. Commerc. Res. **14**(4), 304 (2013)
2. Ghose, A., Ipeirotis, P.G., Li, B.: Designing ranking systems for hotels on travel search engines by mining user-generated and crowdsourced content. Mark. Sci. **31**(3), 493–520 (2012)

3. Chen, X., Faviez, C., Schuck, S., Lillo-Le-Louët, A., Texier, N., Dahamna, B., Huot, C., Foulquié, P., Pereira, S., Leroux, V.: Mining patients' narratives in social media for pharmacovigilance: adverse effects and misuse of methylphenidate. Front. Pharmacol. **9**, 541 (2018)
4. Zhou, X., Wan, X., Xiao, J.: Representation learning for aspect category detection in online reviews. In: Twenty-Ninth AAAI Conference on Artificial Intelligence (2015)
5. Zhou, X., Tao, X., Rahman, M.M., Zhang, J.: Coupling topic modelling in opinion mining for social media analysis. In: Proceedings of the International Conference on Web Intelligence, pp. 533–540 (2017)
6. Chen, Z., Mukherjee, A., Liu, B.: Aspect extraction with automated prior knowledge learning. In: Proceedings of the 52nd Annual Meeting of the Association for Computational Linguistics (Volume 1: Long Papers), pp. 347–358 (2014)
7. Ibrahim, N.F., Wang, X.: Mining social network content of online retail brands: a machine learning approach. In: Proceedings of the 11th European Conference on Information Systems Management, ECISM, vol. 2011, pp. 129–138 (2017)
8. van Altena, A.J., Olabarriaga, S.D.: Predicting publication inclusion for diagnostic accuracy test reviews using random forests and topic modelling. In: CLEF (Working Notes) (2017)
9. Kar, A.K.: What affects usage satisfaction in mobile payments? Modelling user generated content to develop the "digital service usage satisfaction model. Inf. Syst. Front, pp. 1–21 (2020)
10. Schuckert, M., Liu, X., Law, R.: Hospitality and tourism online reviews: recent trends and future directions. J. Travel Tour. Mark. **32**(5), 608–621 (2015)
11. Suleman, K., Vechtomova, O.: Discovering aspects of online consumer reviews. J. Inf. Sci. **42**(4), 492–506 (2016)
12. Dessai, N.S.F., Laxminarayanan, J.A.: A topic modeling based approach for mining online social media data. In: 2019 2nd International Conference on Intelligent Computing, Instrumentation and Control Technologies (ICICICT), vol. 1, pp. 704–709 (2019)
13. Liu, B.: Opinion mining and sentiment analysis (2011)
14. Akhtar, N., Zubair, N., Kumar, A., Ahmad, T.: Aspect based sentiment oriented summarization of hotel reviews. Procedia Comput. Sci. **115**, 563–571 (2017)
15. Shatnawi, S., Gaber, M.M., Cocea, M.: Text stream mining for massive open online courses: review and perspectives. Syst. Sci. Control Eng. Open Access J. **2**(1), 664–676 (2014)
16. Kim, S., Zhang, J., Chen, Z., Oh, A.H., Liu, S.: A hierarchical aspect-sentiment model for online reviews. In: AAAI (2013)
17. Xiong, S., Wang, K., Ji, D., Wang, B.: A short text sentiment-topic model for product reviews. Neurocomputing **297**, 94–102 (2018)
18. Lu, B., Ott, M., Cardie, C., Tsou, B.K.: Multi-aspect sentiment analysis with topic models. In: 2011 IEEE 11th International Conference on Data Mining Workshops, pp. 81–88 (2011)
19. Puspaningrum, A., Siahaan, D., Fatichah, C.: Mobile app review labeling using lda similarity and term frequency-inverse cluster frequency (TF-ICF). In: 2018 10th International Conference on Information Technology and Electrical Engineering (ICITEE), pp. 365–370 (2018)
20. Mukherjee, A., Liu, B.: Aspect extraction through semi-supervised modeling. In: Proceedings of the 50th Annual Meeting of the Association for Computational Linguistics (Volume 1: Long Papers), pp. 339–348 (2012)
21. Bahja, M., Lycett, M.: Identifying patient experience from online resources via sentiment analysis and topic modelling. In: Proceedings of the 3rd IEEE/ACM International Conference on Big Data Computing, Applications and Technologies, pp. 94–99 (2016)
22. Kee, Y.H., Li, C., Kong, L.C., Tang, C.J., Chuang, K.L.: Scoping review of mindfulness research: a topic modelling approach. Mindfulness, pp. 1–15 (2019)

23. Chehal, D., Gupta, P., Gulati, P.: Implementation and comparison of topic modeling techniques based on user reviews in e-commerce recommendations. J. Ambient Intell. Hum. Comput., pp. 1–16 (2020)
24. Chen, N., Lin, J., Hoi, S.C., Xiao, X., Zhang, B.: AR-miner: mining informative reviews for developers from mobile app marketplace. In: Proceedings of the 36th International Conference on Software Engineering, pp. 767–778 (2014)
25. Bi, J.W., Liu, Y., Fan, Z.P., Zhang, J.: Wisdom of crowds: conducting importance - performance analysis (IPA) through online reviews. Tour. Manage. **70**, 460–478 (2019)
26. Irawan, H., Akmalia, G., Masrury, R.A.: Mining tourist's perception toward Indonesia tourism destination using sentiment analysis and topic modelling. In: Proceedings of the 2019 4th International Conference on Cloud Computing and Internet of Things, pp. 7–12 (2019)
27. Wang, W.: Sentiment analysis of online product reviews with semi-supervised topic sentiment mixture model. In: 2010 Seventh International Conference on Fuzzy Systems and Knowledge Discovery. vol. 5, pp. 2385–2389 (2010)
28. Lucini, F.R., Tonetto, L.M., Fogliatto, F.S., Anzanello, M.J.: Text mining approach to explore dimensions of airline customer satisfaction using online customer reviews. J. Air Trans. Manage. **83**, (2020)
29. Moghaddam, S., Ester, M.: ILDA: interdependent LDA model for learning latent aspects and their ratings from online product reviews. In: Proceedings of the 34th International ACM SIGIR Conference on Research and Development in Information Retrieval, pp. 665–674 (2011)
30. Brody, S., Elhadad, N.: An unsupervised aspect-sentiment model for online reviews. In: Human Language Technologies: The 2010 Annual Conference of the North American Chapter of the Association for Computational Linguistics, pp. 804–812 (2010)
31. Liu, B., Zhang, L.: A survey of opinion mining and sentiment analysis (2012)
32. Wang, W., Feng, Y., Dai, W.: Topic analysis of online reviews for two competitive products using latent Dirichlet allocation. Electron. Commerc. Res. Appl. **29**, 142–156 (2018)
33. Genc-Nayebi, N., Abran, A.: A systematic literature review: opinion mining studies from mobile app store user reviews. J. Syst. Softw. **125**, 207–219 (2017)
34. Zhao, X., Jiang, J., Yan, H., Li, X.: Jointly modeling aspects and opinions with a MaxEnt-LDA hybrid (2010)
35. Moro, S., Pires, G., Rita, P., Cortez, P.: A text mining and topic modelling perspective of ethnic marketing research. J. Bus. Res. **103**, 275–285 (2019)
36. Guerreiro, J., Rita, P.: How to predict explicit recommendations in online reviews using text mining and sentiment analysis. J. Hosp. Tour. Manage. **43**, 269–272 (2020)
37. Bansal, B., Srivastava, S.: Hybrid attribute based sentiment classification of online reviews for consumer intelligence. Appl. Intell. **49**(1), 137–149 (2019)
38. Bi, J.W., Liu, Y., Fan, Z.P., Cambria, E.: Modelling customer satisfaction from online reviews using ensemble neural network and effect-based Kano model. Int. J. Prod. Res. **57**(22), 7068–7088 (2019)
39. Xianghua, F., Guo, L., Yanyan, G., Zhiqiang, W.: Multi-aspect sentiment analysis for Chinese online social reviews based on topic modeling and HowNet lexicon. Knowl. Based Syst. **37**, 186–195 (2013)
40. Jia, S.S.: Motivation and satisfaction of Chinese and US tourists in restaurants: a cross-cultural text mining of online reviews. Tour. Manage. **78**, (2020)
41. Bagheri, A., Saraee, M., Jong, F.D.: ADM-LDA: an aspect detection model based on topic modelling using the structure of review sentences. J. Inf. Sci. **40**(5), 621–636 (2014)
42. Titov, I., McDonald, R.: Modeling online reviews with multi-grain topic models. In: Proceedings of the 17th International Conference on World Wide Web, pp. 111–120 (2008)

43. Özdağoğlu, G., Kapucugil-Ikiz, A., Çelik, A.F.: Topic modelling-based decision framework for analysing digital voice of the customer. Total Qual. Manage. Bus. Excell. **29**(13-14), 1545–1562 (2018)
44. Eickhoff, M., Neuss, N.: Topic modelling methodology: its use in information systems and other managerial disciplines (2017)
45. Guo, Y., Barnes, S.J., Jia, Q.: Mining meaning from online ratings and reviews: Tourist satisfaction analysis using latent Dirichlet allocation. Tour. Manage. **59**, 467–483 (2017)
46. Vanhala, M., Lu, C., Peltonen, J., Sundqvist, S., Nummenmaa, J., Järvelin, K.: The usage of large data sets in online consumer behaviour: a bibliometric and computational text-mining-driven analysis of previous research. J. Bus. Res. **106**, 46–59 (2020)
47. Kim, Y.B., Lee, J., Park, N., Choo, J., Kim, J.H., Kim, C.H.: When Bitcoin encounters information in an online forum: using text mining to analyse user opinions and predict value fluctuation. PLoS ONE **12**(5), (2017)
48. Nikolenko, S.I., Koltcov, S., Koltsova, O.: Topic modelling for qualitative studies. J. Inf. Sci. **43**(1), 88–102 (2017)
49. Archak, N., Ghose, A., Ipeirotis, P.G.: Deriving the pricing power of product features by mining consumer reviews. Manage. Sci. **57**(8), 1485–1509 (2011)
50. Dai, X., Spasic, I., Andres, F.: A framework for automated rating of online reviews against the underlying topics. In: Proceedings of the SouthEast Conference, pp. 164–167 (2017)
51. Blei, D.M.: Probabilistic topic models. Commun. ACM **55**(4), 77–84 (2012)
52. DiMaggio, P., Nag, M., Blei, D.: Exploiting affinities between topic modeling and the sociological perspective on culture: application to newspaper coverage of US government arts funding. Poetics **41**(6), 570–606 (2013)
53. Grimmer, J.: A Bayesian hierarchical topic model for political texts: measuring expressed agendas in Senate press releases. Pol. Anal. **18**(1), 1–35 (2010)
54. Jacobi, C., Atteveldt, W.V., Welbers, K.: Quantitative analysis of large amounts of journalistic texts using topic modelling. Digit. J. **4**(1), 89–106 (2016)
55. Zhao, W., et al. A heuristic approach to determine an appropriate number of topics in topic modeling. In: BMC Bioinform. **16**, 8 (2015)
56. Lancichinetti, A., Sirer, M.I., Wang, J.X., Acuna, D., Körding, K., Amaral, L.A.N.: High-reproducibility and high-accuracy method for automated topic classification. Phys. Rev. X **5**(1), (2015)
57. Blei, D.M., Ng, A.Y., Jordan, M.I.: Latent Dirichlet allocation. J. Mach. Learn. Res. **3**, 993–1022 (2003)
58. Alghamdi, R., Alfalqi, K.: A survey of topic modeling in text mining. Int. J. Adv. Comput. Sci. Appl.(IJACSA) **6**(1) (2015)
59. Brocke, J.V., Mueller, O., Debortoli, S.: The power of text-mining in business process management (2016)
60. Mahmood, A.A.: Literature survey on topic modeling (2009)
61. Elgesem, D., Steskal, L., Diakopoulos, N.: Structure and content of the discourse on climate change in the blogosphere: the big picture. Environ. Commun. **9**(2), 169–188 (2015)
62. Koltsova, O., Koltcov, S.: Mapping the public agenda with topic modeling: the case of the Russian LiveJournal. Policy Internet **5**(2), 207–227 (2013)

An Implementation and Combining of Hybrid and Content Based and Collaborative Filtering Algorithms for the Higher Performance of Recommended Sytems

B. Geluvaraj$^{(\boxtimes)}$ ⓘ and Meenatchi Sundaram

Garden City University, Bengaluru, India
geluvaraj171382@gcu.ac.in,
meenatchi.sundaram@gardencity.university

Abstract. This article tells about the RS categories and HRS concepts with block diagram and finding out similarity metrices by using the equations and and understanding the datasets and dividing the Train/Test data and road map of hybrid algorithm and categories of algorithms used in RS and how to build HRS and method of combining CB and CF and Hybrid algorithm with customized algorithm by implementing it and evaluating the algorithms accuracy, sparsity and diversity and making a experimental setup on the the SurpriseLib library and loading of non identical algorithms and dataset and examining the results and comparing them against the research objectives and finding whihc algorithms yields the finest results by plotting the graphs for better understanding of the algorithms efficiency.

Keywords: Recommended systems (RS) · Hybrid recommended systems (HRS) · Content-based filtering (CBF) · Collaborative filtering (CF) · Cosine similarity (CosSim)

1 Introduction

As the HRS takes the best of 2 or 3 systems that is made of user data input and report recommendation based on merging by analysing data. A system that combines CBF and CF could take advantage from both, the representation of the content, as well as the similarities among users, but it will combine its disadvantages as well, that is why hybridization is often made out of two or more models [1]. A hybrid approach combines 2 types of information, while it is also possible to use the recommendations of the 2 filtering techniques independently, so the different outputs are still linear for the analysis, and can be combined based on its weight, score or rating, as it will receive the highest weights, scores and ratings respectively. So in this paper will look into Hybridization techniques and solving problem techniques and results on the basis of different types of algorithms [2].

© Springer Nature Switzerland AG 2021
N. Chaubey et al. (Eds.): COMS2 2021, CCIS 1416, pp. 99–111, 2021.
https://doi.org/10.1007/978-3-030-76776-1_7

2 Literature Survey

2.1 Content Based Recommenders (CBR)

In these different varieties of algorithms items are first symbolized by their attributes. The ratings can be taken from indirect activities of the user like item read, bought, clicked or directly by requesting the user to rate the items. This prototype of user ratings on item is then implementing to any new item via their attributes to promote recommendations. A proper adoption of this is CB filtering where in some exact cases are built around item attributes on which user particulars is grasped and then suggestion is implemented. The benefit of CB recommenders is that they work good even without a large set of users.

2.2 Collaborative Filtering (CF)

CF is based on two basic beliefs.

1. Users fondness are unique stable or remain identical with each other over time.
2. The system is developed in a such a way that it lies with in the field of consistency.

   There are two main types of CF as below:

2.2.1 User-user

The fundamental aim of a user-user CF recommender is to select a proximity of clients who are alike and then scoring various products for the clients to generate a RS. Ex: building a client profile through the Product ratings and procured that have made and then using this to calculate likeness with other user and depending on the ratings that these users have given on other products it sends you RS that consumer may like.

2.2.2 Item-item

Here the likeness is calculated between products via their ratings. When a user rates a particular item, then based on the above likeness RS are created. Ex: when you rate a product highly, displaying other items that were also rated highly in that area.

3 Hybrid Recommended Systems Concept

In the process of achieving the recommendations outcome, the scholars they made a fusion of techniques to construct HRS, which strives to take over merits and eradicates the demerits. Usually HRS incorporate numerous recommendation techniques jointly to attain a homogeneous effect greater than the sum of their separate effects. Inspite the fact there are numerous recommendation approaches that are handful to blend for the better outcomes [3].

Weighted: Possibly it is the most elementary framework of HRS. Considering the items scored individually by each consolidate recommenders where the end outcome is a straight mixture of the median outcomes. Distinctively, observed that factual average is utilized to regulate the finest values for each section. The CBR are able to generate prediction on any product, but CF only scores a product if it is already rated by the genuine users [4].

Mixed: These HRS technique produce a maverick set of recommendations for all the items in the inventory, and mixes the evaluated possibilities in advance which is not known the user [5].

Switching: In this method, whenever the beginning approach fails to yield the expected outcome, then succeeding is applied till we yield the expected outcome. This method usually selects the approach based on the type of item and the user [6].

Feature Combination (FC): Setup that emanates the feature fusion technique retains only one RS component, which is carried out by a subsequent component. Instead of handling the characteristics of the furnishing component individually, they are placed directly into the algorithm of the attested RS [7].

Feature Augmentation (FA): FA is practiced when there is a well-orchestrated essential section. But which demands additional information about the roots. And always the most of the user interfaces expects predictions in actual time when the process is running, But FAs are implemented offline and FAs usually sums up the tiny pieces of features to the initial recommenders [8].

Cascade: Cascade models make possible assortment entirely with the essential predictions, and engaging the succeeding recommender utterly to perfect item ratings [9].

Meta-Level: This engages a prototype cultured by the contributing RS as input for the verified one. Although the common illustration reminds on FA approaches, there exists a notable variance allying both prototypes. Instead of furnishing the actual recommender with supplement benefits [10].

4   Categorization of Hybrid Recommended Systems

4.1   Monolithic Hybrids

This category depends on feature augmentation at the same time it is distributed by content boosted collaborated filtering. Which is where the content features and additional ratings are created [10] (Fig. 2).

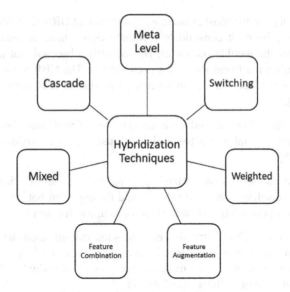

Fig. 1. Hybrid Recommended Systems

Monolithic Hybrids

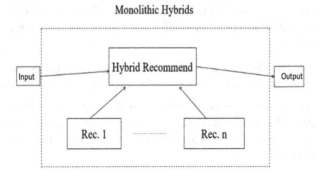

Fig. 2. Monolithic Hybrids

4.2 Parallelized Hybrids

Its outputs depend on the several existing implementations, combine at the same time. Its vastly designed on monolithic hybrid and their weight can be learnt dynamically. It is also called interpreter switch in a special case of dynamic weight [11] (Fig. 3).

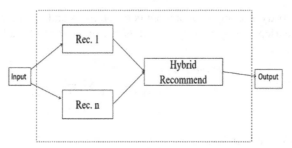

Fig. 3. Parallelized Hybrids

4.3 Pipelined Hybrids

It processes some inputs for subsequent recommender making the possibility to work in cascade and its refinement of recommendation lists [12] (Fig. 4).

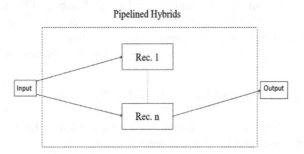

Fig. 4. Pipelined Hybrids

5 Similarity Metrices

It is the ability to discover users matching to you or items matched to items you've liked. we can apply the same techniques to measuring matching based on behaviour data. if you have a bunch of characteristics associated with people or things, you can think of each attribute as a dimension and think of similarity as the angle. The big challenge in measuring these similarities based on the behaviour data is the sparsity of the data we're working with.

5.1 Cosine Metrices

it is applicable mostly to compute matching between users and its ratings. It computes the difference the users rating for an item and their average rating for all items.

$$CosSim(x, y) = \frac{\sum_i x_i y_i}{\sqrt{\sum_i x_i^2} \sqrt{\sum_i y_i^2}}$$

5.2 Adjusted Cosine Metrices

One is the adjusted cosine metrices and its applicable mostly to computing the matching between users found on their ratings. Its found on the notion that dissimilar users may have dissimilar baselines that they are working from.

$$CosSim(x, y) = \frac{\sum ((x_i - \bar{x})(y_i - \bar{y}))}{\sqrt{\sum_i (x_i - \bar{x})^2} \sqrt{\sum_i (y_i - \bar{y})^2}}$$

if you replace x with x_i minus X bar, and replaced Y with Y sub i and Y bar. X bar means the average of all user X's ratings, and Y bar means the average of all user Y's ratings. So, all that's different here from conventional cosine similarity is that we are looking at the variance from the mean of each users ratings, and not just the raw rating itself.

6 Road Map for Hybrid Recommended Systems

Step 1: First we will upload matrix content then we will calculate CosSim similarity.
Step 2: Build title to ID and ID to title mappings
Step 3: Working the relevant metadata of the movies.
Step 4: Extract IDs and assign them to the Datasets.
Step 5: Applying Sorting and Filtering techniques to turn the recommendations according to the example chosen.

7 Train/Test of Dataset

The Dataset used in this research is from MovieLense dataset which is managed by GroupLens community. Here we used 100K dataset which contains 100000 ratings from 1 to 5 stars from 980 clients and 1700 cinemas and also small demographic information such as age, gender and genres of the movies for the clients and also items we use random and sequence aware functions for splitting data into train and test 90% of the data will be used for training and 10% of the data will be used for testing based on the timestamp.

8   Building Customized Algorithm and Evaluation on the Top of SurpriseLib

1. Create a new class that inherits from AlgoBase (which holds up all the algorithms) custom algorithm job is to predict ratings and also its necessary for evaluating accuracy offline.
2. Estimate function is implemented on the class which predicts the ratings for the item which user passed in.
3. Later creating a new class called Evaluated algorithm it introduces new function called Evaluate that runs all of the metrices in Recommended metrices on that algorithm. Which makes it easy to measure accuracy, coverage, Diversity, RMSE and MAE.
4. Evaluation data class is which is used to load MovieLens dataset and creates all the train/test data will be sliced by Evaluated algorithm and now we can evaluate data by wrapping of all the algorithms with evaluated algorithm instance then call the same function name by passing evaluation data instance with the data set and evaluate all the algorithms and measure your objectives and compare the results with different recommender algorithms.

9   Evaluation of Recommender Systems

The most important stage of the RS in which choosing a right algorithms for a problem defined is most difficult task. Because sometimes the algorithm choosen may function stronger to the dataset choosen and might function weaker on the different dataset. So its difficult job to decide what kind of approach to be performed during evaulation process and Accuracy outcomes are the most evlauted objective in this history of RS [13]. Let's look into the process of evaluation, both users watching the same movies obtained different recommendations, such as the content and the order and analysing slightly larger dataset and try different types of recommendations based on the customer reviews and watch [14]. Supplying distinctive data to the RS in better recommendation assistance, but may generate the complication of data solitude an safety. Experiment with new recommender system algorithms, evaluating them, and comparing them against each other. Surpriselib has a Python base class called AlgoBase. Fundamentally, a class is just a collection of functions organized under some name. That class can also have variables associated it. can instantiate an instance of a class object, which lets around a copy of a classes functions and the data in its variables under a single name. for example, here we have an SVD class which inherits from the AlgoBase base class. That means that our SVD class may have functions and data specific to the SVD recommender algorithm, but it also has access to the functions and data defined in the AlgoBase base class. It's just a way to maintain consistent interfaces with all of our different recommender algorithms [10]. For example, the AlgoBase base class defines the function names, fit and test, which are used to train and to test each algorithm. SVD, Content KNN, RBM, Random Hybrid and any custom algorithm might be developed that inherits from AlgoBase

10   Step by Step Implementation and Experimental Setup of Recommender Systems Algorithm

Step 1: Creating a new class that inherits from AlgoBase, and as far as SurpriseLib is concerned, your algorithm has one job, to forecast ratings. As intimated, SurpriseLib is constructed throughout the framework of forecasting the ratings of each movie and each user, and offering back the prime predictions as recommendations and its essential for estimating accuracy offline [15].

Step 2: Creating a Customized recommender algorithm that can approach variables corelated with that occurnace. Coming forward it apprenhand user tags and an item tags. So, when estimate function is called it's asking to forecast a rating for the user and item flown in. ID's that are used internally, and must be delineated back to the fresh user and item ID's in your origin data [16].

Step 3: The customized recommender algorithm just predicts a rating of three stars for absolutely everything and everybody. for commencing the Algorithm class object, which just calls the base classes init function, Need some setup in preparation. all those different evaluation metrics implemented earlier in Recommender Metrics class to the algorithms to work with [17]. So to do that, need to generate a new category of function called Evaluated Algorithm. It establishes a fresh role called Evaluate that runs all of the Recommender Metrics on the algorithm. So, this class makes it easy to measure accuracy, sparsity, Cold start diversity, and everything else on a given algorithm.

Step 4: The functions in the Recommender Metrics class lets slice up training data into train and test splits in various different ways [18]. That's what Evaluation Data class is for. It takes in a Dataset, which might come from class that loads MovieLens data for example, and creates all the train/test splits needed by Evaluated Algorithm class. Evaluated Algorithm will use all the functions defined in Recommender Metrics to measure accuracy, Sparsity, diversity.

Step 5: Compare different recommender algorithms Evaluator class just takes in a raw dataset, say from MovieLens [19], and the first thing it does is create an Evaluated Dataset object from it that it uses internally. Then, just call Add Algorithm for each algorithm want to compare. This creates an Evaluated Algorithm under the hood within the Evaluator.

11   Result and Discussions

Finally, the Results are here after the experimental setup we are comparing SVD, or singular value decomposition, against random recommendation, Content KNN (K nearest neighbour algorithm, Restricted Boltzmann Machine (RBM), Hybrid algorithm with one customized algorithm [20]. About these metrics in terms of accuracy and as per natural phenomenon more accuracy is better, but the actual numbers for Root Mean Squared Error (RMSE) and Mean Absolute Error (MAE) are measuring error, the opposite of accuracy. So it's good that SVD and Hybrid algorithms has lower RMSE and MAE than the all other recommender algorithms [21] Algorithms are predicting movie ratings using what's normal distribution cantered around the average rating value, Diversity Sparsity is also lower with SVD and Hybrid. Evaluating Customized recommendation algorithms and combining multiple recommendation algorithms together, which can sometimes be a very powerful technique.

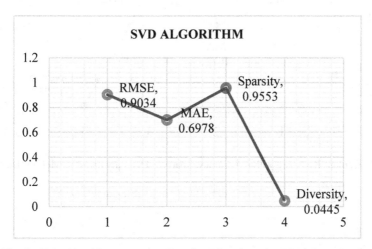

Fig. 5. SVD Algorithm Accuracy, Sparsity, Diversity using MovieLens Dataset

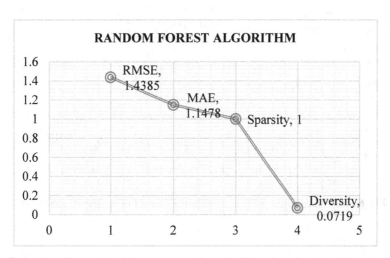

Fig. 6. Random Forest Algorithm Accuracy, Sparsity, Diversity using MovieLens Dataset

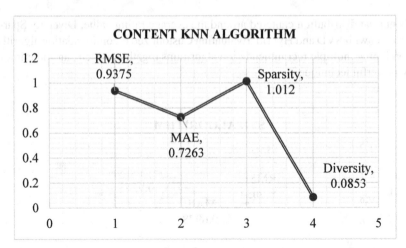

Fig. 7. Content KNN Algorithm Accuracy, Sparsity, Diversity using MovieLens Dataset

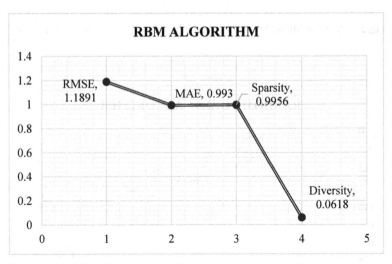

Fig. 8. RBM Algorithm Accuracy, Sparsity, Diversity using MovieLens Dataset

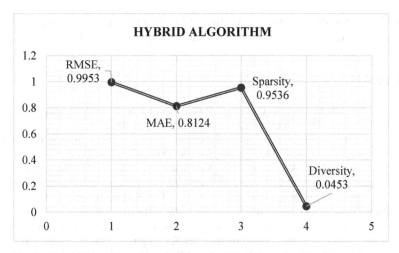

Fig. 9. Hybrid Algorithm Accuracy, Sparsity, Diversity using MovieLens Dataset

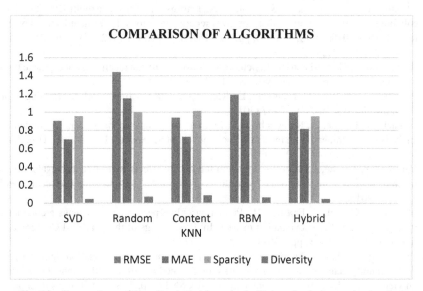

Fig. 10. Comparison of Results plotted in a single Picture for better understanding

12 Conclusion

In this article we discussed about RS categories types and HRS Concepts and caegorites of HRS, finding the similarity between the items and users road map of HRS and Dividing the training and testing dataset. building the customized algorithm and combing with different algorithms and making it hybrid and setting up experimental environment for different algorithms and finding the results for the dataset choosen and analyzing the results and evaluating, As per the results SVD and Hybrid algorithms shows the best results with customized algorithm and still the fine tuning of the customized algorithm can yeild the better results which will be discussed in my next article.

References

1. Ricci, F., Rokach, L., Shapira, B., Kantor, Paul B. (eds.): Recommender Systems Handbook. Springer, Boston (2011). https://doi.org/10.1007/978-0-387-85820-3
2. Aggarwal, C.C.: Neighborhood-based collaborative filtering. Recommender Systems, pp. 29–70. Springer, Cham (2016). https://doi.org/10.1007/978-3-319-29659-3_2
3. Alshammari, G., Jorro-Aragoneses, J.L., Kapetanakis, S., Petridis, M., Recio-García, J.A., Díaz-Agudo, B.: A hybrid CBR approach for the long tail problem in recommender systems. In: Aha, David W., Lieber, J. (eds.) ICCBR 2017. LNCS (LNAI), vol. 10339, pp. 35–45. Springer, Cham (2017). https://doi.org/10.1007/978-3-319-61030-6_3
4. Alshammari, G., Jorro-Aragoneses, J.L., Kapetanakis, S., Polatidis, N., Petridis, M.: A switching approach that improves prediction accuracy for long tail recommendations. In: Bi, Y., Bhatia, R., Kapoor, S. (eds.) IntelliSys 2019. AISC, vol. 1037, pp. 18–28. Springer, Cham (2020). https://doi.org/10.1007/978-3-030-29516-5_3
5. Alshammari, G., Kapetanakis, S., Polatidis, N., Petridis, M.: A triangle multi-level item-based collaborative filtering method that improves recommendations. In: Pimenidis, E., Jayne, C. (eds.) EANN 2018. CCIS, vol. 893, pp. 145–157. Springer, Cham (2018). https://doi.org/10.1007/978-3-319-98204-5_12
6. Armentano, M.G., Christensen, I., Schiaffino, S.: Applying the technology acceptance model to evaluation of recommender systems (51), 73–79 (2015)
7. Bremer, S., Schelten, A., Lohmann, E., Kleinsteuber, M.: A framework for training hybrid recommender systems, pp. 30–37 (2017)
8. Jannach, D., Lerche, L., Kamehkhosh, I., Jugovac, M.: What recommenders recommend: an analysis of recommendation biases and possible countermeasures. User Model. User Adapt. Interact. 25(5), 427–491 (2015b)
9. Jannach, D., Lerche, L., Jugovac, M.: Item familiarity effects in user-centric evaluations of recommender systems. In: Poster Proceedings of the 9th ACM Conference on Recommender Systems (2015a)
10. Maksai, A., Garcin, F., Faltings, B.: Predicting online performance of news recommender systems through Richer evaluation metrics. In: Proceedings of the 9th ACM Conference on Recommender Systems, pp. 179–186 (2015)
11. Cao, C., Ni, Q., Zhai, Y.: An improved collaborative filtering recommendation algorithm based on community detection in social networks. In: Proceedings of the 2015 Annual Conference on Genetic and Evolutionary Computation, (ICCSNT), pp. 1–8 (2015). https://doi.org/10.1145/2739480.2754670
12. Craw, S., Horsburgh, B., Massie, S.: Music recommendation: audio neighbourhoods to discover music in the long tail. In: Hüllermeier, E., Minor, M. (eds.) ICCBR 2015. LNCS (LNAI), vol. 9343, pp. 73–87. Springer, Cham (2015). https://doi.org/10.1007/978-3-319-24586-7_6
13. Fleeson, W., Jayawickreme, E., Jones, A.B.A.P., Brown, N.A., Serfass, D.G., Sherman, R.A., Matyjek-, M.: The use of the genetic algorithms in the recommender systems. J. Pers. Soc. Psychol. 1(1), 1188–1197 (2017). https://doi.org/10.1111/j.1469-7610.2010.02280.x
14. Barraza-Urbina, A., Heitmann, B., Hayes, C., Carrillo-Ramos, A.: XPLODIV: an exploitation-exploration aware diversification approach for recommender systems. In: Proceedings of the 28th International Florida Artificial Intelligence Research Society Conference (2015)
15. Harper, F.M., Konstan, J.A.: The MovieLens Datasets: history and context. ACM Trans. Interact. Intell. Syst. 5(4), 19:1—19:19 (2015a). https://doi.org/10.1145/2827872

16. Harper, F.M., Konstan, J.A.: The MovieLens Datasets: history and context. ACM Trans. Interact. Intell. Syst. 5(4), 19:1–19:19 (2015b). https://doi.org/10.1145/2827872
17. Johnson, J., Ng, Y.-K.: Enhancing long tail item recommendations using tripartite graphs and Markov process. In: Proceedings of the International Conference on Web Intelligence - WI 2017, pp. 761–768 (2017)
18. Wang, S., Gong, M., Li, H., Yang, J.: Knowledge-base d systems multi-objective optimization for long tail recommendation, **104**, 145–155 (2016)
19. Shen, K., Liu, Y., Zhang, Z.: Modified similarity algorithm for collaborative filtering, pp. 378–385 (2017). https://doi.org/10.1007/978-3-319-62698-7
20. Kumar, R., Sharan, A.: Personalized web search using browsing history and domain knowledge. In: 2014 International Conference on Issues and Challenges in Intelligent Computing Techniques (ICICT), pp. 493–497 (2014). https://doi.org/10.1109/ICICICT.2014.6781332
21. Laveti, R.N., Ch, J., Pal, S.N., Babu, N.S.C:.2016 IEEE 23rd International Conference on High Performance Computing Workshops A Hybrid Recommender System using Weighted Ensemble Similarity Metrics and Digital Filters (2016). https://doi.org/10.1109/HiPCW.201 6.14

Event-Related Potential Classification Based on EEG Data Using xDWAN with MDM and KNN

Abu Saleh Musa Miah[1]([✉]), Mumtahina Afroz Mouly[1], Chandrika Debnath[1],
Jungpil Shin[2], and S. M. Sadakatul Bari[1]

[1] Bangladesh Army University of Science and Technology, Saidpur, Bangladesh
[2] School of Computer Science and Engineering, The University of Aizu, Aizuwakamatsu,
Fukushima 965-8580, Japan
jpshin@u-aizu.ac.jp

Abstract. A way of measuring a brain response during cognitive, sensory, or motor event is called event related potential (ERP). Electroencephalography (EEG) data during ERP can be used to cognitive operations. Recently, to classify ERP from EEG signal has begun to apply a compact convolutional neural network (EEGNet) but its performance depends on the data size.

To discriminate between correct and incorrect ERP responses of a subject here a classification algorithm with smoothing of xDAWAN spatial filtering method is proposed. A spatial filtering xDAWAN method extracted only true ERP signal from EEG signal by increasing signal to noise ratio and discarding noise. We have reduced the dimension of the true ERP data by applying Riemannian geometry. Riemannian geometry calculated covariance matrix from true ERP data and all covariance data mapped into a euclidean space called tangent space and produced Riemannian feature vector. Finally, feed this Riemannian feature vector by a machine-learning algorithm to predict ERP response. As a machine-learning algorithm, we used here specially K-nearest neighbor (KNN) and Minimum Distance to Mean (MDM) as a classifier. To evaluate our model, here used EEG data, which contains data for left ear auditory, right ear auditory stimulation and left visualization, right visualization stimulation. xDAWAN is effective due to EEG is a narrow and noisy signal. Performance of Riemannian geometry also not depend on noisy or data size. Our model achieved better performance than other did specially EEGNet. We believe our model will be considered as a great invention in this research domain.

Keywords: K-nearest neighbor (KNN) · Event related potential (ERP) · Electroencephalography (EEG) · Minimum distance to mean (MDM) · xDAWAN · EEGNet

1 Introduction

A Brain-Computer Interface (BCI) is a device that can communicates with a machine through brain signals without muscle and nerve [1]. The human brain contains billions

© Springer Nature Switzerland AG 2021
N. Chaubey et al. (Eds.): COMS2 2021, CCIS 1416, pp. 112–126, 2021.
https://doi.org/10.1007/978-3-030-76776-1_8

of neurons, making up a large complex network which processes body's activity signal information. Flow of electrical current is changed across the membranes by neurons. Electrical and magnetic fields generated by the current for those changes are recorded with small electrodes attached on the scalp surface. To evaluate the electrical activity in the brain, a test is used which is called electroencephalogram (EEG) test. EEG signal is used in various sectors. In medical diagnosis, EEG signal is used for detecting diseases like brain death, sleep disorder, Alzheimer's, epilepsy, mobile robots, artificial limbs, communication devices, BCI-triggered rehabilitation devices, adaptive automation, task difficulty adaptation, detection of errors and so on those are discussed in [2–4]. Also, signal to process, and machine learning is some of the challenging aspects of Brain-computer interfacing (BCI). For BCI, one of the promising events is Motor Imagery (MI) to elicit typical Electroencephalography (EEG) from within the sensorimotor cortex. When a subject thinks of moving, motor imagery helps to classify the movement, which is very useful in medical field for rehabilitation [5]. During the different movement of imagination, central beta and mu rhythms features are used in MI-BCI.

Event related potential (ERP) is one of the most commonly application in EEG based BCI task as oddball paradigm [6, 7]. User can responds for any specific event by counting the occurrence number and press a button this called event related potential (ERP) [7] and that is observed in EEG. P300 and N100 are the electrophysiological components of ERP. Using these ERP component classifies the user stimulus indicates the instruction or command that user want to enter and heeding. ERP contains multiple stimuli, which can be symbols, or tones appear randomly [8, 38]. Contained stimuli some are target stimuli (user pay attention) among several stimuli and some are non-target stimuli (user does not pay attention to the stimulus) [9]. The stimuli that contained ERP can be auditory, left-auditory, right-auditory [10], tactile [11], it can be visual like as columns of letters and flashing rows [12, 13], left visual, right visual, scenery, objects, or faces [14, 15], it can be geometric shapes [16]. "Oddball" task design is one of the most common denominator and ERP is an EEG base BCI system [17].

It is well know that, the raw EEG signals are so narrow, noisy with different types of artifacts some muscular activity, cardiac activity, and eye blinking eye blinking etc. [18]. Therefore, to remove noise and the artifact need some preprocessing steps. Preprocessing of high dimensional data results in noise-free and artifact less data, by using machine learning classification algorithm it can be converted into commands [19].

Generally speaking, There are five processing stages in a BCI which is main [20]: a information gathering stage, which is able to record neural information; a signal processing stage, a feature extraction stage, where significant information can be extracted from the neural information; a classification stage, which is used for the explain of a decision that is made by the data; and a feedback stage. BCI paradigm has same stages, like signal processing stage [21], feature extraction stage [22] and classification stage [23]. BCI system always evolve into new an application domains, if possible to find robust feature extracted strategies, will only remaining to grow [24, 25].

This paper, first for preprocessing we propose a spatial filter namely xDAWN, that is created a pseudo-channel by a linear combination of the original dataset. Then we proposed a Riemannian geometry algorithm namely riemannian tangent space mapping(TSM) to produce a effective feature vectored from xDAWN output. Finally, we applied a K-nearest neighbor (KNN) algorithm to classify our ERP feature vectored into auditory and visual stimuli. In addition, we experimented another machine learning algorithm Minimum Distance to Mean (MDM) method on the xDAWN output feature vector. This paper we organized as follows, Sect. 2 discussed about ERP related existing work and motivation, Basic structure of proposed methodology describe in Sect. 3, Sect. 4 describe about result and discussion and finally discussed about conclusion and future work.

2 Related Work

Due to the narrow, high dimensionality and noise contamination of the raw data, classification of ERP data is not easy. To discriminate among the ERP data there has been developed many technique. First, Tsoi et al. employed a single channel of EEG data to calculate feature vector by using Autoregressive model(AR) coefficient [26].They feed the feature vector to a multilayer neural network model. Vasios C et al. also deployed Autoregressive model(AR) coefficient with neural network to classify ERP data [27]. These model-orders among 3 to 10 only. Researchers need more information from human brain single channel information is not enough for experiment. Anderson CW et al. developed a model where he replaced the AR model by the Multivariate Autoregressive (MVAR) model [28, 29]. The feature vector were trained to a feed forward neural network and classification accuracy is improved to 91%. Rakotomamonjy et al. developed an ensemble of various support vector machine (SVM) classifier based on automatic channel selection method [30, 31], another researcher Hoffmann et al. employed an approach of boosting [32]. To overcome the lack of information and other problems convolution neural network(CNN) have gained attraction recent years in ERP classification domain. H. Cecotti et al. first applied CNN to classify ERP data [12, 33]. They collected their data dimension like a tensor dimensions $N_{electrodes} \times N_{samples}$ and feeding data into a first hidden spatial convolution layer, then second layer produce 5 time feature maps, which worked as down sampling and time convolution with a fixed length kernel, throw a fully connected layers and output layer produced two neuron which represent target and non-target stimuli. To improve performance accuracy, Lawhern et al. proposed compact convolution neural network for classifying the ERP data, they made a EEG specific model which composed of feature extraction from ERP data based on depth wise and separable convolution [25, 34]. They compared EEGNet, for both cross-subject and within-subject to error-related negativity responses (ERN), P300 visual-evoked potentials(ERP), sensory motor rhythms (SMR) and movement-related cortical potentials (MRCP). They showed EEGNet achieved good accuracy comparably reference algorithm but problem is accuracy is better when only limited training data is available. In addition, the accuracy of CNN to classify target and non-target stimuli is not very good. To improve the accuracy of ERP based BCI spatial filter are used for preprocessing the signal that is create a pseudo-channels by a linear combination of original electrode channel [35]. Blankertz, et al. proposed a spatial filter namely common spatial pattern(CSP) [36], and another spatial filtering method xDAWAN [39]. Moreover, these optimizing spatial filter to improve the classification accuracy need more learning data, performance of ERP classification is degraded if learning data is few [37]. To solve the degradation problem Hiroshi Higashi et al. developed regularization approach for the xDAWAN algorithms [38]. B. Rivet et a. implemented spatial filter xDAWAN approach with a unsupervised machine learning algorithm namely Bayesian linear discriminant analysis (BLDA) classifier [39]. They used a spatial enhancement significantly to reduce the feature dimension to improve accuracy. The main drawback of the method is need to additional work to improve performance of the P300-speller BCI that increased the computational complexity and time complexity. Another challenging problem is that, for better performance should be need to know the target and non target stimuli. To overcome all drawbacks to enhance the event related potential (ERP) for the BCI. In the proposed approach we designed a riemannian geometry based Tangent space mapping (TSM) [41–43] subspace technique for the xDAWAN algorithm which is one of the major algorithm for ERP-EEG data. Our subspace Riemannian geometry technique considered data belongs to a curve space and project all data from curve space to tangent space. Finally, we have applied KNN machine learning algorithm. It exploits the stimuli of left visual, write visual, left auditory, and left auditory. Also, we experimented the study in a more robust way.

3 Data Description

Depending on the EEG feature of interest, BCIs are generally classified into two types of dataset [43]: event-related and oscillatory. Event-Related Potential (ERP) BCIs are designed to detect a high amplitude and low frequency EEG response of a known, time-locked external stimulus. Oscillatory BCIs use the signal strength of specific EEG frequency band for external control and are usually asynchronous [25]. In this study, we have used "MNE-sample-data" dataset that is recorded using BCI-2000 system [44].Name of the dataset is MNE-sample-data set which contains 4 types of stimuli Left visual, Left Auditory, Right visual, Right Auditory. This ERP dataset recorded from 109 healthy people, for each people 64 electrode placed on the scalp recording time and 14 runs on each subject in European data format (EDF) format. We collected this from physionet [45] [https://files.osf.io/v1/resources/rxvq7/providers/osfstorage/59c0e26f9ad5a1025c4ab159?version=5&action=download&direct].

4 Proposed Methodology

In this paper, first we read the dataset then we have applied xDAWN as a spatial filter and applied a machine learning algorithm namely Minimum Distance to Mean (MDM) method. Same way, we have applied xDAWAN as a spatial filter to our dataset, then we applied a riemannian geometry to produced the effective feature from xDAWAN feature and lastly we applied K-nearest neighbor, Support vector machine(SVM), Bayesian theorem, Random forest(RF) algorithm for the multiclass classification problem.In our working procedure is, at first we set parameters and necessary setup for reading the raw data. After reading epochs (300 epoch works here) data, we extract the raw data and splitting the data into train, validate data, test (25% and 50). In EEGNet portion, we convert the labels to one-hot-encoding. We convert data to NCHW (trials, kernels, channels, samples) format. Compiling the model, we set the optimizers, count the number of parameters and a valid path for the system to record model checkpoints as well. Finally, we fitted the model and the optimal weight to the model. After this process, we get a classification accuracy that is the accuracy of the EEGNet model. After that, we set up pipeline and reshape back to (trials, channels, samples). In the Riemannian Geometric based riemannian tangent space mapping (TSM) approaches with xDAWN filtering portion, we train a classifier that is our implemented KNN, SVM, RF, Bayesian theorem classification technique.

According to the process, we get another comparable classification accuracy and plot a confusion matrices for both EEGNet, xDAWN+RG+ML (ML means KNN, SVM, RF, Bayesian) and xDAWN throw MDM model to compare the performance accuracy. The experimented approach are shown in Fig. 1. Figure shown three models, first model is EEGNet this is the existing model. second Model name is xDAWN+RG+ML where RG means Riemannian geometry, and Machine learning means KNN, SVM, RF, Bayesian machine learning and third model is xDAWN+MDM. The classification accuracy of xDAWN spatial filtering with Riemannian Geomatry (RG) using KNN have has given more satisfactory than the classification accuracy of EEGNet.

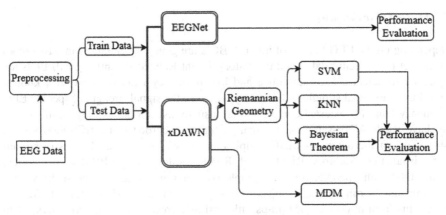

Fig. 1. Proposed methodology

4.1 EEGNet Model: Compact Convolutional Neural Network (Compact-CNN)

To estimate the advantage of convolution neural network or deep learning first we experiment using a compact convolution model [25, 35, 47]. In the model first performed temporal convolutions with the kernel weights, that is computed using data. The network first layer worked as a mimic a band pass frequency filter, then, to reduce the data dimension we uses depthwise spatial convolution as a spatial filter. As these convolution not fully connected with previous outputs, the main benefit of depthwise spatial convolution is decreasing the number of trainable parameters to fit easily. In our model, internal mechanism gives a direct communication way to training spatial filters for each temporal filter, as a consequences, easily generated efficient extraction of frequency-specific spatial filters. Compact CNN or EEG net can be found as a visualization in Fig. 2. Here we collected a mne sample EEG data, having 60 channels and 151 sample. For evaluating EEGNet with our collected as a parameter we have used kernel is 32, data label is 4, number of temporal filter(F1) is 8, number of spatial filter or depth multiplier(D) is 2 and number of pointwise filters (F2) is 16 [25, 38].

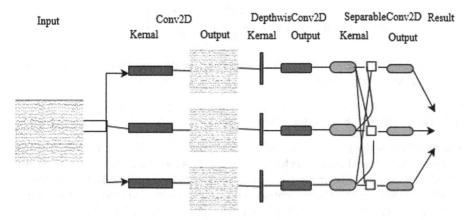

Fig. 2. EEGNet model

4.2 xDAWN Spatial Filtering

xDAWN spatial filtering is used to reduce the dimension of EEG signal and also increase the discriminate between noise data and signal data in a dataset [39, 47, 48]. Here we review the xDAWAN spatial filter [25].

Let $P_j(t)$ is our loaded an ERP-EEG data that is recorded at time t by the jth electrode and consider $P \in \mathbb{R}^{N_t \times N_c}$ is a recorded signal with time samples N_t and channels N_c. Assumed among EEG data the actual ERP data is $Q \in \mathbb{R}^{N_k \times N_c}$, where Q contains ERP waveform at each individual electrode and N_k duration. Finally, evoked potential of P300 elicit target stimuli from the dataset P by following model Eq. 1.

$$P = DQ + Ns \tag{1}$$

Here D is a Toeplitz matrix little bit change of diagonal matrix dimension is $N_t \times N_c$ and Ns is the noise matrix dimension is same as D. Here N is also an EEG signal but not ERP data N can be eye blinking or some kind of artifacts. Let artifact N is produced by a Gaussian distribution, the actual ERP can be computed by a least squares estimates following model

$$\hat{Q} = \arg \max_{Q} \|P - DQ\|_2^2$$

Solution $\hat{Q}$ is given by Eq. (2)

$$\hat{Q} = \left(D^T D\right)^{-1} D^T P \tag{2}$$

Another term Ns_p noise spatial filters are defined by $W \in \mathbb{R}^{N_t \times N_f}$, this filter applied to P by $\hat{P} = PW \in \mathbb{R}^{N_t \times N_f}$ the main target of the design the filter to W can maximizes the signal-to-signal-to-plus-noise = ratio (SSNR) of P. Above concept is are implemented by the generalized Rayleigh quotient Eq. (3)

$$\hat{W} = \arg \max_{w} \frac{Tr\left(W^T Q^T D^T D \hat{Q} W\right)}{Tr\left(W^T P^T P W\right)} \tag{3}$$

We can use QR factorization with a singular value decomposition [49] to solve the above optimization problem.

4.3 xDAWAN with Riemannian Geometry

Our proposed model gives a smoothness of the spatial filter xDAWAN in spatial domain by producing a spatial feature vector from the filter vector. Spatial feature vector is produced by Riemannian geometry based tangent space mapping method. Once xDAWAN produced an accurate ERP data from noisy data, Riemannian geometry generated a spatial feature vector from accurate ERP data by mapping accurate ERP data into a linear space name tangent space. From the Eq. 1 $(P = DQ + Ns)$ given dataset P and true ERP dataset is Q. xDAWAN generated true ERP dataset Q and Noise Ns. Riemannian geometry first calculates the covariance matrix of true ERP data Q, Then assume covariance matrix belongs to a curve space or Riemannian manifold and it's a symmetric positive definite covariance matrix. By using Riemannian distance, all data from covariance matrix mapped into a space name tangent space and produced a Riemannian feature space G.

4.4 Classification

We apply machine learning classification algorithm to classify the Riemannian feature vector G that is came from xDAWAN via Riemannian geometry. We used here two kind of classification algorithm. First type, SVM, RF, KNN are used Riemannian feature and second type is MDM used only on xDAWAN output. Classification algorithm MDM used directly xDAWAN feature vector that is Q but SVM, RF, KNN are used Riemannian feature G.

xDAWAN with Riemannian Feature Based Classification: KNN, SVM, RF
KNN
To classify our feature vector G we used here k-nearest neighbors algorithm (k-NN) machine learning algorithm, which is a non-parametric classification algorithm. The concept of KNN is a plurality vote of its neighbors based on K. If the value of K is one, then the trial is assigned to the class of single nearest neighbor else number of trials is assigned to the most common classes among the k-nearest neighbor by majority voting.

Support Vector Machine
Support Vector Machine are overseeing learning models with related learning algorithms that analyze the feature G used for classification and resistance analysis. It is highly

preferred by many because it creates significant accuracy with low computing power. The linear function output is taken by SVM. We define the data into one class if the output is greater than 1 and also define the data into another class if the output is greater than −1.

Random Forest
For classifying the geometry feature vector G, we also used Random Forest machine learning algorithm as a classifier [19]. Random forest is a lithe, stress-free to use machine learning algorithm that products, even without hyper-parameter tuning, a unlimited result most of the time because of its simplicity and multiplicity. The "forest" it sizes, is an group of decision trees, usually trained with the "bagging" method. The universal idea of the bagging method is that a combination of learning models growths the overall result. Another great quality of the random forest algorithm is that it is very relaxed to measure the relative reputation of each feature on the guess. Internal mechanism of this algorithm is that, for build up a decision tree its calculate gini index and information gain from riemannian feature vector G. Multiple trees are created to classify 4 ERP label in accordance with their feature attributes, Individual tree generates a classification result and store them as for a appropriate class, finally, chosen one of the tree from the all the trees for classification.

xDAWAN Feature Based Classification: MDM
This the supervised machine learning algorithm, we used here to classify our ERP data based on nearest centroid using xDWAN feature vector Q. According to the true ERP data, estimated a centroid for four given classes. Thus, according to the nearest centroid, the class is affected for each new point.

5   Result and Discussion

After splitting the EEG data into training and test data, we got 72-trial point as a test data. We evaluated this test data with our trained model, and got a excellence performance accuracies. Here we have experimented 4 models, one of the method xDAWAN with Riemannian geometry throw KNN (XGK) model generated good performance accuracy [96%], that is higher than the other existing work.

   To assess the proposed model based on the result we generated confusion matrix for each model. In Fig. 3 shows the confusion matrix for xDWAN with EEGNet model. This is the existing model [24] but we also shown here for compare with our proposed model. Here shown the xDWAN with Compact-CNN (EEGNet) classification performance. Best performance acquired this model on the auditory-right stage where 92.9% trials correctly classified and only 7.1% trial miss classified. In addition, less performance produced at the stage of auditory left, correctly classified 68.4% trial and misclassified 31.6% trials. The accuracy of the EEGNet model achieved 89% shown in Table 5 and Fig. 4.

   Table 1 shows the confusion matrix for xDWAN with Riemannian geometry throw SVM (XRSVM) model. XRSVM model produced maximum performance at the stage of visual left and visual right where its correctly classified 100% trials and misclassified

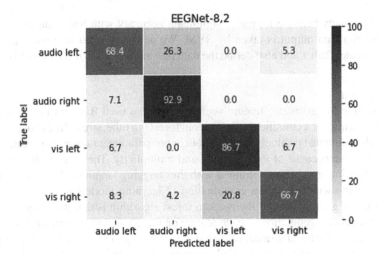

Fig. 3. Confusion matrix of EEGNet

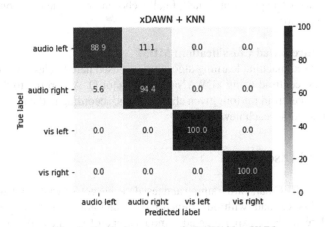

Fig. 4. Confusion matrix of xDAWAN + KNN

0.0% trials, same as bad performance shows at the auditory right stage where misclassified 16.7% trials and correctly classified only 83.3% trials. So we can decide this model is a good model in the domain. Although, in the accuracy table, Table 5 shows the 93% accuracy is achieved by this model. Table 2 presents the confusion matrix for xDAWAN with Riemannian geometry throw RF (XRRF) model. Where shows this model did good performance at the stage of stage of visual left and visual right where its classified 100% trials and no misclassified trials. Moreover, bad performance is achieved at the stage of auditory left where misclassified 26.7% trials and correctly classified. On the accuracy table shows XRR model generated 85.0% accuracy over all stage. So based on the confusion matrix and accuracy table we can say XRRF model is not very good model in this domain.

Table 1. ConfusionMatrix:xDWAN + SVM

Stage	a-left	a-right	v-left	v-right
a-left	83.3	11.1	00.0	5.6
a-right	10.6	89.5	00.0	00.0
v-left	00.0	00.0	100	0.00
v-right	00.0	0.00	00.0	100
Stage	a-left	a-right	v-left	v-right

Table 2. Confusion Matrix: xDAWAN + RF

Stage	a-left	a-right	v-left	v-right
a-left	73.3	26.7	00.0	00.0
a-right	27.3	68.2	00.0	04.5
v-left	00.0	00.0	100	00.0
v-right	00.0	00.0	00.0	100

Table 3 represents the confusion matrix of xDWAN with Riemannian geometry throw Bayesian classification (XRBayes) model. The table says, XRBayes model performed best at the visual left and visual right stages, where it's classified correctly 100% trials without misclassified any trials. Accuracy table shows this XRB model produces 85% accuracy. Table 4 presents the confusion matrix of our proposed method-1 xDAWAN with Riemannian geometry throw MDM (XMDM) model. Table shown XMDM model achieved maximum performance at visual left and visual right stage of EEG data where it's correctly classified 100% trials without misclassified any trials. But at the performance is declined at auditory right stage where misclassified 15% trials. In accuracy table shows the XMDM model produced 93% accuracy.

Table 3. Confusion Matrix:xDAWN + Bayes

Stage	a-left	a-right	v-left	v-right
a-left	70.6	29.4	00.0	00.0
a-right	25.0	70.0	00.0	05.0
v-left	00.0	00.0	100	0.00
v-right	00.0	0.00	00.0	100

Table 4. Confusion Matrix: xDAWN + MDM

Stage	a-left	a-right	v-left	v-right
a-left	88.2	11.8	00.0	00.0
a-right	10.0	85.0	00.0	05.0
v-left	00.0	00.0	100	0.00
v-right	00.0	0.00	00.0	100

Figure 3 shows the confusion matrix of our proposed method-1 xDAWAN with Riemannian geometry throw KNN (XRKNN). The figure shown the proposed method achieved best performance at visual left and visual right stages where it correctly classified 100% trials and no misclassified any trials. However, performance is declined at auditory left stage where misclassified 11.1% trials. Accuracy Table 3 and Fig. 5 shows that XRKNN model generated 96% accuracy.

Table 5 shows the comparative accuracy table of our proposed method-1, proposed method-2 with EEGNet [24] and other existing model. We have shown a confusion matrix of EEGNet where for some stage this model generated a good performance than reference algorithms, But the stage where large training data is available that time performance of the EEGNet is reduced.

Table shows our proposed method-2 xDWAN with Riemannian geometry and KNN (XRK) generated 96%, which is best accuracy of this field. Also proposed method-1 XRM achieved 93% accuracy which is also a good method. Moreover, we demonstrate

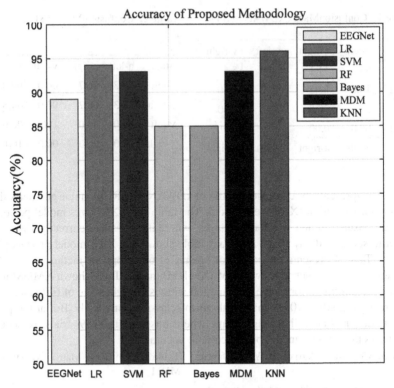

Fig. 5. Comparative accuracies of proposed methodologies

Table 5. Accuracy table

Method name	Accuracy[%]
EEGNet Version 8.2	89.00% [24]
xDWAN with ReimannainGeometry and LR (XRL)	94.00%
xDWAN with ReimannainGeometry and SVM(XRS)	93.00%
xDWAN with ReimannainGeometry and RF (XRR)	85.00%
xDWAN with ReimannainGeometry and Bayes (XRB)	85.00%
xDWAN with ReimannainGeometry and MDM (XRM)	93.00% (Proposed Method-1)
xDWAN with ReimannainGeometry and KNN (XRK)	96.00% (Proposed Method-2)

different ways to visualize the content of proposed method and accuracy. A comparison graph shown in Fig. 4 where performance bar graph suggests that proposed method-1 XRKNN and proposed method-2 XRMDM are robust enough for learning a wide variety of interpretable features in the range of BCI tasks. We observed that evaluation output of the proposed model is bad due to large training data or noisy data.

6 Conclusion and Future Work

In the paper, we proposed a new model to improve the performance of evoked potential responses by target stimuli in an oddball paradigm. The proposed algorithm generated a subspace of the event related potential (ERP) P300 by providing the best signal to noise ratio (SNR). A well know theory is that accuracy of evoked related potential is increased if possible to taking into account the signal and noise. Here xDAWAN spatial filter consider only signal not noise, also large dimension of feature vector reduces the accuracy of machine learning while used here riemannian geometry to reduce the data dimension used to predict words. We used K-nearest neighbor (KNN) method to classify the produced feature vector. We also implemented MDM classifier to improve performance accuracy. From the above procedure, the accuracy could not be found accurately. The data set used in this research is manually made. We cannot tell if this procedure will work completely accurate. Tried to add real data for better accurate calculation, but couldn't do it because of the short time procedure. But we tried to add sample data that are close to real life data to calculate the measurement. To further enhance the performance the ERP-EEG data more work should be considered. Moreover, selection of efficient EEG channel should be considered, that will be leading to improve the more ergonomic BCI. In future We will try to increase the accuracy as possible. We will try to make a specific app with this research. In future, the working processed should be continued. So that others who does this research can find it easier by having more data and information's.

References

1. Wolpaw, R., Birbaumer, N., McFarland, D.J., Pfurtscheller, G., Vaughan, T.M.: Brain-computer interfaces for communication and control. Clin. Neurophysiol.: Off. J. Int. Fed. Clin. Neurophysiol. **113**(6), 767–791 (2002)
2. Miah, A.S.M., Rahim, M.A., Shin, J.: Motor-imagery classification using riemannian geometry with median absolute deviation. Electronics **9**, 1584 (2020)
3. MacDonald, D.B.: Electroencephalography: basic principles and applications. In: International Encyclopedia of the Social & Behavioral Sciences, 2nd edn. (2015)
4. Novak, D.: Biomechatronic applications of brain-computer interfaces. Segil, J. (ed.) Handbook of Biomechatronics, Chap. 5. Academic Press, pp. 129–175. ISBN 9780128125397. http://www.sciencedirect.com/science/article/pii/B9780128125397000088
5. Zhang, X., Yong, X., Menon, C.: Evaluating the versatility of EEG models generated from motor imagery tasks: an exploratory investigation on upper-limb elbow-centered motor imagery tasks. PLoS ONE **12**(11), (2017). https://doi.org/10.1371/journal.pone.0188293
6. Lotte, F., et al.: A review of classification algorithms for EEG-based brain-computer interfaces: a 10-year update. J. Neural Eng. **15**(3), (2018)
7. Squires, K., Petuchowski, S., Wickens, C., Donchin, E.: The effects of stimulus sequence on event related potentials: a comparison of visual and auditory sequences. Percept. Psychophys. **22**(1), 31–40 (1977)
8. Blundon, E.G., Rumak, S.P., Ward, L.M.: Sequential search asymmetry: behavioral and psychophysiological evidence from a dual oddball task. PLoS ONE **12**(3), (2017). https://doi.org/10.1371/journal.pone.0173237
9. Farwell, L.A., Donchin, E.: Talking off the top of your head: a mental prosthesis utilizing event-related brain potentials. Electroencephalogr. Clin. Neurophysiol. **70**(6), 510–523 (1988)

10. Carabez, E., Sugi, M., Nambu, I., Wada, Y.: Convolutional neural networks with 3D input for P300 identification in auditory brain-computer interfaces. Comput. Intell. Neurosci. **2017**, 8163949 (2017)
11. Kodama, T., Makino, S.: Convolutional neural network architecture and input volume matrix design for ERP classifications in a tactile p 300-based brain-computer interface. In: 2017 39th Annual International Conference of the IEEE Engineering in Medicine and Biology Society (EMBC), pp. 3814–3817 (2017)
12. Cecotti, H., Graser, A.: Convolutional neural networks for P300 detection with application to brain-computer interfaces. IEEE Trans. Pattern Anal. Mach. Intell. **33**(3), 433–445 (2011)
13. Shan, H., Liu, Y., Stefanov, T.: A simple convolutional neural network for accurate P300 detection and character spelling in brain computer interface. In: Proceedings of the Twenty-Seventh International Joint Conference on Artificial Intelligence, IJCAI 2018, pp. 1604–1610. International Joint Conferences on Artificial Intelligence Organization (2018)
14. Liu, M., Wu, W., Gu, Z., Yu, Z., Qi, F., Li, Y.: Deep learning based on batch normalization for P300 signal detection. Neurocomputing **275**, 288–297 (2018)
15. Manor, R., Geva, A.B.: Convolutional neural network for multi-category rapid serial visual presentation BCI. Front. Comput. Neurosci. **9**, 146 (2015)
16. Das, R., Maiorana, E., Campisi, P.: Visually evoked potential for EEG biometrics using convolutional neural network. In: 2017 25th European Signal Processing Conference (EUSIPCO), pp. 951–955 (2017)
17. Pereira, A., Padden, D., Jantz, J., Lin, K., Alcaide-Aguirre, R.: Cross-subject EEG event-related potential classification for brain-computer interfaces using residual networks (2018). https://doi.org/10.13140/rg.2.2.16257.10086
18. Nicolas-Alonso, L.F., Gomez-Gil, J.: Brain computer interfaces, a review. Sensors **12**, 1211–1279 (2012). https://doi.org/10.3390/s120201211
19. Joy, Md.M.H., et al.: Multiclass MI-task classification using logistic regression and filter bank common spatial patterns. In: Chaubey, Nirbhay, Parikh, Satyen, Amin, Kiran (eds.) COMS2 2020. CCIS, vol. 1235, pp. 160–170. Springer, Singapore (2020). https://doi.org/10.1007/978-981-15-6648-6_13
20. Nicolas-Alonso, L.F., Gomez-Gil, J.: Brain computer interfaces, a review. Sensors **12**(2), 1211 (2012)
21. Bashashati, A., Fatourechi, M., Ward, R.K., Birch, G.E.: A survey of signal processing algorithms in brain–computer interfaces based on electrical brain signals. J. Neural Eng. **4**(2), R32 (2007)
22. McFarland, D.J., Anderson, C.W., Muller, K.R., Schlogl, A., Krusienski, D.J.: BCI meeting 2005-workshop on BCI signal processing: feature extraction and translation. IEEE Trans. Neural Syst. Rehabil. Eng. **14**(2), 135–138 (2006)
23. Lotte, F., Congedo, M., L'ecuyer, A., Lamarche, F., Arnaldi, B.: A review of classification algorithms for EEG-based brain–computer interfaces. J. Neural Eng. **4**(2), R1 (2007)
24. Zander, T.O., Kothe, C.: Towards passive brain–computer interfaces: applying brain–computer interface technology to human–machine systems in general. J. Neural Eng. **8**(2), (2011)
25. Lawhern, V., Solon, A., Waytowich, N., Gordon, S., Hung, C., Lance, B.: EEGNet: a compact convolutional network for EEG-based brain-computer interfaces. J. Neural Eng. **15**, 056013 (2016). https://doi.org/10.1088/1741-2552/aace8c
26. Tsoi, A.C., So, D.S.C., Sergejew, A.: Classification of electroenchephalogram using artificial neural networks. In: Cowan, J.D., Tesauro, G., Alspector, J. (eds.) Advances in Neural Information Processing Systems, San Francisco, CA. Morgan Kaufmann. vol. 6, pp. 1151–1180 (1994)

27. Vasios, C., Papageorgiou, C., Matsopoulos, G.K., Nikita, K.S., Uzunoglu, N.: A decision support system of evoked potentials for the classification of patients with first-episode schizophrenia. German J. Psychiatry **5**, 78–84 (2002)
28. Anderson, C.W., Stolz, E.A., Shamsunder, S.: Multivariate autoregressive models for classification of spontaneous electroencephalographic signals during mental tasks. IEEE Trans. Biomed. Eng. **45**(3), 277–286 (1998)
29. Franaszczuk, P.J., Blinowska, K.J., Kowalczyk, M.: The application of parametric multichannel spectral estimates in the study of electrical brain activity. Biol. Cybern. **51**(4), 239–247 (1985)
30. Rakotomamonjy, A., Guigue, V.: BCI Competition III: Dataset II Ensemble of SVMs for BCI P300 Speller. IEEE Trans. Biomed. Eng. **55**(3), 1147–1154 (2008)
31. Muller, K.-R., Mika, S., Ratsch, G., Tsuda, K., Scholkopf, B.: An introduction to kernel-based learning algorithms. IEEE Trans. Neural Netw. **12**(2), 181–201 (2001)
32. Hoffmann, U., Garcia, G., Vesin, J.-M., Diserens, K., Ebrahimi, T.: A boosting approach to P300 detection with application to braincomputer interfaces. In: IEEE EMBS Conference on Neural Engineering (2005)
33. Rawat, W., Wang, Z.: Deep convolutional neural networks for image classification: a comprehensive review. Neural Comput. **29**(9), 2352–2449 (2017)
34. Hassan, M., Shamas, M., Khalil, M., El Falou, W., Wendling, F.: EEGNET: an open source tool for analyzing and visualizing M/EEG connectome. PLoS ONE **10**(9), (2015). https://doi.org/10.1371/journal.pone.0138297
35. Woehrle, H., Krell, M.M., Straube, S., Kim, S.K., Kirchner, E.A., Kirchner, F.: An adaptive spatial filter for user-independent single trial detection of event-related potentials. IEEE Trans. Biomed. Eng. **62**(7), 1696–1705 (2015)
36. Blankertz, B., Tomioka, R., Lemm, S., Kawanabe, M., Muller, K.-R.: Optimizing spatial filters for robust EEG single-trial analysis. IEEE Sig. Process. Mag. **25**(1), 41–56 (2008)
37. Rivet, B., Cecotti, H., Perrin, M., Maby, E., Mattout, J.: Adaptive training session for a P300 speller brain-computer interface. J. Physiol. Paris **105**(1–3), 123–129 (2011)
38. Higashi, H., Rutkowski, T.M., Tanaka, T., Tanaka, Y.: Smoothing of xDAWN spatial filters for robust extraction of event-related potentials, pp. 1–5 (2016). https://doi.org/10.1109/apsipa.2016.7820750
39. Rivet, B., Souloumiac, A., Attina, V., Gibert, G.: xDAWN algorithm to enhance evoked potentials: application to brain-computer interface. IEEE Trans. Biomed. Eng. **56**(8), 2035–2043 (2009). https://doi.org/10.1109/tbme.2009.2012869
40. Miah, A.S.M., Islam, M.R., Molla, M.K.I.: Motor imagery classification using subband tangent space mapping. In: International Conference on Computer and Information Technology-2017 held on University of Asia Pacific, Dhaka, Bangladesh (2017)
41. Miah, A.S.M., Islam, M.R., Molla, M.K.I.: EEG classification for MI-BCI using CSP with averaging covariance matrices: an experimental study. In: International Conference on Computer, Communication, Chemical, Material and Electronic Engineering (IC^{4}ME^2 2019), Bangladesh (2019)
42. Miah, A.S.M., Ahmed, S.R.A., Ahmed, M.R., Bayat, O., Duru, A.D., Molla, M.K.I.: Motor-Imagery BCI task classification using riemannian geometry and averaging with mean absolute deviation. In: International Scientific Meeting of Electrical-Electronics & Biomedical Engineering & Computer Science EBBT 2019 held on Istanbul Arel University, 24–26 April 2019, Kemal Gözükara Campus in Istanbul Arel University, Turkey (2019)
43. Beres, A.M.: Time is of the essence: a review of electroencephalography (EEG) and event-related brain potentials (ERPs) in language research. Appl. Psychophysiol. Biofeedback **42**, 247–255 (2017). https://doi.org/10.1007/s10484-017-9371-3

44. Schalk, G., McFarland, D., Hinterberger, T., Birbaumer, N.R., Wolpaw, J.: BCI2000: a general-purpose Brain-Computer Interface (BCI) system. IEEE Trans. Biomed. Eng. **51**, 1034–1043 (2004). https://doi.org/10.1109/tbme.2004.827072

45. Goldberger, A., et al.: PhysioBank, PhysioToolkit, and PhysioNet: components of a new research resource for complex physiologic signals. Circulation **101**(23), E215–E220 (2000)

46. Waytowich, N., et al.: Compact convolutional neural networks for classification of asynchronous steady-state visual evoked potentials. J. Neural Eng. (2018). SP - 066031, IS - 6, VL - 15, SN - 1741-2560, SN - 1741-2552

47. Rivet, B., Cecotti, H., Souloumiac, A., Maby, E., Mattout, J.: Theoretical analysis of xDAWN algorithm: application to an efficient sensor selection in a P300 BCI. In: Proceedings of EUSIPCO-2011, pp. 1382–1386, Barcelona. IEEE (2011). https://ieeexplore.ieee.org/doc ument/7073970

48. Rivet, B., Souloumiac, A., Gibert, G., Attina, V.: P300 speller" Brain-Computer Interface: Enhancement of P300 evoked potential by spatial filters. In: Proceedings of European Signal Processing Conference (EUSIPCO), Lausanne, Switzerland, August 2008

49. Ferracuti, F., et al.: A functiona source separation algorithm to enhance error related potentials monitoring in noninvasive brain-computer interface. Comput. Methods Prog. Biomed. **191**, (2020)

Oil Spill Discrimination of SAR Satellite Images Using Deep Learning Based Semantic Segmentation

V. Sudha[1]($^{\boxtimes}$) ⓘ and Anna Saro Vijendran[2] ⓘ

[1] Department of Computer Science, Sri Ramakrishna College of Arts and Science, Coimbatore, Tamil Nadu, India
[2] School of Computing, Sri Ramakrishna College of Arts and Science, Coimbatore, Tamil Nadu, India

Abstract. This study examined the effective network architecture to discriminate oil spills from look-alikes using deep learning-based semantic segmentation. Data were collected from three different SAR satellites, ENVISAT, ALOSPOL-SAR, and TERRASAR. To ensure better accuracy, different characteristics of SAR satellites were analyzed based on spatial and temporal resolution. Semantic segmentation helps in finer inference by making dense predictions from labels of each class. Before entering into the segmentation phase, image preprocessing is done for effective segmentation results. The image Preprocessing phase includes log normalization, hybrid median filter, and scaling. Oil spill discrimination is done by Semantic segmentation using CNN and deeplabv3plus with pretrained RESNET18 on three different satellite images with the high-level and low-level dataset. It is observed that a high-level dataset of TERRASAR images outperforms rather than another SAR dataset. The comparison technique reveals that the proposed DeeplabV3plus segmentation has resulted in a great accuracy of 99% and is considered as the effective segmentation technique for oil spill discrimination.

Keywords: Synthetic aperture radar · Semantic segmentation · Convolution neural network · Deeplabv3plus · Log normalization · Hybrid median filter

1 Introduction

An oil spill is a major issue in the current environment. It was a major problem at the ocean level. To detect oil spilled area there are several methods used including satellite or airborne techniques. Rather than satellite or airborne, radar technology is used mostly since 1970. In order to produce better oil spill monitoring, the following requirements are needed, i.e., high temporal, spatial, and spectral resolution. SAR meets all these requirements and it can also use even in bad weather conditions. So, it is a more effective instrument in the case of oil spill detection. SAR has certain limitations due to speckle noise and radar cross-section changes. It can be avoided by using filtering and normalization approaches. Thus, in this paper, the major aim is to analyze the semantic segmentation capabilities of CNN and DeepLabV3plus to discriminate oil

© Springer Nature Switzerland AG 2021
N. Chaubey et al. (Eds.): COMS2 2021, CCIS 1416, pp. 127–139, 2021.
https://doi.org/10.1007/978-3-030-76776-1_9

spills in different satellite images. Models trained in three different satellite datasets using ENVISAT ASAR, ALOS POLSAR and TerraSAR-X with a swath width of 400, 350 and 260. TerraSAR-X has average spatial and temporal resolution. While ENVISAT data is comparably lower spatial resolution makes oil spill discrimination a challenging task. TerraSAR-X data has a higher resolution and its performance is comparatively good.

Semantic image segmentation made a progress with the emergence of the deep learning approach. The approach used in this paper is FCN and DeepLabV3plus, to make segmentation of image more accurate and faster. Generally, Data augmentation is used to train the data and also it transforms the existing data by applying transformations such as translation, masking, rotation, warping, resizing, etc. It is used to prevent overfitting and balance the classes within the database [4]. Here data augmentation is not used, instead preprocessing is done with the datasets. Emergence DCNN, in the following aspects: 1. Fully convolutional network, 2. How to sample, 3. FCN along with the CRF method, 4. The convolution approach widened, 5. Pyramid method, 6. Multi-level features and multi-stage methods, 7. Methods that are supervised, supervised weak [17].

2 Related Work

Ilango and Marudhachalam (2011) proposed a different hybrid noise reduction technique to eliminate Gaussian noise, with a topology approach [5]. Chen et al. (2016) shows that domain noise reduction techniques are several times faster than CRF inference that is solid as semantic segmentation, accurately capturing objects [1]. Topouzelis and Singha (2016) shows that, to avoid detection errors radar images with different wavelengths mostly C, L and X bands can be used [8]. Chen (2016), incorporated multi scale features with FCN to obtain better semantic segmentation. It performs better in average- and max-pooling and also helps in visualizing the features at different positions and scales [3]. Yang, Li et al. (2017), used both fuzzy based ontology approach for semantic concepts. This method performed well [19].

Oscar Garcia- Pineda et al. (2017), concluded that TerraSAR-X of highest resolution and RADARSAR of moderate resolution can detect oil slicks in and around sea [14]. Guo et al. (2018) used semantic segmentation using CNN that not only identifies dark spots in SAR images, but also predicts oil spill under high noise and fuzzy boundary conditions. Segnet and FCN8 show high stability and tolerance of adding and multiplication noise, although the overall FCN8S performance is not as good as a Segnet. The process of training is monitored, and the training depends on a large number of label images. Label production is not only time consuming and tiring in the data preparation stage, but also the effects of training can be easily influenced by human factors. [7]. Wurm et al. (2019) used transfer learning which is the advanced deep learning approach to segment slum areas and observed high accuracy [11].

Krestenitis et al. (2019) Proposed DCNN segmentation models and concluded that this method is more efficient in oil spill discrimination. The latest increase from the Deep lab architecture, named DeepLABV3 + extended earlier version by adding an effective, but simple decoder, to improve the results of the segmentation, which produces a distinctive object limit. DeepLABV3 + clearly outperformed the previous version, although smaller batch size was used in the training process. It must be highlighted that the DeepLABV3 + model increases testing accuracy [12]. Sornam (2017), used ostu method for segmentation and Back Propagation Network for classifying oil spills and look-alikes. It produced the improved results [16]. Orfanidis et al. (2018) proposed DCNN for oil spill identification and obtained accurate result. Deep CNN is new that does not require any feature extraction and can semantically annotate the area in the SAR image. In addition, deployed models are modified well, aimed at reducing the total computational cost and operational time. [6].

Ghorbani and Behzadan (2020) employed deep learning models, namely VGG-16 and masked R-CNN to locate oil spills. It yields average precision and recall of 61% and 70%. The introduction of objects in an image can be done in the form of image classification (e.g., determining the object) or object detection (i.e., determine the location and mark the object limits). To train the CNN model for object recognition, a large number of training data and optimal model parameters (a.k.a., hyperparameters) are desirable. However, the scarcity of annotation data for detection of oil spills and marine objects raises a challenge to train a high-performance CNN model. The potential solution for this problem is to train models on data from other domains, and then train the network on the primary domain data. In the Deep Learning (DL), this process is called Transfer Learning [20]. Yekeen (2020), developed an oil spill detection model using computer vision based on deep learning and concluded that the deep learning-based segmentation performs good rather than other approaches. The accuracy of CNN is higher in the introduction, detection, and segmentation of objects and its ability to localize the Instance that is being considered which allows the detection of oil spills in the complex scenario [17]. Zeng and Wang (2020), Based on VGG-16, the OSCNet is designed to detect oil spill using Spaceborne SAR datasets [9].

3   Problem Formulation

According to Ajadi, Lipschitz-Regularity, and Multiscale Techniques performed well in detecting oil spills [15]. Even though the problem that occurred in discrimination still exists due to dark phenomena, that lead to misclassification. The problem identified is formulated below and the proposed methodology is implemented to overcome normalization and resolution constraints.

- Issue in discrimination of oil spill from other ocean features like biogenic silks.
- Simulation of data sets is carried under controlled conditions such as limited wind velocity range, limitations in spill shaping.
- High wind conditions which lead to foam and spindrift are not examined.
- Normalization techniques that have a positive impact on spill shape and size should be implemented.

4   Image Datasets

The experimental dataset is obtained from the Gulf of Mexico Oil spill that occurred on April 20, 2010. The ENVISAT dataset with VV Polarization channels, The TerraSAR-X StripMap image (6.5 m resolution), and the ALOS POLSAR StripMap image (3 m resolution) were acquired during the oil leak in the Gulf of Mexico. The three different SAR satellite dataset is used and their characteristics are shown in Table 1.

Table 1. Characteristics of SAR Image

Satellite sensors	Spectral bands	Spatial resolution (m)	Temporal resolution (day)	Swath width	No of datasets
TERRASAR-X	X	18.5	11	260	3
ENVISAT ASAR	C	30	3	400	25
ALOSPOLSAR-2	L	6	14	350	25

5　Proposed Method

SAR dataset occurs with speckle noise. It is difficult to identify oil spills from looka-likes due to dark spots. Image Preprocessing is necessary to resolve issues in oil spill discrimination due to noise and dark spots. Scaling of images is important for semantic segmentation for labeling images. The experiment includes a comparative analysis of two different semantic segmentation networks, that is CNN and DeeepLabV3plus.

5.1　Image Preprocessing

Image Preprocessing includes the following stages:

Log Normalization
In oil spill discrimination, dark features play a major role. The log normalization is used to enhance the dark regions rather than clipping the white regions. The log-normalization considers a normal or near-normal pixel value and the normalization of the image is more skewed under dark areas than the original data. Another main usage of log-normalization is, it helps in the identification of dark features more accurately that helps in the further segmentation process.

$$x' = \log(x + 1)$$

Here x' and x is a value of pixels. The value 1 is added to avoid the infinity values.

Hybrid Median Filter
The HMF is the enhanced version of the median filter. It helps in noise removal and also in edge preservation of the image while smoothing. The HMF is an NXN box filter of nonlinear class that easily removes noise and preserves edges. The HMF applies the median technique several times with varying window shapes for all elements of the image. The HMF finds medians of horizontal, vertical and diagonal of pixels.

$$B = hmf(Image, N)$$

The above formula filters an image using a NXN box. In comparison with other filters, the median filter has better edge-preserving characteristics. The performance metrics used to compare HMF with other filters are listed in Table 2.

Table 2. Performance metrices for filters

Performance measures	Formula
Mean square error	$MSE = \frac{1}{mn} \sum_{i=0}^{m-1} \sum_{j=0}^{n-1} [I(i,j) - K(i,j)]^2$
Mean absolute error	$MAE = \frac{1}{mn} \sum_{i=0}^{m-1} \sum_{j=0}^{n-1} [|I(i,j) - K(i,j)|]$
Peak signal to-noise ratio	$PSNR = 20log10(MAE) - 10\,log\,10(MSE)$
Structural similarity index measure	$SSIM(x, y) = \frac{(2\mu_x\mu_y + c_1)(2\sigma_{xy} + c_2)}{(\mu_x^2 + \mu_y^2 + c_1)(\sigma_x^2 + \sigma_y^2 + c_2)}$
Image enhancement factor	$IEF = \frac{\sum_{i=0}^{m-1} \sum_{j=0}^{n-1} [N(i,j) - O(i,j)]^2}{\sum_{i=0}^{m-1} \sum_{j=0}^{n-1} [D(i,j) - O(i,j)]^2}$

Scaling
Images obtained from ENVISAT, TERRASAR, and ALOS POLSAR have different pixel range. Scaling images to the same range will make images contribute more evenly to labeling operation in semantic segmentation. Without scaling, segmentation is not possible.

$$O = \text{imresize(Image, } [m\ n])$$

The above formula returns image O after applying specified number of rows and columns [m n] in input image

5.2 Semantic Segmentation

CNN
Semantic segmentation attempts to label each pixel of the image into pre-determined classes. A pixel is encoded to find local features specific to the class thru convolution. A decoder network combines these class-specific features. The labels are masked to obtain the ground truth of the images and also called as Image masking. A mask consists of all the pixels belonging to the particular class. The first set of images contains preprocessed ENVISAT images in Fig. 1. The second set consists of masks of ENVISAT images Fig. 1.

This semantic segmentation network consists of a downsampling and upsampling design as shown in Fig. 2. Downsampling reduces the spatial resolution of an image,

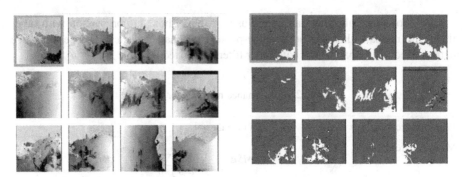

Fig. 1. Preprocessed and masked image of ENVISAT

so that storage space in the transmission process is reduced. Upsampling increases the spatial resolution of an image. CNN consists of sequence of layers, and every layer performs some transformation to another through an activation function. The layers used to build CNN architectures are Convolutional Layer, ReLU, Max Pooling Layer, Softmax, and Pixel Classification Layer.

- Image Input Layer [227 × 227 × 3] have the raw pixel values of the image of width 227, height 227 with 3 dimensions.
- Convolution layer gets 227 × 227 input values that use 3 × 3 filters with a stride of 1 and matches the features in the image.
- The rectified linear activation function or ReLU is a linear function that retains white pixels and vanishes black pixels.
- MaxPooling layer will perform a downsampling operation by calculating the maximum value in a feature map.
- Transpose Convolution layer performs 4 × 4 deconvolution in which every pixel is multiplied with the kernel and projected onto the output space.
- Softmax function outputs probability distribution values and that probabilities sum to 1.
- A pixel classification layer outputs the labeled pixel and ignores undefined pixel labels.

DEEPLABV3 PLUS
In this section, the built-in Resnet-18 architecture is used to segment the oil spill. Res-Net-18 is a modified CNN by adding 18 deep layers. The pretrained network can classify 1000 categories of objects in images. Proposed ResNet-18 architecture is shown in Fig. 2, It also contains Convolutional layer, MaxPool layer, batch normalization, rectified linear unit activation layer like CNN [13]. Atrous convolution controls the resolution as well as allows us to identify the object boundaries by combining DCNN [2].

6   Performance Measures

In this proposed method, the noise reduction in SAR images is performed using Hybrid Median Filter (HMF) filter. It is compared with other filters like Mean, Median, Weiner,

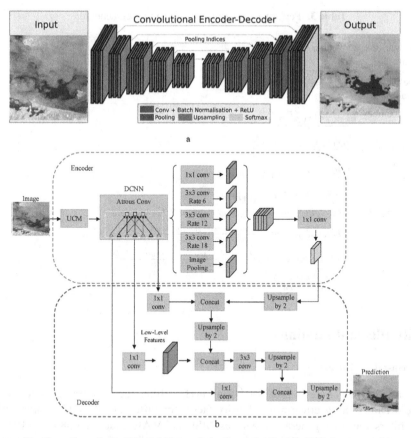

Fig. 2. a-Convolution Neural Network, b-shows the DeepLabV3plus network

Gaussian, fast non-local filter using five performance metrics such as MSE, MAE, PSNR, SSIM, IEF as shown in Table 2. The performance of semantic segmentation using CNN and DeepLabV3plus was evaluated on the ENVISAT, TERRASAR, and ALOSPOLSAR images, including oil spills and another ocean background. The dataset is preprocessed and pixel-level ground truth labelling is done with all images having 512×512 pixels in size. The experiment is done using 50 images with 2 different classes of objects. In addition, our method is mainly to evaluate the performance of three SAR satellite images. In this paper, the performance measures such as global accuracy, mean pixel accuracy, intersection over union, weighted IoU and BFScore are examined. The calculation formula is as follows in Table 3:

Table 3. Performance metrices for semantic segmentation

Performance measures	Formula
Global accuracy	$\frac{TP+TN}{TP+TN+FP+FN}$
Mean accuracy	$\frac{\left(\frac{TP}{TP+FN}\right)+\left(\frac{TN}{TN+FN}\right)}{2}$
IOU or Jaccard similarity coefficient	$\frac{Oil+background}{2}$ $Where:\ Oil = \frac{TP}{TP+FN+FP}$ $Background = \frac{TN}{TN+FN+FP}$
Weighted IOU	$oil\ weight\ X\ oil + background\ weight\ X\ background$ $Where:oil\ weight = \frac{number\ of\ pixels\ belonging\ to\ oil}{total\ number\ of\ pixels}$ $background\ weight = \frac{number\ of\ pixels\ belonging\ to\ background}{total\ number\ of\ pixels}$
BF score	$\frac{2x(precision+recall)}{precision+recall}$

7   Results and Findings

7.1   Based on Filters

SAR satellite images are preprocessed using an HMF filter. It gives more accurate results. Table 4 shows the average noise density factor for different filters. Comparing with other filters, the HMF generates the lowest MSE and MAE values of 8.38 and 6.105 and ensures the highest level of PSNR, SSIM and IEF value. Figure 3 shows the noise density comparisons of HMF with other filters. The HMF achieves better results compared to other filters.

Table 4. Comparison of filter using performance metrices

Filter	Performance metrics				
	MSE	MAE	PSNR	SSIM	IEF
MEAN	10.264	6.485	54.486	0.264	2.909
MEDIAN	12.167	6.812	53.646	0.253	1.802
WIENER	13.226	7.471	53.803	0.074	0.454
GAUSSIAN	11.206	6.029	54.046	0.205	0.138
FNLF	8.693	6.181	55.375	0.275	5.218
HMF	8.38	6.105	55.553	0.282	10.556

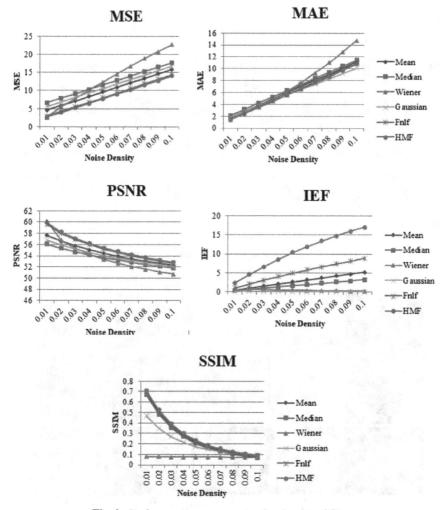

Fig. 3. Performance measures on noise density of filters

7.2   Based on Datasets

In this paper, three different satellite images are used. Figure 5 shows the sample images and their segmented result. The results are obtained based on the spatial and temporal resolution of the dataset. Table 5 shows the performance measures of the different datasets. ENVISAT dataset which has higher temporal resolution has low accuracy compared to the other two datasets. The ALOSPOLSAR and TerraSAR-X which have high spatial resolution produce a better result.

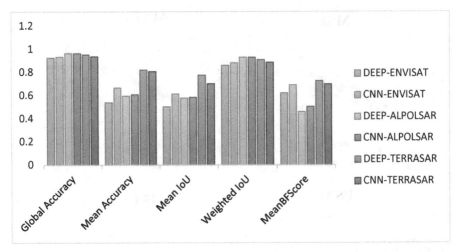

Fig. 4. Comparative analysis of semantic segmentation

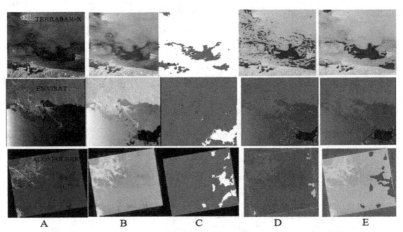

Fig. 5. Results of semantic segmentation A-Original Image, B-Preprocessed Image C-Ground Truth D-CNN E-DeepLabV3Plus

7.3 Based on Segmentation

The semantic segmentation with deep learning approach performance is evaluated for oil spill discrimination in different remotely sensed data sets with varying characteristics. The performance of CNN and DeepLabV3Plus is evaluated for the two classes. The maximum value of the epoch range is 100. The hyperparameters used in training networks were sgdm (Stochastic Gradient Descent with Momentum) optimizer and Cross-Entropy Loss function. Totally six experiments were performed using CNN and DeepLabV3Plus semantic segmentation approach on three different datasets. The performance of this model is done using a softmax cross-entropy loss function. Semantic segmentation based on the DeepLabV3Plus and TerraSAR-X, ALOSPOLSAR dataset have

Table 5. Performance measures of semantic segmentation using CNN and DeepLabV3Plus

Performance measures	DEEP-ENVISAT	CNN-ENVISAT	DEEP-ALPOLSAR	CNN-ALPOLSAR	DEEP-TERRASAR	CNN-TERRASAR
Global accuracy	0.9264	0.9343	0.96453	0.9632	0.95164	0.9372
Mean accuracy	0.5387	0.6655	0.5957	0.607	0.8186	0.805
Mean IoU	0.5017	0.6133	0.5771	0.5833	0.7745	0.7002
Weighted IoU	0.8588	0.8819	0.9307	0.93	0.9088	0.8861
MeanBFScore	0.6211	0.6897	0.4596	0.5028	0.725	0.696

performed well. The Table 5 shows the performance measures of semantic segmentation for all six experiments (Fig. 4).

8   Conclusion

In this paper, oil spill discrimination using semantic segmentation is carried on using robust CNN and Deeplabv3plus models. In deep learning, various pretrained architectures have been proposed for image segmentation. From previous works, and also by evaluating the characteristics of CNN and DeepLabV3Plus architecture, the DeepLabV3Plus with its tailored characteristics is used to solve a given problem. The performance measures are compared using three different satellite images based on temporal and spatial resolution. This study concluded by comparing the results of CNN and deeplabv3plus using pretrained renet18 layers, TerraSAR-X Images performs well in discriminating oil spill from lookalikes. On the other hand, the dataset which has high spatial resolution yields good accuracy. Further implementation can be done to overcome issues in label images for semantic segmentation.

References

1. Chen, L.C., Barron, J.T., Papandreou, G., Murphy, K., Yuille, A.L.: Semantic image segmentation with task specific edge detection using CNNS and a discriminatively trained domain transform. In: IEEE Conference on Computer Vision and Pattern Recognition, pp 4545–4554 (2016)
2. Chen, L.C., Papandreou, G., Kokkinos, I., Murphy, K., Yuille, A.L.: Deep lab: semantic image segmentation with deep convolutional nets, atrous convolution, and fully connected CRFs. arXiv preprint arXiv:1606.00915 (2016)
3. Chen, L.C., Yang, Y., Wang, J., Xu Yuille, A.L.: Attention to scale: scale-aware semantic image segmentation. In: IEEE Conference on Computer Vision and Pattern Recognition, pp. 3640–3649 (2016)
4. Garcia-Garcia, A., Orts-Escolano, S., Oprea, S.O., Villena-Martinez, V., Garcia-Rodriguez, J.: A review on deep learning techniques applied to semantic segmentation. arXiv:1704.068 57v1 [cs.CV] (2017)
5. Ilango, G., Marudhachalam, R.: New hybrid filtering techniques for removal of Gaussian noise from medical images. ARPN J. Eng. Appl. Sci. 6(2), 8–12 (2011). ISSN 1819-6608
6. Orfanidis, G., Ioannidis, K., Avgerinakis, K., Vrochidis, S., Kompatsiaris, I.: A deep neural network for oil spill semantic segmentation in SAR images. In: 25th IEEE International Conference on Image Processing (ICIP) (2018). https://doi.org/10.1109/icip.2018.8451113
7. Guo, H., Wei, G., An, J.: Dark spot detection in SAR images of oil spill using segnet. Appl. Sci. 8, 2670 (2018). https://doi.org/10.3390/app8122670
8. Topouzelis, K., Singha, S.: Oil Spill Detection: Past and Future Trends (2016). https://www.researchgate.net/publication/304496256
9. Zeng, K., Wang, Y.: A deep convolutional neural network for oil spill detection from spaceborne SAR images. Remote Sens. 12, 1015 (2020). https://doi.org/10.3390/rs12061015
10. Mohan1, E., Sivakumar, R.: Denoising of satellite images using hybrid filtering and convolutional neural network. Int. J. Eng. Technol. 7(4.6), 462–464 (2018)
11. Wurm, M., Stark, T., Zhu, X.X., Weigand, M., Taubenböck, H.: Semantic segmentation of slums in satellite images using transfer learning on fully convolutional neural networks. ISPRS J. Photogramm. Remote Sens. 150(2019), 59–69 (2019)

12. Krestenitis, M., Orfanidis, G., Ioannidis, K., Avgerinakis, K., Vrochidis, S., Kompatsiaris, I.: Oil spill identification from satellite images using deep neural networks. Remote Sens. **11**, 1762 (2019)
13. Alif, M.A.R., Ahmed, S., Hasan, M.A.: Isolated Bangla handwritten character recognition with convolutional neural network. In: International Conference of Computer and Information Technology (ICCIT) (2017)
14. Garcia-Pineda, O., Holmes, J., Rissing, M., Jones, R., Wobus, C., Svejkovsky, J., Hess, M.: Detection of oil near shorelines during the deepwater horizon oil spill using synthetic aperture radar (SAR). Remote Sens. **9**, 567 (2017). https://doi.org/10.3390/rs9060567
15. Ajadi, O.A., Meyer, F.J., Tello, M., Ruello, G.: Oil spill detection in synthetic aperture radar images using Lipschitz-regularity and multiscale techniques. IEEE J. Select. Top. Appl. Earth Obs. Remote Sens. **11**, 2389–2405 (2018)
16. Sornam, M.: Oilspill: and look-alike spots from SAR imagery using OTSU method and artificial neural network. Int. J. Eng. Technol. Manag. Res. (2017). https://doi.org/10.5281/zenodo.1065293, ISSN 2454-1907
17. Yekeen, S.T., Yusof, K.B.W., Balogun, A.L: A novel deep learning instance segmentation model for automated marine oil spill detection, ISPRS J. Photogramm. Remote Sens. **167**, 190–200 (2020)
18. Liu, X., Deng, Z., Yang, Y.: Recent progress in semantic image segmentation. Artif. Intell. Rev. (2018). https://doi.org/10.1007/s10462-018-9641-3
19. Yang, Y., Li, Y., Yang, Y., Ma, J.: Detection of oil spill and look-alike from SAR imagery based on ontology and kernel fuzzy C-Means. In: International Conference on Information Science and Control Engineering (2017). https://doi.org/10.1109/ICISCE.2017.64
20. Ghorbani, Z., Behzadan, A.H.: Identification and instance segmentation of oil spills using deep neural networks. In: 5th World Congress on Civil, Structural, and Environmental Engine (2020)

Sentiment Analysis of Bangla Language Using Deep Learning Approaches

Muntasir Hoq(✉) ⑩, Promila Haque⑩, and Mohammed Nazim Uddin⑩

East Delta University, Chattaogram, Bangladesh
{muntasir.h,promila,nazim}@eastdelta.edu.bd

Abstract. Emotion is the most important gear for human textual communication with each other via social media. Nowadays, people use text for reviewing or recommending things, sharing opinions, rating their choices or unlikeness, providing feedback for different services, and so on. Bangladeshi people use Bangla to express their emotions. Current research based on sentiment analysis has got low-performance output by using several approaches on detecting sentiment polarity and emotion from Bangla texts. In this study, we have developed four models with the hybrid of Convolutional Neural Network (CNN) and Long Short Term Memory (LSTM) with various Word Embeddings including Embedding Layer, Word2Vec, Global Vectors (Glove), and Continuous Bag of Words (CBOW) to detect emotion from Bangla texts (words, sentences). Our models can define the basic three emotions; happiness, anger, and sadness. It will make interaction lively and interesting. Our comparisons are bestowed against CNN, LSTM with different Word Embeddings, and also against some previous researches with the same dataset based on classical Machine Learning techniques such as Support Vector Machine (SVM), Naïve Bayes, and K-Nearest Neighbors (K-NN). In our proposed study, we have used Facebook Bangla comments for a suitable dataset. In our study, we have tried to detect the exact emotion from the text. And in result, the best model integrating Word2Vec embedding layer with a hybrid of CNN-LSTM detected emotions from raw textual data with an accuracy of 90.49% and F1 score of 92.83%.

Keywords: CNN · LSTM · NLP · Sentiment analysis · Bangla language

1 Introduction

Social networking is one of the most popular means of communication. The foremost well-known one is Facebook where individuals of all ages from distinctive communities over the world are associated. People express their emotions by providing posts on social media, such as their likings, disliking, favorite brands, and product reviews. On Facebook, most Bangla users use Bangla in their posts and comments because they can express their exact emotions and feel free to write texts in Bangla. In this paper, feelings in post and comments on Facebook written in Bangla language will be analyzed in such a way as to reflect and explain it in a meaningful manner.

© Springer Nature Switzerland AG 2021
N. Chaubey et al. (Eds.): COMS2 2021, CCIS 1416, pp. 140–151, 2021.
https://doi.org/10.1007/978-3-030-76776-1_10

Multiple techniques can be applied to analyze the data. Sentiment analysis has proved to be profitable in this case as it can detect the emotion, attitude, and polarity that are hidden in words. Using this sentiment, a company can understand their consumer what they want and what more can be added. Buyers can know about their client satisfaction.

Most of the works on sentiment analysis in NLP have been focused on English language. But Sentiment analysis in Bangla language and topic modeling both are new ideas. Sentiment Analysis (SA) in Bangla has an extensive province of posterior possibilities with deep learning. So in this study, we have worked on Bangla textual data obtained from Facebook comments on various topics. The proposed method preprocesses the imbalanced dataset to get a balanced one by removing punctuations, alphanumeric and duplicate words. Our proposed model is implemented with a hybrid of CNN-LSTM framework which can use any Word Embedding as an external layer to identify three basic emotions including: happy, sad, angry. Different Word embedding's used with the hybrid model including Embedding layer, Word2Vec, CBOW, GloVe. Due to an imbalanced dataset, we have been capable of defining only three different types of emotions. No previous work has been done on sentiment analysis using Deep Learning approach with hybridization of CNN-LSTM model in Bangla language as of our knowledge. So our proposed method is the first of its kind.

The remainder of the paper is arranged as follows. In the Sect. 2, we give a summary of the related work conducted in this domain. Section 3 describes how the data was collected, stored, and describes the methodologies that are used in this study, Sect. 4 described the experimental results and comparison with different traditional and state-of-the-art disciplines, and Sect. 5 briefly draws the findings and future directions of research.

2 Related Work

Because of its socio-commercial value, Sentimental analysis has become a hot research topic these days. The number of works on sentiment analysis has been rising by a significant amount in recent years. In [1], the study showed an approach for detecting sentiments from tweet data using deep convolutional neural networks. Several Machine Learning and Deep Learning techniques have been employed in [2] and detected Bangla text which are multi-type abusive. Besides, there have worked with new stemming rules for Bangla language which resulted in better. In [3] the dataset has three categories: positive, negative, and ambiguous and they have worked on LSTM using two types of loss functions. In this work, their dataset is substantial and textual for both Bangla and Romanized Bangla. In [4], they have worked for three categories of opinion: positive, negative, and neutral for Bangla textual movie reviews. In [5] neural network approach is used for emotion detection. They [6] have followed others and adopted distance supervision. Using Bangla WordNet, they have defined six different types of emotions. They have planned to reduce the noisy data from the web. By using LSTM on the noisy nature of Bangla toxic texts, it is possible to get better accuracy [7]. Toxic comment means detecting threats, spam, and vulgar words. In [8], they collect data from Bangla, English, and Romanized Bangla from YouTube comments and they have defined both classifying (positive, negative, neutral) a Bangla sentence and basic six different emotions detection from text. But they have skipped the comments that have more than 30 words. Many sentences in Bangla language can express their final emotion at the end of the sentence. So, if it is wanted to understand the exact emotion, needs to take a long sentence that contains more than 30 words. In this paper [9] they have used Word2vec for detecting top-ranked words or sentences. But for embedding layer it should have good vocabulary. For creating a vocabulary, will need a large dataset that are not available for Bangla language. For creating a dataset, one needs to create data manually and collect automatic data [10]. In [12], a Bangla text corpus was used that contains textual data from Facebook groups on different topics, mainly user comments. They used the same dataset and the same number of emotions as the proposed work, but they have used Naïve Bayes Classifier. In this study [13], attention-based CNN is used for the first time in Bangla sentiment analysis with an accuracy of 72.06%. Regarding LSTM networks with advanced layers, [14] this study achieves an accuracy of 94%. In [15], the authors have worked with several DL techniques and with two different datasets and shown some promising comparisons among all the models. In [8], they collect data from Bangla, English and Romanized Bangla from YouTube comments and they have defined both classifying (positive, negative, neutral) a Bangla sentence and basic six different emotions detection from text. But they have skipped the comments that have more than 30 words. Many sentences in Bangla language can express their final emotion at the end of the sentence. So, if it is wanted to understand the exact emotion, needs to take long sentence that contains more than 30 words.

In sentiment analysis, capturing local features is also important along with capturing the context of words in a sentence with long term dependency. Researches done in this field have not thoroughly explored this region. We have tried to overcome this problem with our proposed hybrid model of CNN-LSTM.

3   Methodology

Many algorithms have been used to solve sentiment analysis and polarity. Each proposed work has used different types of algorithms to solve problems. Most of the approaches have been given high accuracy while classifying English words. We have used different embedding layers, word2vec, CBOW, and Glove for developing Bangla CNN, LSTM, and our proposed CNN-LSTM models to detect emotions from Bangla language texts and have tried to improve accuracy than the existing accuracy.

Sentiment detection can be done in three ways: Sub Sentence Level, Sentence Level, and Document Level Analysis. In our proposed method we have followed the document level analysis because we have seen many people express their exact emotion at the end of the text. And few people show their emotion by only using a single sentence and very few people express their emotion by using only one sentence. By using document-level analysis, we have detected exact emotion from our Facebook comment dataset. We have continued annotation based on this document-level analysis. In the current section, an overview of our study is described. Figure 1 illustrates the step-wise architecture of the proposed model.

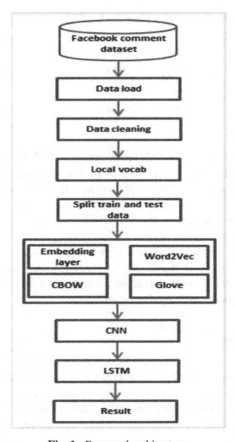

Fig. 1. Proposed architecture.

3.1 Database Formation

This is the initial phase of the analysis process. The dataset we used for this work consists of a large number of textual comments of different users collected from three Facebook groups by using Facebook graph API. We have collected the dataset developed in this study paper [11]. From six emotions and 5640 annotated data from 32000 comments, due to imbalanced data we chose to detect three basic emotions excluding other emotions. The selected emotions are: happy, sad, and angry emotions.

Table 1 provides the class labels, and the amount of data we have used.

In the preprocessing stage, the dataset was processed and cleaned as follows:

- Class labels were removed from the dataset.
- Texts have been split into tokens by white space
- Punctuations have been removed from each token.
- Bangla stop words were removed that are available in our file. The difference in token length can be seen as before removing stop words token length was 48892

Table 1. Emotion Class level and amount of data

Class level	Amount of data
Happy	1000
Sad	1000
Angry	1000

- After removing Bangla stop words token length is 48889. So, stop words are those words that are repeated mostly. Stop words do not play any role. These are like a preposition, conjunction, etc. The list of Bangla stop words were obtained from an open-source project[1].
- Vocab file was created using our clean textual data.

Our processed data contains comments where one comment contains a minimum of 1 word and a maximum of 148 words. In this study [8], the comments were skipped that have 30 words but many comments express emotions at the end of the text. For this reason, we have taken both small and large comments.

3.2 Word Embedding

Word embedding is a feature learning and language modeling technique in NLP. It is required for representing words and documents using dense vector representation. We have used several popular words embedding for sentiment analysis from the text. These are Embedding layer, CBOW, Glove, and Word2vec. In this study, using these word embedding layers, features are extracted and fed into the proposed model to detect emotions from textual data.

Embedded Layer. Firstly, we have used an embedding layer with defined library functions. For developing the model, we have loaded the vocab file created at the database formation phase and the training comments (happy, angry, and sad). Then the training document for integers sequence has been loaded by using Keras API. Then we have defined pad sequence adding empty words to the text for the same length and the X and Y training-testing, that is the transformation of actual string to a number. We have categorized levels 0, 1 & 2 for happy, sad, angry emotions respectively. 80% of data has been used for training and the remaining 20% is for testing. In our embedding layer, we have used 100-dimensional vector space and vocab_size for the number of words in our vocabulary and max_length for input length.

Word2vec. In Word2Vec embedding, words are represented with features which are vector based to capture the similarity. Hence similar words are likely to have similar vectors. The word similarities are calculated with the help of Cosine Similarity Function from the word vector values. The Cosine Similarity function is given below:

$$similarity = cos\theta = \frac{\bar{a} \cdot \bar{b}}{|\bar{a}| \cdot |\bar{b}|} \tag{1}$$

Here, $\bar{a}$, and $\bar{b}$ are two word vectors.

These similarity values range from a lowest of -1 and a highest of 1. In our word2vec model, we have passed the clean sentence and defined embedding vector space 100 and the number of neighbor word 5 as the window size. We have used workers 4 for the number of threads when fitting the model. After that, we have defined min_count 5 that means the number of counted words occurrence. Finally, a word2vec file has been created where we have found the data as ASCII code.

CBOW. In this proposed method, CBOW model has been created by using gnsim library that is special for word2vec. The working procedure has been followed the same as word2vec except min_count is considered 1 in this case. As this method works based on the probability of words so the length of the vocabulary is different than word2vec which works based on finding similar word to word. The result has been saved in ASCII code format to be used for the CNN, LSTM and CNN-LSTM model.

Pre-trained GloVe (Global Vectors). We have used a pre-trained Bangla glove file that has 100-dimensional space. It generates an ASCII code text file. We have used this file with our model. Glove works based on word co-occurrence probability. Let, co-occurrence count is X whose entries is X_{ij}. We have tabulated the number of times where word j occurs in the context of the word i. Suppose, $X_i = \sum_k X_{ik}$ be the number of times and any word can occur in context word i. Now, in the end, we have found Pij $= P(j|i)$ and we can write it Xij|Xi.

3.3   Convolutional Neural Network (CNN)

At first, we have added a method for sequence. Every Keras model using a build or customized sequential class is for a linear stack of layers. Then we have added our embedding layer where we define vocab size, dimensional vector space, and input length. Then, we have defined Convolution layer1D where we have defined filter size and kernel size and activated RELU (rectified linear activation function). Here, filter size has been used for parallel field word processing and relu use for transferring and summing the weight from the input node to output for the input. After that, we have added pool size, flatten method where the pool size variable has been used for a hyperparameter for our CNN model and have flattened the input that does not affect by batch-size. Then we have added a dense function where we have activated relu and sigmoid with a different value. We have seen the output in a 2D vector where features extracted by CNN in back-end multilayer perceptron interpret the CNN feature. We have used the sigmoid function for output values where 0 for happy emotion, 1 for sad emotion, and 2 for angry emotion. Then, we have added the compile method in our model where we define loss, optimizer, and metrics. We have used the binary cross-entropy loss function to classify binary classification problems. We had to keep track of the loss that is produced in training time. For this reason, we have implemented the "adam" optimizer function. After this procession, our training model has got fitness. So, we have defined testing wherein training period testing data were not seen. We have used 200-dimensional vector space with 32 filters (parallel fields for processing words) and a kernel size of 8 with a rectified linear (relu) activation function. We have used a 12582-word size vocab file. Dimensional space can be used 50, 100, 150 it depends on data length.

3.4 Long Short-Term Memory (LSTM)

LSTM is suitable for analyzing time-series data and can remember several states that we needed. It has got a record for natural language text compression and can be trained as supervised training. As LSTM is a feedback network, it can reduce error by backtracking and changing weight. In LSTM, memory units handle a period dependency. It has four units: Cell, Input gate, Output gate & Forget gate.

According to Fig. 2, we can see there is three input where two inputs have come from the previous state. One is h_{t-1}, that has come from previous LSTM, and another is C_{t-1}, which is a memory and it has come from the previous time step. One of the important parts is the gate, where one is the forget gate and another is the memory gate.

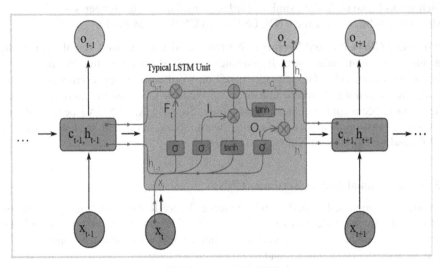

Fig. 2. A typical LSTM

The generic equation for LSTM can be described as follows:

$$i_t = \delta\left(W^i x_t + U^i h_{t-1}\right) \tag{2}$$

$$f_t = \delta\left(W^f x_t + U^f h_{t-1}\right) \tag{3}$$

$$o_t = \delta\left(W^o x_t + U^o h_{t-1}\right) \tag{4}$$

$$c_t = \tan h\left(W^c x_t + U^c h_{t-1}\right) \tag{5}$$

$$c_t = i_t \odot \tilde{c}_t + f_t \odot \tilde{c}_{t-1} \tag{6}$$

$$h_t = o_t \odot \tan h(c_t) \tag{7}$$

Here, i_t represents the input gate, f_t represents forget gate, o_t represents the output gate, δ represents the sigmoid function. W^i, W^f, W^o, W^c, U^i, U^f, U^o, U^c represent the weight matrices and x_t is the vector input to timestep t, h_t current is exposed hidden state and memory cell state is c_t, $\odot$ this is the element-wise multiplication.

In our study, we have built an LSTM model where we have defined embedding size 100 and the embedding method which contains vocab size, embedding size, and input length. We have added a dropout of 0.4 where dropout has reduced the over fitting. We have added a compilation method that we also have used on CNN. After that, we have fitted the training data and used batch size 32 and epoch 15 with validation data.

3.5 CNN-LSTM

In general, LSTM is better for text classification. But in text classification probably a small dataset can vanish the power of LSTM. CNN has its efficacy at learning the local features and spatial structure of textual data and adding a CNN after embedding layers which fed into an LSTM network helps to acquire the global and sequenced characteristics of the input textual data. For this reason, we have created a hybrid model by using CNN and LSTM that has been shown in our proposed methodology. Basically, in our hybrid model (CNN-LSTM) we have pooled a CNN and feed that into LSTM. We have used an embedding layer and used a single Conv1D pooling layer that has helped LSTM to run faster.

In this study, an extensive experiment is done to show that our proposed model outperforms other models in terms of detecting emotions. In this work, for mathematical analysis, for programming Python is used. We have used Google Colab for the simulation.

4 Result and Analysis

In this section, we have discussed the achievement of our proposed method. Some tables and figures are given here, where different kinds of models and their accuracy and F1 scores are shown. We have done our work by defining 80% training and 20% testing from our dataset that have real-time data. Our dataset contains 3000 Facebook comments that have been collected from three different Facebook groups and we have tried to predict three basic emotions: happiness, anger, and sadness from the data. We have implemented CNN for Bangla language and our proposed algorithm is LSTM and we also have made a hybrid model that contains CNN-LSTM.

In Table 2, we can see the result of CNN model where we have used different embedding layers for developing a good Bangla CNN. For our 80% training and 20% testing splitting data, we have got the highest accuracy by using pre-trained Bangla glove embedding. On the other hand, we have got a higher F1-score for CBOW embedding.

In Table 3, we have provided the result of LSTM model where we have got the same accuracy as well as F1-score for Word2vec, CBOW, and Glove embedding.

The result of our CNN-LSTM hybrid model by using different embedding layer has been shown in Table 4.

In CNN-LSTM hybrid model, we have got the best accuracy and F1-score by using Word2vec embedding. We did not get a good result by using only the embedding layer in our three models.

Table 2. Accuracy and F1-score for different embedding layer in CNN model

Model	Accuracy	F1 score
Embedding layer	56.67%	46.74%
Word2vec	82.50%	85.49%
CBOW	83.33%	87.14%
Glove	84.00%	84.46%

Table 3. Accuracy and F1-score for different embedding layer in LSTM model

Model	Accuracy	F1 score
Embedding layer	33.33%	16.67%
Word2vec	66.67%	80.00%
CBOW	66.67%	80.00%
Glove	66.67%	80.00%

Table 4. Accuracy and F1-score for different embedding layer in CNN-LSTM model

Model	Accuracy	F1 score
Embedding layer	33.33%	16.67%
Word2vec	90.49%	92.83%
CBOW	86.00%	88.88%
Glove	80.16%	83.16%

The output of our classifier can be evaluated in terms of accuracy. Therefore, the results of the classifier are measured in terms of accuracy, F1-scores, and AUC curve. Accuracy can be defined as:

$$Accuracy = \frac{Number\ of\ correct\ predictions}{Total\ number\ of\ predictions\ made} \qquad (8)$$

To calculate F1-score, a confusion matrix is expressed as in Table 5 to understand the binary classifier predictions with tp, fp, tn, fn as true positive, false positive, true negative, and false negative respectively.

From the confusion matrix, F1-score can be defined as:

$$Precision = \frac{tp}{tp + fp} \qquad (9)$$

$$Recall = \frac{tp}{tp + fn} \qquad (10)$$

Table 5. Confusion Matrix for different embedding layer in CNN-LSTM model

	Emotion 1 predicted	Emotion 2 predicted
Emotion 1 actual	tp	fn
Emotion 2 actual	fp	tn

$$F1 - score = \frac{2 \times Precision \times Recall}{Precision + Recall} \qquad (11)$$

In Fig. 3 the differences in AUC score among our models have been shown. As the result of the embedding layer is less than the baseline, it has not been shown in the Figure.

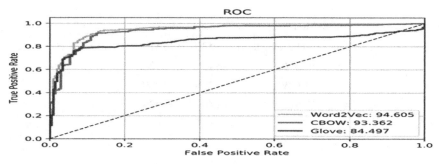

Fig. 3. AUC score CNN-LSTM model

From Table 2, 3, and 4 the best result has been found from the word2vec CNN-LSTM model. CBOW CNN, LSTM, and CNN- LSTM model also have almost equal accuracy and F1 score in the case of 80% training and 20% testing data split. We have provided both accuracy and F1 score. Because accuracy has been showing the ratio of correctly predictive all observations. We have used it because our all classes are equally important. We also have shown F1 score because it is a mean of Precision and Recall as well as it has given an excellent performance for incorrectly classified cases rather than accuracy.

We have developed four models and got the best result by using word2vec embedding. That model has reduced our time and space complexity and provided us the highest accuracy. Alongside 80-20 splitting for the training and testing data depicted in Table 4, we have split 70% training and 30% testing data in Table 6 then, 75% training and 25% testing data in Table 7. Basically, we have got the best result in Word2vec CNN-LSTM model for splitting 80% training and 20% testing data with an accuracy of 90.49% and an F1 score of 92.83% for three basic emotions from 3000 Bangla comments by using Word2vec hybrid model (CNN-LSTM). They have [12] used the same dataset for the same three emotions, but their overall accuracy was 78.6% which is lower than our proposed method. In this paper [11], they have got 77.16% by using only 301 sentences and defined only two basic emotions. We have tried to implement the best model rather than the existing model. In [12], they also have used the same dataset but we have got a better result using our hybrid model for three emotions.

Table 6. Word2vec CNN-LSTM model (70% training & 30% testing data)

Model	Accuracy	F1 score
Embedding layer	44.53%	36.51%
Word2vec	77.67%	84.94%
CBOW	77.44%	82.54%
Glove	82.40%	87.33%

Table 7. Word2vec CNN-LSTM model (75% training & 25% testing data)

Model	Accuracy	F1 score
Embedding layer	44.53%	36.51%
Word2vec	86.13%	89.12%
CBOW	83.20%	88.26%
Glove	82.40%	87.33%

5   Conclusions

Our effort was to give priority to identify the right way to define the emotion from text accurately and to create something that has not been done yet. In Bangladesh, people use social media for sharing their emotion, branding their products, sharing information. It is very tough to get exact emotion in Bangla language because people express the same emotion writing it by using different structures. It is difficult to retrieve emotion from texts; the area of English language consists most of the works. Our first contribution is to create a hybrid Bangla language CNN-LSTM model and the second contribution is to get a better result than the existing models. We have also created Bangla language CNN and LSTM. Now when people will work with the Bangla language, they can use it. It will reduce their time. We have created the hybrid model with different Word Embedding's to find the best model that will provide us higher accuracy and reduce loss. We have built a model can detect emotion with a good accuracy that has been shown in the result part. Due to imbalanced dataset, there aroused some problems. And hence we had to work with only three emotions, but in our future study, we would like to create our balanced dataset and would like to work with more emotions. Negations can be handled too for better performance.

References

1. Sarkar, K.: Sentiment polarity detection in bengali tweets using deep convolutional neural networks. J. Intell. Syst. **28**(3), 377–386 (2019). https://doi.org/10.1515/jisys-2017-0418
2. Emon, E.A., Rahman, S., Banarjee, J., Das, A.K., Mittra, T.: A deep learning approach to detect abusive Bengali text. In: 2019 7th International Conference on Smart Computing & Communications (ICSCC) (2019). https://doi.org/10.1109/icscc.2019.8843606
3. Hassan, A., Mohammed, N., Azad, A.: Sentiment Analysis on Bangla and Romanized Bangla Text (BRBT) using Deep Recurrent models, October 2016. https://arxiv.org/abs/1610.00369. https://www.researchgate.net/publication/308831680_Sentiment_Analysis_on_Bangla_and_Romanized_Bangla_Text_BRBT_using_Deep_Recurrent_models/citation/download
4. Banik, N., Rahman, M.H.H.: Evaluation of naïve bayes and support vector machines on bangla textual movie reviews. In: 2018 International Conference on Bangla Speech and Language Processing (ICBSLP), pp. 1–6 (2018). https://doi.org/10.1109/ICBSLP.2018.8554497. https://ieeexplore.ieee.org/document/8554497
5. Abdul-Mageed, M., Ungar, L.: EmoNet: Fine-grained emotion detection with gated recurrent neural networks. In: Proceedings of the 55th Annual Meeting of the Association for Computational Linguistics, vol. 1, Long Papers, Vancouver, Canada, pp. 718–728 (2017). https://doi.org/10.18653/v1/p17-1067
6. Das, D., Bandyopadhyay, S.: Developing Bengali WordNet Affect for Analyzing Emotion (2010). https://www.semanticscholar.org/paper/Developing-Bengali-WordNet-Affect-for-Analyzing-Das-Bandyopadhyay/cb8e29ffe894321a34aa50d302d022f207e5a73a
7. Banik, N., Rahman, Md.: Toxicity Detection on Bengali Social Media Comments using Supervised Models, November 2019. https://doi.org/10.13140/RG.2.2.22214.01608
8. Irtiza Tripto, N., Eunus Ali, M.: Detecting multilabel sentiment and emotions from Bangla youtube comments. In: 2018 International Conference on Bangla Speech and Language Processing (ICBSLP), Sylhet, pp. 1–6 (2018). https://doi.org/10.1109/icbslp.2018.8554875
9. Abujar, S., Masum, A.K.M., Mohibullah, M., Ohidujjaman, Hossain, S.A.: An approach for Bengali text summarization using Word2Vector. In: 2019 10th International Conference on Computing, Communication and Networking Technologies (ICCCNT), Kanpur, India, pp. 1–5 (2019). https://doi.org/10.1109/icccnt45670.2019.8944536
10. Canales, L., Strapparava, C., Boldrini, E., Martinez-Barco, P.: Intensional learning to efficiently build up automatically annotated emotion corpora. IEEE Trans. Affect. Comput. 1–1 (2017). https://doi.org/10.1109/taffc.2017.2764470
11. Rahman, M.A., Seddiqui, M.H.: Comparison of classical machine learning approaches on Bangla textual emotion analysis. ArXiv:190707826 *Cs.* http://arxiv.org/abs/1907.07826 (2019). Accessed 19 Mar 2020
12. Azmin, S., Dhar, K.: Emotion detection from Bangla text corpus using Naïve Bayes classifier. In: 2019 International Conference on Electrical Information and Communication Technology (ECIT), Khulna, 1–5 Dec 2019. https://doi.org/10.1109/eict48899.2019.9068797
13. Sharmin, S., Chakma, D.: Attention-based convolutional neural network for Bangla sentiment analysis. AI Soc. (2020). https://doi.org/10.1007/s00146-020-01011-0
14. Ahmed, A., Yousuf, M.A.: Sentiment analysis on Bangla text using Long Short-Term Memory (LSTM) recurrent neural network. In: Kaiser, M.S., Bandyopadhyay, A., Mahmud, M., Ray, K. (eds.) Proceedings of International Conference on Trends in Computational and Cognitive Engineering. Advances in Intelligent Systems and Computing, vol. 1309. Springer, Singapore (2021). https://doi.org/10.1007/978-981-33-4673-4_16
15. Rahman, M., Haque, S., Saurav, Z.R.: Identifying and categorizing opinions expressed in Bangla sentences using deep learning technique. Int. J. Comput. Appl. **176**(17), 0975–8887 (2020)

Networking and Communications

Bit Error Rate Analysis of Optical Switch Buffer in Presence of Dispersion and Optical Amplifier Noise

Utkarsh Shukla[1]([✉]) [iD], Niraj Singhal[1] [iD], Pronaya Bhattacharya[2] [iD], and Rajiv Srivastava[3] [iD]

[1] Department of Computer Science and Engineering, School of Engineering and Technology, Shobhit Institute of Engineering and Technology, Deemed-to-be-University, Meerut, 250110, India

[2] Department of Computer Science and Engineering, Institute of Technology, Nirma University, Ahmedabad 382481, Gujarat, India
pronoya.bhattacharya@nirmauni.ac.in

[3] Indian Institute of Technology, Jodhpur, Rajasthan, India

Abstract. In modern data centers, recently optical interconnects are heavily deployed to manage the performance bottlenecks, owing to the inherent nature to support large-scale bandwidth at low-latencies. Due to this, optical communication has gained popularity in recent studies. However, at the physical layer, information bits are transferred through optical signals that use very narrow Gaussian pulses, normally generated by a mode lock laser. As these pulses propagate in the optical fiber, the generated power of the pulses deteriorates and thus the detrimental effect of pulse broadening takes place. Due to this, inter-symbol interference occurs at the physical layer, which results in high information loss at different data-center applications. To address the mentioned limitation, dispersion compensated fibers can be used to narrow the pulse broadening via wide Gaussian vectors. Thus, to address the challenges, the paper proposes a scheme to compensate for the detrimental effect of dispersion and amplifier noise on fiber delay lines based on the optical buffer. In simulations, it has been found that buffer fiber length cannot be ignored (as done in past studies) for power budget analysis. It is also found that buffer design is a complex problem, and successful buffer implementation depends on the number of bits stored bit rate, and dispersion, and losses of the buffer.

Keywords: Optical switch · FDL · Dispersion · Power budget

1 Introduction

The past decade has witnessed an unprecedented rise in multimedia traffic that has leveraged new technological innovations to support the ever-growing demand for data-centric applications. To support the paradigm shift, routing of data through optical networks, supported by optical components is required. The current electrical networks are limited

© Springer Nature Switzerland AG 2021
N. Chaubey et al. (Eds.): COMS2 2021, CCIS 1416, pp. 155–167, 2021.
https://doi.org/10.1007/978-3-030-76776-1_11

by bandwidth and line-rate limitations and are thus not scalable in the near future. However, all-optical communication is much-hyped and market deployments are far from reality [1]. The present optical components and nodes are mainly point-to-point interfaces, where the switching operations are carried out in the electrical domain. Thus, at the physical layer, there are noise and non-linear losses, and data exchange suffers from high energy dissipation for the interconversion of data from electrical-to-optical domains, and vice versa at edge nodes at sender and receiver [2, 5]. Thus, modern data centers are faced with stringent challenges of switching conversions that hinder the optimum utilization of bandwidth through telecom networks. Also, once the data is aggregated at rack servers, they face stringent bottlenecks in data forwarding. Figure 1 depicts the timeline of the present electrical technology, and the future envisioned all-optical networks. By 2030, it is expected that there would be a convergence to hybrid networks combining the best of both worlds-electrical and optical forwarding. With hybrid networks, the quest is also towards building scalable and resilient all-optical data centers.

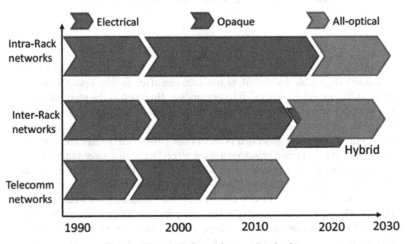

Fig. 1. Timelines for various technologies

Owing to the inherent complexity, and magnitude of scaling-up the network components, the transition to optical devices and counterparts is not an easy task. Moreover, optical storage elements are not into production deployments, and thus optical buffering of optical bursts, and optical packets is not possible. To support the buffering nature, fiber-delay lines are built as recirculator elements that move the data through delay lines, with the difference in slot units and pulse durations, to achieve a pulse locking loop [3]. Also, to forward data from specified input to output slots in the optical switches, point-to-point interconnections are set-up through arrayed waveguide grating that supports tunable wavelength convertors for real-time wavelength conversion. Thus, optical switching supports dynamic wavelength division multiplexing. To support the high-end wavelength parallelism, a hybrid buffer-based switch is designed where data moves in the optical domain while data control operations are performed using electronic processors [4]. In a similar context, researchers globally have proposed optical switch designs that cater to the need of dispersion, and fiber losses, based on selective buffering mechanisms [5–15]. The proposed switches support diverse parameters and pre-conditions to manage and orchestrate the network traffic at the Top-of-Rack based interconnections. Optical racks are differentiated as intra-rack and inter-rack communication based on the managed network traffic. In case the traffic is managed internally, it is intra-rack, and if traffic is balanced between racks it is inter-rack [20, 22]. The design analysis of the optical switch was proposed in [16], and later on, similar analysis has been carried out on many switch designs. The switch design analysis is equally applicable to feed-forward [5], feed backward [9–13], bufferless, and for re-circulating [10–18] type buffers. Each switch design has its own set of advantages and limitations in handling the optical traffic.

1.1 Novelty

Researchers in the past have analyzed the detrimental effects of the dispersion in optical channels. However, efficient techniques of management of dispersion effects are limited, as huge data is aggregated, which results in higher bit rates and pulse broadening takes place briskly. To address the limitation, and fill the research gap, the paper proposes an optical switch design that uses components that minimizes the dispersion effect. The switch considers the physical analysis based on fiber length, with splice losses, which is neglected in earlier state-of-the-art approaches. The switch analysis is proposed in terms of parameters like power, noise, and bit-error-rates (BER), and it is established that the length of the fiber and the effect of dispersion have a big impact in designing an efficient switch buffer.

1.2 Research Contributions

The following are the research contributions of the paper-

1. A switch design is proposed to address re-circulations in available buffer, where packets can be stored for longer durations, with a Gaussian pulse launch seeded to the input of the switch and the effect of dispersion is computed.
2. Based on the Gaussian distribution, a suitable mathematical analysis of the switch is carried out for the physical layer, and power dissipation is computed.
3. Simulations are carried out in a detailed manner to measure the losses incurred at the physical and link-layer through the measurement of BER of the switch, and noise-related factors.

1.3 Layout

The remainder of the article is now organized as follows. Section 2 discusses the proposed switch design and the mathematical analysis of the switch. Section 3 discusses the performance evaluation of the switch in terms of physical layer performance parameters, and finally, Sect. 4 concludes the paper.

2 The Proposed Optical Switch Design

In this section, we propose the recirculating-type buffer switch design, where packets can be stored for longer durations [21]. In Fig. 2, non-contending packets are directly passed through the switch, and the packets that experience contention are placed in the buffer till the contention at the output line is resolved. To achieve the functionality, we place fiber delay lines (FDLs) in the buffer that presents the optical delay slots, based on the packet length. The slots lengths are kept in the range of 1 to m packets durations. Let the length of the packet be 'L', then the maximum length of the FDL is 'mL', and if a packet re-circulates 'K' times then the total traverse distance is mLK.

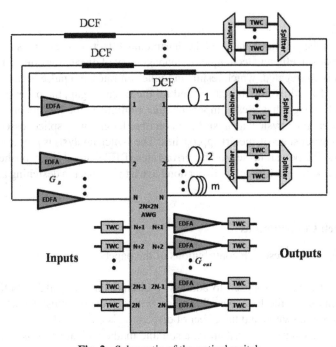

Fig. 2. Schematic of the optical switch

During the packet recirculations, the switching loss that occurred can be computed as follows-

$$A_C = A_{AWG}A_{Splitter}A_{TWC}A_{Combiner}A_{EDFA}A_F \qquad (1)$$

Consider a Gaussian pulse launch at the input of the fiber then input pulse can be written as

$$F(0, t) = A_0 \exp\left[-\frac{\tau^2}{2\tau_0^2}\right] \qquad (2)$$

The pulse propagation within the fiber is modelled by non-linear Schrödinger equation and read as [19]

$$\frac{\partial A}{\partial z} + \beta_1 \frac{\partial A}{\partial t} + \frac{i}{2}\beta_2 \frac{\partial^2 A}{\partial t^2} = i\gamma |A|^2 A \tag{3}$$

The term $\frac{i}{2}\beta_2 \frac{\partial^2 A}{\partial t^2}$ accounts for chromatic dispersion while the term $i\gamma |A|^2 A$ accounts for fiber non-linearity. As in optical switch, small pieces of dispersion compensated fibers (DCF) are used, therefore the non-linear effect that arises due to DCF can be neglected.

The evolve pulse at distance 'z' can be written as described in [4]

$$|F(z,t)| = A_0 \left[\frac{\tau_0^4}{\tau_0^4 + (k_0'' z)^2} \right]^{1/4} \exp \left[-\frac{(t - k_0' z)^2 \tau_0^2}{2(\tau_0^4 + (k_0'' z)^2)} \right] \tag{4}$$

where we use the property $|\tau_0^2 + jk_0'' z| = \sqrt{\tau_0^4 + (k_0'' z)^2}$. The effective width is determined from the argument of the exponent is depicted as follows [4]:

$$\tau^2 = \frac{\tau_0^4 + (k_0'' z)^2}{\tau_0^2} \Rightarrow \tau = \left[\tau_0^2 + \left(\frac{k_0'' z}{\tau_0} \right)^2 \right]^{1/2} \tag{5}$$

Thus, the pulse width is broadened with increasing distance z. The amplitude decreases due to inverse relationship [4]. The peak maximum amplitude is depicted as follows

$$|F|_{\max} = A_0 \left[\frac{\tau_0^4}{\tau_0^4 + (k_0'' z)^2} \right]^{1/4} \tag{6}$$

Therefore power and effective width of the pulse after one circulation in module 1, is

$$P_{1,1} = \left(A_{AWGA} A_{Splitter} A_{TWC} A_{Combiner} A_{EDFA} A_F G_{1,1} \right) \left[\frac{\tau_0^4}{\tau_0^4 + (k_0'' L)^2} \right]^{1/2} P_{in}$$
$$+ n_{sp}(G_{1,1} - 1)h\nu B_o \tag{7}$$

$$\tau = \left[\tau_0^2 + \left(\frac{k_0'' L}{\tau_0} \right)^2 \right]^{1/2} \tag{8}$$

In the above equation $P_{in} = A_0^2$.

Therefore the power of the power pulse after one circulation in module m, is

$$P_{1,m} = \left(A_{AWGA} A_{Splitter} A_{TWC} A_{Combiner} A_{EDFA} A_F G_{1,m} \right) \left[\frac{\tau_0^4}{\tau_0^4 + (k_0'' mL)^2} \right]^{1/2} P_{in}$$
$$+ n_{sp}(G_{1,m} - 1)h\nu B_o \tag{9}$$

The effective pulse width is

$$\tau = \left[\tau_0^2 + \left(\frac{k_0'' mL}{\tau_0} \right)^2 \right]^{1/2} \tag{10}$$

Therefore the power of the power pulse after 'K' circulations in module 1 is

$$P_{K,1} = \left(A_{AWG} A_{Splitter} A_{TWC} A_{Combiner} A_{EDFA} A_F G_{K,1} \right)^K \left[\frac{\tau_0^4}{\tau_0^4 + (k_0'' KL)^2} \right]^{1/2} P_{in}$$
$$+ K n_{sp} (G_{K,1} - 1) h v B_o \tag{11}$$

The effective pulse width is

$$\tau = \left[\tau_0^2 + \left(\frac{k_0'' KL}{\tau_0} \right)^2 \right]^{1/2} \tag{12}$$

Therefore the power of the power pulse after 'K' circulations in module m is

$$P_{K,m} = \left(A_{AWG} A_{Splitter} A_{TWC} A_{Combiner} A_{EDFA} A_F G_{K,m} \right)^K \left[\frac{\tau_0^4}{\tau_0^4 + (k_0'' mKL)^2} \right]^{1/2} P_{in}$$
$$+ K n_{sp} (G_{1,m} - 1) h v B_o \tag{13}$$

The effective pulse width is

$$\tau = \left[\tau_0^2 + \left(\frac{k_0'' mKL}{\tau_0} \right)^2 \right]^{1/2} \tag{14}$$

Referring Eq. 6 to 13, the length of module 1 is given by

$$L = \frac{cb}{nB}. \tag{15}$$

The description and values of the parameters are given in Table 1 [7]. The length of 'm'th module is

$$L^m = m \frac{cb}{nB}, \tag{16}$$

Similarly, the length traversed in the mth module after K re-circulations is

$$L^m(K) = mK \frac{cb}{nB} \tag{17}$$

Based on the above formulation in Fig. 3(a), bits vs. lengths are plotted for different data rates. It is evident from the figure that upto 10^5 bits length, the distance is less than a km, but as the size of the packets increases (i.e., more number of bits) fiber length also increases. For 60 km, the data rate is around 40 Gbps. It is also important to note that

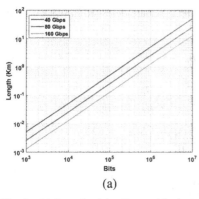 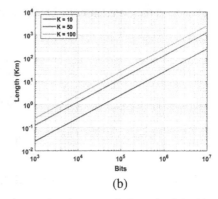

(a)   (b)

Fig. 3. (a) Length of the fiber vs bits in a packet under varying data rates (b) Length of the fiber packet under varying re-circulation counts

as the bitrate increases the length of the fiber decreases. But as the data rate increases the required pulse duration decreases ($T \sim 1/B$), again narrow pulse will disperse more. In Fig. 3(b), bits vs. fiber length are plotted while considering recirculation count as 10, 50, and 100. Here, it is clear that as the number of re-circulations increases, the length of the fiber increases, where the length can grow upto some 1000 km.

Referring to Eqs. (9) to (16), the important term is $k_0'' L = -1.2DL$, now by using dispersion compensated fiber using

$$D_1 L_1 + D_2 L_2 = 0, \tag{18}$$

$$L_1 + L_2 = L$$

In the above equation D_1, L_1 and D_2, L_2 are dispersions and length of the normal and DCF fiber respectively.

$$\frac{dD_1}{d\lambda} L_1 + \frac{dD_2}{d\lambda} L_2 = 0 \tag{19}$$

Using dispersion compensated fiber, the power of the signal can be written as

$$P_{K,m} = \left(A_{AWG} A_{Splitter} A_{TWC} A_{Combiner} A_{EDFA} A_F G_{K,m}\right)^K P_{in}$$
$$+ K n_{sp}(G_{1,m} - 1) h\nu B_o \tag{20}$$

In the above equation fiber loss, A_F is given by

$$A_F(dB) = 0.2 \times L_1 + 0.6 \times L_2 + 8 \times L_s \tag{21}$$

where L_1 is the length of normal fiber while L_2 is the loss of dispersion compensated fiber.

$$P_{K,m} = P(K) + P_{sp}(K) \tag{22}$$

For bit b the different noise components at the receiver are depicted in [6], and are presented as follows.

$$\sigma_s^2 = 2qRP(K)B_e$$

$$\sigma_{sp-sp}^2 = 2R^2 P_{sp}(K)(2B_o - B_e)\frac{B_e}{B_0^2}$$

$$\sigma_{sig-sp}^2 = 4R^2 P(K)\frac{P_{sp}(K)B_e}{B_0}$$

$$\sigma_{s-sp}^2 = 2qRP_{sp}(K)B_e$$

$$\sigma_{th}^2 = \frac{4K_B T B_e}{R_L} \tag{23}$$

The total noise variance for bit b is formulated in [12], which is presented as follows.

$$\sigma^2(b) = \sigma_s^2 + \sigma_{sp-sp}^2 + \sigma_{sp-sig}^2 + \sigma_{s-sp}^2 + \sigma_{th}^2 \tag{24}$$

$$BER = Q\left(\frac{I(1) - I(0)}{\sigma(1) + \sigma(0)}\right) \tag{25}$$

$$Q(z) = \frac{1}{\sqrt{2\pi}}\int_z^\infty e^{-\frac{z^2}{2}}\,dz \tag{26}$$

in this case $I(1) = RP(1)$ and $I(0) = RP(0)$ respectively denote the sampled photocurrents at the receiver end for the corresponding bits 1 and 0, and R depicts the responsivity at the receiver transmitter [7].

3 Performance Evaluation of the Proposed Switch

The simulation for the evolution of the Gaussian pulse is done in MATLAB, using the FFT technique, the total number of points in the time window is considered to be 1024 while taking the initial pulse width as 4 ps, and bit period of 10 ps. Table 1 presents the simulation parameters. Here the results are plotted for z = 10 km and z = 50 km. the evolution of the Gaussian pulse is solved using the split-step Fourier method. The evolution of the pulse as it moves along the fiber is shown in Fig. 5. The initial pulse of FWHM of 4 ps is considered and the power of 1 mW. After the propagation for a distance of 10 km, the FWHM is 9 ps and power is 0.43 mW. Similarly, after traversing a distance of z = 50 km, power is around 0.1 mW. This is the critical value in optical communication as the decision threshold is set $P_{Th} = \frac{P(1)+P(0)}{2}$. It is further noticeable that in optical systems OOK (On-Off keying) is employed. Therefore for a bit '1' a fixed power pulse is launched and for bit '0' no pulse is launched. As we have taken $P(1) = 1$ (mW). The threshold level will lie at 0.5.

Table 1. List of the Parameters [7]

Symbol	Parameter	Value
τ_0	Initial pulse FWHM	4 ps
P_{in}	Initial power	varies
D_1	dispersion coefficient [in ps/nm-km]	-15
D_2	dispersion coefficient [in ps/nm-km]	300
k_0''	Normalized constant	$-1.2D$
n_{sp}	Population inversion factor	1.4
G	A gain of the amplifier	20 dB
B	Bit rate	1GHz
n	Refractive index of the fiber	1.45
R	Responsively	1.28 A/W
e	Electronic charge	1.6×10^{-19} C
B_e	Electrical bandwidth	20GHz
B_0	Optical bandwidth	40GHz

Hence, it is clear from Fig. 4(a) that, dispersion compensation is a must. BER of the pulse after one circulation in module 1, is shown in Fig. 4(b) under dispersion compensation, it is important to note that as the bit rate increases the BER improves, due to lesser fiber length and consequently low loss. The acceptable limit of BER in most optical communication systems is $\leq 10^{-9}$. The poorest BER performance is observed for data rates of 40 Gbps and the recorded BER is 6.21×10^{-10} at the power of 290 μW. For the data rates of 80 Gbps, the required BER level is achieved at the power level of 80 μW, and for the data rates of 160 Gbps, the same is achieved at the power level of 40 μW.

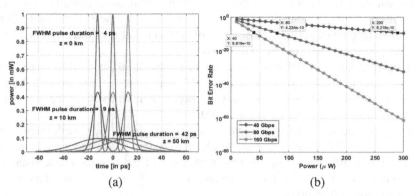

(a)   (b)

Fig. 4. (a) Evolution of Gaussian Pulses for different distances (b) Power vs. BER (b $= 10^7$)

In Fig. 5(a), power vs. BER is shown for the different re-circulation count for a data rate of 80 Gbps. Here, the value of the re-circulation count (K) is considered to be 10, 50, and 100, and results are presented for the first module of length 'L'. The first result is shown while considering 'K' as 10, i.e., in the first module data takes a maximum of 10 re-circulations. Here, to attain acceptable BER, the minimum required power is 0.75 mW. Next, we have considered the value of K as 50, now the required power level increases to 3.75 mW, and for $K = 100$, the required power increases to 7.5 mW, therefore, the required power increases due to increase in number of recirculations in buffer slots.

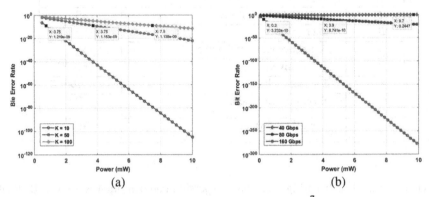

Fig. 5. (a)Power vs. BER under varying circulation counts (b $= 10^7$) (b) Power vs. BER under varying data rates (b $= 10^7$)

In Fig. 5(b), power vs. BER is shown, under different data rates, while considering 'm' $= 4$, therefore the length of the fiber is 'mL', and loss of the fiber also increases, as depicted in the Eq. (20). Power is considered to be 1 to 10 mW and data rates of 40, 80, and 160 Gbps. For 40 Gbps, the BER is very high and it is not advisable to use optical storage of data as at 40 Gbps. Data can be easily stored in a complementary metal-oxide-semiconductor (CMOS) chip that supports the additional overhead of optical to electronic conversions among the edge and the core nodes. At the data rate of 80 Gbps, the required amount of power is close to 4 mW and in the case of the data rate of 160 Gbps, the power required is close to 0.35 mW.

In Fig. 6(a), power vs. BER is shown, for a data rate of 80 Gbps, while considering 'm' $= 4$, therefore the length of the fiber is 'mL'. Here, power is considered to be 1 to 400 mW for $K = 10$, the required amount of power is 40 mW, for K $= 40$ power is 190 mW which increases to 380 mW for $K = 100$.

In Fig. 6(b), power vs. BER is shown, for a data rate of 160 Gbps, while considering 'm' $= 4$ and $K = 10$'. Here, power is considered to be 0 to 5 mW and packet sizes are considered to be 10^6 and 10^7 bits. For the packet size of 10^7 bits, the required amount of minimum power is 2.9 mW, and for a packet size of 10^6 bits, the required amount of minimum power is 0.28 mW.

Therefore, the above simulation demonstrates that as the allowed numbers of re-circulations increase, the required amount of the power also increases, and to avoid

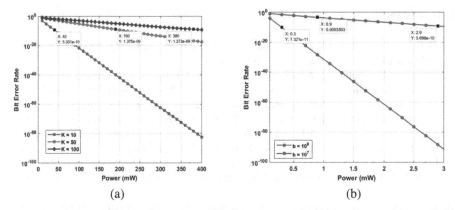

Fig. 6. (a) Power vs BER for different values of K (b) Power vs. BER for fixed data rate of 160 Gbps, and K = 10.

detrimental effects of nonlinearity power should be kept below 1 mW. It is not possible to use an optical buffer for the data rate of 40 Gbps and the required amount of power will be huge (~Watts). For the storage of 10^7 bits at the data rate of 80 Gbps unit length buffer ($m = 1$, where all the delay lines are of unit length) packets can stay in the buffer for 10 re-circulations. The variable delay lines buffer can be used at the data rate of 160 Gbps with the storage of 10^6 bits. In a nutshell, if the packet size is reduced then the variable delay line buffer can be used effectively.

4 Conclusions and Future Work

Current communication technology is migrating from electronic to optical. However, this migration is slow due to the technological limitations of optical communications (absence of tunable wavelength converters (TWC) and 3R regeneration. In optical communication role of an optical switch is vital thus many designs are proposed for resolving contentions at the switch node. However, to resolve the contention, an optical number of delay slots are required as more optical components induce unwanted noise and nonlinear effects that need to be evaluated at the physical, and link-level switch analysis. At the network layer, based on the amount of buffer, packet losses are computed. For analysis of physical layer losses- power, noise, and BER analysis is done. However, the analysis done in past has neglected the effect of dispersion on stored bits, which is an important parameter in high-speed communication. In this paper, we have carried out a power budget analysis while considering dispersion compensated fibers. It is found that dispersion compensated fibers have a great impact on the overall design of the buffer. It is also found that by adjusting stored bits and data rate ratio variable-length buffer can be utilized neglecting fiber non-linear effects.

As part of the future scope of the work, the authors would like to investigate the effects of buffer design for multiple cascaded switches, with due consideration to dispersion compensated fibers.

References

1. El-Bawab, T.S., Shin, J.D.: Optical packet switching in core networks: between vision and reality. IEEE Commun. Mag. **40**(9), 60–66 (2002)
2. Srivastava, R., Bhattacharya, P., Tiwari, A.K., Pathak, V.K.: Optical data centers router design with fiber delay lines and negative acknowledgement. J. Eng. Res. **8**(2), 165–176 (2020)
3. Singh, A., Tiwari, A.K., Bhattacharya, P.: Bit error rate analysis of hybrid buffer-based switch for optical data centers. J. Opt. Commun. (2019). https://doi.org/10.1515/joc-2019-0008
4. Bhattacharya, P., Tiwari, A.K., Ladha, A., Tanwar, S.: A proposed buffer based load balanced optical switch with AO-NACK scheme in modern optical datacenters. In: Singh, P.K., Panigrahi, B.K., Suryadevara, N.K., Sharma, S.K., Singh, A.P. (eds.) Proceedings of ICETIT 2019. LNEE, vol. 605, pp. 95–106. Springer, Cham (2020). https://doi.org/10.1007/978-3-030-30577-2_8
5. Kachris, C., Tomkos, I.: A survey on optical interconnects for data centers. IEEE Commun. Surv. Tutorials **14**(4), 1021–1036 (2012)
6. Srivastava, R., Gupta, V., Singh, Y.N.: Gain dynamics of EDFA in loop buffer switch. Opt. Switch. Network. **8**(1), 1–11 (2011)
7. Bhattacharya, P., Singh, A., Kumar, A., Tiwari, A.K., Srivastava, R.: Comparative study for proposed algorithm for all-optical network with negative acknowledgement (AO-NACK). In: Proceedings of the 7th International Conference on Computer and Communication Technology, pp. 47–51. ACM (2017)
8. Srivastava, R., Mangal, V., Singh, R.K., Singh, Y.N.: A modified photonic switch architecture based on fiber loop memory. In: 2006 Annual IEEE India Conference, pp. 1–5. IEEE (2006)
9. Shukla, V., Jain, A., Srivastava, R.: Physical layer analysis of arrayed waveguide based optical switch. Int. J. Appl. Eng. Res. **9**(21), 10035–10050 (2014)
10. Srivastava, R., Bhattacharya, P., Tiwari, A.K.: Dual buffers optical based packet switch incorporating arrayed waveguide gratings. J. Eng. Res. **7**(1), 1–15 (2019)
11. Shukla, V., Srivastava, R.: WDM fiber delay lines and AWG based optical packet switch architecture. In: Proceedings of National Conference on Innovative Trends in Computer Science Engineering (ITCSE-2015), pp. 47–49 (2015)
12. Singh, A., Singh, R., Bhattacharya, P., Pathak, V.K., Tiwari, A.K.: Modern optical data centers: design challenges and issues. In: Giri, V., Verma, N., Patel, R., Singh, V. (eds.) Computing Algorithms with Applications in Engineering. Algorithms for Intelligent Systems. Springer, Singapore (2020). https://doi.org/10.1007/978-981-15-2369-4_4
13. Singh, A., Tiwari, A.K., Srivastava, R.: Design and analysis of hybrid optical and electronic buffer based optical packet switch. Sādhanā **43**(2), 19 (2018)
14. Shukla, M.P., Srivastava, R.: Arrayed waveguide grating and re-circulating buffer based optical packet switch. J. Opt. Commun. (2018). https://doi.org/10.1515/joc-2018-0160
15. Bhattacharya, P., Tiwari, A., Singh, A.: Dual-buffer-based optical datacenter switch design. J. Opt. Commun. (2019). https://doi.org/10.1515/joc-2019-0023
16. Singh, O., Khare, M.R., Sharma, S., Srivastava, R.: Q function aware optical packet switch with low packet loss rate. J. Eng. Sci. Technol. **12**(3), 622–635 (2017)
17. Shukla, U., Singhal, N., Srivastava, R.: A large-capacity optical switch design for high-speed optical data centers. J. Opt. Commun. (2019). https://doi.org/10.1515/joc-2019-0217
18. Srivastava, R., Singh, R.K., Singh, Y.N.: Design analysis of optical loop memory. J. Lightwave Technol. **27**(21), 4821–4831 (2009)
19. Patel, R.B., Kothari, D.K.: Design and evaluation of 3.9 Tb/s (39 ch. × 100 Gb/s) hybrid transmission Multi-carrier WDM Optical System. Int. J. Microwave Opt. Technol. **13**(5), 442–453 (2018)

20. Kumar, R., Tripath, A.: Cross-layer optimization and cascadability of optical switches in fiber optic data networks. J. Opt. Commun. **1** (2018). https://doi.org/10.1515/joc-2018-0142
21. Shukla, V., Jain A., Srivastava, R.: Performance evaluation of an AWG based optical router. Opt. Quant. Electron. **48**(1) (2016)
22. Singh, A., Tiwari, A.K., Pathak, V.K, Bhattacharya, P.: Blocking performance of optically switched data centers. J. Opt. Commun. (2021). https://doi.org/10.1515/joc-2020-0263

Experimenting with Scalability of Software Defined Networks Using Pyretic and Frenetic

Manasa Kulkarni[1], Bhargavi Goswami[2(✉)], and Joy Paulose[1]

[1] CHRIST (Deemed to be University), Bangalore, Karnataka, India
[2] Queensland University of Technology, Brisbane, QLD, Australia
bhargavi.goswami@qut.edu.au

Abstract. Managing a corporate network has always been a challenge. The network consists of a variety of devices right from routers and switches to the firewalls. Centrally controlled Software Defined Networks has always been proposed as a solution to the current limitations of the traditional networks as it redefines the network. It has overcome the traditional networking limitations by separating the data and control plane. A new modular programming language is introduced that focuses on specifying the network policies for high-level abstractions that are embedded and implemented using Python on Software Defined Networks. In this paper, the authors throws light on the Frenetic, one of the high-level programming language which assess and implement the Pyretic policies to evaluate the performance of Software Defined Network by implementing and observing the scalability aspect of the futuristic SDN corporate networks. The experiment is being performed over the various topologies which range from 100 to 1000 nodes and further analyzing the Pyretic behaviour based on the obtained experimental results to demonstrate the scalability aspect of SDN based corporate networks. A diverse set of networking topologies are experimented by emulating SDN using Mininet and Iperf.

Keywords: Corporate networks · SDN · Pyretic · Frenetic · Mininet · iPerf · Network policy · Topologies · Gnuplot

1 Introduction

Network management is an error-induced task that includes various complexities and fragility if it is not managed properly. Networking involves integrating and configuring many individual tasks into one component which is written in multiple individual tasks. Until recently, the condition was difficult to set up all the devices, and configurations that were tightly coupled. In traditional networking, if there is any fault or a change in the network, the networking devices had to be replaced with another networking devices [1]. Switches, routers, firewalls were considered as separate devices earlier and it was quite difficult to replace and

© Springer Nature Switzerland AG 2021
N. Chaubey et al. (Eds.): COMS2 2021, CCIS 1416, pp. 168–192, 2021.
https://doi.org/10.1007/978-3-030-76776-1_12

secure those devices being costly [2]. SDN has replaced the controls and configuration by software rather than replacing the entire device. SDN has overcome the majority of the demerits of traditional networking. SDN introduces the feasibility to write multiple programs separately and merge them as a single bundle. SDN is one of the new emerging technologies in network management which promises to improve the monitoring of networks through dynamic programmability [3].

As a promising solution, languages like Pyretic and Frenetic can play a major role in implementing high-level abstraction on top of networking components in SDN [4]. Pyretic is recommended for southbound and Frenetic is for northbound functionalities which will facilitate network policy implementation through programming in SDN [5]. But, does the set of pyretic and frenetic programmable network functionality perform efficiently, resisting through fault tolerance to the growing network? This has been the major concern of the corporates which is stopping them from taking a plunge in investing into the huge SDN based infrastructure.

In this paper, Pyretic based network policy is implemented and demonstrated while scaling the network and bringing the network to bottleneck circumstances testing its stress and strain caliber. The biggest challenge was to imbibe the network policies on the entire SDN network through programmability [6]. The Frenetic and Pyretic languages are used together to impose high level abstraction on the application layer to achieve implementation of network policies that control the network while using the resources optimally [1,4,5]. The topologies are designed in the manner that includes widely used infrastructure trends in corporate. Initially, testing the network fault tolerance capabilities of smaller networks of 100 nodes, once the smaller networks are full proof in working condition the nodes are gradually added developing medium scale networks of 500 nodes. Further, addition of nodes continues until the network comes to a bottleneck situation reaching up to 1000 nodes. Using profound SDN network generation [7,8] and research tools such as pyretic, mininet, xterm, iperf and gnuplot, the entire set of experiments is emulated and tested rigorously followed by discussion on results and drawing the conclusion [9]. Thus, through this research authors provide a clear picture of futuristic networks by demonstrating the performance of pyretic and frenetic based SDN networks for small to large scale companies and help them in decision making regarding the best fit topology for their specific requirements.

The rest of the paper is organized in the following manner. Section 2 describes the architecture of the SDN. Section 3 discusses the Network policy implementation in SDN using Frenetic and Python. Section 4 provides details about tools and techniques of implementation. Section 5 describes the Experimental scenarios and apparatus. Section 6 provides details of the obtained results and discussions over the performance metrics. Section 7 concludes the research followed by References.

2   Related Work

In this section, the current approaches in Software Defined Networking are introduced by providing the necessary groundwork in the SDN languages and its policies by providing in detail the necessary context information. Frenetic is one of the query language for packet-forwarding policies.

2.1   SDN – Software Defined Networks Architecture

SDN is exciting innovation which simplifies the management and redefines the networks [10]. As discussed in the above section, SDN has overcome numerous demerits from traditional networking [11]. SDN facilitates useful APIs and higher-level abstractions [12]. It has an impact on future networks for placing the networking on a strong foundation. Benefits of SDN are majorly modularity, portability, efficiency, assurance, and simplicity [13].

SDN architecture majorly consists of various components: Networking devices that are "Data Plane", SDN controller which comes under "Control Plane", Southbound Interface API, Northbound Interface API, Application and Services and Network Operating System (NOS). Data Plane consists of physical and virtual networking devices. The main objective of the data plane is forwarding the packets. Control plane controls all the data plane devices via SDN Controller. It has the ability to control all the applications that are present in the application layer. The controller plays a vital role in communication with the lower and upper layers, which has a high capability to control all the functionalities. SDN Controller communicates with the SDN Switches with the help of Southbound APIs [14,15]. So far what is discussed about SDN is closely related to the provided SDN architecture in Fig. 1.

SDN separates the planes from the control plane which acts as the "brain" of the system and the data plane which acts as the "muscle" of the system. The Data plane receives the packets and further forwards the packets based on the flow-table. The control plane updates the flow table to specify where the packets should go. Data Plane processing is being done by the networking devices and the control plane processing is done by the controller. Southbound Interface is the interface between the controller and the networking devices (Data Plane). Northbound Interface is the interface between the controller and the application plane. Openflow switches are a part of SDN architecture that is directly programmable, agile, centrally managed, and programmatically configured. The agile system of SDN controls the network dynamically to meet the changing needs of the data traffic. SDN lets the network managers configure, secure, and manage the network resources with the help of automated SDN programs [16,17].

2.2   Frenetic: A Network Programming Language

Recent research has been considered for providing a variety of services. The languages used in today's networking lacks the modern features. In this paper,

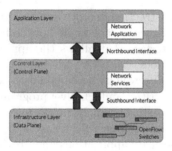

Fig. 1. SDN Architecture

author's throw light on the Frenetic, which is one of the high-level programming language for the distributed collection of switches. Author's present several contributions in this paper like: presenting a language-design, implementation of the language, and further analysing the key limitations of the language.

2.3   Modular SDN Programming with Pyretic

SDN is creating exciting new possibilities for developers of network applications. In this paper, author's throw light on the new network language called Pyretic, which is a Python-based framework that allows programmers to build sophisticated SDN applications. Further, describes the applications for Open-Flow Switches and Controllers. In addition, the authors address the policies that make Pyretic a simple and dynamic language in the field of networks.

2.4   Research Gap and Motivation

Pyretic is an unexplored dynamic networking language with a varied set of policies for SDN based network switches [2,18]. Even though a lot of literature states that it fits well the SDN requirements, real life scenarios are not implemented in the form of various topologies in current state of art. As per the authors claim, rigorous experimentation and testing using Pyretic is not done yet. This inspires us to fill this research gap by performing the experiment in three different scenario's and test the prominent cost influential parameters while increasing the scalability for the real-time corporate networks. The impact of Throughput, Jitter and Latency is high on network infrastructure implementation cost. therefore, these parameters are analysed in this paper to know the calibre of scalability of the Pyretic based SDN that are further tested in a keen aspect. After performing the experiment, we realized that the Pyretic tries to remove the barrier for creating numerous SDN applications which is a novel contribution by the researchers in current time.

3   FRENETIC and PYRETIC

Frenetic is the programming language for SDNs [2]. Programming the OpenFlow is not easy. OpenFlow is tied to the underlying hardware i.e. Southbound APIs

[2]. It allows the low-level abstraction in order to match the flow rules. Controllers see an event where the switches do not know how to handle it. But we need a high-level programming interface that allows the applications to talk with the controller. This opens the doors for network administrators cum developers to write these applications and develop the capabilities on the top of OpenFlow [18]. If the applications are written in high-level programming languages such as; Python, those applications need not to perform the low-level switch modifications to implement policies of abstractions [19]. Those applications work ideally on large switch abstraction, security applications and provide services. Northbound API provides a solution to the programming interface which helps the systems to program the network [2,19].

3.1 Frenetic

Best example of the programming language that is in northbound API is "Frenetic". It is also similar to SQL query language. Frenetic is present on the northbound API which allows the programmer to count the number of bytes and updates the counter every 60 s. Frenetic acts as an umbrella for SDN languages which majorly focuses on language designing and compiler implementation. There are two members of the Frenetic family they are: Pyretic and Frenetic Ocaml. Pyretic is embedded and implemented in Python. Frenetic Ocaml is embedded and implemented in Ocaml. It declares network policy and it is hardware independent. Frenetic has numerous features such as abstraction, returning a stream, aggregating the size of packets, filter using the high-level patterns, traffic monitoring and many more. The language "Pyretic" follows the theory of Frenetic [2,19].

3.2 Pyretic (Python + Frenetic)

Pyretic is one of the members of the Frenetic family of SDN programming languages. Pyretic is a Python-embedded programming language in SDN that is also programmer friendly. Pyretic is the SDN language and runtime. Pyretic focuses on how to specify the network policy at high-level rather than implementing it on the low-level OpenFlow rules. Pyretic is specifically implemented for the entire network at once. It helps in SDN modular programming. In traditional OpenFlow programming, the programmer cannot write the application modules separately instead forcing the programmers to merge the multiple programs without committing any mistakes. Pyretic integrates all the networking policies together and runs it as one application. Most importantly, SDN controllers allow the programmers to program in low-level API ie; "Assembly Language". Here, the programmer has to manipulate the bit patterns. This demerit is overcome which induces many additional features to make the work feasible and efficient. Pyretic suits for APIs and languages, traffic monitoring, sampling, testing, debugging, verification, virtualization of the network. It acts well when the system challenges for the scalability, fault-tolerance, performance, consistency, and upgradability [2,19].

Pyretic allows the operators to write the complex network policies as a function independently. It allows an operator to describe the packets including AND, OR and NOT operations. It provides the capabilities to specify and modify the virtual packet headers as metadata. In short, a pyretic program can combine multiple policies together making use of composition operators, parallel composition, and sequential composition. Finally, the pyretic provides the facility to create a dynamic policy by offering a rich topology-abstraction [2, 19].

3.3   Pyretic Network Policies

One of the major problems associated with high-level programming is the higher level of abstraction which involves writing the multiple modules. Finally, all these modules needed to be combined to form a single individual module to achieve the goal. To achieve this goal, we need composition operators that specify how these individual modules should be composed or combined into one application. Frenetic is one of the programming languages which is well-suited for the northbound APIs. In pyretic, all these networking policies are the functions that are used to map the packets with the other packets.

Composing Network Policies with Pyretic. As discussed in the above section, the high level of abstraction needs to have multiple modules where each of the modules is affected with the same traffic. There are two different ways to compose the policies. Parallel composition performs the operations simultaneously whereas, sequential composition performs one operation at a time and then operates on the next operation. For example, if one wishes to forward the traffic but also wants to count how much the traffic is being forwarded then, those two operations can be performed in parallel. Another way, performing the operations one after the other then it is considered as sequential composition. Generating Network load followed by the Load Balancing is the best example of sequential composition.

3.4   Pyretic Features

Pyretic offers a bundle of features. Firstly, it can take the input packets and further return the packets to their respective destination. It allows the implementation of network policy as a function. Secondly, the pyretic is the notion of Boolean predicates which do not allow the simple conjunction expressions such as AND, OR and NOT. It makes the programmer easier to refer to the packet locations. It helps to tag the packets which are present in the different locations in the program by applying specific functions on it. Pyretic provides composition operators such as parallel and sequential composition as discussed in the above section. Main features of pyretic include policy composition, predicates on packets, network policy as function and virtual packet headers. Let us understand the important Pyretic features in detail. In contrast, Pyretic makes writing complex policies easy.

Network Policy as a Function. The controller application defines the policy for the network in time at any moment. A traditional OpenFlow program includes the explicit logic that creates and sends installation rule messages to the switches and the registers. Pyretic, on the other hand, masks this low-level information by permitting the programmers to articulate the policies as compact, abstract functions. This will take a packet as an input and it returns a set of new packets to different locations. If it returns an empty set, then it corresponds to the packet drop. If a single packet return corresponds forwarding the packet to a new location. Multiple packet return corresponds to a multicast i.e., it takes input as a packet, returns packets at different locations.

Programmers can easily write one line that takes a packet which is located at any port on any switch in the network as an input i.e. flood(), where flood() is interpreted as a function. Pyretic programmers can write even more sophisticated policies for the fragment of policies which can be used for more pyretic features. In contrast, OpenFlow policies are bit patterns and in Pyretic, the polices are the functions that map packets to the other packets. Table 1 includes the list of network policies which are within the scope of the objectives of this research paper.

We make use of predicate policies (match and conjunction) to distinguish between the packets. Modification policies (fwd) are being used to change the header content or to change the location of the packets. Composition operators (+ for parallel composition and >> for sequential composition).

Table 1. Lists of Pyretic policies

Syntax	Summary
identity	It returns the original packet
drop/none	It returns an empty set
match (f = v)	It identifies the field f and matches v, else drops it
fwd (a)	It modifies (port = a)
flood ()	It returns one packet for each port on the network spanning tree.
modify (f = v)	It returns the packet with field f which is set to v

From Bits to the Boolean Predicates. An OpenFlow rule corresponds with a bit pattern of packets where each bit is a 0, 1 or "don't care". It is difficult to formulate a strategy with respect to bit patterns. Pyretic allows the programmers to write simple predicates which are of the form match (f = v), where f is the demanding field and v is the abstract value. Further, programmers can construct more complicated predicates making use of Boolean operators '&' (and) '—'

(or), and ' ' (not). All these predicates serve as filters. The packets need to pass through the filter. If the packet passes through the filter, it means it satisfies the predicate. If the incoming packet across the filter does not satisfy the predicate then it is dropped and Pyretic matches the function output of the packet or does nothing depending on the predicate.

Parallel and Sequential Composition. Composition makes it easy for the policies to build on one another. An application controller needs to perform multiple tasks such as: routing, load balancing, monitoring and access control. These all major tasks can affect the traffic handling. In traditional OpenFlow programming, multiple modules were being written separately and when all the modules were merged, led to interference of modules with each other. It so happens that one module might overwrite the rules of other modules, as a result, the module drops the significant packets which need to be sent to the destination address instead of getting dropped. Pyretic offers two composition operators to combine the policies in parallel and sequential manner. These two compositions are for composing complex policies.

Sequential Composition
Sequential composition (>>) c. It treats the output or resultant value of one policy as input for the next operation. For example: match (tip = '3.3.4.6') >> fwd(1). Here, the packets are passing through the filter in sequence with the forwarding policy fwd(1). That is; all the packets which are passed through the filter are being forwarded to the outport 1. Example includes: Firewall and switch.

Parallel Composition
Parallel composition (+) operates simultaneously alongside. It can combine the two policies and give a better result. A routing policy "P" can be expressed as; P = (match(dstip = '2.2.2.3') >> fwd(2)) + (match(dstip = '2.2.2.4') >> fwd(3)). The packets which are destined to 2.2.2.3 will be sent to the out port 2 and the packets which are destined to 2.2.2.4 will be sent to the out port 3. Example includes: counting, forwarding. In order to understand the parallel composition.

Traffic Monitoring. Traffic monitoring is all about the network flow monitoring which is being handled by a program, which keeps track of all the devices that are connected in the network. Traffic monitoring is a difficult job which depends on two major factors: QoS (Quality of Service), and Network Bandwidth. In the traditional OpenFlow programs, collecting the traffic statistics involves installing the rules and issuing the queries to poll these counters responses when they arrive and further needed to be combined across multiple rules and it was a tedious task.

In Pyretic, network monitors are simple policies that may be joined as a simple type of policy. Pyretic monitors the raw packets, packets count, and byte counts i.e. when a programmer creates a new query and forwards it requesting it to restrict web-traffic. The runtime system handles the low-level queries which are polling the counters, receiving the responses, combining the result, and composing the query implementation.

Topology Abstraction. This feature is said as "A Legacy Gateway Replacement". The controller application written in traditional OpenFlow programming for one switch cannot be easily ported to run over the distributed collection of switches. It is difficult to share the switch with other packet-processing applications. Load-balancer programs would help to overcome these problems. Whereas a good and best solution to overcome this problem is to make use of topology abstraction i.e. partition of the application into two pieces. a) One which does load balancing before as if the load balancer is being implemented on a big switch, which is connected to the hosts and further routes to lower level. b) Secondly, the load balancer is re-usable on any network of switches and it can be operated on any network. In order to develop this kind of scenario, Pyretic offers a library for topology abstraction that can represent multiple underlying switches as one single switch or can be derived alternatively, on underlying switches as multiple derived virtual devices.

Dynamic Policies. Query policies are often used to drive the changes after the implementation dynamically as per the requirement. These policies have vital behavior which changes over time according to the programmer's specification. The policies whose forwarding behavior changes and which are represented as the timeseries of the static policies. These policies, therefore, change the response to network change and further, query policies drive changes to the other policies. Dynamic policies have a behavior which occasionally changes over time. Query policies are being used to drive the changes to the dynamic policies. Mainly the policies dynamically change as per the changes are made in the queries.

4   Tools, Techniques and Simulation Environment

To conduct this experiment, Frenetic and Pyretic is used along with Mininet [20], xTerm [21], iPerf [22] and gnuplot [23]. Mininet is used as a simulator along with a POX controller as the SDN controller. The experiment is conducted on Virtual Machine (VM) with Linux Ubuntu platform. Table 2 provides the information about the specifications and configurations of VM and exact versions of tools used during the experimentation.

Table 2. Lists of Pyretic Policies

Tools	Configuration
Operating system	Ubuntu 14.04 LTS
Processor	2 CPUs
Memory	4 GB
Virtual machine	VM Ware Workstation 15 Pro
Mininet	2.2.0
Iperf	Version 3
Pyretic	64 bit VM
Gnuplot	5.2 (Stable)
Xterm	Xterm-351
Python	3.7

5   Experimental Procedure

Scalability of the Pyretic needs to be checked by creating the network emulation, with the help of Mininet. The switch (OpenFlow) is being used to create visual topology. It is necessary to write the python script which generates the desired customized topology. One of the objectives of the experiment is to test the Pyretic with numerous topologies like linear, single, reversed and custom (star, mesh and tree). Mininet is one of the best SDN based network emulators which creates the virtual hosts, switches, controllers and further connects all these components together. In this section step by step pyretic and SDN network generation is demonstrated.

There are several modes to run the Pyretic: a) interpreted i : mode "i" means, every packet is being processed in the controller runtime and it is useful for debugging. b) reactive r0: rules are being pushed actively to the switches based on the Pyretic policy. c) proactive p0: rules are being pushed to switches based on Pyretic policy. Generally, the highest performance mode is made currently available.

5.1   Running Pyretic with Mininet

Step 1: Open a new terminal using the command Ctrl + Alt + t and enter into the pyretic folder using the command cd pyretic/. After entering into the pyretic folder, update and install the additional packages in order to run the Pyretic. The command to update the packages is sudo apt-get update. Step 2: Run the controller using the command ./pyretic.py −m p0. If there is any error pop-up for the specific module, then install the module. In general, when the pyretic is run for the first time the error "no module named yappi" is being popped. To solve the error, install the module error by using the command sudo pip install yappi. After installing the module, run again and check the controller run.

It asks to mention the modules. We can start the Pyretic using the following command ./pyretic.py –m p0 pyretic.modules.mac_learner and the Pyretic starts running on the POX controller. MAC learner module is used for the dynamic policies and it is used to learn where the hosts are located. It is an effective module which works very well for the shortest path routing and multicast trees. The MAC learning module sees the network as one "Big Switch" and one of its ports being connected with the underlying hardware device/physical network. Below is the figure which shows the Pyretic being connected to the frontend, run over POX controller.

Next step is running Pyretic with Mininet and configuring the Mininet emulator with the Pyretic and POX controller. Open a new terminal using the command Ctrl + Alt + t. Type the topology command to start running the topology. Type the topology command to run the mininet for example "sudo mn –topo linear,3 –controller=remote, ip=192.168.56.133, port=38916". Test the connectivity between the host by command: h1 ping h2. For checking all the links command: pingall. If the ping is through, the frenetic and pyretic based SDN is up and running.

5.2   Generating Topologies

Topology is the arrangement of networking components connected optimally in accordance with the physical infrastructure. It determines the physical and logical layout of the network. There are numerous topologies which can be generated. But, the most conspicuous necessity is to find out the best fit topology that suits the Pyretic with POX for the corporate environment. To get a better insight of the topology, understanding the topologies is necessary. Every topology has its own pros and cons. Every topology has its own function and performs according to their physiological aspects. Figure 2 describes the base structure which is expanded to include large scale nodes from 100 to 1000.

Single Topology. Single Topology is one of the topology types which is connected to a single switch and which is further having multiple hosts. It is connected to one OpenFlow switch and k-hosts. The command to run the single topology is sudo mn –topo single, 100 –controller=remote, ip=192.168.56.133.

Linear Topology. Linear Topology connects with k-switches and k-hosts, which are connected to a single switch and which share a common cable line to transfer the data. Every switch is connected with each host. The command to run the linear topology is sudo mn –topo linear, 100 –controller=remote, ip=192.168.56.133.

Tree Topology. As the name suggests, it is a different structure which connects with its branches of a tree. It has a parent node which is connected with the two child nodes and further each child node branches to two sub child nodes. The command to run this topology is sudo mn –topo tree, 100 –controller=remote,

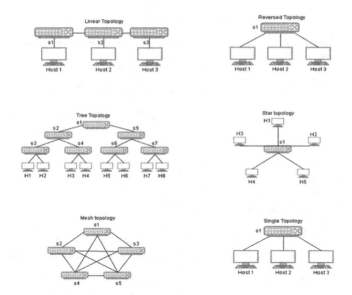

Fig. 2. Basic topologies considered for the Pyretic and Frenetic based SDN Networks scaling from 100 to 1000 nodes

ip=192.168.56.133. There is another way to run tree topology and design it with the help of depth and fanout. The command for tree topology is sudo mn –topo tree, 2, 10 –controller=remote, ip=192.168.56.133 where depth=2 and fanout=10.

Reversed Topology. Reversed Topology is quite similar to the single topology but it works in a reversed manner and it is connected in a reverse way. The command to run this topology is sudo mn –topo reversed, 100 –controller=remote, ip=192.168.56.133

Mesh Topology. Mesh Topology is the one where every device is interconnected with each other. It has multiple connections. It is widely used for the best distribution of the network. It is not a built-in topology therefore, we need to generate it using custom topology. It needs to be run from the custom folder present in the mininet folder. The command to run this custom topology is sudo mn –custom mesh.py –controller=remote, ip=192.168.56.133, port=38916.

Star Topology. Star Topology is one of the special types of topology which individually connects to the central node. It is also a custom topology, it is not a built-in topology. The command to run this topology is similar to tree topology along with its file name sudo mn –custom star.py –controller=remote, ip=192.168.56.133, port=38916. Figure 3 provides the insight of the python based code of custom topology where demonstration includes two topologies, mesh (left) and star (right).

```
/*** Mesh Topology***/                              /*** Star Topology*** /|
class OVSBridgeSTP( OVSSwitch ):                    def emptynet():
    prio = 1000                                         net = Mininet( topo=None, build=False )
    def start( self, *args, **kwargs ):                 info( '*** Adding controller\n' )
        OVSSwitch.start( self, *args, **kwargs )        net.addController('c0', controller=RemoteController,ip="192.168.56.133",port=38916)
        OVSBridgeSTP.prio += 1                          info( '*** Adding hosts\n' )
        self.cmd( 'ovs-vsctl set-fail-mode', self, 'standalone' )    hosts=[]
        #self.cmd( 'ovs-vsctl set-controller', self )   for h in range(100):#change here for number of hosts
        self.cmd( 'ovs-vsctl set Bridge', self,             hosts.append('h%s' % (h+1))
                  'stp_enable=true',                    info( '*** Adding switch\n' )
                  'other_config:stp-priority=%d' % OVSBridgeSTP.prio )    switches = []
switches = { 'ovs-stp': OVSBridgeSTP }                  for i in range(6):#change here for number of switches
class test(Topo):                                           switches.append('s%d' % (i+1))
    "Demo Setup"                                        for h in hosts: #create hosts
    def __init__( self, enable_all = True ):                globals() [h]= net.addHost(h)
        "Create custom topo."                           for s in switches:#create switches
                                                            globals() [s] = net.addSwitch(s, cls=OVSSwitch)
        Topo.__init__( self )                           info( '*** Creating links\n' )
                                                        i=n=0;
        # Init values                                   for h in hosts:
        switches = 10     # total switches                  net.addLink(h,switches[i])
        cons = 1          # connections with next switch    n+=10
        if cons >= switches:                                if(n==10):#number of host per switch
            cons = switches - 1                                 i+=1
        hosts = 30        # nodes per switch                    n=0
                                                        net.addLink(s1,s6)
        # Create host and switch                        net.addLink(s2,s6)
        # Add link :: host to switch                    net.addLink(s3,s6)
        for s_num in range(1,switches+1):               net.addLink(s4,s6)
            switch = self.addSwitch("s%s" %(s_num))     net.addLink(s5,s6)
            for h_num in range(1,hosts+1):              net.addLink(s1,s2)
                host = self.addHost("h%s" %(h_num + ((s_num - 1) * hosts)))    net.addLink(s2,s3)
                self.addLink(host,switch)               net.addLink(s3,s4)
                                                        net.addLink(s4,s5)
        # Add link :: switch to switch                  net.addLink(s5,s1)
        for src in range(1,switches+1):                 info( '*** Starting network\n' )
            for c_num in range(1,cons+1):               net.start()
                dst = src + c_num                       for s in switches:
                if dst <= switches:                         globals() [s].cmd('ovs-vsctl set bridge %s stp-enable=true' % (s))
                    print("s%s" %src,"s%s" %dst)        info( '*** Running CLI\n' )
                    self.addLink("s%s" %src,"s%s" %dst) CLI( net )
                else:                                   info( '*** Stopping network' )
                    dst = dst - switches                net.stop()
                    if src - dst > cons:
                        print("s%s" %src,"s%s" %dst)    if __name__ == '__main__':
                        self.addLink("s%s" %src,"s%s" %dst)    setLogLevel( 'info' )
topos = { 'test': ( lambda: test() ) }                  emptynet()
```

Fig. 3. Custom topology snippet of Mesh and Star Topology

5.3 Traffic Generation and Logging Network Events

This section includes the step by step procedure of graph generation with the help of Iperf and Mininet. Iperf is a network measurement tool, which tests the traffic, and checks the performance of the network. Iperf gives the detail of delay, throughput and bandwidth. Here, analysing the performance based on these parameters and performing the task at TCP and UDP. Xterm provides a platform for generating client server architecture on SDN networks, which helps the hosts to connect through commands. Below are the steps followed to obtain logs to analyse the topologies for TCP protocol and UDP protocol. Step 1: Open a terminal using the command Ctrl+Alt+T Step 2: Run the topology as discussed in the above sections and once the topology execution is run type pingall to make sure all the links are running. Step 3: Type xterm h1 h2 which opens two xterm emulators h1 and h2. Step 4: Goto the h2 terminal of the xterm and type the command iperf3 -s -p 5566 -w 5000 -i 1 > result. Here -w is the window size which is used only for the TCP, -s is the server mode, -p is the port number of the iperf server, -i is the interval on which the server will measure the traffic and result is the output file where the data will be stored. It means, this command is executed at the server end. Along with this is command, another command needs to be run at the client. Step 5: Next, goto the h1 terminal of the xterm and type the command iperf3 -c 10.0.0.2 -p 5566 -w 5000 -t 150. Here -c is the client mode, -p is the port number of the iperf client, -t is the time in seconds ie; the command executes for 150 s. Step 6: Once the step 4 and step 5 starts running successfully then, goto the mininet terminal and type h1 ping h2 > resultant.txt. Here, this command stores the latency data into the text file later we can filter the data and check its correctness. Step 7: Once the data are being stored into the output file, the next step is to filter the data and plot the graph. The command to filter the values is cat result | grep sec | head -150 | tr - ' ' | awk '{print $2,$5}' > new_result. Here, new_result is the filtered data output file which contains 150 data values. This data is ready for plotting the graph. Step 8: In order to calculate the jitter, bandwidth and data transfer, there is a need to run the iperf server in the UDP mode and further store the data into the file. The command used to run at the h2 terminal which is the iperf server is iperf 3 -s -u -p 5566 -w 5000 -i 1 > result. Step 9: Along with this command need to run another command in the iperf client i.e.; h1 terminal. The command is iperf3 -c 10.0.0.2 -u -b 10M -p 5566 -w 5000 -t 150. Here, -u is the UDP traffic, -b sets the maximum bandwidth, -p is port, -w is for setting buffer socket buffer size and -t is for setting the duration of test and in our case, it is 150 s. Once the execution is completed and the data is being retrieved into the file then filter the data as discussed in step 7 and store the resultant data into a new output file. Step 10: Once the execution stops then goto the mininet terminal and press Ĉ to stop the execution and filter the latency values according to the command provided in step 7. Similarly, filter the values of Jitter and Throughput from the result file and plot the graph. In the next sections, a deep dive of plotting the graph with the help of graph script and analysing the graph based on the Throughput, Jitter and Latency parameters is described.

5.4   Graph Generation

This section provides the resultant performance metrics obtained during the experimentation in the form of graphs. The purpose is to try maximum possible topological diversity while scaling the network from 100 to 1000 nodes to support decision making for corporate networks. Step by step while imposing diverse networking conditions, incrementing nodes gradually. The experiment is run for 150 s on a fixed note to observe the variations. The values are captured and analysed with crucial networking parameters. To have a better insight into the performance metrics, the experiment is classified into TCP and UDP protocols for 100, 500 and 1000 nodes representing small, medium and large scale corporate networks. Making use of GNUPLOT to plot the graphs for the different scenarios.

Graph Script provided in Fig. 4 gets executed after running the GNUPLOT and it needs to be modified as per the requirements of the individual parameter and scenario. But the below commands are very necessary for plotting the graph. Figure 7 describes one of the graph generation scripts for 1000 nodes.

6   Performance Metrics and Result Discussions

Scenario 1 is running the Pyretic for 100 nodes and checking its correctness and scalability for 6 different topologies. The Pyretic is run for six major topologies

```
set terminal png
set output 'UDP_Resultant_1000_nodes.png'
set title "Topologies run over UDP protocol for 1000 nodes"
set xrange[0:150]
set xtics 10
set yrange[0:250]
set ytics 25
set xlabel "Time (in seconds)"
set ylabel "Throughput (in MBytes)"
set style data line
set grid
set key box
plot "Single_topology" with line,"Linear_topology" with line,
"Reversed_topology" with line, "Mesh_topology" with line,
"Tree_topology" with line, "Star_topology" with line
```

Fig. 4. Graph Script for generating graphs for the topology comparison

to check its scalability. Scenario 2 is running the Pyretic for 500 nodes and Scenario 3 is running the Pyretic for 1000 nodes. The throughput and latency are the major features under observation. Again, the tests are conducted for real time and reliable connections. Therefore, TCP and UDP, two different types of flows are observed for all the three scenarios. For TCP flows, latency is observed and for UDP flows, jitter is observed during the experiment. Results are being represented with the help of graphs. Different factors are measured and checked to find out the performance of the Pyretic using POX. We analyse the performance based on the different parameters like: Throughput, Jitter and Latency.

6.1 Throughput

Throughput is the measure of the data packets sent over the network to the destination address. Its capacity is measured in bits per seconds or MBytes. It is the transfer of the data in the network. Throughput is calculated for TCP and UDP protocols for 100, 500 and 1000 nodes. From Figs. 5, 6, 7, 8, 9 and 10 throughput graphs are plotted for UDP and TCP.

UDP Throughput. Considering the UDP throughput for 100–500 nodes, it can be observed that the performance of small to large scale corporate scenarios perform at the average of 150 MBytes for all the topologies except linear and star. With increasing nodes, the performance of linear topology further degrades whereas star topology remains consistent but lower in comparison of other topologies. But, on contrast, the star topology performs equivalent to other topologies once the network scales to 1000 nodes and linear topology performance also improves; however, still linear topology remains lower than remaining efficient topologies.

TCP Throughput. Considering the throughput graph provided in Figs. 8, 9 and 10, we recommend small business to avoid linear topology. The spikes

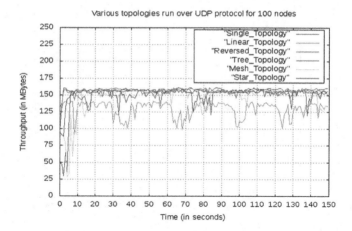

Fig. 5. UDP Throughput v/s Time for connectionless real time traffic for 100 nodes.

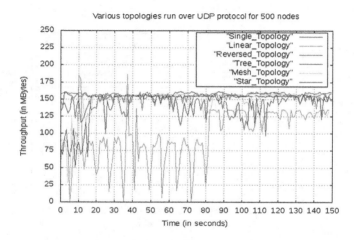

Fig. 6. UDP Throughput v/s Time for connectionless real time traffic for 500 nodes.

observed during the first 70 s clearly indicate that stability and reliability requirements of connection oriented flows cannot be met by linear topology for small
scale SDNs. While gradually scaling to medium and large scale networks, linear topology performs at par with the other topologies. However, with large
scale networks, performance of reversed topology degrades drastically and cannot recover until 120 s and therefore, reversed topology is not recommended for
large scale networks. After observing the overall performance of multiple topologies, dynamic and hybrid networking requirements of business can be fulfilled by
tree topology which performs better for real-time as well as reliable networks.

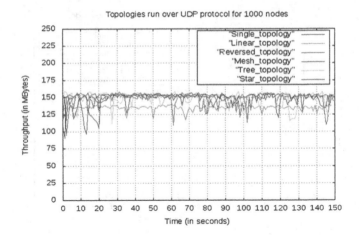

Fig. 7. UDP Throughput v/s Time for connectionless real time traffic for 1000 nodes.

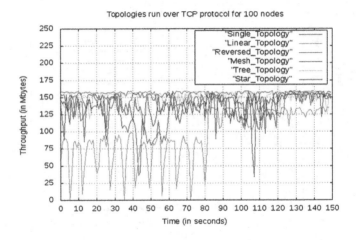

Fig. 8. TCP Throughput v/s Time for connection-oriented traffic for 100 nodes.

6.2   Jitter

Jitter is the small delay value during the transmission. It is measured and captured for 150 s. As discussed in the "running mininet and generating the graph" section, we have filtered the data for UDP protocol. It is measured in milliseconds and its unit is ms. We analyse jitter for 100, 500 and 1000 nodes for UDP realtime flows. Figures 11, 12 and 13 provides insight upon the jitter behaviour by the scaling network. For the 100 nodes SDN network, the jitter remains lower than 0.06 ms with the incident of few spikes by linear, mesh, reversed and star topologies. When the network scale to 500 nodes, the instability is depicted by all the topologies crossing the range of 0.08 ms. Once 1000 nodes density is reached, the jitter stability is obtained and in presence of few projections by mesh, reversed

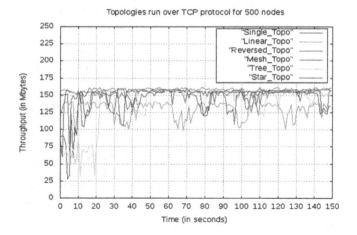

Fig. 9. TCP Throughput v/s Time for connection-oriented traffic for 500 nodes.

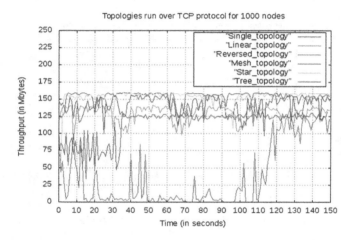

Fig. 10. TCP Throughput v/s Time for connection-oriented traffic for 1000 nodes.

and linear topologies. During entire experiment, the SDN network stays stable because average jitter always remains lower than 0.05 irrespective of scale of the network.

6.3 Latency

It is also called "Network Delay" for determining delay imposed for connection-oriented flows such as TCP. It is measured from the time the packet is sent to the destination ie; RTT (Round Trip-Time) which is measured in ms. There might be latency in the network based on various factors like: packet size, transmission media and poor signal strength. Figures 14, 15 and 16 provides the clear view of the topologies distributed into two groups, one range from 0.06 ms to 0.14 ms

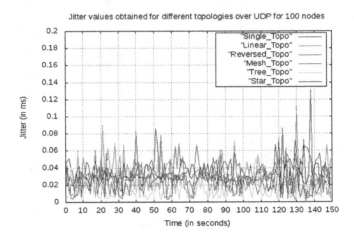

Fig. 11. UDP Jitter v/s Time graph of connectionless Real Time traffic for 100 nodes.

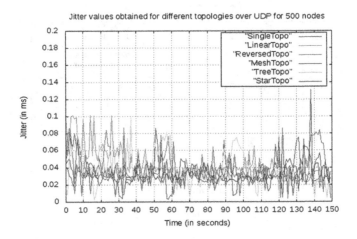

Fig. 12. UDP Jitter v/s Time graph of connectionless Real Time traffic for 500 nodes.

and another from 0.02 ms to 0.07 ms. From the connection oriented flows latency graph of 100 nodes, high latency group members are single, linear, reversed and mesh; whereas, low latency group includes tree and star. When the network scales to 500 nodes, the gap between the two groups reduces still the better performing topologies are the same, star and tree. When the network further scales to 1000 nodes, that group vanishes and all the topologies appear in the same range of 0–0.07 ms with very few incidence of spikes. Therefore, considering the overall small to large scale networks, tree and star topology behaves better for connection oriented flows.

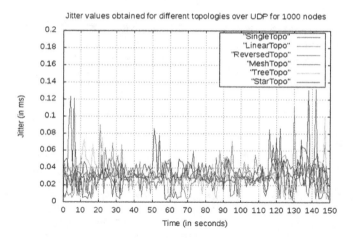

Fig. 13. UDP Jitter v/s Time graph of connectionless Real Time traffic for 1000 nodes.

After discussing the overall performance of all the three scenarios being rigorously tested with a variety of topologies, the average mean is computed as shown in Table 3, providing us the clear picture indicating that latency and jitter decreases with scaling network; whereas, optimum resource utilization happens at middle level networks up to 650 nodes.

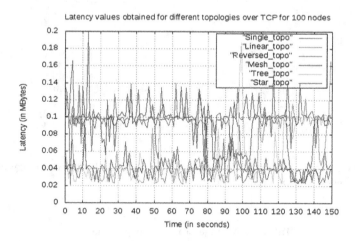

Fig. 14. TCP Connection-oriented network with 100 nodes faced latency as represented in latency v/s time graph.

Author's have performed the experiment for three different scenario's and tested the key network performance parameters that represents diversified near to real-time corporate topologies. The average values were calculated to further

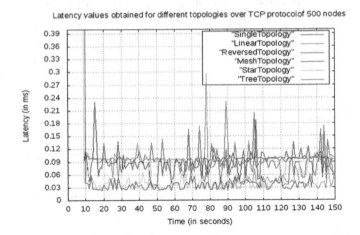

Fig. 15. TCP Connection-oriented network with 500 nodes faced latency as represented in latency v/s time graph.

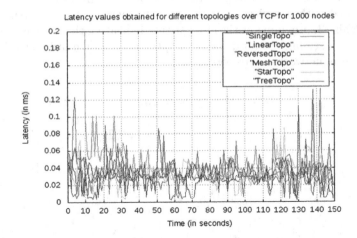

Fig. 16. TCP Connection-oriented network with 1000 nodes faced latency as represented in latency v/s time graph.

Table 3. Average of resultant parameters

Scenario	Number of nodes	Throughput (MBytes)	Jitter (ms)	Latency (ms)
First	100	13539.8	0.041	0.297
Second	500	16071.4	0.021	0.204
Third	1000	15563.2	0.095	0.176

analyse the result of the experiment statistically represented in Table 3. Average Throughput obtained is presented in column 3 for all the three scenarios and it was observed that- when the number of nodes increases gradually, the average throughput also increases. Average Jitter is measured and represented in column 4 of Table 3. Jitter improves while there is an increase in the number of nodes. Lastly, the average latency is calculated and represented in the last column of Table 3, which has shown a positive result. It was observed that as the number of nodes increases, latency reduces. Overall, second scenario outperforms remaining scenarios in all the three aspects and therefore, second scenario is recommended to businesses intending to shift to SDN based infrastructure.

7   Conclusion

This paper has investigated frenetic and pyretic based software defined networks focusing on scaling with a diverse set of topologies. This paper proposes the network policy implementation using programmable networks through languages like frenetic and pyretic. The implementation is rigorously tested for three different scaled networks ranging from small scale to large scale corporate environments. The gaps between advanced technology and its adaptability lies due to lacuna of statistical and simulation based implementation of futuristic SDN networks, which is filled by providing the insight on process of implementation and performance evaluation for all kinds of corporate networks. Results of three scenarios provides the support for decision making by corporate investors improving the efficiency and confidence on adapting to the improved technological advancements. After conducting this research we can conclude by stating following facts based on the research outcomes. Small and medium scale businesses depending upon real-time traffic should avoid linear and star topology. Star topology improves performance with scaled networks upto 1000 nodes but overall linear topology must be avoided by real-time networking businesses. Tree topology and single topology performs better with scaling networks along with diverse networking requirements of real-time as well as reliable networks. Average jitter remains lower than 0.04 ms irrespective of the scale of the networks. Other than a minimal number of events of jitter spikes observed by all the topologies. Corporate world having high demand for real-time data transmission is recommended to use tree topology and single topology. Latency behaviour is distributed into two groups until medium scale networks; however, they merge into a single group gradually reaching a large scale of 1000 nodes. Also, the performance of latency improves with the scaling networks.

Thus, this paper contributes to a) corporate world for decision making, b) network administrators with demonstration on network policy implementation using frenetic and pyretic languages on SDN based networks, c) researchers can carry forward this research concept by converting complex networking functionalities to software based functionalities using frenetic and pyretic. Finally, the simulation provided will inspire newbees to join the journey of software defined networks and contribute to the world of research and technology.

8   Future Work

Considering the future perspective, the research team intends to make the use of maximum accessibility of the Pyretic functionality for network policy implementation. This study has shown profound results for a varied set of nodes and a diverse set of topologies. The plan is to extend this research for the exploration of policy implementation of the data-plane by providing the data plane functionality using pyretic. This work can be extended further by making ease of Traffic Engineering and Topology read.

Conflict of Interest. Manasa Kulkarni, Bhargavi Goswami and Joy Paulose declare that there is no conflict of interest.

Funding. This research not funded by any body for conducting this research.

References

1. Goswami, B., Asadollahi, S.S.: Enhancement of LAN infrastructure performance for data center in presence of network security. In: Lobiyal, D.K., Mansotra, V., Singh, U. (eds.) Next-Generation Networks. AISC, vol. 638, pp. 419–432. Springer, Singapore (2018). https://doi.org/10.1007/978-981-10-6005-2_44
2. Goswami, B., Wilson, S., Asadollahi, S., Manuel, T.: Data visualization: experiment to impose DDoS attack and its recovery on software-defined networks. In: Anouncia, S.M., Gohel, H.A., Vairamuthu, S. (eds.) Data Visualization, pp. 141–160. Springer, Singapore (2020). https://doi.org/10.1007/978-981-15-2282-6_8
3. Asadollahi, S., Goswami, B.H.: Revolution in existing network under the influence of software defined network. In: Proceedings of the 11th INDIACom, New Delhi, India, pp. 1012–1017. IEEE (2017)
4. Reich, J., Monsanto, C., Foster, N., Rexford, J., Walker, D.: Modular SDN programming with pyretic. Technical Reprot of USENIX (2013)
5. Foster, N., et al.: Frenetic: a network programming language. In: ICFP 2011, 19–21 September, Tokyo, Japan (2011)
6. Khan, M.A., Goswami, B., Asadollahi, S.: Data visualization of software-defined networks during load balancing experiment using floodlight controller. In: Anouncia, S.M., Gohel, H.A., Vairamuthu, S. (eds.) Data Visualization, pp. 161–179. Springer, Singapore (2020). https://doi.org/10.1007/978-981-15-2282-6_9
7. Kumar, A., Goswami, B., Augustine, P.: Experimenting with resilience and scalability of WiFi Mininet on small to large SDN networks. Int. J. Recent Technol. Eng. **7**(6S5), 201–207 (2019)
8. Manuel, T., Goswami, B.H.: Experimenting with scalability of Beacon controller in software defined network. Int. J. Recent Technol. Eng. **7**(5S2), 550–555 (2019)
9. Sameer, M., Goswami, B.: Experimenting with ONOS scalability on software defined network. J. Adv. Res. Dyn. Control Syst. **10**(14-Special Issue), 1820–1830 (2018)
10. Asadollahi, S., Goswami, B., Sameer, M.: Ryu controller's scalability experiment on software defined networks. In: IEEE International Conference on Current Trends in Advanced Computing (ICCTAC), Bangalore, pp. 1–5 (2018). https://doi.org/10.1109/ICCTAC.2018.8370397

11. Asadollahi, S., Goswami, B., Raoufy, A.S., Domingos H.G.J.: Scalability of software defined network on floodlight controller using OFNet. In: 2017 International Conference on Electrical, Electronics, Communication, Computer, and Optimization Techniques (ICEECCOT), Mysuru, pp. 1–5 (2017). https://doi.org/10.1109/ICEECCOT.2017.8284567

12. Nadeau, T.D., Gray, K.: SDN: Software Defined Networks, 1st edn., pp. 9–20. O'Reilly Media Inc, Newton (2013)

13. Kreutz, D., Ramos, F.M.V., Esteves Verissimo, P., Esteve Rothenberg, C., Azodolmolky, S., Uhlig, S.: Software-defined networking: a comprehensive survey. Proc. IEEE **103**(1), 14–76 (2015). https://doi.org/10.1109/jproc.2014.2371999

14. Sharma, P.K., Tyagi, S.S.: Improving security through Software Defined Networking (SDN): an SDN based model. Int. J. Recent Technol. Eng. **8**(4), 295–300 (2019). https://doi.org/10.35940/ijrte.d6814.118419

15. Asadollahi, S., Goswami, B.: Experimenting with scalability of floodlight controller in software defined networks. In: 2017 International Conference on Electrical, Electronics, Communication, Computer, and Optimization Techniques (ICEECCOT), Mysuru, pp. 288–292 (2017). https://doi.org/10.1109/ICEECCOT.2017.8284684

16. Asadollahi, S., Goswami, B., Sameer, M.: Ryu controller's scalability experiment on software defined networks. In: 2018 IEEE International Conference on Current Trends in Advanced Computing (ICCTAC), pp. 1–5. IEEE, February 2018

17. Monsanto, C., Reich, J., Foster, N., Rexford, J., Walker, D.: Composing software-defined networks. In: USENIX NSDI (2013)

18. Mousa, M., Bahaa-Eldin, A.M., Sobh, M.: Software defined networking concepts and challenges. In: 2016 11th International Conference on Computer Engineering & Systems (ICCES), Cairo, pp. 79–90 (2016). https://doi.org/10.1109/ICCES.2016.7821979

19. Kumar, A., Goswami, B., Augustine, P.: Experimenting with resilience and scalability of Wifi Mininet on small to large SDN networks. Int. J. Recent Technol. Eng. (IJRTE) **7**(6s5), 201–207 (2019). SCOPUS

20. Manuel, T., Goswami, B.H.: Experimenting with scalability of beacon controller in software defined network. Int. J. Recent Technol. Eng. (IJRTE) **7**(5S2), 550–555 (2019). SCOPUS

21. Hoang, D.B., Pham, M.: On software-defined networking and the design of SDN controllers. In: 2015 6th International Conference on the Network of the Future (NOF), Montreal, QC, pp. 1–3 (2015). https://doi.org/10.1109/NOF.2015.7333307

22. Das, S., Goswami, B., Asadollahi, S.: Investigating software-defined network and networks-function virtualization for emergent network-oriented services. IJIRCCE **5**(2), 201–205 (2017). DOI: doi.org/10.15680

23. Goswami, B., Asadollahi, S.: Performance evaluation of widely implemented congestion control algorithms over diversified networking situations. In: ICCSNIT - 2016, Pattaya, Thailand. Open Access (2016)

24. Goswami, B., Asadollahi, S.: Performance evaluation of widely implemented congestion control algorithms over diversified networking situations. In: ICCSNIT – 2016, Pattaya, Thailand. Open Access (2016)

25. Frenetic & Pyretic: Networking Language (2020). http://www.frenetic-lang.org/pyretic/. Accessed Sep 2020

26. OpenFlow: FloodLight controller (2020). http://www.projectfloodlight.org/. Accessed Sep 2020

27. Python: scripting network topologies (2020). https://www.python.org/. Accessed Sep 2020
28. Mininet: emulator (2020). http://mininet.org/. Accessed Sep 2020
29. Xterm: emulator (2020). https://invisible-island.net/xterm/. Accessed Sep 2020
30. IPERF: networks tool (2020). https://iperf.fr/. Accessed Sep 2020
31. Gnuplot: graph tool (2020). http://www.gnuplot.info/. Accessed Sep 2020

Design and Implementation of Lightweight Dynamic Elliptic Curve Cryptography Using Schoof's Algorithm

Ansh Tyagi[1]([✉]) [iD], K. K. Soundra Pandian[2]([✉]) [iD], and Shamsuddin Khan[2] [iD]

[1] Indian Institute of Information Technology, Sonepat, India
tyagiansh23@gmail.com
[2] Ministry of Electronics and Information Technology, O/O CCA, New Delhi, India
soundra.pandian.cca@nic.in

Abstract. Security and efficiency for resource constrained devices using lightweight cryptography techniques is still a problem. It is important to make these devices secure from the intruders and communicate with them securely. Elliptic Curve Cryptography (ECC) comes out to be a major contender to solve this problem as it provides the security using smaller key length. Since the conventional ECC works on predefined and fixed curves, the elliptic curves are analysed thoroughly since the emergence of ECC. This paper, proposes an implementation of dynamic elliptic curves which are secure and feasible for Internet of Things (IoT) devices and other devices which require lightweight cryptography for security. The experimental results show the feasibility and efficiency of the algorithm used to generate dynamic curve for cryptography. Also, a new curve will be generated at each runtime. It would be nearly impossible for intruders to exploit and retract information from the devices. Hence, the proposed technique is more secure and practically efficient for resource constrained devices.

Keywords: Elliptic Curve Cryptography (ECC) · Elliptic Curve Discrete Logarithm Problem · Elliptic curve

1 Introduction

This decade has seen the emergence of Internet of Things (IoT) and other resource-constrained devices coming in use in our daily life. An IoT is network of devices or "Things" like a wearable watch, LEDs, cellphone are connected over a network. Due to the availability of cheap internet and also the emergence of technology like 5G, more than 20 billion IoT devices will come in action by the end of this year. This advent has led to a high demand of storing and sharing data with these devices. The data is shared over a network hence the question of how secure these devices are arises. These devices are vulnerable and provide opportunities to the intruders to invade the privacy [13]. Many cryptographic algorithms and techniques have been developed to prevent this, one of them is elliptic curve cryptography (ECC), which uses a shorter key-length but provides

© Springer Nature Switzerland AG 2021
N. Chaubey et al. (Eds.): COMS2 2021, CCIS 1416, pp. 193–204, 2021.
https://doi.org/10.1007/978-3-030-76776-1_13

a security equivalent to Rivest-Shamir-Adleman (RSA) [14] cryptosystem of larger key-length. These tiny devices are designed with 8 or 16 bit microprocessor and have low power consumption and have a limited bandwidth [22]. Storage is another factor in which an IoT lags behind; many of these devices are made with limited storage. ECC proves to be useful in providing the security goals like authenticating, message integrity and confidentiality in the case of IoT since ECC has a low data-requirement, it allows to use smaller, faster and cheaper cryptoprocessor which can be embedded into small IoT devices as well [15]. Recent studies by many researchers have also proposed better and efficient ECC processor architecture designs [16] which can be embedded in the IoT. Many curves are predefined by NIST standards [18]. Many attempts have been made on hardware and software implementation of predefined ECC in embedded domains in the past years. But these curves require heavy computation which are difficult to computed in IoT and resource-constrained devices and since these curves are predefined, many cryptanalyst have analysed the curves. The main operation which makes ECC difficult to crack is its Elliptic Curve Point Multiplication (ECPM), which requires heavy computation. But with smaller prime number it can easily be computed on an IoT device with less processing power and proves to be more efficient. Elliptic Curve Discrete Logarithm Problem (ECDLP) makes it difficult for the intruder to crack the Private Key. The work proposed mitigates the problem of using the traditional predefined curves which are intensively analysed and discussed upon. Also the problem of using fixed prime number for developing a random private curve. Each time a signal or data needs to be shared over a network a new set of parameters for the elliptic curve a generated and thus ECC takes place. Thus this paper, provides a different approach which develops a new Elliptic Curve on each runtime for the Elliptic Curve Cryptosystem and makes it dynamic in nature.

2 Design and Idea of Elliptic Curve Cryptography

2.1 Basic Idea Behind Elliptic Curve Cryptography

Elliptic Curve Cryptography is based on the idea of Elliptic Curve Discrete Logarithm Problem (ECDLP) [1], one of the difficult problems present in mathematical theories. Rivest-Shamir-Adleman (RSA) is based on factor decomposition problem [1]. Since computing power is increasing with the time it will be easier to solve these problems. However it is still a challenge with resource constrained devices. ECDLP is a distinct case of the Discrete Logarithm Problem (DLP) [2]. DLP can be defined as: Given a group G, a generator g of the group and an element of group G, to find the discrete logarithm to the base g of h in group G, For example: if the group is Z_7^* the generator is 3, then the discrete logarithm of 6 is 3 because $3^3 \equiv 6 \bmod 7$. However DLP is not always hard, the difficulty of the problem depends on the choice of group. For example: preferred choice of groups in cryptosystem based on ECDLP or discrete logarithm are Z_p^*, where p are large prime number. ECDLP [2] is a special case for DLP in Elliptic curves which can be stated as: Let E be an elliptic curve over finite field F_p. Suppose there are points $P, Q \in E(F_p)$, find n such that $Q = nP$.

2.2 Limitation in Other Techniques

ECC is considered to be light-weight as compared to other public-key cryptography techniques like RSA [3], Diffie-Hellman [20] and others. ECC requires a lesser key-size to provide the same level of security as compared to RSA with a larger key-size [4]. Moreover the ECDLP makes ECC more secure than RSA. Hence, ECC is considered to be idle and feasible for IoT [17] and resource-constrained devices. Also the classical ECC is performed on the fixed curves. Such unified curve system can be easily challenged by cryptoanalysis. Hence to increase the security the key size needs to be increased. Such approach is practically inefficient for devices with limited resources. Moreover the selection of secure elliptic curve is a tedious job for the users. Selecting curves from the group of NIST recommended curves [5] rewinds us back to the problem of larger key sizes. Thus the classical approach is impractical and insecure for the resource-constrained devices [19, 21].

3 Preliminary Work

This section includes the basic concepts of elliptic curve and cryptography based on elliptic curve. Few point operations on the curves are (i) Point Addition, (ii) Point Doubling, (iii) Scalar Multiplication.

3.1 Elliptic Curves

An elliptic curve is a group of points which satisfies the Eq. (1) as under:

$$y^2 = x^3 + ax + b \tag{1}$$

Where a, b are constants in the Eq. (1) [6]. The equation given in (1) can either be defined on real, integers, complex or any finite field. These curves are non-singular, i.e. curve does not contain any point where the curve ceases to be well-behaved in a particular way, iff the Eq. (2) hold algebraically true:

$$-16\left(4a^3 + 27b^2\right) \neq 0 \tag{2}$$

Graphically represented elliptic curves are not ellipses and have different properties than ellipses. Shapes of curve vary according to the discriminant given in Eq. (2). Few examples of the graphs are shown in Fig. 1.

In the given figure the curves are defined on real numbers and are non-singular as first curve's discriminant is positive, i.e. $64 > 0$, and in the second curve the discriminant is negative, i.e. $-432 < 0$, the difference in the shape is evident.

In Elliptic Curves over a finite field F_p the order of curve n is the total number of points on the curve which include a special point at infinity, O_∞, which is also the identity element. Some curves form non-overlapping cyclic subgroups while some form a single cycle group [7]. In the first case the points split into h cyclic subgroups each of order r, h is called the cofactor and the relation between n, hr is $n = hr$.

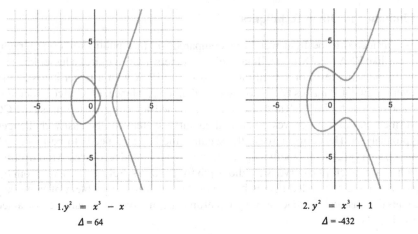

1. $y^2 = x^3 - x$
   $\Delta = 64$

2. $y^2 = x^3 + 1$
   $\Delta = -432$

Fig. 1. Shapes of elliptic curves

3.2 Point Addition

- Addition Law is commutative as well as associative

$$P + Q = Q + P$$

$$(P + Q) + R = P + (Q + R)$$

- Let $P = (x_1, y_1)$ & $Q = (x_2, y_2)$ and $L(x) = mx + c$ be the line joining P and Q, where m is the slope of the line, then $P + Q + R = 0$ where $R = (x_3, y_3)$
- The sum of P and Q is the reflection of the point R
- The coordinates the reflection of R are as follows:

  - $x = m^2 - x_1 - x_2$
  - $y = m(x_1 - x) - y_1$ (Fig. 2)

- Point Doubling: It refers to adding the same point twice i.e. let $P = (x_1, y_1)$ then $2P = P + P$ then:

  - $m = \frac{3x_1^2 + a}{2y_1}$
  - $x = m^2 - 2x_1$
  - $y = m(x_1 - x) - y_1$ (Fig. 3)

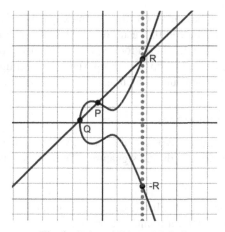

Fig. 2. Point addition of P & Q

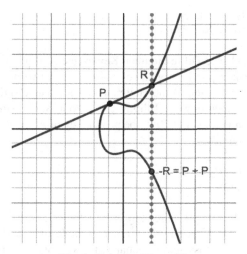

Fig. 3. Point doubling of P

3.3 Scalar Multiplication

Given a curve $E : y^2 = x^3 + ax + b$, Scalar multiplication can be defined as the operation to repeatedly adding a particular point over the curve itself. It can be denoted as:

$$\underbrace{nP = P + P + P \ldots + P}_{n \; times}$$

If $nP = O_\infty$ holds true, n is defined as the order [8] of point P. In ECC, this operation helps in generating a trapdoor function or a one-way function. It sets up the base for creating the ECDLP on the curve E over F_p. ECDLP can be defined as: For a curve $E|F_p$, let P and Q be two points on the curve if $kP = Q$, holds true the problem is to find k if P and Q are known. ECDLP is considered harder than DLP in finite field. The fastest algorithm to solve ECDLP has the worst-time complexity to be $O(\sqrt{p})$ over the field F_p. The shorter key length are indeed the result of absence of sub-exponential algorithms which results in choosing smaller fields for crypto systems using DLP. Some algorithm to solve ECDLP is Shank's Baby Step Giant Step Algorithm, Pohlig-Hellman Algorithm newer algorithms use index calculus which results in sub-exponential solutions.

3.4 Elliptic Curve Cryptography

Elliptic Curve Cryptography is a type of public-key cryptosystem. Elliptic Curves can be used in key-exchange as well as digital signature. The following is the basic procedure to implement ECC:

- Publicly known entities are the Elliptic Curve Equation, i.e. equation constants a, bp, elliptic group and the generator point/base point G.
- Alice and Bob generate a public and a private key:

  - Private Key $\in \left[1, p-1\right]$
  - Public Key $=$ Private Key $*$ G

- Elliptic Curve (EC) based Diffie-Hellman Key exchange is a key agreement scheme which is used to share public-private key pair between two parties. Elliptic Curve Diffie Hellman (ECDH) and Diffie-Hellman Key Exchange (DHKE) are different only because of one operation, i.e. Elliptic Curve Point Scalar Multiplication instead of modular exponentiations. Let $P_A P_B$ be private key of Alice and Bob respectively, the key shared is as follows:

  - Alice computes $P_A(P_B * G)$
  - Bob computes $P_B(P_A * G)$

  Since both are equal, the final shared key is $P_A * P_B * G$.
- EC based ElGamal Cryptography is another example of how dynamically EC are being used in other cryptosystem to enhance the security. In this cryptosystem the message is encoded into a point on the curve. Letssay, P_M is that point. The cipher is a point with the coordinates:

$$C_M = \{P_A G, (P_M + P_A * p_B)\}$$

  Where, P_A is private key of Alice and p_B is the public key of Bob

- At Bob, the y_{C_m} can be computed as $(P_M + P_A * P_B * G)$, where $P_A * G$ is x_{C_M}. Hence, decryption is as such:

$$P_M = y_{C_M} - P_B x_{C_M}$$

- There are many more cryptosystem and many more schemes that can be linked with Elliptic Curves. The Elliptic Curve Digital Signature Algorithm (ECDSA) [9] is also an example of the versatile nature of Elliptic Curves to authenticate users.

3.5 Schoof's Algorithm

In the early days of elliptic curves, counting the number of points [10] was done by naive approach, which is the least preferred one. In this it is iterated through all the elements of the finite field over p and keeping the count of the elements which satisfy the Elliptic Curve equation. For a larger p this approach is not feasible for resource constrained devices as it has a booming time complexity which would indeed result into failure and a limitation for the purpose.

René Schoof in 1980s proposed the first polynomial time method to count the number of points on an elliptic curve $E(F_p)$. This approach is quite feasible and fast for resource constrained devices. It has a time complexity of $O(n^{5+o(1)})$ where $n = logp$ and space complexity to be $O(n^3)$. This approach exploits Hasse's Theorem, which describes a range of finite possible values for #$E(F_p)$. This technique describes #$E(F_p) = p + 1 - t$, where p is the prime number and t is the trace of Frobenius modulo many small primes l. Trace of Frobenius is obtained by Chinese remainder theorem. In 1990s Noam Elkins and A.O.L Atkin improved the Schoof's Algorithm [11] making its time complexity to be $O(n^{4+o(1)})$ and space complexity to be $O(n^3 logn)$.

4 Proposed Dynamic Elliptic Curve Cryptography

The implementation was done on SageMath [12] open-source software in Python Language on MacBook Pro, 6-core i7 processor with overclocking of 2.6 GHz, 16 GB RAM, 4 GB AMD Radeon 5300 M GPU. The following is the algorithm to produce dynamic elliptic curve at each runtime.

4.1 Randomising the Constants

The elliptic curve equation i.e. Eq. (1) has 3 constants i.e. a, b and p, where a is the coefficient of x, b is the constant in the equation while p is the prime number over which the field is formed. With the help of Pseudo Random Number Generator (PRNG) we can generate random integers a, bp and form an elliptic curve over a finite field. The constants a and b are generated such that the curve is not singular i.e. the discriminant is not equal to zero. For a smaller machine with constrained resources and lack of technical specifications, smaller bit length a, bp can be generated in order to randomise the constants for the equations and produce a whole new elliptic curve at each runtime.

4.2 Counting the Points of Elliptic Curve

One of the difficulties to produce an elliptic curve is to count the number of points. Elliptic curve with a prime order n is considered to be hard to solve, therefore the number of points on the curve should be prime in order to increase the security of our dynamic elliptic curve. Moreover if n is prime number then DLP problem is also hard to solve.

Now, using Schoof's or SEA Algorithm [8] order of the curve is counted, and checked whether the elliptic curve which has being formed is having a prime order to make sure that it is secure to use.

4.3 Randomly Choosing a Generator Point

Generator point is used to generate all the other points on the curve. Selecting the correct base point is essential in constructing a secure elliptic curve for cryptography. If the cofactor (h) of the curve comes out to be 1 then every point in the curve is a generator point. For selecting a secure curve $h \leq 4$, for h to be equal to 1 the whole group is selected as one cyclic group and the order of any point is equal to the total number of the points on the curves. The relation is as such $\#E(F_p) = nh$. To select a base point for the curve with $h > 1$, follow the following steps:

1. Select a random point Q on the curve $E(F_p)$.
2. Verify $hQ \neq O_\infty$, if not select the point again.
3. Now, Verify $nQ = O_\infty$, if not goto the first step.
4. Return Q as the base point with order n

Generator point plays an important role in elliptic curve cryptosystem and can be considered as building blocks for the ECDLP problem in the ECC. Hence it should be carefully selected. Taking the security point of view, the order should be a large prime number and cofactor equal to 1. The "Bitcoin" curve uses *secp256k1* curve, having a large prime number as its order and its cofactor equal to 1.

4.4 Flowchart

The proposed implementation is shown in the Fig. 4, through a flowchart. For Elliptic Curve Cryptography 6 constants are defined that are (p, a, b, G, n, h) [23], where p is defined as the prime number over which the curve is formed, a and b are the constants shown in Eq. (1), G is the base point or the generator, n is the order of the curve, h is the cofactor. The algorithm starts with randomizing the constants for the elliptic curve equation given in Eq. (1). If the curve comes out to be singular i.e. Eq. (2) does not hold true, repeat the randomization. Once, the Eq. (2) holds true for a triad (p, a, b) initialise the curve.

Schoof's or SEA algorithm is used to count the points on the curve in polynomial time. SageMath provides implementation of SEA algorithm. Elliptic curves with prime number of points are considered to be secure. Since the elliptic curve will be of a prime order group hence h, cofactor will be equal to 1. Therefore by the equation: $\#E(F_p) = nh$, we conclude that $\#E(F_p) = n$ and every point on the curve will be a generator point. Therefore, randomly select a generator point to generate all the other points on the curve.

The algorithm fulfils the prerequisites of ECC implementation. For IoT like devices user can produce a smaller bit-length constant. Smaller bit-length will indeed result in smaller key length but it will have faster computation speed. Moreover, the elliptic curve produced can only be used for one-time. Public and Private key pair can be generated for the curve generated. A number randomly chosen from $[1, p - 1]$ can be defined as the private key for the cryptography. A n-bit private key can also be generated by specifying the lower bound to be smallest n-bit number and upper bound to $(p - 1)$. Public key can be defined as the scalar product of the private key and the Base Point, G. Since, every point on the curve is a multiple of G, public key will also lie on the curve. With the newly

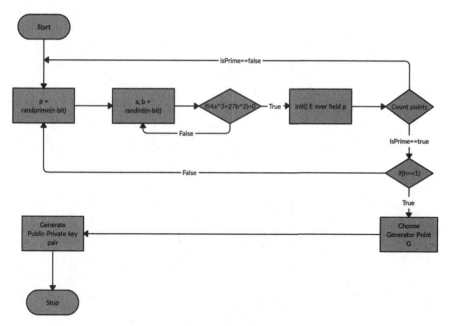

Fig. 4. Flowchart

made cryptosystem, messages can be encoded, decoded and authenticated through the principles of Elliptic Curve Cryptosystem. This algorithm is dependent on bit-length of prime number and Pseudo Random Number Generator (PRNG). Hence, for secure cryptosystem a larger bit-length prime number and secure PRNG should be used.

5   Results

These results are based on the implementation done on a specific machine. These results may vary for different devices but provides strong ECDLP based cryptosystem. The results generated show the different bit security achieved by the algorithm with the average time taken by it.

Since the algorithms work on PRNG, the algorithm runtime is random too, therefore an average of 50 observations have been recorded. Clearly from the Table-1 it can be deduced that a 32-bit size key would be an apt choice for a device with limited resources like an IoT.

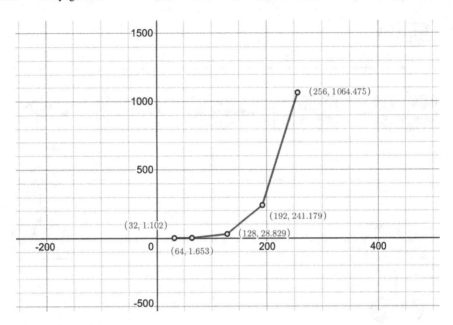

6 Conclusion

In this paper, a new approach has been proposed in which secure dynamic elliptic curves are generated for practical use of Elliptic Curve Cryptography in IoT and other resource-constrained devices. In this technique the conventional approach to implement the ECC with predefined curves has been bypassed. The results show the efficiency of the algorithm and also the limitation in this approach. According to observations shown in Table 1 the time taken for resource-constrained devices to generate 256 bit key length would not be feasible in terms of time, as the time complexity of this algorithm is exponential in nature. Whereas for smaller key-size the approach seems to be perfect in terms of time as well as the security provided by it. Also, having a new curve makes it difficult for the intruder to access the information and exploit it. The dynamic nature of curves at each runtime, removes the barrier of using a fixed curve which have been analysed in the past. This technique solves the security issue in most of the IoT which require lightweight cryptography and resource constrained devices.

Table 1. Security level v/s time taken comparison

S.no.	Security level	Average time taken (in secs)
1	32-bit	1.102 s
2	64-bit	1.653 s
3	128-bit	28.829 s
4	192-bit	241.179 s
5	256-bit	1064.475 s

References

1. Bai, Q.-H., Zhang, W.-B., Jiang, P., Lu, X.: Research on "Design Principles of Elliptic Curve Public Key Cryptography and Its Implementation". In: 2012 International Conference on Computer Science and Service System, pp. 1224–1227 (2012)
2. Changyu, D.: Discrete Logarithm Problem. In: Math in Network Security. Imperial College of London, UK, Ch. 06, Sec. 2
3. Dindayal, M., Dilip, K.Y.: RSA and ECC: a comparative analysis. Int. J. Appl. Eng. Res. **12**(19), 9053-9061 (2017), ISSN 0973-4562
4. Kumar, A., Tyagi, S.S.: A comparative study of public key cryptosystem based on ECC and RSA. Int. J. Comput. Sci. Eng. **3**(5), 1904–1909 (2011)
5. Lily, C., Dustin, M., Andrew, R., Karen, R.: Recommendations for Discrete Logarithm-Based Cryptography: Elliptic Curve Domain Parameters. NIST SP 800-186 (Draft) (2019)
6. Hailiza, K.: Generating Elliptic curves modulo p for cryptography using mathematicas-oftware. In: 2010 Seventh International Conference on Computer Graphics, Imaging and Visualization, pp. 92–96 (2010)
7. Svetlin, N.: Elliptic curve cryptography. In: Practical Cryptography for Developers, ISBN: 9786190008705, Ch. 8, Sec. 4
8. Kim, Y.H., Bahr, J., Neyman, E., Taylor, G.: On orders of elliptic curves over finite fields. Rose-Hulman Undergraduate Math. J. **19**(1), Article 2 (2018)
9. Olorunfemi, T.O.S, Alese, B.K., Falaki, S.O., Fajuyigbe, O.: Implementation of elliptic curve digital signature algorithms. J. Softw. Eng. **1**, 1–12 (2007)
10. Ritzenthaler, C.: Point counting on elliptic curves. Ch. 02, pp. 11–14 (2009)
11. Schoof, R.: Counting points on elliptic curves over finite fields. Journal de Théorie des Nombres de Bordeaux **7**, 219–254 (1995)
12. Stein, W.A.: SageMath v9.1, May 2020. [Online]
13. Arora, V., Tyagi, S.: Analysis of symmetric searchable encryption and data retrieval in cloud computing. Int. J. Comput. Appl. **127**(12), 46–51 (2015)
14. Kumar, A., Tyagi, S.S.: A study based on asymmetric key algorithms. In: Proceedings of National Seminar on AIC at DCTM, Palwal (2011)
15. Tyagi, S.S., Chauhan, R.K., Kumar, A.: A new approach for key expansion in passport protocol using chebyshew and AES algorithms. In: Proceedings of 3rd International Conference on Advance Computing and Communication Technologies (2008)
16. Kudithi, T., Sakthivel, R.: High-performance ECC processor architecture design for IoT security applications. J. Supercomput. **75**, 447–474 (2019)
17. Hasan, H., et al.: Secure lightweight ECC-based protocol for multi-agent IoT systems. In: 2017 IEEE 13th International Conference on Wireless and Mobile Computing, Networking and Communications (WiMob), pp. 1–8. Rome (2017) https://doi.org/10.1109/wimob.2017.8115788
18. Brown, M., Hankerson, D., López, J., Menezes, A.: Software implementation of the NIST elliptic curves over prime fields. In: Naccache, D. (ed.) Topics in Cryptology—CT-RSA 2001. CT-RSA 2001. Lecture Notes in Computer Science, vol. 2020. Springer, Heidelberg (2001). https://doi.org/10.1007/3-540-45353-9_19
19. Andrea, H., Norbert, D., Christian, K., Christian, S., Tomaz, F.: Hardware/software co-design of elliptic-curve cryptography for resource-constrained applications. In: Proceedings of the 51st Annual Design Automation Conference (DAC '14).Association for Computing Machinery, pp. 1–6. New York, NY, USA (2014)
20. Diffie, W., Hellman, M.: New directions in cryptography. IEEE Trans. Inf. Theory 644–654 (1976)

21. Lu, C., Chen, Y., Bian, Z.: An implementation of fast algorithm for elliptic curve cryptosystem over GF(p). J. Electron. (China) **21**, 346–352 (2004)
22. Noori, D., Shakeri, H., NiaziTorshiz, M.: Scalable, efficient, and secure RFID with elliptic curve cryptosystem for Internet of Things in healthcare environment. EURASIP J. Info. Secur. **2020**, 13 (2020)
23. Lara-Nino, C.A., Diaz-Perez, A., Morales-Sandoval, M.: Elliptic curve lightweight cryptography: a survey. IEEE Access **6**, 72514–72550 (2018). https://doi.org/10.1109/access.2018.2881444

QRP: QPSO Based Routing Protocol for Energy Efficiency in Wireless Body Area Networks

Satyam Sharma[✉] [iD]

DAV University, Jalandhar, India

Abstract. In contemporary times, Wireless Body Area Networks has arisen as a new area for tracking, identification, examining and treatment of multiple deadly diseases in patients. It is designed by grouping biosensors that might either be implanted or fixed outwards over anyone's body, for scrutinization of myriad body parts. In it, the biosensor nodes are pinioned to different body parts to examine the health or specific bodily functions such as blood pressure, respiratory levels, heart rate, etc. Energy utilizations prove to be major roadblock for WBANs as replacing, re-energizing these biosensors might cause discomfort for the person bearing them. The contemporary research is mainly centered on minimizing the energy utilization in body area networks. For the purpose of energy conservation, we append QPSO, in order to find the shortest, energy-efficient route, in our wireless body area network. The proposed technique uses a relay node along with a multiple-hops technique. For the purpose of achieving better results, a quantum behaved PSO based routing protocol (QRP) is put forth to optimize a fitness function. The performance of QRP is analyzed and compared with existing protocols namely, M-ATTEMPT, SIMPLE and PSOBAN. Our experimental results show significant improvements in packet success rates as our proposed protocol achieves an increased throughput over the aforementioned protocols. Similarly, our protocol achieves much higher transmission rates, lesser path loss and retains more residual energy as well.

Keywords: Wireless body area networks · Routing · Multiple-hop · Remnant energy · Fitness function

1 Introduction

In the fast-paced life, there exist myriad things which have contributed towards a sedentary lifestyle. Consequently, the occurrence of various earlier unknown diseases has significantly increased. So, the need for a robust and reliable health monitoring system is the need of the hour [1–3]. Wireless BANs adhere to a category, called external monitoring health care systems (eHealth), which are used to perform local monitoring and controlling. A WBAN system offers long term health monitoring without hindering day-to-day activities. WBANs are concurrently operating, less-energy, low-ranged network. It comprises of various different types of biosensors. They possess the capability of accumulating physiological data, namely electroencephalography (EEG), electrocardiography (ECG), arterial pressure, blood sugar, temperature, etc. [4–6]. Low-Power

© Springer Nature Switzerland AG 2021
N. Chaubey et al. (Eds.): COMS2 2021, CCIS 1416, pp. 205–221, 2021.
https://doi.org/10.1007/978-3-030-76776-1_14

utilization is acknowledged as one of the most significant as well as a challenging task in WBAN systems. In nearly every Wireless BAN devices, battery cells primarily supply power. They are also the most abundant components as far as weight and capacity are concerned, in comparison with other parts. In this paper, we intend to elevate Wireless BANs in terms of overall exhaustion of energy. Specific attention is laid on relaying. Our optimum routing strategy focuses on minimalizing exhaustion of energy and escalating the longevity as well. Figure 1 illustrates 3-tier architecture of WBAN.

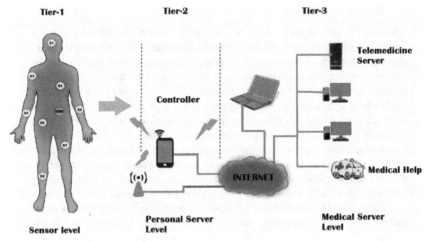

Fig. 1. 3-Tier Architecture of WBAN.

2   Related Work

Avoiding energy-squandering is one of the paramount concerns that still exists in WBAN. Higher Energy levels contribute to prolonged network life. Many researchers have designed various protocols, keeping these factors in mind. Wu et al. [7] apply P.S.O to find out superlative location of the relay nodes. A path with lowest levels of specific absorption rate (SAR) is chosen for this purpose. In [8], N. Bilandi has given a routing paradigm, PSOBAN, to pick out relaying designations. In [9], Kaur et al. put forward two protocols OCER as well as E-OCER. In OCER, optimization is done by employing genetic algorithm, and it is multiple-objective cost function. Kanchan et al. [10] put forth a quantum-inspired clustering methodology (QPCINL). The quantum inspired algorithm was chosen because lesser parameters are needed. Comparisons were made with LEACH and PSO-ECHS. Nadeem [11] introduced, SIMPLE, in which a technique is devised for selecting the forwarder. It is observed that the throughput achieved by SIMPLE is higher than M-ATTEMPT. In [12] J. Yan et al. A new routing scheme OEABC is proposed. Simulations indicate it's efficacy, when it is compared with ACO and genetic algorithm. Results show that OEABC has a rapid convergence rate. Kalaiselvi et al. [13] analyzed that untrusted sensors hindered network functionality. So, they have optimized the trust features using genetic algorithm, after being drawn out. In order to tackle health issues for pilgrims, in an overcrowded environment like Hajj, researchers in [14] gave routing mechanisms based on BA to manage power utilizations. In [15], a technique is given for selecting an appropriate path to enhance remnant energy-levels. Some new-found meta-heuristics are, Black Widow [16], Harris hawks [17], Group teaching optimization [18], Coyote optimization algorithm [19], etc.

2.1 Novelty

In our research work, we put forward a quantum PSO based energy efficient routing protocol (QRP) to enhance the remnant energy-levels within biosensors, since energy conservation is a critical factor that can affect the longevity of the network. For that purpose, a relaying sensor node is selected to decrease the energy utilization among the nodes. The selection is done by comparing with the threshold energy-levels. During the selection, the distance of sink is evaluated from the nodes. The sensor node whose energy-level is greater than the threshold energy is chosen as a relay node.

The quantum PSO is chosen because it amalgamates the useful features of quantum computing and PSO. The quantum PSO, is a nature inspired algorithm, which has fewer control parameters to adjust during the position-updating phase and it uses only one parameter, position vector, unlike other existing algorithms, which can be controlled using the contraction-expansion coefficient (α) that enables it to have a much greater scope for exploration as well as exploitation, depending upon its value. The value of α thus decides the position of the particle in the state-space, and it also helps in avoiding entrapment in local minima.

3 Preliminaries

3.1 Particle Swarm Optimization

In conventional PSO [20], every particle p is defined by a position vector $x = \left(x_1, x_1, x_1, \ldots x_D\right)$ which signifies a solution in the state-space and also a velocity vector $v = \left(v_1, v_2, v_3, \ldots v_D\right)$ accountable for exploring. Suppose 'M' signifies population of swarm, 'D' stands for state-space dimensionality. After each iteration, the positions and velocities of every swarm member are updated as follows:

$$v_{i,d}^{k+1} = wv_{i,d}^k + c_1v_{i,d}^k\left(pbest_{i,d}^k - x_{i,d}^k\right) + c_2R_{i,d}^k\left(gbest_{i,d}^k - x_{i,d}^k\right) \tag{1}$$

$$x_{i,d}^{k+1} = x_{i,d}^k + v_{i,d}^{k+1} \tag{2}$$

($1 \leq i \leq N$) and ($1 \leq d \leq D$), $v_{i,d}^k$ and $x_{i,d}^k$ denote velocity as well as position during k-iteration. $pbest_{i,d}^k$, and $gbest_d^k$ denote locally as well as globally best values for particles during k-iteration. w signifies inertial weight, and $c1$ and $c2$ represent acceleration coefficients. $r_{i,d}^k$ and $R_{i,d}^k$ denote random numbers distributed uniformly over (0, 1) interval.

The updating is continued till feasible value for $gbest_d^k$ is found. Evaluation of $pbest_{i,d}^k$ and $gbest_d^k$ is done, as shown below:

$$pbest_{i,d}^k = p_{i,d}^k, \text{ if fitness}\left(p_{i,d}^k\right) < \text{fitness}\left(pbest_{i,d}^k\right)$$
$$= pbest_{i,d}^k, \text{ else} \tag{3}$$

$$gbest_d^k = p_{i,d}^k, \text{ if fitness}\left(p_{i,d}^k\right) < \text{fitness}\left(gbest_d^k\right)$$
$$= gbest_d^k, \text{ else} \tag{4}$$

3.2 Quantum-Inspired Particle Swarm Optimization

In Accordance with trajectory analysis [21, 22], the PSO algorithm convergence might be attained, when every particle approaches their neighborhood attractor $p_i = \left(p_{i,1}, p_{i,2}, \ldots, p_{i,Dim}\right)$; for that co-ordinates can be denoted by

$$p_{i,d}^k = \varphi_d^k \times pbest_{i,d}^k + \left(1 - \varphi_d^k\right) \times gbest_d^k \tag{5}$$

where, $\varphi_d^k = c_1 r_{i,d}^k / \left(c_1 r_{i,d}^k + c_2 R_{i,d}^k\right)$

The Q-PSO is designed by above-mentioned interpretation. Every member of Quantum PSO is considered to be particle roaming round. The likelihood for it to appear on x_i^k during iteration k is decided using a probability-density function [23–25]. Flight of every particle is determined by Monte-Carlo's method as:

$$r_{i,d}^{k+1} = p_{i,d}^k + a\left|x_{i,d}^k - mbest_d^k\right| \ln\left(\frac{1}{u_{i,d}^k}\right),$$
$$\text{if randv greater than or equal to 0.5} \tag{6}$$

$$r_{i,d}^{k+1} = p_{i,d}^k - a\left|x_{i,d}^k - mbest_d^k\right| \ln\left(\frac{1}{u_{i,d}^k}\right),$$
$$\text{if randv is less than 0.5}$$

α indicates contraction expansion parameter; both $randv$ as well as $u_{i,d}^k$ signify random no. between (0, 1); $mbest$ signifies the mean-best:

$$mbest_d^k = \left(\frac{1}{M}\right) \sum_i^M pbest_{i,d}^k \tag{7}$$

A technique called time-deviating diminishing technique [26] is generally adopted to differ the value of α:

$$\alpha_v = \alpha_1 + \frac{(\alpha_0 - \alpha_1) \times (T - k)}{T} \tag{8}$$

where α_0 and α_1 denote maximal and minimal values for α, respectively; k denotes current search iteration; T denotes maximum iterations.

Table 1. The deployment of Biosensor nodes on the human body

Biosensor nodes	Position (x, y)	
	'x' co-ordinate	'y' co-ordinate
S1	0.55	1.00
S2	0.25	1.00
S3	0.28	0.20
S4	0.48	0.25
S5	0.30	0.50
S6	0.50	0.50
S7	0.45	1.30
S8	0.35	0.90
Sink	0.40	1.10

4 Materials and Methods

A fitness function for the Quantum PSO based approach is defined to represent the routing objective and also, a multi-objective optimizing methodology is devoted to our model. The model (a) discovers the optimal solution for the framework and (b) analyses, assesses the outcomes of network parameters on the results acquired.

4.1 Networking Model

In this paper, a Wireless BAN is devised, in which octad biosensors $S_1, S_2, S_3, \ldots, S_8$, and a sink are positioned on a person's body. After deployment, every node is assumed to be immobile. All are assigned to carry out varied, specific tasks at regular time intervals. Each node has to sense and transmit data to sink by discovering the minimal path. The deployment scheme of bio-sensor nodes, represented in Table 1.

4.2 Energy Model

The energy model used in [27] has been used. The amount of energy utilized can be evaluated by Eq. (9).

$$E_{Tr} = \varepsilon_{transmitter} \times \rho + \varepsilon_{amp} \times \delta^2 \times \rho \tag{9}$$

The energy utilized for data receival can be evaluated by Eq. (10).

$$E_{Rec} = \varepsilon_{receiver} \times \rho \tag{10}$$

Since data is transmitted through the skin, some overheads might arise, due to hindrance of the skin, called human pathloss-coefficient $\left(PL_{coeff}\right)$. Thus, it must be inducted in the equations. The net energy utilized following inclusion of PL_{coeff}, is evaluated by Eq. (11).

$$E_{Tr} = \varepsilon_{transmitter} \times \rho + \varepsilon_{amp} \times PL_{coeff} \times \delta^2 \times \rho \qquad (11)$$

Comprehensively, the energy utilized by the biosensor node for receival and transmitting is defined by Eq. (12).

$$E_{total} = E_{Rec} + E_{Tr} \qquad (12)$$

where,

E_{Tr}:	Transmission energy
E_{Rec}:	Reception energy
$\varepsilon_{transmitter}$:	Energy utilized by transmitter
$\varepsilon_{receiver}$:	Energy utilized by receiver
ε_{amp}:	Energy utilized by Amplifier
δ:	Distance between source sensor node to destination
PL_{coeff}:	Path loss coefficient
ρ:	No. of bits in data packet

4.3 Path-Loss Model

Path loss signifies decrementation of the power density of an E-M wave during propagation. It [9] expresses signal attenuation amidst a transmitting node as well as receiving node as a function of propagation distance and various other parameters. The total path loss incurred during the data transmission is given by Eq. (13).

$$PL = 10log_{10}\left(\frac{d_P}{d_t}\right) + Pl_0 \qquad (13)$$

$$\text{where,} \quad Pl_0 = 10log_{10}(4\pi d_t/\lambda)$$

PL:	Path loss
d_P:	Path distance
d_t:	Threshold distance
λ:	Wavelength

4.4 Proposed Approach

The proposed quantum behaved PSO based approach (QRP) to improve energy efficiency in WBAN which amalgamates the useful points of quantum computing and standard PSO. The main advantage of our quantum PSO based approach is that during updation of positions, just a single parameter suffices i.e., position vector. Quantum PSO based Routing Protocol (QRP) comprises of the following steps:

1. Position Updating.

2. Comparison of sensor nodes energies with threshold energy.
3. Relay Node Selection.
4. Selection of the shortest path for transmission.
5. Repeat the same procedure until all nodes die.

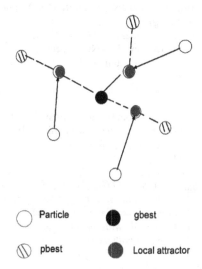

○ Particle   ● gbest

⦻ pbest   ● Local attractor

Fig. 2. Search behaviour of Q-PSO.

The updations of the particle positions are done using Quantum PSO, and the selection of the relay is done by comparing with threshold energy-level. During relay selection, the distance of sink is evaluated from the nodes. The sensor node whose energy-level is greater than the threshold energy is chosen as a relay node. The pros of using Quantum PSO for updation of positions is that not many parameters are needed; instead, position vector is the only requirement.

Fitness Function. A criterion, is presented, to select the relaying sensor node for QRP. A Relaying sensor node is selected to decrease the energy utilization among sensor nodes. The computation of the fitness values for all nodes is done. According to the fitness, decision is made whether a node should be chosen to become a relay node or not. *Fitness Function* is described as the ratio of the length of distance between sink and a sensor and the remnant energy of biosensor. The Fitness function is evaluated using Quantum PSO. The *Fitness Function* [11] to calculate corresponding *Fitness value* of node i is given by:

$$Fitness\ Function(i) = \frac{Distance\ (i)}{Residual\ Energy\ (i)} \tag{14}$$

Updation of Position of Particles. The updation of particle position is made by quantum-PSO [28]. The concept of quantum computation inspires it. According to quantum mechanics, a particle's likelihood to appear at any random location in the state-space, is decided according to its probability density function. The updations are done by employing Eq. (6). Figure 2 is illustrating searching behaviour of QPSO. The pseudocode for QRP algorithm is illustrated in Fig. 3.

Algorithm: *Quantum PSO based Routing Protocol (QRP) for Energy Efficiency.*
Input: Biosensor Nodes $S = [S_1, S_2, \ldots, S_n]$
Number of dimensions, D = No. of Sensor Nodes
Maximum number of iterations, T
Swarm Size M
[Fitness value calculated using fitness function (14)]
Steps:
Step1: For $i = 1$ to population size of swarm M
Step2: Randomize position of each particle $x[i]$;
Step3: Calculate $x[i]$; $l_{best}[i] = x[i]$
        end for
        do
Step4: $g_{best} = argmin(f(l_{best}))$
Step5: Calculate mean best, m_{best} by using step (3)
Step6: For $i = 1$ to population size of swarm
Step7: Calculate $p[i]$ with step (1)
Step8: Update $x[i]$ with step (2)
Step9: If $(f(x[i]) < (f(l_{best}[i]))$
Step10: $l_{best}[i] = x[i]$
      end if
    end for
Step11: Stop after reaching T

Fig. 3. Pseudocode of QRP

5 Results and Discussions

To assess the efficacy of our Quantum PSO based routing protocol (QRP), we have compared its performance with the M-Attempt, SIMPLE and PSOBAN on the same framework. The simulations for our Protocol were carried out and results were plotted on MATLAB R2017a [29] in accordance with the network parameters, as mentioned in Table 2. The parameters of QPSO and PSO are mentioned in Table 3.

The performance metrics used are as follows:

- **Throughput**: The throughput is the triumphant dispatch of data packets to the sink over a WBAN.
- **Residual Energy**: The amount of energy still left over with each node, after performing varied, specific tasks within the network.
- **Network Lifetime**: It is the instant at which first node in WBAN runs out of energy for sending data, because losing a node means, the WBAN could lose some of its functionalities.

Table 2. Different parameters of network

S. no	Parameters	Value
1	Initial energy	0.6 J
2	$\varepsilon_{receiver}$	$36.1 * 10^{-9}$ J/bit
3	$\varepsilon_{transmitter}$	$16.7 * 10^{-9}$ J/bit
4	ε_{amp}	$1.97 * 10^{-9}$ J/bit
5	Voltage	1.9 V
6	Dc Current for receiver, $I_{receiver}$	$18 * 10^{-3}$ A
7	Dc Current for transmitter, $I_{transmitter}$	$10.5 * 10^{-3}$ A
8	Packet size	4000 bits
9	Frequency	2.4 GHz
10	PL_{coeff}	3.38
11	Wavelength, λ	0.125 m
12	Rounds	10000
13	Biosensor nodes	8

Table 3. Parameters of QPSO and PSO.

Parameters	Value
Number of particles, M	100
C1	1.0
C2	1.0
Number of iterations, T	100
Dimensions, D	8
Initial (maximal) value of Contraction – Expansion (CE) Coefficient, α_0	0.9
Final (minimal) value of Contraction – Expansion (CE) Coefficient, α_1	0.08
Inertia weight, w	0.9

- **Path Loss:** It is the decrementation of the energy density of an E-M wave during propagation.
- **Packets sent to sink:** The packet sent signifies total packets directed to sink (destination), over course of transmission.
- **Packet Dropped:** The packet drop is basically, the loss of packets transmitted to the sink(destination) over the course of transmission.

5.1 Throughput

The throughput is the triumphant dispatch of data packets to the sink over a WBAN. The protocol QRP attains a massive upsurge in the throughput rate than PSOBAN, SIMPLE and M-ATTEMPT, as evident in Fig. 4.

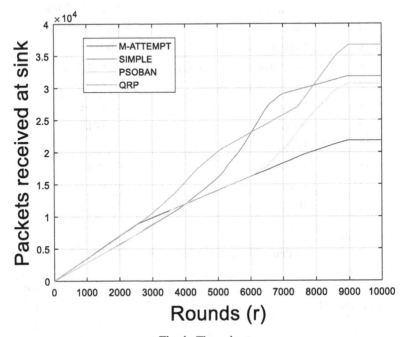

Fig. 4. Throughput

QRP achieves a much higher packet success rate, i.e., 36678 packets over PSOBAN, SIMPLE and M-ATTEMPT, having 30900, 31811 and 21819 packets per 10,000 rounds, respectively. This is because Quantum behaved particle swarm Optimization successfully discovers the route with the shortest length within the WBAN for data transmission. Since it has fewer control parameters to adjust, the contraction-expansion coefficient (α) enables it to have a much greater scope of exploration as well as exploitation, depending upon its value. The value of α thus decides the particle's location in the state-space. As for PSOBAN, both position as well as velocity parameters, are taken into account.

5.2 Residual Energy

The amount of energy still left over with each node, after performing different operations within the WBAN, is called the residual or remnant energy. As stated earlier, Quantum PSO has fewer control parameters to adjust, exploration is increased significantly, chances of confinement in the local optimum are reduced as well. So, our proposed routing protocol, QRP, deploys the policy of selection of relaying biosensor according to the Eq. (14), via. the shortest distance from a node to sink, and as a result, the pathway that is obtained contributes to enhanced energy saving. The simulations convey that at about 7000 rounds, QRP retains 8.75% more residual energy levels than PSOBAN, 52.34% more residual energy than SIMPLE and 22.97% more residual energy levels than M-ATTEMPT. While roughly at 8000 rounds, QRP retains 9.82% more residual energy levels than PSOBAN, 37% more residual energy than SIMPLE and 26.2% more residual energy levels than M-ATTEMPT i.e., greater energy conservations, than others (Fig. 5).

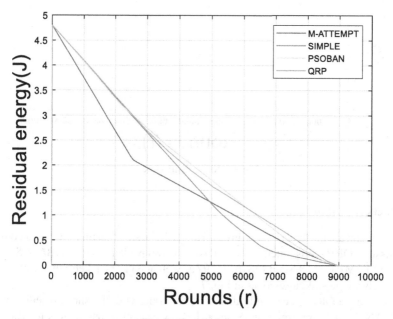

Fig. 5. Residual energy

5.3 Network Lifetime

QRP, is pitted against the existing PSOBAN, M-ATTEMPT and SIMPLE protocol. From Fig. 6, it's obvious that QRP has an enhanced networking-lifetime than PSOBAN and M-ATTEMPT as its foremost biosensor perished way afterwards than the other two. In comparison with SIMPLE protocol, the rearmost node of QRP perishes afterwards. It is so, as in QRP, the transmissions take place only when the biosensors possess higher remnant energies and also least distanced. The foremost and rearmost node of PSOBAN perish at 3800 and 8995 rounds, respectively. As for M-ATTEMPT and SIMPLE, the foremost and rearmost nodes perish at 2493 and 8974 rounds as well as 5325 and 8962 rounds, respectively. The QRP shows considerable improvement, as its foremost and rearmost node perish at 4349 and 8972 rounds, respectively.

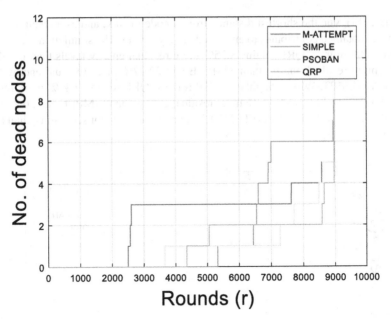

Fig. 6. Network lifetime

5.4 Packets Sent to Sink

The packet sent are the total packets directed towards the sink (destination), over course of transmission. QRP sends much higher packets, 52480 packets over PSOBAN, SIMPLE and M-ATTEMPT which send 43876, 45397 as well as 31173 packets per 10,000 rounds respectively to the sink, as evident in Fig. 7.

It is because QRP successfully discovers the route with the shortest length within the WBAN for data transmission. Since it has fewer control parameters to adjust, the contraction-expansion coefficient (α) enables it to have a much greater scope of exploration as well as exploitation, depending upon its value. The value of α thus decides the particle's location in the state-space. As for PSOBAN, both position as well as velocity parameters, are taken into account. Similarly, SIMPLE and M-ATTEMPT have lesser stability period i.e. lesser alive nodes than QRP, so the packets sent to the sink are much lesser.

5.5 Packet Dropped

The packet drop is basically, the loss of packets transmitted to the sink (destination) over the course of transmission. As QRP detects the shortest path much quicker than PSOBAN, SIMPLE as well as M-ATTEMPT, by better exploring and exploiting the state-space, the data transmission rates are ought to be higher. Whenever the data transmission rates are massive, some amount of loss of the data packets is always there. As stated above, since the data transmission rate of QRP is much greater, loss of packets over the network is inevitable, as seen in Fig. 8. Therefore, in contrast with QRP; PSOBAN,

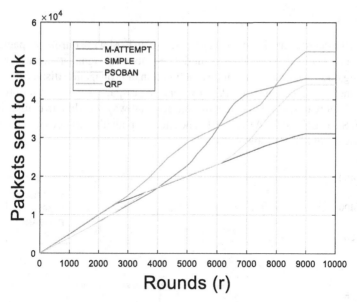

Fig. 7. Packets sent to sink

SIMPLE and M-ATTEMPT send much lesser number of packets to the sink; thus, the packet drops are comparatively lesser in these routing protocols.

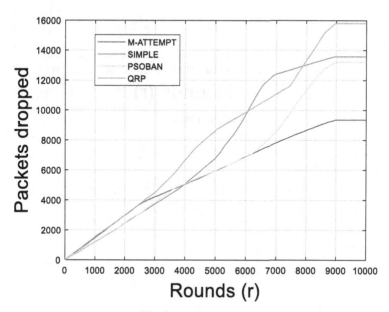

Fig. 8. Packet dropped

5.6 Path-Loss

Path loss is the decrementation of energy density of an E-M wave during propagation. It is measurable in 'decibel'. The path loss model describes the signal attenuation between a transmitting node and a receiving node as a function of propagation distance and various other parameters. Since Quantum PSO explores state-space way better, it optimises the fit. fun. with more efficacy and detect the shortest pathway speedily, in comparison with PSOBAN, SIMPLE and M-ATTEMPT. The shortest path, thus assures much lesser path loss, as evident in Fig. 9 (Table 4).

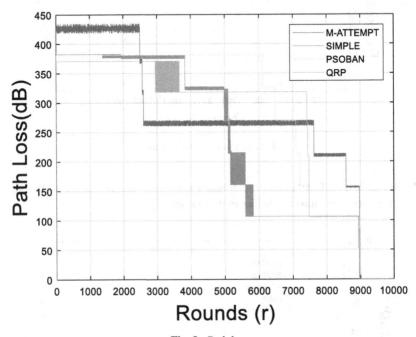

Fig. 9. Path loss

Table 4. Different parameters for comparison of M-ATTEMPT, SIMPLE, PSOBAN and QRP

Parameters	Protocols	M-ATTEMPT[11]	SIMPLE[11]	PSOBAN [8]	Proposed QRP
No of rounds at which first sensor node dies		2493	5325	3800	4349
No of rounds at which last sensor node dies		8974	8961	8995	8972
Packets sent		31173	45397	43876	52480
Packets received		21819	31811	30900	36678
Packets dropped		9354	13585	12976	15802
Residual Energy (J)	At 1000 rounds	3.745736	4.08104	4.06992	4.09545
	At 2000 rounds	2.68955	3.36658	3.3661	3.390105
	At 3000 rounds	1.95298	2.65572	2.64584	2.68793
	At 4000 rounds	1.60381	1.94456	2.2095	2.092102
	At 5000 rounds	1.25457	1.22981	1.702876	1.593058
	At 6000 rounds	0.90439	0.65980	1.2652	1.186839
	At 7000 rounds	0.55496	0.26131	0.697207	0.784665
	At 8000 rounds	0.23512	0.12719	0.3990	0.49715
	At 9000 rounds	0	0	0	0
	At 10000 rounds	0	0	0	0
Path-Loss (dB)	At 2000 rounds	428.69	380.65	372	370.74
	At 4000 rounds	264.68	327.30	372	318.06
	At 6000 rounds	262.94	106.67	372	318.06
	At 8000 rounds	211.90	106.67	109.2	105.55
	At 10000 rounds	0	0	0	0

6   Conclusion and Future Scope

In our research paper, we proposed a quantum behaved PSO based routing protocol, QRP. The QPSO algorithm is selected because it makes use of only single parameter, positional vector, where PSO makes use of both positional and velocity. Fitness function used, in this work, is the ratio of the length of distance between sink and a biosensor and the remnant energy of biosensor. The biosensor node having least function value is chosen relay, to transmit data through the shortest route. To justify its efficacy, performance of QRP is analyzed and compared with prevailing contemporaries namely, M-ATTEMPT, SIMPLE and PSOBAN. The protocol performance is compared in terms of energy utilization, throughput, packets sent to sink, packet drop, path loss, and total network lifetime. The simulations show that our algorithm outperforms SIMPLE, M-ATTEMPT and PSOBAN in the above-mentioned performance metrices. Our experimental results show significant improvements in packet success rates as our proposed protocol achieves an increased throughput of 18.69% over PSOBAN, 15.3% over SIMPLE and 68.1% over M-ATTEMPT respectively. Similarly, our protocol achieves much higher transmission rates as packets sent by QRP are 19.61% more than PSOBAN, 15.6% more than SIMPLE and 68.35% more than M-ATTEMPT respectively. The results also show that at about 8000 rounds, QRP experiences 50.19% lesser path loss than M-ATTEMPT, 3.4% lesser than PSOBAN and 1.05% lesser path loss than SIMPLE. The results also indicate that at about 8000 rounds, QRP retains 9.82% more residual energy levels than PSOBAN, 37% more residual energy than SIMPLE and 26.2% more residual energy levels than M-ATTEMPT i.e., greater energy conservation, in comparison with others. Thus, promoting increased energy-efficiency and prolonged performance of the WBAN. In future work, we will focus on comparison with other existing routing protocols as well as developing new routing strategies.

References

1. Raja, K.S., Kiruthika, U.: An energy efficient method for secure and reliable data transmission in wireless body area networks using RelAODV. Wireless Pers. Commun. **83**(4), 2975–2997 (2015). https://doi.org/10.1007/s11277-015-2577-x
2. Movassaghi, S., Abolhasan, M., Lipman, J., Smith, D., Jamalipour, A.: Wireless body area networks: a survey. IEEE Commun. Surv. Tutorials **16**(3), 1658–1686 (2014). https://doi.org/10.1109/SURV.2013.121313.00064
3. Shakya, A., Mishra, M., Maity, D., Santarsiero, G.: Structural health monitoring based on the hybrid ant colony algorithm by using Hooke-Jeeves pattern search. SN Appl. Sci. (2019). https://doi.org/10.1007/s42452-019-0808-6
4. Chen, M., Gonzalez, S., Vasilakos, A., Cao, H., Leung, V.C.M.: Body area networks: a survey. Mobile Netw. Appl. **16**(2), 171–193 (2011). https://doi.org/10.1007/s11036-010-0260-8
5. Ling, Z., Hu, F., Wang, L., Yu, J., Liu, X.: Point-to-point wireless information and power transfer in WBAN with energy harvesting. IEEE Access **5**(c), 8620–8628 (2017). https://doi.org/10.1109/ACCESS.2017.2695222
6. Shi, W.V., Zhou, M.: Body sensors applied in pacemakers: a survey. IEEE Sens. J. **12**(6), 1817–1827 (2012). https://doi.org/10.1109/JSEN.2011.2177256
7. Wu, T.Y., Lin, C.H.: Low-SAR path discovery by particle swarm optimization algorithm in wireless body area networks. IEEE Sens. J. **15**(2), 928–936 (2015). https://doi.org/10.1109/JSEN.2014.2354983
8. Bilandi, N., Verma, H.K., Dhir, R.: PSOBAN: a novel particle swarm optimization based protocol for wireless body area networks. SN Appl. Sci. (2019). https://doi.org/10.1007/s42452-019-1514-0
9. Kaur, N., Singh, S.: Optimized cost effective and energy efficient routing protocol for wireless body area networks. Ad Hoc Netw. **61**, 65–84 (2017). https://doi.org/10.1016/j.adhoc.2017.03.008
10. Kanchan, P., Shetty, D.P.: Quantum PSO algorithm for clustering in wireless sensor networks to improve network lifetime. In: Advances in Intelligent Systems and Computing, vol. 814, pp. 699–713. Springer, Berlin (2019). https://doi.org/10.1007/978-981-13-1501-5_62
11. Nadeem, Q., Javaid, N., Mohammad, S.N., Khan, M.Y., Sarfraz, S., Gull, M.: SIMPLE: Stable increased-throughput multi-hop protocol for link efficiency in Wireless Body Area Networks. In: Proceedings - 2013 8th International Conference on Broadband, Wireless Computing, Communication and Applications, BWCCA 2013, pp. 221–226 (2013). https://doi.org/10.1109/BWCCA.2013.42
12. Yan, J., Peng, Y., Shen, D., Yan, X., Deng, Q.: An artificial bee colony-based green routins mechanism in WBANs for sensor-based E-healthcare systems. Sensors (Switzerland), **18**(10) (2018). https://doi.org/10.3390/s18103268
13. Kalaiselvi, K., Suresh, G.R., Ravi, V.: Genetic algorithm based sensor node classifications in wireless body area networks (WBAN). Cluster Comput. 1–7 (2018). https://doi.org/10.1007/s10586-018-1770-6

14. Ali, G. A., Murtaza, S., Al Masud, R.: Routing optimization in WBAN using Bees Algorithm for overcrowded Hajj environment. Int. J. Adv. Comput. Sci. Appl. **9** (2018). www.ijacsa.the sai.org
15. Ahmed, S., et al.: Co-LAEEBA: cooperative link aware and energy efficient protocol for wireless body area networks. Comput. Hum. Behav. **51**, 1205–1215 (2015). https://doi.org/10.1016/j.chb.2014.12.051
16. Hayyolalam, V., Pourhaji Kazem, A.A.: Black Widow Optimization Algorithm: A novel metaheuristic approach for solving engineering optimization problems. Eng. Appl. Artif. Intell. **87**, 103249 (2020). https://doi.org/10.1016/j.engappai.2019.103249
17. Heidari, A.A., Mirjalili, S., Faris, H., Aljarah, I., Mafarja, M., Chen, H.: Harris hawks optimization: algorithm and applications. Future Gener. Comput. Syst. **97**, 849–872 (2019). https://doi.org/10.1016/j.future.2019.02.028
18. Zhang, Y., Jin, Z.: Group teaching optimization algorithm: A novel metaheuristic method for solving global optimization problems. Expert Syst. Appl. 113246 (2020). https://doi.org/10.1016/j.eswa.2020.113246
19. Qais, M.H., Hasanien, H.M., Alghuwainem, S., Nouh, A.S.: Coyote optimization algorithm for parameters extraction of three- diode photovoltaic models of photovoltaic modules. Energy **187**, (2019). https://doi.org/10.1016/j.energy.2019.116001
20. Shi, Y., Eberhart, R.C.: Empirical study of particle swarm optimization. In: Proceedings of the 1999 Congress on Evolutionary Computation, CEC 1999, vol. 3, pp. 1945–1950 (1999). https://doi.org/10.1109/CEC.1999.785511
21. Li, R., Wang, D.: Clustering routing protocol for wireless sensor networks based on improved QPSO algorithm. In: International Conference on Advanced Mechatronic Systems, ICAMechS, 2017- December, pp. 168–172 (2018). https://doi.org/10.1109/ICAMechS.2017.8316529
22. Clerc, M., James, K.: The Particle Swarm—Explosion, Stability, and Convergence in a Multidimensional Complex Space. Ieee Trans. Evol. Comput. **6**, 58–73 (2002)
23. Sun, J., Feng, B., Xu, W.: Particle Swam Optimization with Particles Having Quantum Behavior (n.d.)
24. Liu, A.J., Xu, A.W., Sun, A.J.: Quantum-behaved Particle Swarm Optimization with Mutation Operator (2005)
25. Yang, Z.L., Wu, A., Min, H.Q.: An improved quantum-behaved particle swarm optimization algorithm with elitist breeding for unconstrained optimization. Comput. Intell. Neurosci. (2015). https://doi.org/10.1155/2015/326431
26. Sun, J.: Quantum-Behaved Particle Swarm Optimization : Analysis of Individual Particle Behavior and Parameter Selection, **20**(3), 349–393 (n.d.)
27. Heinzelman, W.B., Chandrakasan, A.P., Balakrishnan, H.: An application-specific protocol architecture for wireless microsensor networks. IEEE Trans. Wirel. Commun. **1**(4), 660–670 (2002). https://doi.org/10.1109/TWC.2002.804190
28. Sun, J., Xu, W., Fang, W.: LNCS 4247 - A Diversity-Guided Quantum-Behaved Particle Swarm Optimization Algorithm. LNCS, vol. 4247 (2006)
29. https://www.mathworks.com/products/matlab.html

Investigation of Alibaba Cloud Data Set for Resource Management in Cloud Computing

Kirtikumar Jashavantbhai Sharma$^{(\boxtimes)}$ and Narenda Manorbhai Patel

Birla Vishvakaram Mahavidyalaya, Engineering College, Gujarat Technological University,
Vallabh Vidyanagar 388120, Gujarat, India
{kjsharma,nmpatel}@bvmengineering.ac.in

Abstract. Effective utilization of Cloud computing resources is always part of research trades. Even due to the high carbon footprint of it, it is essential to know the utilization of each resource, like underutilized or over-utilized. Alibaba Cluster Trace Program is published by Alibaba Group. It helps all the people in the field of Cloud be students, researchers to have inside of the characteristics for data centers and the workloads through cluster trace from real production. This paper gives an in-depth analysis of the Alibaba cluster dataset 2017, published in 2018 as part of Alibaba cloud. Mostly two types of workloads are shown in the dataset; one is batch workload (offline Job) another is online workload, which runs in containers. This paper also describes how to calculate overall, offline, and online workload utilizations. Lastly, recent research on the dataset and discussed various scheduling algorithms that could apply for better resource management.

Keywords: Resource management · Cloud computing · Container · Analysis · Scheduling algorithm · Additional alibaba cluster

1 Introduction

Resource management and proper utilization is a crucial parameter in cloud computing services. How to effectively maximize resource use is a challenging issue [7]. To increase the data center efficiency and as cloud datacenter grows on a scale, we need to co-allocation large-scale online service and batch jobs. Existing Cluster Management system has a significant challenge due to the co-allocation. Those challenges includes services and jobs scheduler. If services and Job are tuned with efficient algorithm cluster utilization and efficiency can be increased significantly [5, 7].

A challenge to following research topics for both academics and industry. First, Workload Characterization. Second, the algorithm is to assign workload to machine and CPU cores. It transfers and re-adjust workloads to different machines and CPUs for better resource utilization. For maintaining QoS and failure recovery for online service, Batch Jobs and Online service scheduler has to cooperate. It helps online service and batch jobs schedulers in adjusting resource allocation and hence improving the throughput of batch jobs.

© Springer Nature Switzerland AG 2021
N. Chaubey et al. (Eds.): COMS2 2021, CCIS 1416, pp. 222–233, 2021.
https://doi.org/10.1007/978-3-030-76776-1_15

There are four chapters in this paper. The first chapter about introducing the data set and the need for the dataset study are discussed. In the second chapter, an in-depth study of the dataset is discussed. We will discuss each minute detail of the dataset in the second chapter. The third chapter discussed analysis, correlation of each machine, characterized workload, and last recent work on the dataset.

2   Understanding Ali Baba Dataset

Alibaba cluster-trace-v2017 provide trace data taken from a production cluster in 24 h period [1]. The data includes part of the machines and the workload of the whole cluster. All the included machines can run both online services and batch jobs. Certain information in dataset has been normalized as it is real-time data and there are certain security and confidentiality reasons. Timestamps of each record in the trace contains a value. The value is in seconds and relative to the start of the trace period. Additionally, a zero value represents the event occur before the trace period. In some of the files, there are few fractions of entries (e.g., less than 0.1% in batch_instance.csv) with a negative timestamp, and they also indicate the events that happen before the start time of trace [1].

Measurements of usages, including instances and machine usages, are taken in 60 s and average over 300 s. For confidentiality reasons, they disclose usage data only for 12 consecutive hours.

"Alibaba Cluster Trace" 12 h production servers' cluster information are in the dataset. and includes about 1.3 k machines that run both online services and offline batch jobs (1.5 GB) [1]. Physical server executes Batch jobs and containers executes online services.

The server executes online workload, e.g., Payment, transaction, browsing request by a container. Different instances serve offline workload, e.g., computing service, a batch. Each offline workload has n number of jobs. Each Job has n number of tasks. Each task has n number of instances. Instances are executed on the server (Fig. 1).

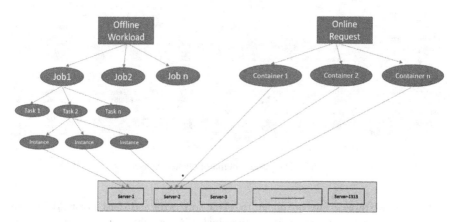

Fig. 1. Offline workload and online workload.

Every machine has unique numeric identifiers for online and service workload in the trace period. Dataset provider has not mentioned service and task names. CPU core count is not normalized but Disk utilization measurements and Memory requests are normalized.

The dataset includes six files: which can be classified into two categories, workload data and Resource data. These detailed specifications can be found in the schema.csv file. Resource Data contains four CSV files, i.e., Server_event.csv, Server_usage.csv, Container_usage.csv and Container_event.csv. Workload data contains two CSV files, i.e., Batch_instance.csv and Batch_task.csv. The CSV files have no header. Each data table is given in CSV format. The schema for all tables are also provided in CSV format in a file called schema.csv.

2.1 Resource Utilization Information

Two tables describe machines: the machine events table and the machine resource utilization table [1].

2.1.1 Machine Events (Server_event.csv)

This CSV file describes the hardware information of each server. As per Fig. 2, a total of 7 attributes in CSV file to represent server information. In this dataset, total 1313 Servers are there with machine id 1 to 1313. Each server has 64 core CPUs and normalized memory, and a hard disk. All machine values of the timestamp attribute are zero, which means all servers are already working conditions before this log is taken.

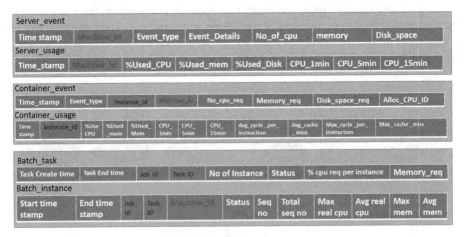

Fig. 2. Database schema of cluster dataset

As an event, three events are added to ADD, soft_error and Hard_error. ADD event means a machine became available to the cluster. All machines in the trace have an ADD event and have a timestamp of value 0 since all machines are added before the trace collection. Soft_error means a machine becomes temporarily unavailable due to software failures, such as insufficient disk space and agent failures. Last, hard_error means a machine becomes unavailable due to hardware failures, such as disk failures. In software and hardware errors, new batch jobs and online services should not be added in the machines, but existing services and jobs may still function normally. Error reasons can be inferred from the event detail field.

Physical capacity of each machine is being reflected as normalized value along each dimension. Normalized value ranges from 0 to 100 for CPU Core and RAM size.

2.1.2   Machine Resource Utilization (Server_usage.csv)

This CSV file describes overall machine resource utilization. The total period is 12 h (12 * 60 = 720 min). For every 5 min interval, one utilization entry is available in the dataset, a total (720/5)144 entries for each 1313 machine.

Total resource utilization of all workloads (batch tasks, online container instances, and operating systems' workloads) in physical machines. It records the CPU usage, memory usage, disk usage, the average Linux CPU load of 1/5/15 minduring a period from 39600 s to 82500 s, and most of the record time interval is 300 s (5 min). Machine utilization is the fraction of 100, reflecting the total resource usage of all workloads, including operating systems.

2.2   Online Service (Container)

All transaction requests and real-time instances are given to containers, a small instance to execute online queries. Two tables describe online service one is service instance event, and another is service instance usage.

2.3   Online Request Table (Container_event.csv)

This table reflects the created online containers and their requested resources, including the assigned CPU cores, memory, and disk space. Container event consists of eight attributes ts: timestamp of event, event: event type includes: Create and Remove, instance_id: online instance id, machine_id, plan_cpu: CPU number requested, plan_mem: normalized memory requested, plan_disk: normalized disk space requested, cpuset: assigned cpuset by online scheduler CPUs delimited by 'l'. A total of 11102 online instances are recorded.

Just one event type, "Create", that is, the online container instance will always exist if it is not killed after being created, which can be considered a long-running job workload. The timestamp for all events is zero, which means it starts before recording time. Machine id is also allocated because of the online event and has higher priorities. While in the offline Job, when the task is requested, the machine is not assigned.

This trace includes only two types of instance events. The online instance creation record for a start is in "create" event records, and the online instance finish record, for instance, is in the "finish" event record. "ts" field has a zero value indicate the container created before the trace period. As the instance creation and removal finish in a few minutes, the start time of instance, creation, and removal can be derived from the finish time.

According to CPU topology and service constraints, the Online scheduler gives unique cpuset allocation to the online instance. There are a total of 64 CPUs in each machine. CPUs 0 to 31 package in same and 32 to 64 package in the same category. CPU 0 and 32 belong to other CPU cores, et cetera. Improvement in the cpuset allocation should be made, like difference interference between instances sharing the same CPU core and package.

2.3.1 Service Instance Usage (Container_usage.csv)

The file has necessary resource utilization information for online container instances, such as CPU usage, memory usage, disk usage, average CPU load, cache misses. Most container resource utilization data is also collected from the 39600 s to 82500 s and 300 s data for resource usage measurement. As total online requests are 11,102 for 144-time intervals, 1,598,688 data must be available in the dataset, but 117,782 rows (8%) data are missing.

Container event consists of twelve attributes ts: start time of measurement interval, instance_id: online instance id, cpu_util: used percent of requested CPUs, mem_util: used percent of requested memory, avg_mpki: average last-level cache misses per 1000 instructions, disk_util: used percent of requested disk space load1 load5 load15, avg_cpi average cycles per instructions, max_cpi: maximum CPI, max_mpki: maximum MPKI.

Service instance utilization like The CPU/mem/disk is relative to the requested resource. Its value can be 0 (no utilization) to 100 (full usage). The Load metric is relative to the assigned CPUs. The CPI and MPKI metrics are measured in 1 s, and five samples are taken to compute the average and maximum values.

2.4 Batch Workload

Two tables describe the batch workload. One is the instance table, and another is the task table. Users submit batch workloads in the form of Job. Multiple tasks may be included in a job. Different tasks execute different computing logic. Functions for a DAG according to the data dependency. Batch workload has smallest unit as instance. Within a task, all instances execute with the same resource request with the same binary file but with different input data.

2.4.1 Task Table (batch_task.csv)

Mostly all offline and computational jobs are treated as batch jobs. It consists of eight attributes create_timestamp: creation time of a task, modify_timestamp: latest state modification time, job_id: unique job id is given to all Job, task_id: all Job has required task, instance_num: number of instances for the task, status: Task states include Ready, Waiting, Running, Terminated, Failed, and Cancelled, plan_cpu: CPU requested for each instance of the task, plan_mem: normalized memory requested for all instance of the task.

Table (total 80553 tasks with no of instance, 11,909,321) contains multiple tasks, and according to the data dependencies, different tasks execute different computing logics.

Multiple instances may execute the same task for different input data using the same binary file.

Task attribute having following values "Failed:" task fails, and "Running:" The Task is being processed, "terminated:" A task goes to 'Terminated' when all its instances are done, "Waiting:" A task is not in initialized yet.

Instance attribute having the following values "Terminated:" An instance is done, "Waiting:" The instance cannot run because dependencies have not finished, "Failed:" An instance fails, and due to some reseon instance stop "Interrupted:" feature introduced for backup.

Here Job id and task id is a unique attribute and it is also reflected in the batch instance table. Job id starts from 0 and up to 12950. While the task begins from 0 to maximum 67988, which means jobs have a minimum of 0 to a maximum 67988 number of tasks. Each task has several instances; it starts from 0 to end with 64486. A total of 80553 rows in the batch task file.

2.4.2   Instance Table (batch_instance.csv)

A batch task that got a chance to run, its information is available in the instance table. When the Task of the Job starts and completes its work reflected in this table, instance table consists of twelve attributes job_id, task_id, end_timestamp: instance end time if the instance ended, start_timestamp: instance start time if the instance is started, machineID: the host machine running the instance, real_mem_max: maximum normalized memory when instance running, real_mem_avg: average normalized memory when instance running, status: Instance states: includes Failed, Running, Terminated, Ready, Waiting, Cancelled, and Interrupted, seq_no: running trials number, starts from 1 and increase by 1 for each retry, real_cpu_max: maximum CPU numbers of the actual instance running,total_seq_no: total number of retries, real_cpu_avg: average CPU numbers of the actual instance running, Due to network problems and machine failure a batch instance may fail. Each record in the instance table record one tries to run. Value 0 will be recorded for the start and end timestamp for some instance status. For example, the instance is in the running and failed status, the start time is non-zero, but the end time is zero. It is in ready and waiting status; all timestamps are zero.

In this file, multiple entries are available for the same job id and task id because multiple instances are there for each Job and task. Dataset does not contain 80% data (80553 * 11,909,321) in the CSV file. It isn't easy to judge the utilization of batch job tasks. Here the actual timestamp is recorded when it started and completed.

The batch's smallest scheduling unit is workload value 0 for some instances in the start and end timestamp. For example, all timestamps are zero when the instance is in ready and waiting status; the start time is non-zero, but the end time is zero when the instance is in failed status. Most of the batch job's completion time is 132,260 and 1067 s. The maximum task is 40, and the maximum Instance 940.

3 Data Analysis

Resource management and utilization are essential parameters of any cloud service provider. This paper analyzes the usage of primary resources, i.e., CPU, Ram, and memory. Mainly two types of requests: offline requests, online requests. Online requests run on the container, and offline Job handled batch-wise.

3.1 Utilization and Summary of Data

This section calculation and method discussed to know the utilization of each request either may be offline or online.

3.2 Overall Utilization

Apart from offline and online, the request machine itself also has a workload. Server_usage CSV file describes overall usage, machine usage, offline, and online workload usage. Figure 3 shows the heat map of the overall utilization of CPU, Memory, and Disk. Heat map produced shows approximately 50% utilization of CPU, more memory utilized, and less disk utilization. Somewhere machine_id between 380 to 569 is not utilized correctly. The workload is not correctly distributed among the server (Figs. 4 and 5).

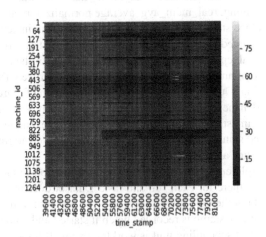

Fig. 3. Heat map of overall utilization for CPU

3.2.1 Container Level Resource Usage Data

To calculating the CPU usage, memory usage, and disk usage of all containers during every interval following algorithm implemented. Every request requires more than one CPU and more memory so that it can be run on multiple servers vice versa; one server handles multiple requests for every 5 min interval usage given. So need of All machine

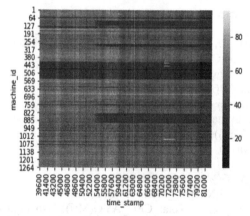

Fig. 4. Heat map of overall utilization for memory

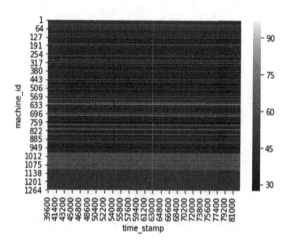

Fig. 5. Heat map of overall utilization of Disk

all timestamp calculation. Each server has 64 cores; accordingly need to calculate the CPU average. Memory value is normalized, so for each container need avg memory usage is required, same applicable to disk utilization (Table 1).

Figure 6, 7 and 8 heat map about the utilization of CPU, memory, and disk of online request (Container). No online request by machin_id from 442 to 568 means that offline batch jobs only utilize the machine. Overall from all heat map containers utilized fewer resources. It required more memory; online jobs are memory intensive.

Table 1. Algortiham to calculte CPU, memory, and disk utilization of all containers

Algorithm: To find CPU, memory, and disk utilization of all containers
Input: All Machine and Container data
Output: Total CPU Usage, Total Memory usage
  Select all machine(M(i))
    Select all container on that machine(C(j))
      Select all timestamp (T(k))
      CPU_AVG(c(i))= %CPU_use (C(j)) * (No of CPU Requested(C(j)))/(Total No CPU(M(i)))
      Mem_Avg(c(i)) = %Mem_use(c(j)) * %Mem_req(c(j))
    Total_CPU_AVG(M(i))= ∑CPU_AVG(C(i))
    Total_Mem_AVG(M(i))= ∑Mem_AVG(C(i))
  Overall_cluster_avg_cpu = Total_CPU_AVG(M(i)) / No_of_Machine
  Overall_cluster_avg_mem = Total_Mem_AVG(M(i)) / No_of_Machine

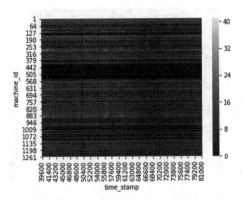

Fig. 6. Heat map of the container (online job) for CPU utilization

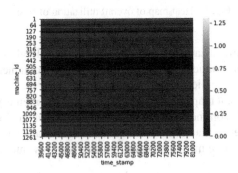

Fig. 7. Heat map of the container (online job) for memory utilization

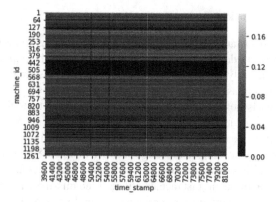

Fig. 8. Heat map of the container (online job) of disk

3.2.2 BATCH Level Resource Usage Data

To find the utilization of batch jobs is straightforward because the overall utilization and online job utilization data are already calculated. From that, easily calculate utilization of batch workload. Heat map of the batch level job shows the offline Job is a more CPU intensive task rather than memory intensive. Formula to find utilization of each resource is

Batch level resource usage = Total usage – Container usage or another way, for each 5 min time stamp, all batch jobs need to consider that have been either started, completed, or running throughout timestamp. We need to consider four types of offline jobs. First, the batch job starts after the timestamp started and before the time stamp is completed (task 1). The second batch job starts before the time stamp and is completed before the time stamp is completed (task 2). Third batch job after time stamp and not compete before the time stamp end time (task 3). Fourth, the batch job starts before the time stamp and does not complete a 5 min time stamp (task 4). Summation of all and take the average of those able to calculate resource utilization of offline jobs (Fig. 9).

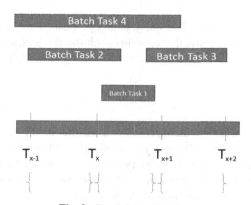

Fig. 9. Batch job utilization.

3.3 Characterized Workload

The online container instances and batch tasks are not running on all the machines in the cloud. More memory demand and long running jobs is for the online containers, the memory usage is relatively stable, on the other hand batch jobs are CPU intensive and fluctuate for most batch tasks are short time duration based jobs.

Following known issues to the current version of the dataset, try to fix them in the next version. Some task_id or job_id is missing in batch_instance.csv. As mentioned in the issue in the batch_instance.csv file, about 85% of the entries are missing. As with task_id and job_id are of start_timestamp in the range between 60000 to 89000. instance_id 9088 and some instance_id in container_usage.csv not appearing in container_event.csv. In the usage information of batch_instance.csv file e some missing data [1].

For resource management, current container technology, e.g., Docker, Kubernetes, and Apache Mesos using basic scheduling methods Round Robin, Bin pack, and Round Robin [8, 9]. We need to apply a new strategy to the reduction of energy consumption in data centers. Current research is based on Weighted based Ensure Quality of services (online and offline job) or method which applies to manage virtual machines. The same method can be useful to manage containers.

3.4 Recent Research for the Dataset

Congfeng jiang, guangjie han discussed workload characterization, resource Utilization, CPU and memory utilization for online request and offline jobs, machine clustering, correlation analysis of CPU and memory utilization [2].

Rui Ren, Lei Wang, Zheng Cao Jinheng Li, Jianfeng Zhan, discussed first data Preprocessing, perform node similarity analysis, workload characteristics, and anomaly analysis [6].

Fengcun Li and Bo Hu by Simulator released with this paper: CloudSimPy-2019. The log data Alibaba cluster v2017 is replayed to the trainee agent. Input dimension of the neural network is 6 is available duration of a task and no of instances of task, reduction in makespan CPU & memory of machine and CPU & memory requirement of task [3].

Miao lin, jiayin wu, weihua bai, and jianqing proposed three multi-objective optimization model, first one improve the reliability of cluster services, second one Balancing a load of a physical node in the cluster and third reducing network transmission cost [4].

4 Conclusion

This paper mainly focuses on utilizing resources, whether online or offline and finds the correlation between machines. The study concludes that offline jobs are more processor-intensive, and online jobs are more memory intensive. Some of the online jobs are not run on any machines, and the same some offline jobs are not run on all machines. An imbalance is the workload distribution, which makes a lot of machines underutilized. Hence, the dataset analysis suggests that the current scheduling algorithm has a scope of improvement to utilize the resources better. The cluster also can be divided further into a sub-cluster to run an appropriate workload. E.g., one server can run 50% offline jobs and 50% online jobs. The above researcher's algorithms might be run on the Alibaba dataset to explore its effective utilization.

Acknowledgment. Many thanks to The Alibaba Cluster Trace Program is published by Alibaba Group for publishing cluster dataset.

References

1. Alibaba: Alibaba Cluster Trace Program. https://github.com/alibaba/clusterdata
2. Jiang, C., et al.: Characteristics of Co-allocated online services and batch jobs in internet data centers: a case study from Alibaba cloud. IEEE Access **7**, 22495–22508 (2019). https://doi.org/10.1109/ACCESS.2019.2897898
3. Li, F., Hu, B.: DeepJS: job scheduling based on deep reinforcement learning in cloud data center. In: Proceedings of the 2019 4th International Conference on Big Data and Computing - ICBDC 2019, pp. 48–53. ACM Press, Guangzhou, China (2019). https://doi.org/10.1145/3335484.3335513
4. Lin, M., et al.: Ant colony algorithm for multi-objective optimization of container-based microservice scheduling in cloud. IEEE Access **7**, 83088–83100 (2019). https://doi.org/10.1109/ACCESS.2019.2924414
5. Liu, B., et al.: A new container scheduling algorithm based on multi-objective optimization. Soft Comput. **22**(23), 7741–7752 (2018). https://doi.org/10.1007/s00500-018-3403-7
6. Ren, R., et al.: Anomaly analysis for co-located datacenter workloads in the Alibaba cluster. arXiv:1811.06901[cs] (2018)
7. Zhou, R., et al.: Scheduling frameworks for cloud container services. IEEE/ACM Trans. Netw. **26**(1), 436–450 (2018). https://doi.org/10.1109/TNET.2017.2781200
8. Apache Mesos: Program against your datacenter like it's a single pool of resources. http://mesos.apache.org/
9. How services work: Docker Documentation. https://docs.docker.com/engine/swarm/how-swarm-mode-works/services/

A Hybrid Approach Based on ACO and Firefly Algorithm for Routing in FANETs

Amrita Yadav[1]([⊠]) [iD] and Seema Verma[2] [iD]

[1] Department of Computer Science, Banasthali Vidyapith, Tonk, India
[2] Department of Electronics, Banasthali Vidyapith, Tonk, India
vseema@banasthali.in

Abstract. The paper proposes Hybrid Ant Colony Optimization and Firefly Algo-rithm for routing solutions in Flying Ad-hoc Networks (FANETs). As routing is one of the major problems in FANETs because of its distinctive characteristics, this paper aims to find the best solution for routing. The proposed algorithm focusses on obtaining the efficient path with the help of ACO (Ant Colony Optimization) and FA (Firefly Algorithm) in ad-hoc networks. It uses a multi-path ACO algo-rithm and finds the optimal path by using the Firefly algorithm. The proposed hybrid algorithm is tested on various performance parameters which are packet delivery ratio, throughput, overhead, and end-to-end delay. The Hybrid algorithm is compared with ACO and FA individually and results showed that the hybrid algorithm outperforms Ant Colony Optimization and Firefly algorithm and proves to be an efficient routing solution for FANETs.

Keywords: Ant colony optimization · Firefly algorithm · Routing · FANET · Nature inspired

1 Introduction

Flying Ad-Hoc Network (FANET) is a network that connects multiple Unmanned Aerial Vehicles (UAVs). These UAVs do not require a fixed infrastructure. FANETs make com-munication easy with every UAVs which are at the ground station as well as which are in the air, this means all the UAVs which are even not in the range of communication may transfer data to the ground station. Various companies are using UAVs to collect information of ground regions and to minimize the cost and time of operation [1]. But there are many issues which can hold back proper communication between them. One of the major issues in a communication network is routing. Maintaining and enduring connectivity in FANETs becomes difficult since the nodes keep on moving at a high speed. Their topology keeps on changing rapidly and hence they may lose connectivity. Previous research consists of designing protocols on the conventional routing protocols in airborne networks. In FANET, the research is still going on to set up a proper commu-nication network between the nodes. There must be a proper routing algorithm between the nodes which ensures proper transmission of packets.

© Springer Nature Switzerland AG 2021
N. Chaubey et al. (Eds.): COMS2 2021, CCIS 1416, pp. 234–246, 2021.
https://doi.org/10.1007/978-3-030-76776-1_16

Nature-Inspired Algorithms (NIA) has taken over all the other traditional routing algorithms and, are found in the area of computing systems for wireless communication. NIA is an algorithm that takes inspiration from biological phenomena so as to aid in computation. These algorithms are based on living organisms' frameworks [2]. Nature-inspired optimization algorithms represent an encouraging solution for explaining complex optimization problems.

NIA is divided into two parts: Genetic Algorithms and Swarm Intelligence.

Genetic algorithms (GA) are a part of evolutionary computing [3]. "Genetic Algorithm is based on Darwin's theory about evolution" [4]. It is an efficient search method that can be used to select paths in a network. A GA is made with a set of solutions, which represents the chromosomes. This set is known as population. Following steps shows the process of GA- Initialization in which population is generated. Selection, where the population is calculated by fitness function. Mutation in which the population from the previous step is added to the mating pool and termination, where once the stopping condition is reached, the algorithm is made to exit.

The other type of algorithm is Swarm Intelligence (SI). Swarm intelligence approach also indicates the results of better performance than using other routing protocols.

SI is a subfield of artificial intelligence related to intelligent behaviour of swarms by interacting with each other for resolving real-world problems by simulating their natural behaviours [5].

It can also be defined as devising of algorithms that are intelligent in nature and are simulated by the behaviour of various animal communities. There are certain algorithms which are upgraded by its improved version and perform better.

The Improved ABC (Ant Bee Colony) algorithm is one such example that works better in real-time [6].

Algorithms inspired by swarm intelligence are flock-based congestion control, based on the behaviour of flock of birds [7], Chicken swarm algorithm, Elephant search algorithm, Cat swarm optimization algorithm etc.

Other SI algorithms include Firefly Algorithm, Cuckoo search Algorithm, Artificial Fish Swarm Algorithm. These algorithms are used in various other domains as well. Some of them are used for routing in wireless networks and have given much better results as compared to conventional algorithms.

SI was introduced in the year 1986. After that many algorithms based on swarm intelligence were started getting explored. Ant Colony Optimization (ACO) is the most commonly used Nature Inspired algorithm (NIA). This algorithm was introduced in the year 1990. The testing of many of the variants of Ant Colony Optimization (ACO) has been done and compared with other algorithms in previous research and it is proved to be comparable and better than many of the routing algorithms on certain parameters. After the tremendous performance of ACO in many ad-hoc networks, another swarm-based NIA was given in 2008, which was named as Firefly algorithm. This algorithm uses the light flashing behaviour of fireflies. Firefly algorithm has also been used in various other ad-hoc networks and have given efficient results.

Since ACO algorithm has been used many times in FANETs, this paper briefly describes how Firefly algorithm can also be used in airborne networks and what makes it more adaptable. Both ACO and FA have proved to be efficient algorithms in different ad-hoc networks. This paper presents the mechanism of both the algorithms to find optimal path and proves to be an effective algorithm.

The paper has five sections. Section 1 presents the introduction of FANETs and NIA. Section 2 describes the Literature work done till now in NIA. Sections 3 and 4 presents the existing algorithms and working of proposed hybrid algorithm. Section 5 describes the parameters and methods used in simulation. The result of the simulation is described in Sect. 6. And lastly Sect. 7 briefly illustrates the conclusion of the paper.

2 Literature Review

Nature Inspired Algorithms have replaced the conventional routing algorithms in flying ad-hoc networks. There are many NIA which gives better results in flying ad-hoc networks when compared to old routing algorithms. In literature, much work has been cited by scholars in the field of NIA which proves that these algorithms are the new age routing solutions which uses artificial intelligence and gives favourable results for routing in FANETs. Following is the literary work which has been done till now using NIA for routing:

Muhammad Saleem (2008) [8], presented the Bee Adhoc algorithm. They showed two performance metrics i.e., routing overhead and route optimality using mathematical models for BeeAdHoc. In another paper, Vasily A. Maistrenko (2016) [9], compared AODV (Ad-hoc On-demand Distance Vector), DSR (Dynamic Source Routing), DSDV (Destination-Sequenced Distance Vector) protocols with AntHocNet in FANET routing. The results showed that with the increasing number of nodes, the packet delivery rate (PDR) becomes higher. The E2E (end-to-end delay) delay is low in AntHocNet with respect to AODV and DSDV. The paper concluded that AntHocNet outperforms AODV and DSDV on the basis of above parameters.

Joe Fiala (2016) [10], this paper shows the comparison MAARA (Multi-agent ant based routing algorithm) with AODV, AntHocNet, DSR in MANET routing, the results show that MAARA outperforms all the above algorithms in terms of PDR and delay.

In the next paper, two SI algorithms were compared with the conventional routing algorithms. A.V.Leonov (2017) [11], compared AntHocNet, BeeAdhoc with DSR, DSDV, AODV in FANET routing.

The results clearly showed that the solutions based on SI algorithms AntHocNet and BeeAdHoc are efficient in comparison with the conventional routing algorithms DSR, DSDV, and AODV.

Ashraf Darwish (2018) [12], in this paper, Bio-inspired computing- BIOA are analyzed, Observation of behavior and reaction of animals, setting assumptions, develop pseudo code, test algorithm. Results showed the integration of chaos theory with BIA to increase the level of performance.

A Nature-inspired scheme for FANETs based on clusters i.e., Bio-Inspired Clustering Scheme (BICSF) was proposed by Khan, A.N., et al (2019) [13]. This scheme uses glow-worm swarm optimization (GSO) and krill herd (KH) together as a hybrid mechanism. In this scheme, the cluster head formation and energy-aware cluster formation are done by the GSO algorithm. The results show BICSF has better results when compared with the other clustering algorithms based on nature-inspired. The results showed improvement in the following parameters: time to build cluster, cluster lifetime, energy consumption, and probability of delivery success.

Another Bio-Inspired recruiting Protocol in FANETs was proposed by Tropea, M., et.al (2019) [14]. The work showed performance of the protocol varying different algorithm parameters. The other algorithm similar to ACO is Bee Colony algorithm. Zhao, B., and Ding, Q. (2019) [15], reports work on the Bee colony algorithm (BCA) in FANET routing. It uses an extended Gauss Markov as its mobility model with the fitness function of BCA. This algorithm is used to identify path for FANETs in a 3D environment. The results show an improved PDR and delay.

Khan, Muhammad et al. (2019) [16] proposed a hybrid algorithm using Bluetooth and Wi-fi technology. The proposed algorithm mainly uses wireless communication technique and was designed for low energy consumption and high rate of transmission of data. The algorithm showed great performance for throughput and end-to-end delay parameters.

A hybrid algorithm based on packet forwarding was proposed by C. Pu and L. Carpenter (2019) [17]. This algorithm uses end-to-end routing and delay tolerant forwarding as it schemes. The simulation is done using OMNeT++. The results indicate that it can be used as a solution for routing in FANETs.

Another Hybrid algorithm for FANETs is proposed by Bhandari, Saurabh & Dudeja, Rajan (2020) [18]. This algorithm uses firefly algorithm with artificial neural network. The algorithm is based on clustering technique and uses SOCS (Hybridization of self-organization clustering scheme). The results are compared with ACO, SOCS, GWO (Glow worm Swarm optimization algorithm. The results of hybrid algorithm give better performance when compared to SOCS (self-organization clustering scheme) in terms of cluster formation and energy consumption and comparable to ACO and GWO.

S. Nath, et al (2020), [19] proposed a hybrid algorithm which uses firefly algorithm and ACO so as to make AODV more efficient. The results show that the suggested routing algorithm can be used as a better path generating algorithm as compared to AntHocNet and BeeAdhoc.

Modified ANtHocNet named as eAntHocNet was given by Khan, Inam, et.al (2020) [20]. It improves the network performance and lowers the energy consumption. The results were compared with DSR, TORA, AntHocNet and shows that it performs better than all the other routing protocols.

Therefore, from the above literature work, we can say that there is a huge need to explore Nature Inspired routing algorithms as they are giving phenomenal results in the area of routing in ad-hoc networks. Also, there is not so much work done on many NIA like firefly algorithm so there are lots of possibilities of considering FA as a routing solution for FANETs.

3   Existing Algorithm

Nature Inspired algorithms because of their ability to mimic the behaviour of insects, are widely been used as a part of artificial intelligence. These algorithms have earlier given comparable and efficient results when compared to conventional routing algorithms. ACO is the most used nature inspired algorithm and has been used in FANETs. Not many Nature inspired algorithms have been touched in this field. Since Firefly has given good response time in other ad-hoc networks, there was a need to use it in FANETs and compare the results with ACO as well.

3.1 Ant Colony Optimization (ACO)

ACO is a swarm intelligence algorithm. It was proposed by Dorigo [10]. It is an optimization technique which mimics the behaviour of ants when they search for food. It finds the shortest path when ants travel from their nest to the food source. Initially ants travel in every direction randomly. While travelling they leave pheromones (a chemical substance) on the path they have taken. All the other predeceasing ants smell the pheromones and get attracted by pheromones to follow the path which have more amount of pheromone. This causes communication between the ants and help them travel to the food source. While travelling there can be an obstacle on the route due to which the length of the path increases. This can distract ants from traveling by the shortest paths but since the concentration of the pheromone of longer path will evaporate and will not last long so the ants will again start travelling by the shortest path.

Therefore, the path can adapt dynamic changes in the environment.

i.   Every arc (i, j) of graph $G(N, A)$ has variable $t(\tau)_{ij}$ as pheromone trail.
ii. Initially constant amount of pheromone is deposited to all the arcs which is

$$t(\tau)_{ij} = 1, \ \forall (i, j) \in A$$

iii. Probability of the Kth ant at node i to j using pheromone trail is:

$$P_{ij}(K) = \begin{cases} \dfrac{t(\tau)_{ij}^{\alpha}}{\sum_{1 \in N_i^k} t(\tau)_{ij}} & \text{if } j \in N_i^k \\[2ex] & \text{if } j \notin N_i^k \end{cases}$$

Where N_i^k is neighbour of ant k at i^{th} node
iv. Neighbours of ith nodes connects all nodes except predecessor nodes.
v.   Pheromone deposited at every iteration is updated by

$$t(\tau)_{ij}(K + 1) = \rho_{t(\tau)_{ij}}(K) + \Delta_{t(\tau)_{ij}}(K)$$

Where $0 \leq \rho < 1$ = evaporation rate of pheromone
$\Delta t(\tau)_{ij}$ = Performance of each ant
vi. Probability of movement of ant K is given by

$$P_{ij}^K = \frac{\left[\tau_{ij}^{(t)}\right]^{\alpha} \left[\eta_{ij}^{(t)}\right]^{\beta}}{\sum \left[\tau_{ij}^{(t)}\right]^{\alpha} \left[\eta_{ij}^{(t)}\right]^{\beta}}$$

Where $\eta_{ij}^{(t)}$ = attractive coefficient

$\tau_{ij}^{(t)}$ = pheromone coefficient

α = coefficient controlling the value of τ

β = coefficient controlling the value of η

Following is the algorithm of ACO [21]:

Algorithm
Initialize ants, parameters of ACO;
while not end condition **do**
    for k=0 to n
        ant k selects source node;
    while solution is not constructed **do**
        ant k selects node having more pheromones;
    end while
    end for
    Update Pheromones;
end while

Algorithm 1: ACO algorithm

3.2 Firefly Algorithm

Firefly algorithm (FA) is another SI algorithm proposed by Xin-She Yang in 2008 [22]. The firefly algorithm uses the behaviour of firefly to find the shortest path and to find minimum response time from source to destination, queuing analysis is done. This algorithm mimics the interaction of fireflies using their flash lights. Fireflies are attracted by another firefly based on their flash lights. Therefore, attractiveness depends on the brightness of fireflies. The brightness also reduces with increase in distance which is based on inverse square law [23] i.e.

$$I \prec 1/r^2$$

The intensity of light at r distance from the initial point can be written as

$$I = I_0 e^{-\gamma r^2}$$

Where γ is the coefficient of light absorption and I_0 is the intensity of light at the source. Likewise, the brightness denoted as β, will be

$$\beta = \beta_0 e^{-\gamma r2}$$

After assigning of brightness, fireflies will start their movement and will get attracted to brighter firefly. The firefly with the brightest light intensity will start its search by moving randomly in its region. So, if there are two fireflies i and j and firefly j is having higher light intensity than the other firefly, the movement of firefly i will take place towards the brighter firefly j which can be given by:

$$x_i = x_i + \beta_0 e_{i,j}^{-\gamma r}(x_j - x_i) + \alpha\varepsilon$$

The movement of fireflies continues with iteration until a terminate condition is reached.

The update of location of fireflies depends on the current performance and not on memory of previous solutions or performances. Also, in this algorithm all the parameters are fixed. This means the behaviour of search will remain same for any state in all iterations.

```
Algorithm
Objfunction f(x)
x= (x₁,....,xₙ)
Initialize fireflies population xᵢ where i=1,2,...,n
Intensity of light I at xᵢ is given by f(xᵢ)
Assign γ as light absorption coefficient
while (t<MaxGen)
for i=1: n-1
for j=i+1: n
if (Iⱼ>Iᵢ), firefly i will travel towards firefly j
end for
end for
Update fireflies.
end while
```

Algorithm 2: Firefly Algorithm

4 Proposed Algorithm

Based on the overview of ACO and Firefly Algorithm in the earlier section, the suggested algorithm using the combination of both the approaches is illustrated.

The optimal route between Source and Destination is selected by using Hybrid Ant Colony Optimization and Firefly algorithm (HACO-FA). This technique is used to select path from multiple alternative parameters which are available. The path selection technique uses ACO to generate multiple paths using pheromones and then based on the light intensity and objective function, the optimal path is identified by using Firefly algorithm. This algorithm takes less time in calculating path and hence delivers the most packets in less time.

Steps:

1. Initialization: Assign x vector for every ant, where i signifies group of values for all m solutions. Pheromone $\tau 0$ is assigned for every ant.
2. Apply ACO: At each iteration ants create solution by moving to every node once. These ants deposit pheromone in every path they travel. Multiple paths will be generated on the basis of pheromones deposited by random moving ants. Pheromone updating will take place and will be stored in a table. At the end of iteration, pheromone values are updated for further iterations to generate most feasible path similar to the previously generated one. Pheromone level at each iteration is given by

$$t(\tau)_{ij}(K + 1) = \rho_{t(\tau)_{ij}}(K) + \Delta_{t(\tau)_{ij}}(K)$$

3. Firefly Algorithm search: This search selects optimal path from the list of paths generated by ACO. It will start the process in following steps:

   i. Initialize swarm of flies- Initial population of firefly is generated x_i, ($i = 1, 2, 3..., n$).

   ii. Variation of light intensity- Change in the light intensity L among the fireflies will take place and is determined by $f(x_i)$.

$$L(x_i) = f(x_i)$$

   iii. Movement of Fireflies- Fireflies will start moving toward the attractive fly which is written as:

$$x_i = x_i + \beta_0 e_{i,j}^{-\gamma r}(x_j - x_i) + \alpha\varepsilon$$

   iv. Reaching the destination- After the maximum number of generations are complete, the search will end.

Algorithm
Input: Population of ACO and FA, parameters of ACO and FA, objective functions
Output: Best objective function value
t=0
Initialize ants by xa, assign $\tau 0$ to each ant
Initialize population of FA by xk
For each generation do
while t<=MaxGen do
Pheromone level updating at each iteration is given by
$t(\tau)_{ij}(K+1) = \rho t(\tau)_{ij}(K) + \Delta t(\tau)_{ij}(K)$
Modify the variables
T=t+1
end while
//if single path is generated by ACO, then end loop and exit
//else Firefly algorithm will start
while t<=MaxGen do
Calculate light intensity by
I(xi)= f(xi)
Movement of firefly towards the brightest fly
$x_i=x_i+\beta_0 e^{-\gamma r}_{i,j}(x_j-x_i)+\alpha\varepsilon$
x_i=xnew
x_j=xmax
t=t+1
Update position of fireflies
end while
end for
return

Algorithm 3: Proposed Hybrid ACO-Firefly algorithm

5 Parameters and Methods

Given below are the simulation parameters and methods used during implementation of the algorithm:

5.1 Simulation Platform

For simulation, network simulator, version ns-3.26 was used. Data used for input in simulation modeling of ACO, Firefly algorithm and Hybrid ACO-FA is given in Table 1.

5.2 Simulation Parameters

See Table 1.

Table 1. Simulation parameters

Parameter	Value
Simulation area	1000 m * 1000 m
Simulator	Ns-3 (Version-Ns 3.26)
Mobility model	Random waypoint mobility model
Channel type	Wireless channel
Protocol	ACO, firefly
Number of nodes	10,50
Packet size	1024 bytes
Simulation time	20 s

5.3 Performance Parameters

The performance of routing algorithms ACO, Firefly is analyzed by the following parameters:

i. *Packet Delivery Ratio:* It can be defined as ratio of total packets received to the total packets sent.
ii. *Throughput*: It is the rate of successful delivery of packets.
iii. *End-to-End delay*: It shows the lag in time between the initial byte sent and last byte received.
iv. *Routing overhead*: It is the routing packets being carried when data is transmitted from source to destination. Less routing overhead shows better network.

6 Results and Discussion

In this paper, the analysis of routing algorithms ACO and Firefly is given. Simulation is performed and comparison of proposed algorithm is done with ACO and FA. According to the results of simulation, the suggested Hybrid algorithm can be a new and effective solution for routing in FANETs.

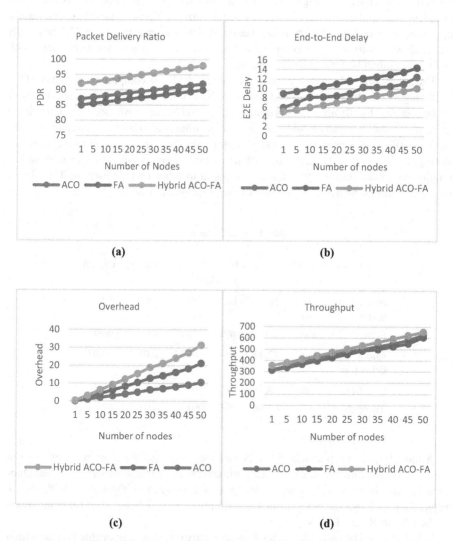

Fig. 1. Comparison of algorithms on different parameters

Figure 1(a) shows that the packet delivery ratio (PDR) is quite high in hybrid algorithm. The proposed algorithm has improved PDR because it finds optimal path from set of multipath in ACO by using Firefly algorithm. This helps in transmitting the packets at a faster and improved rate. Figure 1(b) shows that hybrid ACO-FA is performing considerably better with lesser end-to-end delay when compared to ACO and FA. This is because of the less time taken in finding the path during the hybrid process. In Fig. 1(c) Hybrid algorithm generates lesser number of overhead packets. However, the decrease in overhead is not major when compared with ACO and FA.

Figure 1(d) shows that Hybrid algorithm has the highest throughput which means that it transmits packets at higher rate in comparison to ACO and FA. This is because it takes less time to forward data from one node to another. These values show that Firefly algorithm when compared with ACO gives equivalent values to that of ACO. The results clearly show that firefly gives comparable results on FANETs and when combined with ACO, gives much better results for routing.

The simulation outcomes are shown in Table 2. It shows comparison between ACO, Firefly algorithm (FA) and proposed Hybrid ACO-FA at nodes 10 and 50 respectively. It can be seen that Firefly algorithm is quite efficient and has approximately close results to the results of ACO. It can be said that Firefly algorithm is also apt for routing along with ACO algorithm. The proposed hybrid algorithm has 98% of successful packet delivery and higher than both the algorithms with lesser end-to-end delay. Also, throughput has a major difference and is very high as compared to other two algorithms. This shows how successful is the transmission rate of the proposed algorithm.

Table 2. Simulation results

Algorithms	ACO		Firefly algorithm		Hybrid ACO-FA	
Number of nodes	10	50	10	50	10	50
PDR	88%	92%	86%	90%	93.2%	98%
End-to-end delay (ms)	8.2	12.47	9.94	14.42	6.03	10.07
Overhead	2.1	10.48	2.15	10.75	1.84	10.18
Throughput	370	627.6	365	606.6	410	654.10

Although it has been analyzed that Nature Inspired algorithms are more efficient in comparison with conventional routing algorithms [5], a comparison of the proposed algorithm has also been done with other conventional routing algorithms along with Nature Inspired algorithms. The conventional algorithms which are being used for comparison are AODV, DSR, and DSDV.

In Fig. 2, it can be seen that packet delivery ratio of proposed algorithm is clearly high than the other algorithms. Also, the delay is comparatively less in hybrid algorithm. From the above charts, it is clear that suggested hybrid algorithm outperforms the conventional routing algorithms and can be used as an intelligent routing solution for FANETs.

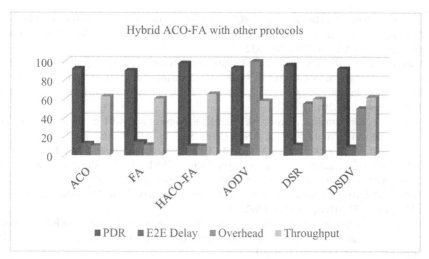

Fig. 2. Comparison of Hybrid ACO-FA with other conventional and Nature Inspired Algorithms

7   Conclusion

This paper introduces a hybrid method for routing in FANETs. Routing in FANETs is an intricate task because of its unique characteristics. The proposed concept uses both ACO and Firefly Algorithm to generate better routing solutions in Flying Ad-hoc Networks. The proposed algorithm has been compared with ACO and FA. Based on the outcomes of simulation, it is found that the suggested Hybrid ACO-FA provides improved results for performance parameters like PDR, E2E delay, throughput and routing overhead. The future work of this research could be enhancing the Firefly algorithm to work more competently in dynamic environment.

References

1. Avellar, G., Pereira, G., Pimenta, L., Iscold, P.: Multi- UAV routing for area coverage and remote sensing with minimum time. Sensors **15**, 27783–27803 (2015). https://doi.org/10.3390/s151127783
2. Mellouk, A., Hoceini, S., Zeadally, S.: A bio-inspired quality of service (QoS) routing algorithm. IEEE Commun. Lett. **15**(9), 1016–1018 (2011)
3. Lin, Q., Song, H., Gui, X., Wang, X., Su, S.: A shortest path routing algorithm for unmanned aerial systems based on grid position. J. Netw. Comput. Appl. **103**, 215–224 (2017). https://doi.org/10.1016/j.jnca.2017.08.008
4. Seetaram,J., Kumar, P.S.: An energy aware genetic algorithm multipath distance vector protocol for efficient routing. In: International Conference on Wireless Communications, Signal Processing and Networking (WiSPNET), Chennai, 2016, pp. 1975–1980 (2016). https://doi.org/10.1109/wispnet.2016.7566488
5. Sahingoz, O.: Networking models in flying Ad-Hoc networks (FANETs): concepts and challenges. J. Intell. Rob. Syst. **74**, 513–527 (2014). https://doi.org/10.1007/s10846-013-9959-7

6. Tian, G., Zhang, L., Bai, X., Wang, B.: Real- time dynamic track planning of multi-UAV formation based on improved artificial bee colony algorithm, pp. 10055–10060 (2018). https://doi.org/10.23919/chicc.2018.8482622

7. Escalante, L.D.S.: Swarm intelligence-based energy saving greedy routing algorithm for wireless sensor networks. In: CONIELECOMP 2013, 23rd International Conference on Electronics, Communications and Computing, Cholula, 2013, pp. 36–39 (2013). https://doi.org/10.1109/conielecomp.2013.6525754

8. Saleem, M., Khayam, S.A., Farooq, M.: Formal modeling of Bee AdHoc: a bioinspired mobile Ad Hoc network routing protocol. ANTS Conference, pp. 315–322 (2008)

9. Maistrenko, V.A., Alexey, L.V., Danil, V.A.: Experimental estimate of using the ant colony optimization algorithm to solve the routing problem in FANET. In: 2016 International Siberian Conference on Control and Communications (SIBCON), pp. 1–10 (2016)

10. Fiala, J.: A Survey of Bio-Inspired Wireless Communication (2016). https://www.cse.wustl.edu/~jain/cse574-16/ftp/biocomm/index.html

11. Leonov, A.: Applying bio-inspired algorithms to routing problem solution in FANET. Bull. South Ural State Univ. Comput. Technol. Autom. Control Radio Electron. **17**, 5–23 (2017). https://doi.org/10.14529/ctcr170201

12. Darwish, A.: Bio-inspired computing: algorithms review, deep analysis, and the scope of applications. Fut. Comput. Inf. J. (2018). https://doi.org/10.1016/j.fcij.2018.06.001

13. Khan, A.N., Aftab, F., Zhang, Z.: BICSF: bio-inspired clustering scheme for FANETs. IEEE Access **7**, 31446–31456 (2019)

14. Tropea, M., Santamaria, A.F., Potrino, G., Rango, F.D.: Bio-inspired recruiting protocol for FANET in precision agriculture domains: pheromone parameters tuning. Wirel. Days WD **2019**, 1–6 (2019)

15. Zhao, B., Ding, Q.: Route discovery in flying Ad-Hoc network based on Bee colony algorithm. IEEE Int. Conf. Artif. Intell. Comput. Appl. (ICAICA) **2019**, 364–368 (2019)

16. Khan, M., Qureshi, I., Khanzada, F.: A hybrid communication scheme for efficient and low-cost deployment of future flying Ad-Hoc network (FANET) **3**, 22 (2019). https://doi.org/10.3390/drones3010016

17. Pu, C., Carpenter, L.: To route or to ferry: a hybrid packet forwarding algorithm in flying Ad Hoc networks, pp. 1–8 (2019). https://doi.org/10.1109/nca.2019.8935011

18. Bhandari, S., Dudeja, R.: HSCS: hybridization of self-organized clustering scheme for flying Ad-Hoc network **10**(3), 13607–13622 (2020). IJMPERDJUN20201296

19. Nath, S., Paul, A., Banerjee, R., Bhaumik, S., Sing, J.K., Sarkar, S.K.: Optimizing FANET routing using a hybrid approach of firefly algorithm and ACO-Lévy flight. In: 2020 IEEE VLSI Device Circuit and System (VLSI DCS), Kolkata, India, pp. 378–383 (2020). https://doi.org/10.1109/vlsidcs47293.2020.9179956

20. Khan, I., Qureshi, I., Aziz, M., Cheema, T., Shah, S.B.: Smart IoT control-based nature inspired energy efficient routing protocol for flying Ad Hoc network (FANET). IEEE Access, 1 (2020). https://doi.org/10.1109/access.2020.2981531

21. Fidanova, S., Roeva, O., Luque, G.: Ant colony optimization algorithm for workforce planning: influence of the algorithm parameters. In: Georgiev, K., Todorov, M., Georgiev, I. (eds.) Advanced Computing in Industrial Mathematics (BGSIAM 2017). Studies in Computational Intelligence, vol. 793, pp. 119–128. Springer, Cham (2019). https://doi.org/10.1007/978-3-319-97277-0_10

22. Yang, X.-S., Xingshi, H.: Firefly algorithm: recent advances and applications. Int. J. Swarm Intell. **1**, 36–50 (2013). https://doi.org/10.1504/IJSI.2013.055801

23. Khan, W., Hamadneh, N., Tilahun, S., Ngnotchouye, J.-M.: A Review and Comparative Study of Firefly Algorithm and its Modified Versions (2016). https://doi.org/10.5772/62472

RC-Security Mechanism to Prevent Attacks on IoT Smart Switch

Jigar Makhija[✉] and V. Anantha Narayanan

Department of Computer Science and Engineering, Amrita School of Engineering,
Coimbatore, India
jm_makhija@cb.students.amrita.edu,
v_ananthanarayanan@cb.amrita.edu

Abstract. Now-a-days the technology advancement has made significant improvement in different sectors of the society. IoT is always having an important role dealing with all these smart devices and their security. One such security issue is DOS attacks which is very frequent in IOT devices. This paper provides a solution to the experiment on a NodeMCU12e based smart switch to prevent and mitigate the attacks executed on wireless embedded devices. The major idea for developing this model is to build a suitable security mechanism for constrained devices which are part of various IOT and CPS applications. The results presented claims that when attacks are executed on the device, further communications would be halted with unidentified IP addresses using Request Capturing Security Mechanism (RCSM).

Keywords: IoT security · Smart switch · Wi-Fi devices · RCSM · Network security

1 Introduction

Internet of Things is capturing the global market. WSN (wireless sensor networks) gives the ease of collaboration between various devices and equipment to communicate with each other, providing platforms for creation of different smart devices that can easily automate manual workload with low cost devices. It also aids in rapidly developing solutions, offering a creative and versatile environment with ease of remote communication. With the use of constrained devices, building security mechanisms is quite a resource expensive task for IoT in terms of energy consumption and processing overheads [1]. The aim is to ensure that these wireless communications devices give both energy efficiency and are robust. We now consider Low-power Lossy Networks (LLNs) implementations for potentially important system scenarios (e.g. Manufacturing plant control, industrial automation), requiring both reliability and security assurances. There are three main security standards that any technology project needs to focus majorly while designing it:

The original version of this chapter was revised: The Author's name has been corrected as "V. Anantha Narayanan". The correction to this chapter is available at
https://doi.org/10.1007/978-3-030-76776-1_20

Confidentiality, Integrity, and Availability, known as the CIA [2]. We should take more responsibility for IoT security loopholes as they are introduced in major sectors such as nuclear power plants, hospitals, industries, and many [3]. Sensor nodes collect data directly from the environment in real-time, and there is a chance that the data could be exposed to malicious users. However, several strategies have been suggested to achieve pool proof security. A practical and efficient technique that can provide perfect security for a client remains a challenge.

Denial-of-Service (DoS) attacks are being used to occupy the system access and preventing the legitimate users from accessing it. Large organizations like banking and government firms deal with critical and highly confidential information. These organizations are usually the most common victims of DoS attacks. IoT applications are extremely vulnerable to this kind of malicious attacks because they are built on top of the network. One of several attacks that are possible on IoT systems is discussed in the paper [4, 5]. DoS and DDoS is already a serious challenge in network operations because it will take over the networks at multiple significant levels. The DoS is effective in blocking the target against its defensive measures because of its multi-to-one attack aspect. It leads to overhead congestion and loss of bandwidth. The challenge is that in spite of having many automated tools available today, which raises the frequency of the attacks as well [6].

Many of the ongoing studies on these problems where the solutions can prevent many types of attacks. Though there are different adversarial attacks that could damage some equipment that supports various other different applications. Hence, this research implementation provides a form of simulation that enables any researcher to apply in IoT applications for testing these types of attacks. Using targeted IoT device, the attacker can upload incorrect data to the server and retrieve legitimate information about the client from the network to which the IoT device is connected [7].

On the other hand, there are a significant number of WSN-related vulnerabilities and security threats have always been identified in various research studies which try to show the potential damage to the reliability, accessibility, and privacy of data in a WSN. Some of these risks are connected in the protocol stack to the network layer. These kinds of attacks involve selective routing, sinkholes, various wormholes, and are intended by malicious checkpoints and traffic exploitation to trigger unwanted behavior in WSN. This all threats are very effective because it allows attackers to sniff and alter data in real-time, attacks such as denial of service (DOS), selective forwarding attacks, collecting data packets, injecting false information into reliable network channels and hijacking the complete routing processes. The risks of wormhole attacks pose new security vulnerabilities that need to be tackled and minimized in order to protect data and privacy of end users [8].

1.1 Impacts of Attack

The assault on DOS and MiTM affects the privacy, reliability and security of the information in the WSN that is part of IoT that could affect the entire network [8].

Impact on Confidentiality: Confidentiality is a function of the Information that guarantees that it can only be accessed by legitimate users for which any unauthorized access is considered infringement. Assuming that all data collection and routing nodes are known in the WSN, including a malicious intruder without authorization, makes the sensitive information accessible and manipulated. Network privacy and information so that the concept of confidentiality is the first to be compromised when unregistered intruders join the WSN, taking advantage of the lack of oversight or prior registration.

Impact on Availability: Accessibility is the information attribute that guarantees that the data flow is not disrupted and that the information is always accessible prior to any consultation or use. When a malicious node hijacks the information, it would be possible to block the source, since when re-doing an identity impersonation, it remains capable of gathering the information through the middle man attack (MiTM) [21] and the possibility of interrupting the data flow, rendering the nodes and routers inaccessible.

Impact on Integrity: Integrity is a feature that ensures the information is free from third-party changes or alterations, and that the data is kept intact from the time it is produced to its final disposal. With the presence of a malicious node in the WSN through a man in the middle (MiTM) attack, it is possible for the attacker to change the original data obtained from the sensors, giving the router nodes additional information. It would change the usual data flow with it.

The paper is organized into the following sections; a summary of other IoT attacks and research work conducted in anomaly detection is given in Sect. 2. In Sect. 3, the overview of the experimental setup along with the framework and model is explained. The results of the experiments are described in Sect. 4 of this article. The limitations of the experiment, conclusions as well as the future scopes are described in Sect. 5.

2 Review on IoT Security Solutions

Based on the literature review it was observed that those who have used the NodeMCU device to collect, analyze and send the sensor data to Raspberry Pi via wireless AP [9] can easily be targeted for collecting the sensitive information or manipulate the device functionality. In [10], researchers suggest an architecture to boost Snort IDS' performance. Nonetheless, there are numerous ways to decrease the efficiency of the Snort-based Intrusion Detection and Prevention as it is available behind the firewall and many real-time embedded systems may not be able to identify and manage the attack.

In [4], the authors claim that DoS attacks in IoT is an ongoing 'research' topic and also gave the basic idea about the monitoring mechanism but these available methodologies only deal with this particular kind of static WSN to analyze the intrusion in which the sensor devices are individually deployed to maintain the constancy. Since these sensor devices are constantly in doubt in various transmission fields with multiple speed rates, the choice of sensor monitoring devices have become a challenge in these researches also shown in [11]. In [12], the paper elaborated the idea about the IoT devices configured with default credentials and that have easy to guess passwords and this increase the risk of botnets acquiring IoT devices. IoT MQTT's existing client and server security mechanism also may be exposed to various security attacks due to MQTT's security weakness given in [13]. A list of network-based defense mechanisms is not yet implemented to prevent DoS attacks where protocol-level attacks like TCP

SYN (synchronize) flood and ICMP (Internet Control Message Protocol) flood attacks are discussed in [14]. In [15], current IDSs do not identify the type of attack that took place. In addition, significant human effort was observed in responding to warnings and assessing the seriousness of an attack without this knowledge. The main challenge is how to secure these devices from physical level attacks, including critical hardware attacks, side channel attacks, reverse engineering attacks, and other attacks on the network, such as attacks on Man-in - the-Middle (MiTM) and Denial-of-Service (DoS) are shown in [16]. In [17], it is claimed that the communication protocol was safe from known attacks. However, the technique presented by the researchers are not completely secured against denial of service and other attacks. The main reason for this was the constant value of identity.

Various researchers gave an idea about different DoS attacks and their classifications. The DoS category is defined in the paper as the level of infrastructure and the level of device bug. The paper addresses another category of DoS attack based on Coercive Parsing, overloaded payload, and flood attack. In Paper, as shown in Fig. 1, DoS attack is classified as bandwidth and resource depletion [18].

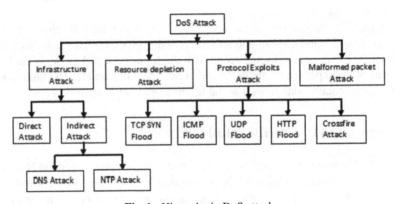

Fig. 1. Hierarchy in DoS attack

2.1 Classification Hierarchy of DOS

Bandwidth Depletion and Flood Attacks

The attacker absorbs all the bandwidth available to the victim by pushing surplus undesired traffic to stop the victim from using the resources. It is possible to utilize many tools to execute these attacks [18]. This assault can be carried out by using the handler-managed zombie machines to redirect the large volume of traffic to the victim computer. This enormous traffic incapacitates the server and utilizes the entire bandwidth.

Amplification Attacks

This attack is initiated by sending the IP address to transmit a large number of packets. In turn, it will send a response from the machines in the broadcast range to the victim unit. Many networked devices, like routers, that uses broadcast features are prone to this kind of attacks. The execution of the attacks to the victim can be launched using zombie machines.

Resource Depletion Attacks

To impoverish the target computer system resources, this type of attack is performed. The benevolent client is therefore not allowed to use the tools.

Protocol Exploit Attacks

The end users network device can be exploited by using different attributes of protocols in many cases an attacker will be able to consume all the excess resources. Examples of this type of attack are PUSH+ACK, TCP SYN and CGI query.

Malformed Packet Attacks

As the name suggests, the payload will be sent by an attacker with the malicious contents in it on the target machines. The execution can be achieved by attacking the IP address (Tables 1 and 2).

Table 1. Objectives of denial-of-service attacks on targeted OSI Levels [19]

OSI layer	Working	Protocols	Areas on targeting DOS	Attacks outcome
7	Creating packets for data. Attachment and access to data. User-defined FTP, SMTP, Telnet protocols	FTP, HTTP, POP3, SMTP	HTTP GET/POST requests capturing	Asset deficit. Excessive use of system resources on the attacked client by services
4	Providing error-free flow of information between nodes, handling message transmission at 1, 2, and 3 layers.	TCP, UDP	SYN-flood, an attack with modified addresses on ICMP requests	Achievement of exceeding the channel width limit or number of permitted connections, violation of network equipment activity

Table 2. Comparison of various IoT network modules

#	WiFly Shield RN131	Wifi Shield HDG204	Huzzah CC3000	ESP8266 ESP-01
Company	SparkFun	Arduino.cc	Adafruit	Espressif
Concurrent sockets	NA	4	4	5
Access point	Yes	Unclear	No	P2P, Soft-AP
Interface	SPI	SPI	SPI	TTL Serial

3 Methodology

RCSM works on any constrained devices (low power & low cost devices). The algorithm is implemented on the device to help it operate in a more intelligent manner. Any unidentified requests will be blocked if it exceeds the limits.

The proposed RCSM algorithm, on the constrained devices, will be acting as a firewall against unauthorized users that are trying to access the device. The algorithm filters the incoming IP addresses based on the payload size and the source port numbers. The classification between a normal and attack activity is carried out in two steps. Firstly, the authorization check occurs based on the IP address of the client. Moreover, if bulk request is identified from the same IP address, the device will disconnect the client automatically. In the second phase, the port number and the payload size will be identified from the incoming request. The unidentified port numbers and uneven payload size would be blacklisted.

3.1 Experimental Setup for the IoT Smart Switch

SMPS is used for voltage conversion of AC power to DC power. So basically, it will be used to transform AC 220 V to DC 5 V.

In the SS-relay, the electromagnet is used to mechanically hand over the loop. The relays are used by a low-power signal to control a circuit or from one signal to control multiple circuits. Based on their role for which they are used, there are many relay classifications. It works on a small electrical current that controls the system capable of handling even large electrical power [20] (Figs. 2 and 3).

Fig. 2. Proposed smart switch with RCSM (Developed in MWN lab).

A current transformer (CT) is used to attenuate or amplify an AC current. In it's secondary, it produces a current that is equal to the current in its primary.

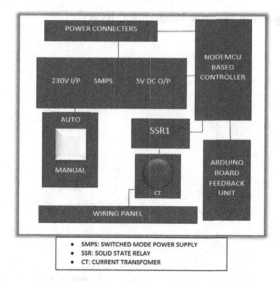

Fig. 3. Smart switch model

3.2 Flow of the Experimental Setup

(Figure 4)

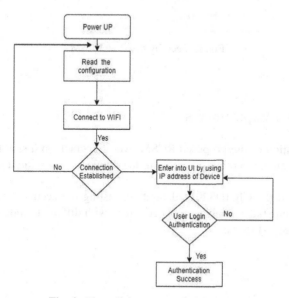

Fig. 4. Flow of the smart switch system

3.3 Request Capturing Security Mechanism (RCSM)

(Figure 5)

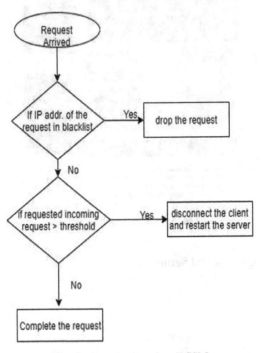

Fig. 5. Security based on RCSM

4 Results and Experiments

The implementation of the proposed RCSM over the attack on a smart switch device established without encryption protocols in the network to provide a solution for the DOS attack.

We have used the CICIDS2017 dataset for testing the accuracy of the proposed algorithm. A comparative analysis was performed with different models and tabulated as shown in Table 3 (Fig. 6).

Table 3. Comparative analysis

Methods	Accuracy
RCSM	99.98
KNN	66.0
SVM	96.2
Random Forest	60.6

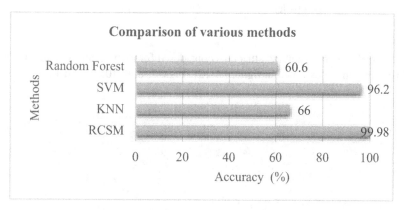

Fig. 6. Comparative analysis of different methods [22].

4.1 Attack Scenario

We have attempted three separate WIFI attacks on this hardware. For the ESP32/8266 they've already fixed most of the vulnerabilities. The first flaw is easy to identify. The access point, when connected to another access point, sends an "AKM suite list" field to the ESP8266 which contains the number of authentication methods available for communication. Since the ESP does not perform bounds-checking on this value, a suspicious fake access point may send a huge number here, probably flooding a buffer, and eventually crashing the ESP. We tried to send a beacon frame or probe response to an ESP8266, which caused it to crash.

The second and third flaws exploit weaknesses in the ESP libraries that manages the extensible authentication protocol (EAP). It is mostly used in corporate and higher protection environments. The first attack will cause the ESP32 or ESP8266 to crash on the EAP-enabled network, but the other will allow the encrypted session to be fully hijacked.

Such EAP attacks are more disturbing than a crash-DOS situation. The hijacking session is riskier but they have already patched the ESP32 codebase, but the newer ESP8266 SDK has not yet been patched. So as of now, the device is fragile if we try to run an ESP8266 on EAP.

The features that were considered in RCSM for identification of attacks are mentioned in Table 4.

Table 4. List of features considered.

Features	Feature type	Data type
Destination port number	Discrete	bigint
Flow duration	Discrete	float
Total length of packets	Discrete	int
Packet length mean	Discrete	float
Average packet size	Discrete	float
Header length	Discrete	float

The correlation between the attributes considered for identification of attacks on the IoT smart switch is described in figure [7–12] (Figs. 7, 8, 9, 10, 11 and 12).

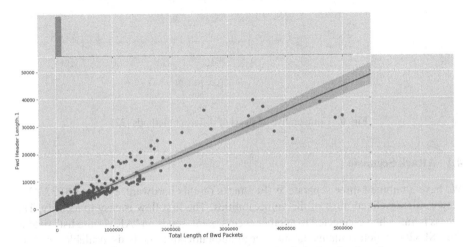

Fig. 7. Correlation between forward and backward packet length.

4.2 Mitigating Attacks

We have tried to implement the request count security mechanism to make the device act more intelligent in a way to identify the incoming requests from various Remote IP's and blocking/disconnecting that IP, if multiple sockets are requested from that same IP with respect to DOS attack but if the authentication level attack is executed to get the user credentials then one solution we come up with was making the ESP device use its HTTPS communication.

And for the testing purpose we tried to find the threshold that how many sockets can be connected at once by connecting multiple devices using ESP and 4–6 are connected.

In addition, we can either limit the incoming request by reconfiguring SDK:

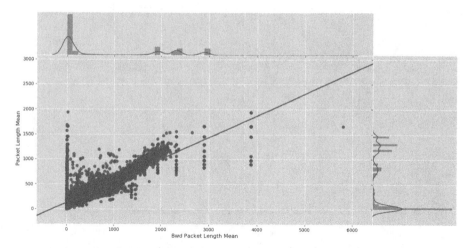

Fig. 8. Correlation between packet length mean and backward packet length mean.

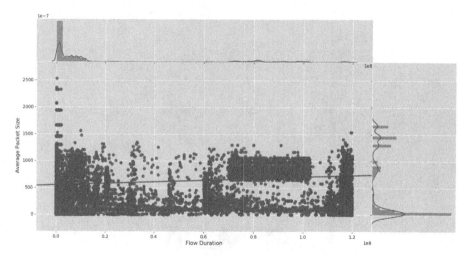

Fig. 9. Correlation between avg. packet size and duration.

Change the sdkconfig.h file overwrite the value and recompile it.

```
#define CONFIG_LWIP_MAX_SOCKETS 8
```

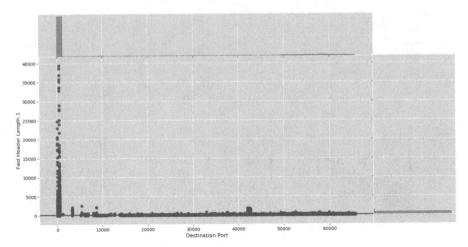

Fig. 10. Correlation between header length and destination port.

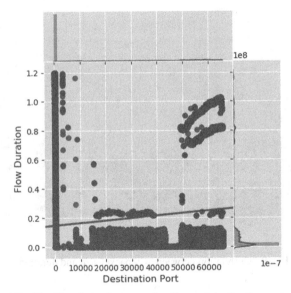

Fig. 11. Correlation between duration and destination port.

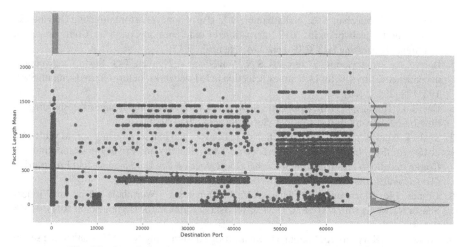

Fig. 12. Correlation between packet length mean and destination port.

5 Conclusion and Future Work

The proposed RCSM algorithm was implemented successfully in constrained devices that captures incoming requests.

The testing of DoS attack was executed and the outcome was able to capture requests from incoming clients on the IoT device and block the unidentified IP addresses that exceeds the request limit. The proposed algorithm was able to achieved a detection rate of 99.98%. This area exposes the susceptibility of wireless devices to various WIFI attacks and leakage of packets. To cover these gaps of the IoT with the available technology, several different areas of security measures for IoT devices must be investigated through intelligent algorithms to identify adversarial attacks. This would also allow end-users to incorporate real-time security on constrained devices. An adversarial security mechanism can be designed and implemented as future work using the signatures and encryption methods to secure the payload across the communication channel. Additionally, several different attacks, such as jamming and hijacking, can be explored to improvise the intrusion detection system.

References

1. Silva, E., Galdino, M., Carmino, J., Bento, A.: An experiment with DDoS attack on NodeMCU12e devices for IoT with T50 Kali Linux. Int. J. Adv. Eng. Res. Sci. **6** (2019). https://doi.org/10.22161/ijaers.6.1.3
2. Dorri, A., Kanhere, S.S., Jurdak, R., Gauravaram, P.: Blockchain for IoT security and privacy: the case study of a smart home. In: 2017 IEEE International Conference on Pervasive Computing and Communications Workshops (PerCom workshops), pp. 618–623. IEEE (2017)
3. Thomas, A., Kumar, G.T., Mohan, A.K.: Neighbor attack detection in internet of things. In: Advanced Computational and Communication Paradigms, Singapore (2018)

4. Anirudh, M., Thileeban, S.A., Nallathambi, D.J.: Use of honeypots for mitigating DoS attacks targeted on IoT networks. In: 2017 International Conference on Computer, Communication and Signal Processing (ICCCSP), pp. 1–4. Chennai (2017)

5. Baig, Z.A., Sanguanpong, S., Firdous, S.N., Van Nhan, V., Nguyen, T.G., So-In, C.: Averaged dependence estimators for DoS attack detection in IoT networks. Future Gener. Comput. Syst. **102**, 198–209 (2020)

6. David, J., Thomas, C.: Efficient DDoS flood attack detection using dynamic thresholding on flow-based network traffic. Comput. Secur. **82**, 284–295 (2019)

7. Shah, T., Venkatesan, S.: Authentication of IoT device and IoT server using secure vaults. In: 2018 17th IEEE International Conference on Trust, Security and Privacy in Computing and Communications/12th IEEE International Conference on Big Data Science and Engineering (TrustCom/BigDataSE), pp. 819–824. IEEE (2018)

8. Gómez, J.R., Montoya, H.V., Henao, A.V.: Implementing a Wormhole Attack on Wireless Sensor Networks with XBee S2C Devices Revista Colombiana de Computación **20**(1), 41–58 (2019)

9. Edward, M., Karyono, K., Meidia, H.: Smart fridge design using NodeMCU and home server based on Raspberry Pi 3. In: 2017 4th International Conference on New Media Studies (CONMEDIA), pp. 148–151. IEEE (2017)

10. Gaddam, R., Nandhini, M.: An analysis of various snort-based techniques to detect and prevent intrusions in networks proposal with code refactoring snort tool in Kali Linux environment. In: 2017 International Conference on Inventive Communication and Computational Technologies (ICICCT), pp. 10–15. IEEE (2017)

11. Deepak, B.D., Al-Turjman, F.: A hybrid secure routing and monitoring mechanism in IoT-based wireless sensor networks. Ad Hoc Netw. **97**, art. no. 102022 (2020)

12. Shah, T., Venkatesan, S.: A method to secure IoT devices against botnet attacks. In: Issarny, V., Palanisamy, B., Zhang, L.J. (eds.) Internet of Things – ICIOT 2019. ICIOT 2019. Lecture Notes in Computer Science, vol. 11519. Springer, Cham (2019)

13. Yerlikaya, Ö., Dalkılıç, G.: Authentication and authorization mechanism on message queue telemetry transport protocol. In: 2018 3rd International Conference on Computer Science and Engineering (UBMK), pp. 145–150. Sarajevo (2018)

14. Jayaraj, P., Jayaraman, B.: DoS attacks on real-time media through indirect contention-in-hosts. IEEE Internet Comput. **13**, 22–30 (2009)

15. Bharot, N., Verma, P., Suraparaju, V., Gupta, S.: Mitigating distributed denial of service attack in cloud computing environment using threshold based technique. Indian J. Sci. Technol. **9** (2016). https://doi.org/10.17485/ijst/2016/v9i38/98811

16. Anthi, E., Williams, L., Slowinska, M., Theodorakopoulos, G., Burnap, P.: A supervised intrusion detection system for smart home IoT devices. IEEE Internet Things J. **6**(5), art. no. 8753563, 9042–9053 (2019)

17. Asghar, M.R., Hu, Q., Zeadally, S.: Cybersecurity in industrial control systems: issues, technologies, and challenges. Comput. Netw. **165**, art. no. 106946 (2019)

18. Ghani, A., Mansoor, K., Mehmood, S., Chaudhry, S.A., Rahman, A.U., Najmus Saqib, M.: Security and key management in IoT-based wireless sensor networks: an authentication protocol using symmetric key. Int. J. Commun. Syst. **32**, (2019)

19. Buriachok, V., Sokolov, V.: Using 2.4 GHz wireless botnets to implement denial-of-service attacks. 1, 14–21 (2018). https://doi.org/10.31435/rsglobal_wos/12062018/5734

20. Lalitha, V.K., Mahalakshmi, B., Madhusudan., S., Srinivasaperumal, M., Srikanth, S., Kumar, S.R.: Smart control of home amenities using Google assistant and clap switch circuit. In: 2019 5th International Conference on Advanced Computing & Communication Systems (ICACCS), pp. 350–352. Coimbatore, India (2019)

21. Bhushan, D., Agrawal, R.: Security challenges for designing wearable and IoT solutions. Intell. Syst. Ref. Lib. **165**, 109–138 (2020)
22. Aamir, M., Rizvi, S.S.H., Hashmani, M.A., Zubair, M., Ahmed, J.: Machine learning classification of port scanning and DDoS attacks: a comparative analysis. Mehran Univ. Res. J. Eng. Technol. **40**(1), 215–229 (2021)

Identifying the Impacts of Node Mobility on Network Layer Based Active and Passive Attacks in Mobile Ad Hoc Networks: A Simulation Perspective

Uthumansa Ahamed[1]($\boxtimes$)(iD) and Shantha Fernando[2](iD)

[1] Department of Physical Sciences, Faculty of Applied Sciences,
Rajarata University of Sri Lanka, Mihintale, Sri Lanka
[2] Department of Computer Science and Engineering, Faculty of Engineering,
University of Moratuwa, Colombo, Sri Lanka
shantha@cse.mrt.ac.lk

Abstract. Ad hoc On-demand Distance Vector Routing (AODV) is a routing protocol that is used in Mobile Ad hoc Network (MANET). Pure AODV protocol is failed to handle the security. In this research, we try to find the answers for the following research questions to upgrade AODV protocol in security concern. I). Does node mobility in a MANET impact the behavior of a malicious node? II). Is node mobility need to be considered when designing appropriate security countermeasures? We used Network Simulator 2 (NS2) for simulations and AODV as routing protocol. Blackhole and Grayhole attacks are selected to study the network layer based Active attacks and Wormhole attack is used for Passive attack. We observed the impacts of each attacks by changing the speed of nodes and the numbers of connected node in the network. We changed the directions of node mobility randomly during the simulation. Though node speed is constant for all nodes. Number of nodes and nodes speed are changed to collect more accurate results. We compared the performances of each network with a controller. Few Performance Matrices (PM) (Packet Delivery Ratio (PDR), End to End Delay (EED) and Throughput) are used to evaluate the network performances. Mobile nodes degrade the network performances. Node mobility either leads to break the links between nodes nor to create new links. Therefore it creates an opportunity to break the link with malicious node. We can screen the malicious node at routing if a routing protocol is equipped with an initial screening mechanism for malicious nodes.

Keywords: Node mobility · Active attacks · Passive attacks · Simulation study

1 Introduction

MANET is a type of Ad hoc Network [1] that is formed by self configurable wireless mobile devices: mobile phones, laptops and other mobile devices. These devices

© Springer Nature Switzerland AG 2021
N. Chaubey et al. (Eds.): COMS2 2021, CCIS 1416, pp. 262–275, 2021.
https://doi.org/10.1007/978-3-030-76776-1_18

are called as nodes. The main character of a MANET is mobile nodes. Source, destination and intermediate nodes are available in MANET [1]. The limited wireless radio range makes source node to depend on number of intermediate nodes to communicate with destination which is not in its' radio range. This nature is called as multi-hop routing. Relatively Low cost of network deployment and opportunistic nature enables MANET into many applications. For instance disaster situations, hostile environments and military operations when infrastructure networks are unavailable [1].

Basically routing protocols are categorized into two: Proactive and Reactive. AODV [2] is an example for reactive routing protocol that is more suitable for MANET [1]. Fundamental characters of MANET are dynamic network topology, open network boundary and infrastructure-less nature. These characters are the reasons for the security threats in a MANET [1]. Therefore pure AODV protocol is insecure for data communications. In order to propose a security mechanism following research questions should be answered. I). Does node mobility in a MANET impact the behavior of a malicious node? II). Is node mobility need to be considered when designing appropriate security countermeasures?

Rest of the paper is organized as follows. Related literature are reviewed in Sect. 2 to identify research gap. State of the art of the node mobility related researches are presented on Sect. 3 to point-out the importance of this study. Section 4 describes about the research methodology. Section 5 expresses the results and discussions in our study. Section 6 explains about the conclusion and proposed future works.

2   Literature Review

Camp, T. et al. [3] presented simulation results by using synthetic mobility models which are used in ad hoc network simulation. The data traffic pattern of the mobility model greatly influences the protocol performances. Moreover they [3] argued that Random Way-point Mobility Model (RWMM) is flexible and it creates a realistic mobility patterns and Random Direction Mobility Model (RDMM) is unrealistic than RWMM. The Boundless Simulation Area Mobility, Gauss–Markov Mobility, Probabilistic Random Walk Mobility Models provide movement patterns that one might expect in the real world. Sharma, G. et al. [4] constructed movement paths using the Voronoi diagram of obstacle vertices that is more realistic movement model through the incorporation of obstacles. Connectivity of the nodes, network density, packet delivery and overhead of the routing protocol are effected because of the mobility model. Bai, F et al. [5] did a study and analyze various mobility models and their effects on MANET protocols. Furthermore they [5] attempted to provide current research status of mobility modeling and analysis. They concluded that a requirement method is needed to select a suitable set of mobility models. Lin, G. et al. [6] proposed a technique that enables accurate derivation of steady state distribution functions for node distance and speed to analyze mobility model based on the renewal theory. This theoretical solution is suitable for speed decay problem of nodes in

RWMM. Atsan, E. et al. [7] provided a hybrid classification for mobility models. They used Random Walk Model (RWM) and RWMM during their simulation study. Simulation results are discussed based on the simulation settings and parameters. They simulated based on the varying number of nodes and size of the simulation area. RDMM and RWM showed worst performance. AODV protocol performed well for boundless simulation area mobility model.

Sharma, G. et al. [4] designed a research to answer three research questions based on the different mobility models and delay capacity relationship. Their study results showed that the mobility models are considered in the literature are in some sense extreme: they either exhibit the smallest critical delays or the largest critical delays among the mobility models. They introduced an idea of critical delay that is studied to identify the tolerated value to enhance the network capacity. They showed that the critical delay is inversely proportional to the length of the node traveled path in same direction [4]. Radha, S. et al. [8] discussed the survey of about different mobility models that are independent and dependent node mobility. They stated that exponential model performs well than the uniform models for expanded speeds and traffic loads. They stated that best performance is possible with the combination of different mobility models. Ting, Z. et al. [9] studied about node mobility model in vehicular communication system. They suggested to use RWMM and RDMM in a simple environment because of its less computational overhead compared to Vehicular mobility model.

Ciullo, D. et al. [10] analyzed the correlated node movement based on the real mobility process. They enforced the Group Mobility model for better network performances than independent node movements. Through the study, they revealed the wide range of correlated node movements help to better performance than the independent nodes movements. Khairnar, V. et al. [11] evaluated the RWMM through a simulation study in a VANET. They stated that MOVE allows to customize the RWMM in a realistic manner. Vasanthi, V. et al. [12] analyzed some mobility models. Their simulation study is based on the RWMM in DSR routing protocol. The study aims to prove the affect of mobility model on the network performances of the simulation. Finally they concluded that simulation results highly dependent on the node mobility model used in the simulation. Zarifneshat, M. et al. [13] attempted to propose modification on the random mobility models and Levy walk mobility model to enhance the simulation node mobility into realistic ones. Their simulation study is based on random mobility model. Through the simulations results they exposed the correlation between occurrence of an accelerated movement and event of mobile node's direction change. Han, G. et al. [14] tried to measure the influences of mobility of the selected nodes in an Mobile Wireless Sensor Network on the DV-hop localization algorithm. RWMM, RDMM and Reference Point Group Mobility models are used for the simulation study [14]. They conclude that RD and RWP mobility models perform well in DV-hop localization algorithm. Moreover, mobility models greatly affect the DV-hop localization algorithm. Othman, N. et al. [15] investigate about the node mobility on node cooperation in MANET. In their study they observed that RWMM and Steady-state RWMM impact similarly on the cooperative nodes. Furthermore Self Similar Least Action Walk Mobility model significantly differ from other two models. Finally they concluded that different mobility models produce different impacts on the network.

Though researchers conducted different studies on the node mobility of the network and different mobility models there are no any study considering on the impacts of node mobility of malicious node.

3   State of the Art

As discussed under literature review section, in 2002, Camp, T. et al. [3] surveyed different mobility models for ad hoc network to illustrate the importance of selecting a mobility model for a simulation. Furthermore relationship between mobility model and the network performances is exposed. In 2003, Jardosh, A. et al. [16] proposed a realistic mobility model by introducing obstacles on the route of node movement. Bai, F. et al. [5] surveyed and examined different mobility models that has unique characters such as temporal dependency, spatial dependency or geographic restriction. In 2004, Lin, G. et al. [6] proposed a new methodology to simulate mobility of nodes with a guaranteed steady state for node movement distribution from the beginning. In 2006, Atsan, E. et al. [7] surveyed and proposed a hybrid classification on existing mobility models. In 2006, Radaha, S. et al. [8] presented a survey which helps researchers to select a research model for the simulation study based on the performance evaluation. Furthermore, they concluded that combination of different mobility model may be more effective for simulations. Sharma, G. et al. [4] analyzed different mobility models by using a framework which evaluates a mobility model by critical delay. In 2009, Ting, Z. et al., [9] presented a comparative study of mobility models on VANET. In 2011, Ciullo, D. et al. [10] concluded from their research study that correlated nodes movements lead to better performance than independent node movement mobility models. In 2012, Vasanthi, V. et al. [12] analyzed different mobility models including entity models. In 2013, Zarifneshat, M. et al. [13] mobility trace produced by a mobility trace generator tool. They used association rule mining concept to find possible correlation between mobile nodes. In 2014, Othman, N. et al. [15] investigated the impacts of few mobility models. In the same year, Han, G. et al. [14] quantified the influence of mobility of a node that moved based on three different mobility models by using DV hop based localization model.

4   Methodology

Computer simulation is considered as the research instrument to collect empirical data such as field experiment do [16]. Table 1 shows parameters that are maintained during the simulations. Attacks are introduced individually to the network to check the impacts separately. Impacts on the network is expressed through the PDR, EED and Throughput. PDR is a ratio between total number of received packets from destination node and total number of packets sent by the source node [1]. EED is a time that is taken by a packet to reach the destination node [1]. Units are in seconds. Throughput is a ratio between total number of successfully received packets by destination node and total time taken to receive all the packets [1]. Units are in bytes per second (bps). The attacks are introduced to the network by modifying the functions of AODV protocol [1]. Grayhole attacks is configured as to drop all packets after a certain period of time. Transmission range in between wormhole nodes are maintained as twice the range of the normal node during the wormhole attack simulations. We considered following assumptions.

- Nodes are identical.
- Configurations are unique for all nodes except wormhole nodes.
- Malicious nodes show abnormal behavior during the communication.

Table 1. NS2 parameters

Parameter	Value
Simulator	NS2 (v.2.35) [17]
Frequency	9.14×10^8 Hz
Bandwidth	2.0×10^6 bps
Antenna/OmniAntenna X, Y, Z	0, 0, 1.5 m
Radio-propagation model	TwoRayGround
Network interface type	Phy/WirelessPhy
Traffic type	Constant bit rate (CBR)
Max packets in Interface Queue	50
Nodes Transmitter range	250 m
Number of nodes	10, 15, 20, 25, 30
Node Speed	0, 5, 10, 15, 20 ms^{-1}
Simulation Area X, Y	1500 m, 2500 m
Simulation time	10 s

5   Results and Discussion

Table 2 contains the average values of each PM of the networks which are affected by different security attacks. In this experiment, node mobility is maintained as zero ms^{-1} in each network. Average values of PM are obtained by averaging each corresponding PM values. Average PDR, EED and Throughput values of the controller network are 50.58%, 0.76 s and 6746.51 bps. According to the results PDR value is decreased on increasing the number of connected nodes in the network. Though, PDR value is increased at last. EED value is increased for increasing the connected nodes amount. Furthermore Throughput value is decreased gradually on increasing number of connected nodes in the network. The reason is, the packets needed to travel through many nodes while increasing the nodes amount.

Due to the effect of Blackhole attack PDR, EED and Throughput of the network are 0.28%, ∞ and 0.33% compared to the controller network. Blackhole node does not allow any data packets but routing packets. PDR and Throughput values are not zero because Blackhole node allows only routing packets. Therefore the Blackhole attack degraded the network performances than all the other network performances.

Wormhole attack enhanced the network performances than other networks including controller network. Because of the higher speed data transferring wormhole tunnel between wormhole nodes. Therefore data packets quickly transfer through the tunnel. Furthermore, wormhole attack is a passive attack which shows no harm or undetectable harm to the network [1]. PDR, EED and Throughput values are 151.60%, 1.31% and 178.41% compared to the controller network.

The network shows intermediate performances in the presence of Grayhole attack. The performances are lower than controller network and higher than the network with Blackhole attack. PDR, EED and Throughput values are 51.30%, 92.67% and 57.23% compared to the controller network.

Table 2. Network performances in zero node mobility

Performance matrices	Controller	Blackhole	Grayhole	Wormhole
PDR	50.58	0.14	25.95	76.68
EED	0.76	∞	0.71	0.01
Throughput	6746.51	22.34	3861.28	12036.26

Figure 1 shows the graph plotted between PDR of different number of connected nodes in the network vs node speed in the presence of Blackhole attack. According to the simulations results, the link between source and Blackhole node is broken and established again at lower number of nodes with higher speed of node mobility. Therefore graph shows slight increase at that point. In the other cases, link breakages did not occur along with the Blackhole node or no any new links are established after a link breakage with Blackhole node.

Figure 2 shows the graph plotted between PDR of different number of connected nodes in the network vs speed of node mobility in the presence of Grayhole attack. According to the simulations results, when the number of connected nodes and the speed are increased the link between the source and Grayhole node breaks. Then a new route is established between source and destination node. Therefore PDR is increased. When the speed of node mobility is very high, PDR values are decreased due to the breakage of the existing links among the nodes.

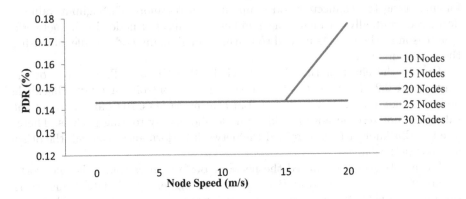

Fig. 1. PDR of the network with Blackhole attack vs node speed

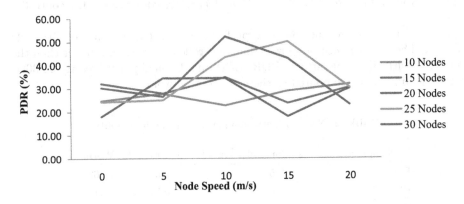

Fig. 2. PDR of the network with Grayhole attack vs node speed

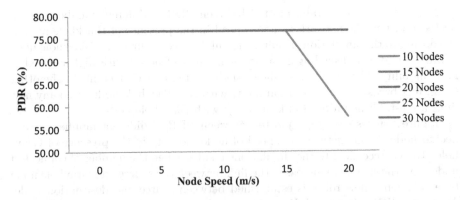

Fig. 3. PDR of the network with Wormhole attack vs node speed

Figure 3 is the graph of PDR value of different number of connected nodes in the network vs speed of node mobility in the presence of Wormhole attack. According to the simulations results when the number of connected nodes and speed of nodes are increased PDR value remains same because of the wormhole tunnel. Though when number of node is low and speed of the node is high the link between the source node and the wormhole node breaks. Therefore PDR value is decreased.

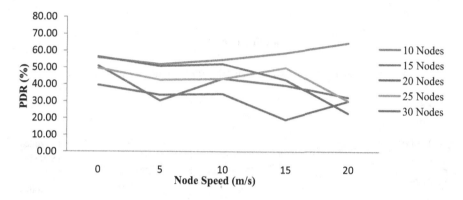

Fig. 4. PDR of controller network vs node speed

Graph between PDR of different number connected of nodes in the network vs speed of node mobility of the controller network is shown in Fig. 4. According to the Fig. 4, though the number of connected nodes are increased, PDR value is decreased. This is because of the higher speed of node mobility increases the links breakage. Therefore amount of data received by destination is decreased. Even when the number of connected nodes are decreased, destination can receive data by new links which are created by higher speed of node mobility.

Figure 5 shows the graph plotted between EED of different number of connected nodes in the network vs speed of node mobility in the presence of Blackhole attack. According to the simulation results, destination node did not receive any data packets either number of connected nodes in the network is increased or speed of node mobility is increased. Therefore all the graphs are lie on zero.

Figure 6 shows the graph plotted between EED of different number of connected nodes in the network vs speed of node mobility in the presence of Grayhole attack. According to the results, when the speed of the node mobility and number of connected nodes in the network are increased links are broken including the link between Grayhole node and the source node. Therefore source node is able to communicate with destination with lowest hop count. Therefore EED is decreased when number of connected node and speed of the nodes mobility are increased.

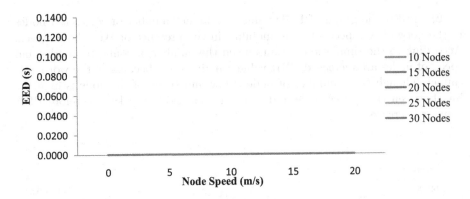

Fig. 5. EED of the network with Blackhole attack vs node speed

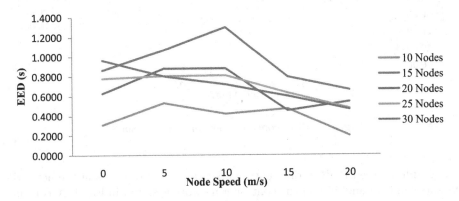

Fig. 6. EED of the network with Grayhole attack vs node speed

Figure 7 shows the graph plotted between EED of different number of connected nodes in the network vs speed of node mobility in the presence of Wormhole attack. According to the results, when the speed of nodes mobility and number of connected nodes in the network are increased links are broken including the link between Grayhole node and the source node. Therefore source node is able to communicate with the destination with lowest hop count. Therefore EED is decreased when number of connected nodes and speed of the nodes mobility are increased.

Figure 8 is the graph between EED of different number of connected nodes in the network vs speed of node mobility of the controller network. According to the results, when the number of connected nodes and the speed of the node mobility are increased the EED value is decreased. This is because with higher number of node and higher node speed existing links are broken and new links are created. Furthermore data packets are reached the destination through newly created shortest route.

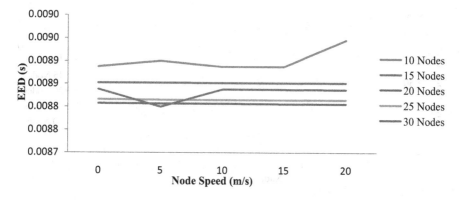

Fig. 7. EED of the network with Wormhole attack vs node speed

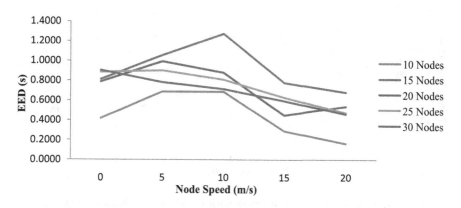

Fig. 8. EED of controller network vs node speed

Figure 9 shows the graph plotted between Throughput of different number of connected nodes in the network vs speed of node mobility in the presence of Blackhole attack. According to the Fig. 9, when the number of connected nodes and the speed of the node mobility are increased the Throughput value remains same. This is because of Throughput of RREQ packets. Furthermore There was no any link breakage between source node and Blackhole node or no any new links are created due to the node mobility. Graph between Throughput of different number of connected nodes in the network vs speed of node mobility of the network which is affected by Grayhole attack is shown in Fig. 10. According to the Fig. 10, when the number of connected nodes and the speed of the node mobility are increased the Throughput value is decreased. This is because of the link between the source and Grayhole node is broken and new links are not formed between source and destination node. Furthermore in lower number of

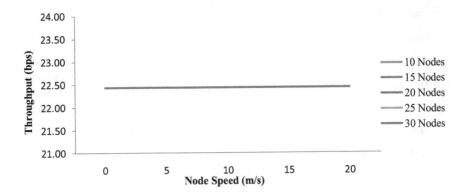

Fig. 9. Throughput of the network with Blackhole attack vs node speed

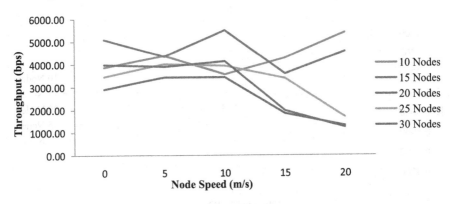

Fig. 10. Throughput of the network with Grayhole attack vs node speed

connected nodes in the network with higher speed of node mobility new links are established between source and the destination node. Therefore Throughput value is increased.

Figure 11 shows the graph plotted between Throughput of different number of connected nodes in the network vs speed of node mobility in the presence of Wormhole attack. Though number of connected nodes in the network is increased and speed of the node mobility is increased Throughput remains same. The reason is Wormhole node are able to maintain the link with source node. Furthermore the link between source node and Wormhole node is broken with the lower number of connected nodes in the network and with the higher speed of node mobility. Therefore Throughput value is decreased. Figure 12 shows the graph plotted between Throughput of different number of connected nodes in the network vs speed of node mobility of the controller network. According to the simulation results, when the number of connected node in the network and the speed of node mobility are increased, Throughput value is decreased. The reason is the link breakage between nodes. Though in the lower number of connected

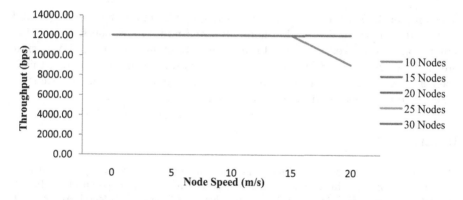

Fig. 11. Throughput of the network with Wormhole attack vs node speed

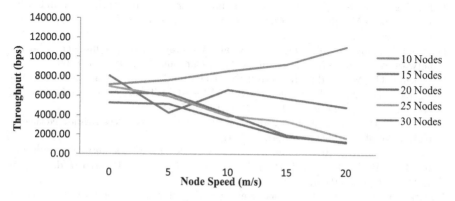

Fig. 12. Throughput of Controller network vs node speed

nodes in the network and higher speed of node mobility Throughput value is increased. Because source node is able to create new and shortest path between destination node.

6   Conclusion and Future Works

Node mobility in the network degrades the MANET performances that differ from one another based on the node speed and direction of the movement. Node mobility leads to occasional link breakage between nodes in the MANET. Therefore link breakage affects the activity of a malicious node. All the nodes including malicious node need to under go for route establishment between source and destination nodes after a link breakage. Therefore node mobility need to be considered when designing appropriate security countermeasures. Because if a routing protocol is equipped with malicious screening mechanisms on route discovery stage then malicious nodes can be screened. Link breakage is favorable for security. Because, It is possible to identify Black hole nodes from the initial screening mechanisms on the routing process. Furthermore, it is helpful to find new shortest path to destination node after the nodes movements. During the simulation we observed that initial route links are maintained in AODV until it breaks. Though, destination node is very close to source node. Therefore, this is opened to another research regarding the existing route verification for shortest path for communication during the communication.

References

1. Ahamed, U., Fernando S.: Identifying the impacts of active and passive attacks on network layer in a mobile ad-hoc network: a simulation perspective. Int. J. Adv. Comput. Sci. Appl. **11**(11) (2020). https://doi.org/10.14569/IJACSA.2020.0111173
2. Perking, C. Royer, E.: Ad-hoc on-demand distance vector routing. In: 2nd IEEE Workshop on Mobile Computing Systems and Applications, LA, USA, pp. 90–100. IEEE (1999)
3. Camp, T., Boleng, J.D., Davies, V., et al.: A survey of mobility models for ad hoc network research. Wireless Commun. Mob. Comput. **2**(5), 483–502 (2002)
4. Sharma, G., Mazumdar, R., Shroff, N.: Delay and capacity trade-offs in mobile ad hoc networks: a global perspective. IEEEs ACM Trans. Netw. **15**(5), 981–992 (2007). https://doi.org/10.1109/TNET.2007.905154
5. F. Bai, F. Helmy, A.: A survey of mobility models. In: Wireless Ad-hoc Networks. University of Southern, California (2004)
6. Lin, G. Noubir, G. Rajaraman, R.: Mobility models for ad hoc network simulation. In: IEEE INFOCOM 2004, Hong Kong, pp. 454–463 (2004). https://doi.org/10.1109/INFCOM.2004.1354517
7. Atsan, E. Özkasap, Ö.: A classification and performance comparison of mobility models for ad hoc networks. In: Kunz, T., Ravi, S. (eds.) ADHOC-NOW 2006, LNCS, pp. 444–457. Springer, Heidelberg (2016). https://doi.org/10.10007/1234567890
8. Radha, A., Shanmugavel, S.: Mobility models in mobile ad hoc network. IETE J. Res. **53**(1), 3–12 (2007)
9. Ting, Z. Jianjun, H. Li, S. Jianfeng, L. Yan, M.: Study on mobility models in vehicular communication system. In: 2009 2nd IEEE International Conference on Broadband Network & Multimedia Technology, Beijing, pp. 57–61 (2009). https://doi.org/10.1109ICBNMT.2009.5347824
10. Ciullo, D. Martina, V. Garetto, M. Leonardi, E.: Impact of correlated mobility on delay-throughput performance in mobile ad-hoc networks. In:2010 Proceedings IEEE INFOCOM, CA, San Diego, pp. 1–9 (2010). https://doi.org/10.1109/INFCOM.2010.5461993
11. Khairnar, V. Pradhan, S.: Mobility models for vehicular ad-hoc network simulation. In: 2011 IEEE Symposium on Computers & Informatics, Kuala Lumpur, pp. 460–465 (2011). https://doi.org/10.1109/ISCI.2011.5958959
12. Vasanthi, V., Hemalatha, M.: Simulation and evaluation of different mobility models in ad-hoc sensor network over DSR protocol using Bonnmotion tool. In: Thampi, S.M., Zomaya, A.Y., Strufe, T., Alcaraz Calero, J.M., Thomas, T. (eds.) SNDS 2012. CCIS, vol. 335, pp. 157–167. Springer, Heidelberg (2012). https://doi.org/10.1007/978-3-642-34135-9_16

13. Zarifneshat, M., Khadivi, P.: Using mobile node speed changes for movement direction change prediction in a realistic category of mobility models. J. Netw. Comput. Appl. **36**(3), 1078–1090 (2013)
14. Han, G., Chao, J., Zhang, C., Shu, L., Li, Q.: The impacts of mobility models on DV-hop based localization in Mobile Wireless Sensor Networks. J. Netw. Comput. Appl. **42**, 70–79 (2014)
15. Othman, N. Hassan, R. Hasan, S.: The impact of mobility models on nodes cooperation in mobile ad hoc networks. In: 2014 IEEE Student Conference on Research and Development, Batu Ferringhi, pp. 1–5 (2014). https://doi.org/10.1109SCORED.2014.7072943
16. Barberousse, A. Franceschelli, S. Imbert, C.: Computer simulations as experiments. Synthese **169**(2012). https://doi.org/10.1007/s11229-008-9430-7
17. Issariyakul, T. Hossain, E.: Introduction to Network Simulator NS2, 2nd edn. Springer, Heidelberg (2012). https://doi.org/10.1007/978-1-4614-1406-3

Simulated Analysis of Double-Gate MOSFET and FinFET Structure Using High-k Materials

Pooja Srivastava[1]($\boxtimes$) and S. C. Bose[2]

[1] Department of Electronics, School of Physical Science, Banasthali Vidyapith, Rajasthan 304022, India

[2] IoT Group, CSIR-CEERI, Rajasthan 304022, India

Abstract. In this paper, the concept of non-conventional transistors has been presented. Both Double-Gate MOSFET and FinFET have tremendous potential for reducing short-channel effects and high leakage current. With the advancement in the nanometer technology, chip density and operating frequency is increasing leading to the more and more power consumption of battery operated portable devices. Hence, to meet all these challenges including scaling, Double-Gate MOSFET and FinFET are the promising substitutes for the bulk CMOS structures. The devices have been developed and are compared to conventional MOSFET structures which provide wider benefits.

Keywords: Short channel effects · Double-Gate MOSFET · FinFET · High-k material · Poly-Si Gate Stack · Metal gate stack · Hafnium Oxide (HfO$_2$) · Zirconium Oxide (ZrO$_2$) · Fermi Level Pinning · Phonon Scattering

1 Introduction

In today's scenario, the hardware for any algorithms is typically first implemented/tested on Field Programmable Gate Array (FPGA) before implementing through Application Specific Integrated Circuit (ASIC) as per requirement. Therefore, the dedicated circuits while retaining or improving the performance ability should also consume as less energy as possible. The architecture of the circuit, the type of transistors used and the technology of the IC are the deciding factors of performance and energy consumption. Semiconductor industries are trying to stick to Moore's law because of commercial benefits which are accrued due to resulting performance improvement inherent in scaling down of planar technologies. While catering to single gate MOSFET (Conventional Transistor-CT), Moore's law is slowly saturating, fuelling the search for other non-conventional transistor (NCT). Current research shows that there are several commercial and performance benefits of NCTs like Double Gate MOSFET (DG-MOSFET), Fin Field Effect Transistor (FinFET) and Junction-less Field Effect Transistor (JLFET) etc. Now a days, technology or minimum channel length goes up to or below 10 nm, so high-quality junctions become necessary. JLFET is a newly born NCT having no junctions and is the possible alternative and promising emerging device to the CT. The present work focuses on the use of NCTs after their appropriate study and analysis to design circuit blocks

© Springer Nature Switzerland AG 2021
N. Chaubey et al. (Eds.): COMS2 2021, CCIS 1416, pp. 276–286, 2021.
https://doi.org/10.1007/978-3-030-76776-1_19

and evaluate their sub-system performance. Such blocks are proposed to be further used for partial or complete schematic implementation of medical and healthcare processing. The proposed research can be implemented in many areas of analog/digital circuit design with ultra low power applications. The researchers can use this concept for below 5 nm technology related circuit design using JLFET with huge cost reduction.

As we know about the Moore's Law which observes that transistor count doubles every two years which is shown in Fig. 1. The scaling beyond 10 nm channel length of bulk Complementary Metal Oxide Semiconductor Field Effect Transistor (CMOSFET) or CMOS structure as shown in Fig. 2, results in various problems such as electrostatic limits, process variation, leakage current, mobility degradation. One of the most important issue is power dissipation which is due to the reduction in the size of CMOS circuits and its continuous scaling. To have a better control over channel and its current intensity by the gate, there is a need of more and more effective and advanced structure of transistors. To meet the International Technology Roadmap for Semiconductors (ITRS) roadmaps requirements, the concept of multi-gate MOSFET is introduced due to increasing complexity and cost of scaling of Si-MOSFET. Before multi-gate, there was substrate engineering which includes partially depleted and fully depleted MOSFET as shown in Figs. 3 and 4. These are ultra-thin body devices where body doping is removed and leakage current is suppressed, but multi-gate device are more scalable such as Double-Gate MOSFET, FinFET, Omega-gate and so on [1–3].

2 Short Channel Effects (SCEs)

Short-Channel Effects are the most important problem of bulk Complementary Metal Oxide Semiconductor Field Effect Transistor (CMOSFET) or CMOS structure which leads to alteration in threshold voltage (V_{TO}) when there is shortening in channel length and hence limitations on electron drift characteristics. The various Short-Channel Effects include Drain-Induced Barrier Lowering, Hot Electron Effect, Impact Ionization, Velocity Saturation, Surface Scattering and Punch through. Hence Double-Gate MOSFET and FinFET structure are the promising devices in reducing Short-Channel Effects [5, 6].

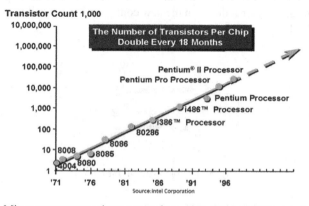

Fig. 1. Microprocessor transistor counts from 1971–2011 and Moore's Law [3]

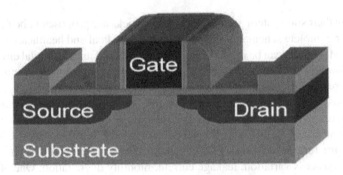

Fig. 2. Conventional bulk CMOS [4]

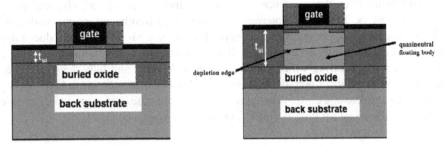

Fig. 3. Partially depleted SOI MOSFET [4]

Fig. 4. Fully depleted SOI MOSFET [4]

3 Double-Gate MOSFET Device Structure

As further scaling cannot be done beyond 10 nm, Double-Gate MOSFET is an alternative to build MOSFET when Lg < 10 nm. There is desirable control of channel from two gates, which reduces the further short-channel effects with improved sub-threshold slope. Figure 5 and 6 shows the structure of Double-Gate MOSFET. There are various circuit problems in this device which are gate-gate alignment and source/drain gate alignment. These problems are further reduced in the new configuration of Double-Gate MOSFET i.e. FinFET [7–9].

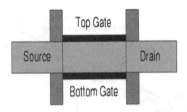

Fig. 5. Double-Gate MOSFET [7]

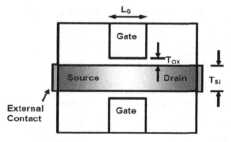

Fig. 6. In Double-Gate MOSFET the oxide thickness, tox = 2 nm, length of gate, Lgate = 100 nm and body thickness, tsi = 100 nm [8]

4   FinFET Device Structure

FinFETs are like field effect transistor, channel is "turned on its edge" and made to stand up as shown in Fig. 7. Both the front and back gate are independently controlled. Width of FinFET is $W = 2 \times n \times h$, where n and h are number of fins and height of FinFET respectively. It has high quality control of short-channel effects in submicron regime [10–12] (Table 1).

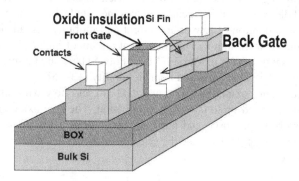

Fig. 7. FinFET gates in self-aligned manner [9]

5   Performance Evaluation by High-k Materials

High-k metal gate stack technology is becoming an apparent substitute for the conventional dielectrics and poly-Si gates, for sub nano-meter range MOSFETs to satisfy the need of both high speed and low power consumption devices. In today's scenario, the SiO_2 layer thickness reaches upto 5 atomic layers due to scaling. This causes oxide breakdown due to hot electron tunneling. This in turn produces the large amount of gate leakage current. Thus, further thinning of SiO_2 was not possible and the dielectrics were replaced by high-k materials. In latest research, the issues like Fermi Level Pinning and Phonon Scattering which impede the use of high-k have been observed and the use of

Table 1. FinFET technology parameters

Parameter	Value
Channel length (L)	30 nm
Gate-Drain (Source) overlap	3.0 nm
Fin height (H_{fin})	30 nm
Fin thickness (t_{si})	8 nm
Oxide thickness (tox)	1.6 nm
Channel doping	10^{15} cm^{-3}
Source/drain doping	2×10^{20} cm^{-3}
Work function (N-FinFET)	4.0 eV
Work function (P-FinFET)	4.6 eV
V_{DD}	0.8 V

high-k dielectric material Hafnium Oxide (HfO_2), Zirconium oxide (ZrO_2) over SiO_2 as dielectric and metal gate over poly-Si gate have been compared.

Materials with high-k dielectric had been chosen as one of the best substitute for the conventional dielectric as it drastically reduces the gate leakage current. But in turn, it comes with the limitation of low drain current and mobility degradation due to the critical issues related with high-k. The significant effects of high-k dielectric material which obstruct its employment in MOSFET over Poly-Si layer are Fermi Level Pinning, Phonon Scattering, Poly Depletion and Poor Reliability [13–15].

A few decades ago, oxide thickness was 100 nm and now with advancement of technology, it has reached up to 0.7 nm in production. The gate oxide layer thickness up to 0.7 A° has been proposed and has only two atomic layer of SiO_2. So far the conventional approach applied to scale the gate dielectric has been reduce t_{ox} to increase C_{ox} as given by Eq. 1

$$C_{OX} = k\varepsilon_0 A / t_{OX} \qquad (1)$$

where the dielectric constant is k, A is area of dielectric and t_{OX} and C_{OX} are thickness and capacitance. As further, scaling is now difficult to decrease the main problem of electron tunneling, that is gate leakage current, so that researchers have turned towards high-k dielectrics. That is use of dielectrics with higher k relative to SiO_2 so that high physical thickness of film (t_{high-k}) and also higher values gate capacitance C_{high-k} can be achieved [16–20].

5.1 Concept of High-k Dielectrics

As explained above, the gate dielectric thickness has to be taken greater than before so as to control the tunneling of electrons that is leakage current and also to evade reliability problems. The dielectric layer generates a high electrical which is critical to control short channel effects and also to make sure that sufficient drain current flows in

MOSFETs. The only solution is thus to replace the silicon oxide with materials having higher dielectric constant to provide the required gate insulation. Among the assortment of high-k materials accessible Nd_2O_3, Gd_2O_3, Y_2O_3, ZrO_2, Er_2O_3, HfO_2, Al_2O_3, Ta_2O_5, TiO_2, La_2O_3, $LaAlO_3$, CeO_2 [21] etc. are under investigation for alternate gate dielectric. A parameter Equivalent Oxide Thickness (EOT) is defined for the high-k dielectrics [22]. EOT gives a corresponding thickness of SiO_2 required to get the same amount of gate capacitance as obtained by use of high-k dielectric as given by Eq. 2

$$EOT = t_{high\text{-}k}\left(K_{SiO2}/K_{high\text{-}k}\right) \qquad (2)$$

$t_{high\text{-}k}$ is thickness of high-k dielectric and k_A is dielectric constant of A.

5.2 Choice of High-k Oxide

The selection criterion for dielectric has been set very carefully, in order for the dielectric to be chosen to replace SiO_2, it should:

- High thermodynamic stability
- Excellent interface quality with Si
- Low fixed oxide charge
- Equivalent oxide thickness (EOT)-10 to 15 Å
- Compatibility with other material used in CMOS
- Reliability comparable to SiO_2
- Large band gap suitable band off-sets

5.3 The Observed Design

A. Comparison between SiO_2 and ZrO_2
As shown in Fig. 8, the leakage current of ZrO_2 is much lower than leakage current for SiO_2 for the thickness. Thus, the purpose of using high-k dielectrics instead of SiO_2 has been achieved. Thus a good MOSFET with reliable characteristics can be manufactured with high-k material [23].

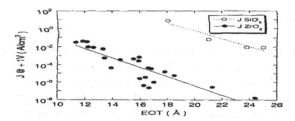

Fig. 8. J vs EOT comparison between SiO_2 and ZrO_2

B. Comparison between ZrO₂ and HfO₂
Overall characteristics were observed to be better in HfO₂-Poly-Si MOS than in ZrO₂-Poly-Si MOS [24]. Figures 9 and 10 have been shown the transistor characteristics of ZrO₂/Poly-Si and HfO₂/Poly-Si transistors.

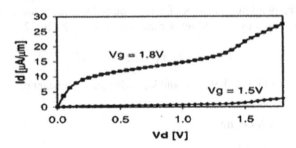

Fig. 9. Characteristics of ZrO₂/Poly-Si transistor

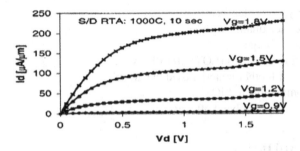

Fig. 10. Characteristics of HfO₂/Poly-Si transistor

C. Comparison between SiO₂/Poly-Si, HfO₂/Poly-Si and HfO₂/TiN Metal Gate
The comparison between three structures namely SiO₂-Poly-Si Gate Stack, HfO₂-Poly-Si Gate Stack and HfO₂-TiN-Metal Gate Stack have been done in this paper [25, 26].

6   Implementation

The design flow used in implementation has been detailed as firstly, there is a need to specify the design specifications of the individual transistors and components have been used. Next is the mesh capture of the design to be made. Then, the device of the design has been created. Simulation is defined as a model or design which define the properties, behaviour and appearance of the system. The simulation of the device has been performed and later on the layout has been designed. Design rule check has been performed on the layout to verify the device characteristics. Extraction of the design has been done to extract parasitic capacitances and resistances.

7 Simulation Results

In this paper, all the simulated analysis has been done by SILVACO TCAD Tool with ATHENA Process Simulator and ATLAS Device Simulator. The model parameters of CMOS for different available devices have been explored and developed.

The Fig. 11 has depicted the net doping profile and material structure for Double Gate MOSFET. Figures 12 and 13 have shown the Drain Current vs Drain Voltage and Drain Current vs Gate-bias Voltage Characteristics of Double Gate MOSFET respectively. Figures 14 and 15 have shown the Drain Current vs Drain Voltage and Drain Current vs Gate-bias Voltage Characteristics of FinFET respectively.

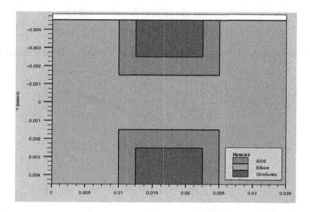

Fig. 11. Process Simulation of Double-Gate MOSFET with materials

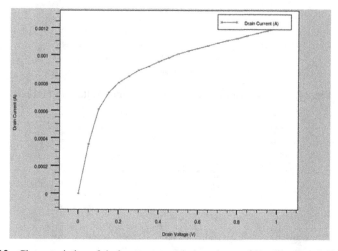

Fig. 12. Characteristics of drain current vs drain voltage of Double-Gate MOSFET

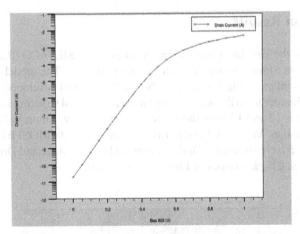

Fig. 13. Characteristics of drain current vs gate bias voltage of Double-Gate MOSFET

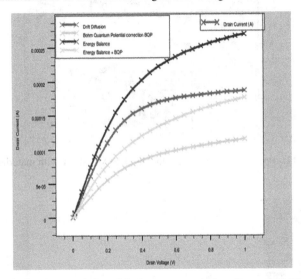

Fig. 14. Characteristics of drain current vs drain voltage of FinFET

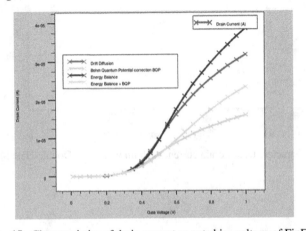

Fig. 15. Characteristics of drain current vs gate bias voltage of FinFET

8 Conclusion

In this work, comprehensive study of short channel effects have been analyzed and different devices like Double Gate MOSFET and FinFET with their characteristics have been simulated and evaluated by Silvaco tool. Result shows that decreasing scaling have reduced the delay times for various structure. There is better electrostatic integrity in Double Gate MOSFET and FinFET over conventional planar bulk MOSFET structure. The advancement of the Silicon in Insulator MOSFET leads to single-gate MOSFET device to multi-gate MOSFET device.

To study the role of dielectric in device performance, 100 nm gate length MOSFET device structures have been used. It was observed that some of parameters like drain current, threshold voltage and mobility which change severely with the use of high-k dielectrics. And these problems can be improved back by replacing Poly-Silicon gate electrode by metal gate. Severe reduction in gate leakage current points towards a new era of unconventional MOSFETs, which use the technique of higher k rather than scaling to achieve smaller devices in the nano-scale regime devices.

9 Future Scope

New advancements in technology of device with extended scaling will continue with further advancement, non-conventional transistor and non silicon material transistor in future. Both the technology will be supporting the new architecture of various multi-gate technology such as FinFET, Tri-gate, Pi-gate, Omega-gate and Gate-all-around. The future studies on Double-Gate MOSFET and FinFET will enhance the performance and low power consumption with significant short channel suppression. These multi-gate devices will provide lower V_{DD}, minimum V_{TH} variability and increase transistor scaling.

High-k dielectrics have held the promise of continual availability of smaller devices. The choice of high-k material is very crucial as gate dielectric is the very heart of MOSFET. There are still a large variety of dielectrics available that are yet to be observed and that can be the solution to researcher's unanswered challenges. As well as various effects that come along with the usage of high-k materials in place of SiO_2 need to be addressed and discussed.

Acknowledgements. This work is supported by Department of Electronics, Banasthali Vidyapith, Rajasthan, India and IoT Group, CSIR-CEERI, Pilani, India.

References

1. Nowak, E.J.: Maintaining the benefits of CMOS scaling when scaling bogs down. IBM J. Res. Dev. **46**(2/3), 169–180 (2002)
2. Moore, G.E.: Cramming more components onto integrated circuits. Electronics **38**(8), 114–117 (1965)
3. International Technology Roadmap for Semiconductors, 2003 Edition, SIA (2003)

4. Pelella, M.M., et al.: Advantages and challenges of high performance CMOS on SOI. In: 2001 IEEE International SOI Conference Proceedings, pp. 1–4 (2001)
5. Gupta, K.A., et al.: The impact of channel-width on threshold voltage for short channel devices. IEEE Circ. Syst. 715–719 (2011)
6. Gupta, K.A., Anvekar, D.K., Venkateswarlu, V.: A Comparative Study and Analysis of Short Channel Effects for 180 nm and new 45 nm transistors. Springer Journal book series in Advance Intelligent and Soft Computing, vol. 178 Series, pp. 377–387 (2012)
7. Pelella, M.M., et al.: Advantages and challenges of high performance CMOS on SOI. IEEE International SOI Conference Proceedings, pp. 1–4 (2001)
8. Kaya, S., Ma, W.: Optimization of RF linearity in DG-MOSFETs. IEEE Electron Dev. Lett. 25(5), 308–310 (2004)
9. Pei, G., Kan, E.C.-C.: Independently driven DG MOSFETs for mixed-signal circuits: quasi-static and non-quasi-static channel coupling. IEEE Trans. Electron Dev. 51(12), 2086–2093 (2004)
10. Wong, H.S.P., Chan, K.K., Taur, Y.: Self-aligned (top and bottom) double gate MOSFET with a 25 nm thick silicon channel. In: IEDM Technical Digest, pp. 427–430 (1997)
11. Kedzierski, J, et al.: Metal-gate FinFET and fully-depleted SOI devices using total gate silicidation. In: IEDM Technical Digest, pp. 247–250 (2002)
12. King, T.J.: FinFETs for nanoscale CMOS digital integrated circuits. In: Proceedings of the International Conference Computer-Aided Design, pp. 207–210 (2005)
13. Zhu, W., et al.: Mobility measurement and degradation mechanisms of MOSFETs made with ultrathin high-k dielectrics. IEEE Trans. Electron Dev. 51(1) (2004)
14. Kerber, A., Cartier, E.A.: Reliability challenges for CMOS technology qualifications with hafnium oxide/titanium nitride gate stacks. IEEE Trans. Dev. Mater. Reliabil. 9(2) (2009)
15. Yang, Y.-L., et al.: Reliability improvement of 28 nm High-k /Metal Gate MOSFET using appropriate oxygen annealing. IEEE Electron Dev. Lett. 33(8) (2012)
16. Wong, H.-S.P.: Beyond the conventional transistor. IBM J. Res. Dev. 46, 133–168 (2002)
17. Lee, B.H., et al.: Gate stack technology for nano-scale devices. Mater. Today 9(6), 32–40 (2006)
18. Rathee, D., et al.: CMOS development and optimization, scaling issue and replacement with high-k material for future microelectronics. Int. J. Comput. Appl. 8(5), 10–16 (2010)
19. Zhao, et al.: Dielectric relaxation of high-k oxides. Nanoscale Res. Lett. 8, 456 (2013)
20. Swapnadip, D., et al.: A study of the characteristic parameters for deep submicron MOSFETs. IUP J. Electric. Electron. Eng. 5(3)2014
21. Qi, W.-J., et al.: MOSCAP and MOSFET characteristics using ZrO2 gate dielectric deposited directly on Si. IEDM Technical Digest, pp. 145–148 (1999)
22. Kim, Y., et al.: Conventional n-channel MOSFET devices using single layer HfO$_2$ and ZrO$_2$ as high-k gate dielectrics with poly-silicon gate electrode. IEDM Technical Digest, pp. 455–458 (2001)
23. Shashank, N., Basak, S., Nahar, R.K.: Design and simulation of nano scale high-K based MOSFETs with poly silicon and metal gate electrodes. Int. J. Adv. Technol. 1(2) (2010)
24. Chau, R., Datta, S., Doczy, M., Doyle, B., Kavalieros, J., Metz, M.: High-k metal–gate stack and its MOSFET characteristics. IEDM Tech. Digest 25(6) (2004)
25. Hobbs, C., et al.: Fermi level pinning at the poly-si/metal oxide in trace. In: Symposium VLSI Tech. Digest, pp. 9–10 (2003)
26. Choi, C.-H.: Gate length dependent polysilicon depletion effects. IEEE Electron Dev. Lett. 23(4) (2002)

Correction to: RC-Security Mechanism to Prevent Attacks on IoT Smart Switch

Jigar Makhija(iD) and V. Anantha Narayanan(iD)

Correction to:
Chapter "RC-Security Mechanism to Prevent Attacks on IoT Smart Switch" in: N. Chaubey et al. (Eds.): *Computing Science, Communication and Security*, **CCIS 1416, https://doi.org/10.1007/978-3-030-76776-1_17**

In the originally published version of chapter 17, the name of the Author was incorrect. The Author's name has been corrected as "V. Anantha Narayanan".

The updated version of this chapter can be found at
https://doi.org/10.1007/978-3-030-76776-1_17

Author Index

Printed in the United States
by Baker & Taylor Publisher Services